Motor Vehicle Law and **The Law of Impaired Driving** in North Carolina

by Ben F. Loeb, Jr., and James C. Drennan

2000 Edition

Production and distribution of this publication was made possible by a grant from the Governor's Highway Safety Program.

INSTITUTE *of* GOVERNMENT
The University of North Carolina at Chapel Hill

Originally published as *Traffic and Motor Vehicle Laws of North Carolina,* 1947.

INSTITUTE OF GOVERNMENT
The University of North Carolina at Chapel Hill
∞ This publication is printed on permanent, acid-free paper in compliance with the North Carolina General Statutes.

Printed in the United States of America

ISBN 1-56011-360-X

Printed on recycled paper.

Contents

Foreword / iv
Preface / v
How to Use This Book / vii

Part One **Motor Vehicle Offenses** / 1

Chapter 1 Definitions / 3
Chapter 2 Driver's License Law: Licenses, Permits, Revocations, and Suspensions / 7
Chapter 3 Commercial Driver's License Law / 15
Chapter 4 The Nonresident Violator Compact and Waiver Lists / 19
2000 Waiver List / 20
Chapter 5 Registration, Inspection, and Insurance Violations / 23
Chapter 6 Reckless Driving / 27
Chapter 7 Speeding Offenses / 29
Chapter 8 Racing / 33
Chapter 9 Driving on the Right / 35
Chapter 10 Passing and Being Passed / 37
Chapter 11 Railroad Crossings / 39
Chapter 12 Rules Regarding Intersections and Right-of-Way / 41
Chapter 13 Signals, Following, and Backing / 45
Chapter 14 Stopping and Parking / 47
Chapter 15 Motorcycles and Mopeds / 49
Chapter 16 School Buses / 51
Chapter 17 Pedestrians / 53
Chapter 18 Hit-and-Run / 55
Chapter 19 Other Statutory Offenses / 59
Chapter 20 Vehicular Homicide / 61
Chapter 21 Auto Liability Insurance / 65

Part Two **Impaired Driving Offenses** / 75

Chapter 1 Impaired Driving Offenses, License Sanctions, and Punishments / 77
Chapter 2 Other Impaired Driving Offenses / 103
Chapter 3 Special Provisions Applicable to Impaired Drivers / 115

Appendix A **Punishment Chart for North Carolina Motor Vehicle Offenses / 153**
Appendix B **North Carolina Motor Vehicle Statutes / 187**

Foreword

The Institute of Government carries out its work in many ways—through teaching, advising, and research and writing. We are committed to meeting the needs of our clients and the people you serve. This book exemplifies that value and is reflective of the finest traditions of the Institute. We are proud to offer this new edition of *Motor Vehicle Law* and are confident that readers will find it accurate and helpful to them in understanding this sometimes confusing legal topic.

The Institute has been publishing reference books on motor vehicle law since 1947. This book is the twelfth iteration of that work first done fifty-three years ago. For the past thirty-four years, Institute faculty member Ben F. Loeb, Jr., has been the primary author of these books, and this edition is the eighth he has written. For the last two, he has been joined by his colleague Jim Drennan.

Ben's service to those interested in this subject is noteworthy for both its quality and continuity. It reflects the kind of commitment to service that is the foundation of the Institute of Government. Ben has now moved into a part-time, retired status, and this may well be his last version of this book. So, on behalf of his colleagues, I wish to recognize his extraordinary devotion to this field and to this publication. Thanks, Ben, for a job well done.

Michael R. Smith
Director
Institute of Government
The University of North Carolina at Chapel Hill

Chapel Hill
Winter 2000

Preface

This is the twelfth iteration of a book first published by the Institute in 1947 under the title *Traffic and Motor Vehicle Laws of North Carolina*, as edited by John Fries Blair and others. It is the eighth to have been authored (or coauthored) by Ben Loeb and the second in which Jim Drennan has written the chapters dealing with impaired driving offenses.

Publication of a book with this amount of detail requires the participation of several persons in addition to the authors. Among those were Chapel Hill attorney Beth Tillman Logan, who assisted with the legal research, and two members of the Institute's publications staff: our editor, Leslie Watkins, and designer Michael Brady, who designed the final product (including the cover).

Ben F. Loeb, Jr.
James C. Drennan
Professors of Public Law and Government
Institute of Government
The University of North Carolina at Chapel Hill

Chapel Hill
January 1, 2000

How to Use This Book

This book is divided into two main parts, as follows:

Part One discusses and analyzes the more common North Carolina motor vehicle offenses; Part Two outlines the impaired driving offenses. In addition, Appendix A contains a chart that lists the punishments for most motor vehicle offenses, including offenses that are not discussed in parts one and two.

Each chapter begins with a brief summary of the law on a particular subject, such as speeding, driver's license offenses, and so on. Following this summary is a penalties and points section, which outlines criminal penalties, driver's license penalties, and insurance points for the offenses discussed in the chapter. Driver's license points and insurance points are assigned by the North Carolina Division of Motor Vehicles and the insurance industry, respectively. These are administrative decisions based on point schedules that are not always free of ambiguity. Thus the exact number of points assigned for a particular violation cannot always be determined with absolute certainty.

Sections of Chapter 20 of the North Carolina General Statutes that are cited in parts one and two are set out in numerical order in Appendix B. Since the statement of law that begins each chapter is a summary, it is advisable to read the entire relevant section in Appendix B before arriving at any final conclusions as to a particular question. Statutory changes through the regular 1999 Session of the North Carolina General Assembly are included.

Questions as to impaired driving offenses should be directed to Jim Drennan; all other inquiries, to Ben Loeb.

Part One
Motor Vehicle Offenses

by Ben F. Loeb, Jr.

This part discusses and analyzes the more common motor vehicle offenses and the rules for operating a motor vehicle. These include the various types of driver's licenses and their revocation and suspension; registration and insurance violations; reckless driving, speeding, and racing violations; rules on passing and being passed and on intersections and various rights-of-way; parking violations; hit-and-run offenses; and other statutory offenses.

1 Definitions

Section 20-4.01 of the North Carolina General Statutes (hereinafter G.S.) is the definitions section of the motor vehicle law of North Carolina. Only those definitions that have application throughout G.S. Chapter 20 will be discussed in this chapter. Those that apply only to a particular subject will be analyzed in the chapter dealing with that subject. For example, the definition of *alcohol concentration* will be dealt with in Chapter 1 of Part Two, the portion of the book focusing on impaired driving offenses. The definition of terms involving more general aspects of motor vehicle law will be dealt with in various chapters of this part. For example, the term *license* is discussed in Chapter 2 of Part One.

The definitions that have application throughout Chapter 20 are as follows:

CONVICTION

As a general rule, driver's license revocations, suspensions, and points are legal consequences that result from convictions. Thus a citation or even an arrest do not normally lead to such a consequence until after a *final conviction.* (There are a few exceptions to this rule, such as the thirty-day immediate pretrial civil revocation for an implied consent offense, discussed in Chapter 3 of Part Two.) The word *conviction* is defined by G.S. 20-4.01(4a) in a slightly different manner depending on whether the offense was committed in North Carolina or outside this state. When referring to an offense committed within North Carolina, it means

- a final conviction of a criminal offense, including a no-contest plea;
- a determination that a person is responsible for an infraction, including a no-contest plea;
- an unvacated forfeiture of cash in the full amount of a bond;
- a third or subsequent prayer for judgment continued within a five-year period.

Out-of-state convictions include

- an unvacated adjudication of guilt;
- a determination that a person has violated or failed to comply with a law in a court of original jurisdiction;
- an unvacated forfeiture of bail or collateral deposited to secure appearance in court;
- a violation of a condition of release without bail.

In *Barbour v. Scheidt*,[1] the North Carolina Supreme Court ruled that there is no final conviction when the trial court enters a *prayer for judgment continued.* The court also held that if a defendant appeals, there is no final conviction until the judgment of the trial court is upheld on appeal. As noted above, however, G.S. 20-4.01(4a) has created exception for a third or subsequent prayer for judgment continued within any five-year period.

Of course, motorists do sometimes temporarily avoid a conviction by the simple expedient of not appearing in court. However, provisions now contained in G.S. 20-24.1 provide that the Division of Motor Vehicles (DMV) *must* revoke the driver's license of any defendant who (1) fails to appear in court after a case has been called for trial or hearing or (2) failed to pay the fine, penalty, or court costs ordered by the court. Revocations entered pursuant to the authority of G.S. 20-24.1 are effective on the sixtieth day after the order is mailed or personally delivered to the defendant. In a way, this is a kind of in-state solution to the same problem addressed by the Nonresident Violator Compact for out-of-state residents.

DRIVER OR OPERATOR

In this context the terms *driver* and *operator* are identical in meaning and include any person in actual physical control of a vehicle that is in motion or in which the engine is running.[2] *Most motor vehicle offenses require that the defendant be driving or operating the vehicle.* It should be noted, however, that driving or operating can on occasion be proved by circumstantial evidence. Thus in *State v. Turner*,[3] wherein the defendant was convicted of driving under the influence, driving with a revoked license, and manslaughter, the conviction was appealed on the ground that the state had failed to present sufficient evidence that he was in fact driving the car. The appellate court, however, noting that the defendant was found seated behind the steering wheel of the car with the motor running, ruled that this was sufficient evidence to sustain a driving-under-the-influence conviction.

The defendant in *State v. Mabe*[4] appealed his impaired driving conviction on the ground that he was not "in actual physical control of the automobile" because when he was found, he was either sound asleep or had passed out. The court of appeals made short work of this argument, noting that the defendant was behind the steering wheel with the motor running, evidence enough to bring him within the purview of the driving while impaired (DWI) statute. In at least one case the court has found a defendant to have been operating the vehicle even though the engine was not running at the time the officer arrived. However, the headlights were on, the key was in the ignition, and the hood was warm.[5]

DIVISION

As used herein, the word *Division* (capped) always refers to the State Division of Motor Vehicles (DMV).

---

1. 246 N.C. 169, 97 S.E.2d 855 (1957).
2. *See* subdivisions (7) and (25) of Section 20-4.01 of the North Carolina General Statutes (hereinafter G.S.).
3. 29 N.C. App. 163, 223 S.E.2d 530 (1976).
4. 85 N.C. App. 500, 355 S.E.2d 186 (1987).
5. *See* State v. Mack, 81 N.C. App. 578, 345 S.E.2d 223 (1986).

HIGHWAY AND STREET

Subdivisions (13) and (46) of G.S. 20-4.01 define *highway* and *street* to include the entire width between property or right-of-way lines of every way or place, when any part thereof is open to public use as a matter of right for the purpose of vehicular traffic. The words *highway* and *street,* like the words *driver* and *operator*, are exactly synonymous. This concept is extremely important because *as a general rule the provisions of G.S. Chapter 20 apply only on streets and highways.*

In *Smith v. Powell,*[6] the question presented was whether the area beneath a highway bridge was part of the highway (or a public vehicular area) for purposes of enforcing the motor vehicle law. The court noted that the word *highway* is broader in meaning than the word *roadway*, which is defined in Subdivision (38) of G.S. 20-4.01 as that portion of the highway, exclusive of the shoulder, that is improved, designed, or ordinarily used for vehicular traffic. In finding for the defendant, the North Carolina Supreme Court held that *highway* meant the top surface and not the ground beneath the bridge. In the much earlier case of *State v. Perry,*[7] the court had ruled that a sidewalk is part of a highway and thus that the state's DWI law can be enforced if the vehicle is in that area. The emergency strip adjacent to an interstate highway also has been held to be part of a highway where the state's motor vehicle law can be enforced.[8]

PUBLIC VEHICULAR AREA

As a general rule, G.S. Chapter 20 applies only on public streets and cannot be enforced on private property. But a few motor vehicle offenses, including DWI and reckless driving, apply in public vehicular areas as well as on streets and highways. Subdivision (32) defines *public vehicular area* to include any area generally open to the public for vehicular traffic; this includes any driveway, roadway, street, or parking area on the grounds and premises of

- a public or private hospital, college, school, orphanage, church, or any of the institutions, parks, or other facilities maintained by the state or local government; or
- a service station, store, restaurant, or any other business, residential, or municipal establishment providing parking space to customers or the public; or
- any U.S.–owned property subject to the jurisdiction of North Carolina.

A public vehicular area also includes any beach area used for vehicular traffic as well as subdivision roads whether or not they have been dedicated to the public and their maintenance taken over by the state or city. Excluded from this definition is all private property not generally open to or used by the public.

The courts have taken a rather broad view of what constitutes a public vehicular area. Thus in *State v. Carawan,*[9] a parking lot in a public park was found to be within a public vehicular area, even though the area in question was a grassy field that was used for parking only a few times a year. In *State v. Mabe,*[10] the court found the wheelchair ramp connecting a parking lot to a motel entrance to be a public vehicular area. More recently an appellate court held that a mobile home park meets the definition of *subdivision* and thus that its roads constitute a public vehicular area.[11] Other fairly recent cases concerning the definition of public vehicular area include: *State v. Snyder,*[12]

---

6. 293 N.C. 342, 238 S.E.2d 137 (1977).
7. 230 N.C. 361, 53 S.E.2d 288 (1949).
8. State v. Kelley, 65 N.C. App. 159, 308 S.E.2d 720 (1983).
9. 80 N.C. App. 151, 341 S.E.2d 96 (1986).
10. 85 N.C. App. 500, 355 S.E.2d 186 (1987).
11. State v. Turner, 117 N.C. App. 457, 451 S.E.2d 19 (1994).
12. 343 N.C. 61, 468 S.E.2d 221 (1996).

in which the parking lot of a private club was found to be a public vehicular area; *Corns v. Hall,*[13] wherein the court held that a traffic lane of a shopping center parking lot was a public vehicular area and not a roadway; and *State v. Robinette,*[14] wherein the court found that a car wash parking lot was a public vehicular area and not private property, even though a town ordinance prohibited parking on the premises of the car wash unless the facilities were being used.

As previously noted, several rules of the road can be enforced in public vehicular areas, but such is not the case with driver's license law and many other provisions of G.S. Chapter 20. A person driving with no operator's license or a revoked license cannot be charged unless the motor vehicle is being driven on a public street or highway. Of course serious criminal violations such as second-degree murder and manslaughter (both of which can be committed with a motor vehicle) apply on any state thoroughfare and not only on public streets.

VEHICLE AND MOTOR VEHICLE

Some parts of G.S. Chapter 20, such as rules of the road, apply to all vehicles, whereas other sections, such as driver's license law, apply only to motor vehicles. Therefore the distinction between these terms is important to those who enforce or interpret G.S. Chapter 20 and related provisions of North Carolina law.

A *vehicle* is "every device in, upon, or by which any person or property is or may be transported . . . except devices moved by human power or used exclusively upon fixed rails or tracks." For purposes of G.S. Chapter 20, bicycles are deemed vehicles, and every rider of a bicycle on a street is subject to the laws that are applicable to the driver of a vehicle, except for those laws that by their nature have no application.[15] There is, however, wording in Subdivision (49) that appears to exempt motorized wheelchairs and similar devices from the definition of vehicle.

Motor vehicle is defined by Subdivision (23) of G.S. 20-4.01 to include any vehicle that is self-propelled and any vehicle designed to run on a highway that is pulled by a self-propelled vehicle. Mopeds, as defined in Subdivision (27d1.), are excluded from the definition of motor vehicle but are considered vehicles. In 1967, in the case of *Lowe v. Futrell,*[16] the North Carolina Supreme Court specifically ruled that a bicycle is a vehicle and its rider is a driver within the meaning of the state's motor vehicle law. On the other hand, a person walking along a highway and pushing a handcart is a pedestrian and not the driver of a vehicle within the meaning of the law.[17] Finally, in at least one case, the North Carolina Court of Appeals has ruled that a *mobile home*, because it is designed to be transported along the highway, is a motor vehicle.[18]

---

13. 112 N.C. App. 232, 435 S.E.2d 88 (1993).
14. 124 N.C. App. 212, 476 S.E.2d 387 (1996).
15. G.S. 20-4.01(49).
16. 271 N.C. 550, 157 S.E.2d 92 (1967).
17. Lewis v. Watson, 229 N.C. 20, 47 S.E.2d 484 (1948).
18. Peoples Sav. & Loan Ass'n v. Citicorp. Acceptance Co., 103 N.C. App. 762, 407 S.E.2d 251 (1991).

2 Driver's License Law: Licenses, Permits, Revocations, and Suspensions

Section 20-7(a) of the North Carolina General Statutes (hereinafter G.S.) provides that no person may drive a motor vehicle on a North Carolina street or highway unless he or she has first obtained an appropriate license from the state Division of Motor Vehicles (DMV) and possesses the license while driving the vehicle. North Carolina law now provides for a class A, B, and C regular license and a class A, B, or C commercial license as well as various kinds of learner permits and provisional licenses. This complex system of driver licensing is outlined in the material to follow.[1]

G.S. 20-4.01 defines a Class A motor vehicle as having a combined *gross vehicle weight rating* (GVWR) of at least 26,001 pounds, of which the towed unit has a GVWR of at least 10,001 pounds. This weight rating does not reflect the *actual* weight of the vehicle but rather a *maximum loaded weight* assigned by the manufacturer and therefore cannot be proved simply by weighing the vehicle. Class A would also include a GVWR of less than 26,001 pounds if the vehicle's towed unit weighed at least 10,001 pounds. The most common type Class A motor vehicle is undoubtedly the trailer-truck. Class B motor vehicles include single units that have a GVWR of at least 26,001 pounds; Class C vehicles are usually single motor vehicles, and the definition includes regular automobiles.[2]

As a general rule, a commercial license is required if the vehicle is used for business purposes and a regular license will suffice if the vehicle is for personal use only. In addition G.S. 20-37.16 provides that requirements for a commercial license do not apply to vehicles used for fire fighting or otherwise preserving life or property; nor is a commercial license required for farm vehicles meeting the requirements of G.S. 20-37.16(e). (See Chapter 3 of this part, "Commercial Driver's License Law.")

To obtain a driver's license in North Carolina, the applicant must be a resident of the state and demonstrate the physical and mental ability to safely drive a motor vehicle included in the class of license for which the person has applied.[3] To become licensed, prospective drivers must pass an examination that may include a road test, vision test, written test, and so on. However, the Division of Motor Vehicles (also referred to here as the Division or the DMV) may not require a person who applies to renew a license to take a written or road test unless (a) that person has been convicted of a traffic violation since the license was last issued or (b) the applicant suffers a mental

1. *See* Section 20-4.01(17) of the North Carolina General Statutes (hereinafter G.S.) for the statutory definition of *license*.

2. G.S. 20-4.01(2a) through (2c).

3. G.S. 20-7(b1).

or physical condition that impairs his or her ability to drive a motor vehicle. In addition the Division may not require a person who is at least sixty years old to parallel park a motor vehicle as part of a road test.[4] The Division may impose any restriction deemed advisable on a driver's license. It is unlawful for the holder of a restricted license to operate a motor vehicle without complying with that restriction; doing so is the legal equivalent of driving without a license.[5]

G.S. 20-8 exempts certain individuals from the requirement of having a driver's license. Among these are: (a) any person operating a vehicle that is the property of the armed forces of the United States; (b) anyone driving road machines, farm tractors, or an implement of husbandry temporarily operated on a highway; (c) a nonresident who is at least sixteen years of age and possesses a valid driver's license issued in his or her home state or country; or (d) any person driving a moped if he or she has reached the age of sixteen. A person is guilty of driving without a license—this offense is referred to as *no operator's license* (NOL)—in violation of G.S. 20-7(a) if that person

1. drives
2. a motor vehicle
3. on a highway (or street)
4. without a license for the class of vehicle being driven.[6]

NON-ADULT LEARNER'S PERMITS

A person is not automatically eligible to apply for a North Carolina driver's license by attaining a certain age. A learner's permit and/or provisional license must precede obtaining a regular driver's license. Pursuant to new G.S. 20-11, as rewritten by the 1997 General Assembly, three levels of permits/licenses are now required for drivers between the ages of fifteen and eighteen.

Level One

A person who is at least fifteen years old (but less than eighteen) may obtain a *limited learner's permit* if he or she (a) passes a driver education course, (b) successfully completes a written test administered by the Division, and (c) has a driving eligibility certificate or high school diploma. A limited learner's permit is subject to the following restrictions: (a) a supervising driver must be seated beside the permittee in the front seat of the vehicle when it is in motion; (b) for the first six months after issuance, the permittee may drive only between 5:00 A.M. and 9:00 P.M.; (c) every person in the vehicle must be buckled in a properly fastened safety belt.[7]

Level Two

A person who is at least sixteen years old (but less than eighteen) may obtain a *limited provisional license* by meeting the following requirements: (a) has held a limited learner's permit for at least twelve months, (b) has not been convicted of a motor vehicle moving violation during the preceding six months, (c) passes a road test administered by the Division, and (d) has a driving eligibility certificate or a high school diploma. A limited provisional license is subject to the following restrictions: (a) the licensee may drive without supervision only from 5:00 A.M. to 9:00 P.M. or when driving to or from work, or when driving to or from an activity of a volunteer fire de-

4. G.S. 20-7(c).
5. G.S. 20-7(e).
6. *See* G.S. 20-35(c) for defenses to failing to carry a regular driver's license.
7. G.S. 20-11(b) and (c).

partment, rescue squad, or the like; (b) when the licensee is driving with supervision, the supervising driver must be seated beside the licensee in the front seat of the vehicle whenever it is in motion; and (c) all vehicle occupants must have their safety belts properly fastened.[8]

Level Three

A person who has reached age sixteen (but not eighteen) may obtain a *full provisional license* by meeting the following requirements: (a) has held a limited provisional license for at least six months; (b) has not been convicted of a motor vehicle moving violation for the preceding six months; and (c) has a driving eligibility certificate or high school diploma. The level one and level two restrictions concerning time of driving, supervision, and passenger limitations do not apply to a full provisional licensee.[9]

The *driving eligibility certificate* required by G.S. 20-11 (when the driver does not have a high school diploma) is usually obtained from the driver's school and states that he or she is making satisfactory progress toward obtaining a high school diploma or its equivalent. The holder of one of these provisional licenses or permits must carry it when driving, just as a regularly licensed driver. Also it is unlawful for the licensee to fail to comply with restrictions applicable to the particular license or permit; failure to comply with a restriction concerning the time of driving or the presence of a supervising driver constitutes operating a motor vehicle without a license.[10] New G.S. 20-11(n1) provides that a student can lose the driving eligibility certificate for certain behavior, including assaulting a teacher. When this happens, the Division revokes the license or permit.

ADULT LEARNER'S PERMIT

G.S. 20-7(l) provides for a regular learner's permit for a person who is at least eighteen years old. This permit authorizes a driver to operate a specified type or class of motor vehicle and is valid for a period of eighteen months. The permittee must, while operating the motor vehicle on a street or highway, be accompanied by a person licensed to operate the motor vehicle being driven.

PROVISIONAL LICENSEES

Provisional licensees are defined by G.S. 20-4.01(31a) to include any person under eighteen years of age. Provisional licensees can have their driver's license suspended for offenses that would not result in suspension for an adult driver. Thus under G.S. 20-13(b) the Division *may* suspend the license of a provisional licensee as follows:

(a) For a second moving violation committed within twelve months of the date of a first offense, suspension can be for up to thirty days.
(b) For a third moving violation committed within twelve months of the date of a first offense, suspension may be for up to ninety days.
(c) For a fourth violation committed within twelve months of the date of the first offense, the Division may suspend for up to six months.

In addition to the revocations provided for in G.S. 20-13, the Division *must* revoke the license of a person convicted under G.S. 20-138.3, that is, a person under twenty-one caught driving a motor vehicle after consuming alcohol or drugs. (This revocation is discussed in Chapter 3 of Part Two.) Other grounds for revoking a provisional license are contained in G.S. 20-13.2.

---

8. *See* G.S. 20-11(d) and (e).
9. G.S. 20-11(f).
10. G.S. 20-11(l).

LICENSE SUSPENSIONS

At one time license suspensions in North Carolina were discretionary and revocations were mandatory, but over time these distinctions have increasingly blurred. Under current law *revocation* and *suspension* mean exactly the same thing: termination of the license or privilege to drive.[11] G.S. 20-16 allows, *but does not require*, the Division to suspend licenses for certain designated reasons. Among these are

- accumulating twelve or more driver's license points within a three-year period;
- permitting an unlawful or fraudulent use of the license or permit;
- displaying a license or permit not issued to the driver;
- committing, in another state, an offense that if committed in North Carolina, would be grounds for suspension or revocation;
- transporting alcoholic beverages illegally;
- being convicted of impaired instruction under G.S. 20-12.1;
- being convicted within twelve months of two or more charges of speeding in excess of 55 mph but not more than 80 mph;
- operating a motor vehicle at a speed in excess of 75 mph on a road where the maximum speed is less than 70 mph;
- operating a motor vehicle at a speed in excess of 80 mph on a road where the maximum speed is 70 mph.

The most common reason by far for a license suspension is the accumulation of twelve or more driver's license points.[12] Points range from five for passing a stopped school bus to one for littering. Some offenses, including illegal parking, improper plates, and so on, do not carry points. The first suspension under G.S. 20-16(c) is for not more than sixty days; the second, six months; any subsequent suspension, one year. The length of suspensions other than those for points is set forth in G.S. 20-19 and usually will be for at least six months. As of December 1, 1999, more points are assigned for certain listed violations if the driver was operating a commercial vehicle.

In addition to the *discretionary* provisions of G.S. 20-16, *mandatory* suspensions for certain speeding offenses are required by the provisions of G.S. 20-16.1, under which the Division is to suspend for a period of thirty days the license of any driver convicted of either exceeding the speed limit by more than 15 mph if also traveling in excess of 55 mph or driving in excess of 80 mph at the time of the offense. Upon a first conviction, the trial judge may grant a limited driving privilege for purposes reasonably connected with the health, education, and welfare of the defendant and his or her family. However, a second or subsequent offense occurring within one year of a prior offense results in a sixty-day suspension without the possibility of a limited driving privilege.

Mandatory Revocations

Mandatory revocations are required for some offenses by the provisions of G.S. 20-17. Among these offenses are

- manslaughter (or negligent homicide) resulting from the operation of a motor vehicle;
- impaired driving offenses contained in G.S. 20-138.1 and -138.2;
- any felony in which a motor vehicle was used;
- hit-and-run resulting in personal injury;

---

11. G.S. 20-4.01(36).
12. *See* G.S. 20-16(a)(5) and (c).

- perjury or false statement under oath concerning matters covered by G.S. Chapter 20;
- conviction upon two charges of reckless driving committed within a period of twelve months;[13]
- conviction of reckless driving while engaged in the illegal transportation of intoxicants for sale;
- conviction of using a fictitious name or address in an application for a license;
- death by vehicle;
- conviction of assault with a motor vehicle;
- a second or subsequent conviction of transporting an open container of alcoholic beverages under G.S. 20-138.7;
- a second conviction of driving a commercial vehicle after consuming alcohol;
- conviction of driving a school bus, a school activity bus, or child-care vehicle after consuming alcohol;
- certain criminal behavior, including malicious use of explosives.

As is the case with suspensions under G.S. 20-16, revocation periods are set forth in G.S. 20-19. When a license is revoked under any provision that does not provide a specific revocation period, the revocation is for one year. For repeat offenders of impaired driving laws, a revocation can be permanent, but even then the Division can conditionally restore the license after three years.

Out-of-State Convictions

G.S. 20-23 allows the Division to revoke the license of any North Carolina resident upon receiving notice of that person's conviction in another state of any of the offenses set forth in G.S. 20-26(a). Those offenses covered by G.S. 20-26 include exceeding a speed limit of 55 mph or more by more than 15 mph, driving while a license is suspended or revoked, careless and reckless driving, racing, hit-and-run driving resulting in damage to property, unlawfully passing a stopped school bus, illegal transportation of alcoholic beverages, and all those offenses listed in G.S. 20-17 for which revocation of a license is mandatory in North Carolina. The Division cannot revoke an out-of-state license, but it can revoke a nonresident's privilege to drive in this state.[14]

DRIVING WHILE LICENSE REVOKED

One of the more serious offenses in the North Carolina motor vehicle law is driving while a license is revoked.[15] A person is guilty of driving while license revoked if that person

1. drives
2. a motor vehicle
3. on a highway
4. while his or her driver's license is revoked.

This offense applies only to motor vehicles as defined in G.S. 20-4.01(23) and not to any vehicle. Thus a person whose driver's license has been permanently revoked can ride a bicycle or a moped. The word *highway* as defined by G.S. 20-4.01(13) is identical in meaning to the word *street.*

---

13. The North Carolina Supreme Court has held that the dates of the offenses and not the dates of the convictions are the determinative factor; that the convictions are not within a twelve-month period is of no consequence. *See* Snyder v. Scheidt, 246 N.C. 81, 97 S.E.2d 461 (1957).

14. G.S. 20-22.

15. G.S. 20-28(a).

Driving without a license is not a crime except on a street or highway. It does not apply in a public vehicular area.

G.S. 20-4.01(36) provides that *revocation* or *suspension* mean exactly the same thing, that is, termination of a licensee's or permittee's privilege to drive on the streets or highways of North Carolina. Also G.S. 20-23.1 provides that in any case where the Division would be authorized to suspend or revoke a license but the driver does not have a license, the Division may suspend or revoke the operating privilege. In such a case the provisions of Chapter 20 governing suspensions, revocations, and so on apply, just as if there had been a license to suspend or revoke.[16]

DRIVING WHILE DISQUALIFIED

The offense of driving while disqualified can be committed only in a commercial vehicle and therefore is discussed in Chapter 3, "Commercial Drivers Licenses."

Knowledge of Revocation

In order to be convicted of the offense of driving while a license is revoked, the defendant must know that the license has been revoked.[17] Of course some licenses are surrendered to the court at the time of a conviction. Otherwise notice may be given by the Division pursuant to G.S. 20-48 by deposit in the United States mail or by personal delivery. (The giving of notice by mail is complete upon the expiration of four days after the deposit of the notice.)

Misuse of Driver's License

G.S. 20-30 sets forth numerous violations involving the misuse of a driver's license or learner's permit. Elements of two of the most frequently committed of these offenses are set forth below.

Display of Fictitious License[18]

A person commits this offense by

1. displaying, or causing to be displayed, or possessing
2. a driver's license or learner's permit while
3. knowing the same to be fictitious or canceled, revoked, suspended, or altered.

Display of Another's License[19]

A person commits this offense by

1. displaying or representing as one's own
2. a license or permit
3. not issued to the person displaying same.

Other violations of G.S. 20-30 include using a false name or address in an application for a license or permit, photostating or otherwise reproducing a license or permit, selling or offering for sale any reproduction or simulation of a license or permit, or possessing more than one commer-

---

16. *See* State v. Newborn, 11 N.C. App. 292, 181 S.E.2d 214 (1971).
17. State v. Atwood, 290 N.C. 266, 225 S.E.2d 543 (1976).
18. G.S. 20-30(1).
19. G.S. 20-30(3).

cial driver's license (or both a commercial license and a regular license). New G.S. 20-30(9) makes it a Class I felony to use a license or permit containing a false name in the commission of a felony.

Allowing Violations

G.S. 20-32 makes it unlawful to cause or permit any minor under the age of eighteen to drive on a highway without being licensed as required by Chapter 20. In addition G.S. 20-34 makes it unlawful for a person to knowingly permit a motor vehicle owned by him or her (or under his or her control) to be driven by any person who has no legal right to do so or in violation of the driver's license law.

Grace Period for Driving without a License

G.S. 20-35 makes a violation of the driver's license law a Class 2 misdemeanor. However, a driver may not be convicted of failing to carry a regular driver's license if he or she produces in court a license that was valid at the time of the offense. Also a driver may not be convicted of driving without a regular license if, when tried for the offense, the person shows that

1. at the time of the offense he or she had an expired license and
2. the license was renewed within thirty days of its expiration and
3. the person could not have been charged with driving without a license if he or she had possessed the renewal license when charged with the offense.

In effect this creates a thirty-day grace period for renewing a license.

Penalties and Points

Driving without a license in violation of G.S. 20-7(a) or in violation of a restriction on a license as provided by G.S. 20-7(e) is a Class 2 misdemeanor (pursuant to G.S. 20-35). G.S. 20-16(c) assigns three driver's license points for conviction of driving without a license or of driving with a license that has been expired for more than one year. No insurance points are assigned for failure to have a driver's license in one's possession, provided that the driver does have a valid license. Apparently the failure to secure a driver's license carries only one insurance point (for any other moving violation). (See Chapter 21, "Auto Liability Insurance.")

A person convicted of driving while a license is revoked in violation of G.S. 20-28(a) is guilty of a Class 1 misdemeanor. However, in some cases G.S. 20-28(a1) treats this offense as a *no operator's license* violation when the revocation is solely under G.S. 20-16.5 (immediate civil revocation for implied consent offenses) and the mandatory revocation period is up.

A driver's license is revoked for an additional period of one year for a first offense for violating G.S. 20-28(a), two years for a second offense, and permanently for a third or subsequent offense. Once a revoked driver's license has been restored, a driver who operates a motor vehicle on a highway without maintaining financial responsibility for it can be found in violation of driving without a license. Eight insurance points are assigned for conviction of operating a motor vehicle during a period of revocation or suspension of either the license or the registration.

A violation of G.S. 20-30(7) (sale of false driver's licenses) or G.S. 20-30(9) (use of license in commission of a felony) is a Class I felony. All other violations of G.S. 20-30 are Class 2 misdemeanors; these include possessing a fictitious or revoked license or displaying a license not issued to the person who displays it.[20]

---

20. G.S. 20-35.

3 Commercial Driver's License Law

Commercial driver's licenses are a special case, and this chapter describes the provisions of the 1989 legislation establishing a separate driver's licensing system for commercial vehicle drivers as mandated by the Federal Commercial Motor Vehicle Safety Act of 1986.[1] These requirements are contained in Article 2C of Chapter 20 of the North Carolina General Statutes (hereinafter G.S.).[2] Since April 1992 a special driver's license has been required to operate a commercial vehicle in North Carolina.

CLASSES OF LICENSES

North Carolina now has two distinct categories of driver's licenses, *regular* and *commercial*, each of which comprises a Class A, a Class B, and a Class C. Thus the state now has six different driver's licenses, and to complicate the matter further, endorsements can be added to each.[3] The vehicle weight referred to in the following material is the *gross vehicle weight rating* (GVWR), which for all vehicles is the value *specified by the manufacturer* as the maximum loaded weight of a vehicle. The manufacturer's GVWR usually is found on a plate mounted on the vehicle. The GVWR of a combination vehicle is the GVWR of the power unit plus the GVWR of the towed unit(s). Thus neither the *registered* gross weight of the vehicle nor the vehicle's *actual* weight when put on scales is used to prove its GVWR.[4]

A *Class A commercial license* is the broadest of the three commercial licenses and authorizes the driving of all vehicles except for those that require an endorsement in addition to the license. A combination vehicle that has a gross weight of 26,001 or more pounds and a towed unit of at least 10,001 pounds can be driven only by the holder of a Class A commercial license.[5]

A *Class B commercial license* authorizes the driving of all vehicles except for those that can be driven only by the holder of a Class A commercial license. A single vehicle that weighs 26,001 or more pounds, or a combination vehicle that weighs 26,001 or more pounds with a towed unit that weighs less than 10,001 pounds, can be driven only by the holder of a Class A or a Class B commercial license.[6]

---

1. 49 U.S.C. § 36.
2. G.S. 20-37.10 through -37.23.
3. G.S. 20-4.01; 20-7.
4. G.S. 20-4.01(12a).
5. G.S. 20-4.01(3d)a.
6. G.S. 20-4.01(2b).

A *Class C commercial license* authorizes the driving of all commercial vehicles that do not require a Class A or a Class B commercial license. The two kinds of vehicles that most often fall into this category are those designed to transport sixteen or more passengers (including the driver) and vehicles used to transport hazardous materials and therefore required to have a placard in accordance with Title 49, Part 172, Subpart F of the *Code of Federal Regulations*.[7]

In addition to a commercial driver's license, *endorsements* (provisions specifying particular uses) are required for certain vehicles as follows[8]

H—vehicles carrying hazardous materials
M—motorcycles
N—tank vehicles not carrying hazardous materials
P—vehicles carrying passengers
T—double trailers
X—tank vehicles carrying hazardous materials.

Exemptions from the commercial license are listed in G.S. 20-37.16(e) and include the following:

1. vehicles owned or operated by the Department of Defense (including the National Guard);
2. any vehicle when used as fire-fighting or emergency equipment for the purpose of preserving life or property;
3. farm vehicles that meet certain listed criteria, including being used within 150 miles of the farm;
4. vehicles for personal use, including recreational vehicles.

COMMERCIAL VEHICLE DRIVING DISQUALIFICATION

G.S. 20-4.01(5a) defines *disqualification* as withdrawing the privilege to drive a commercial motor vehicle. G.S. 20-17.4 lists those offenses for which a disqualification is required; they include

- a first conviction of G.S. 20-138.1 (driving while impaired) that occurred while driving a noncommercial motor vehicle,
- a first conviction of G.S. 20-138.2 (driving a commercial motor vehicle while impaired),
- a first conviction of G.S. 20-166 (hit-and-run) involving a commercial vehicle,
- a first conviction of a felony in the commission of which a commercial motor vehicle was used,
- refusal to submit to a chemical test when charged with an implied consent offense (as defined in G.S. 20-16.2) that occurred while driving a commercial motor vehicle,
- a second or subsequent conviction of driving a commercial vehicle after consuming alcohol.[9]

Commission of one of the offenses listed above results in disqualification to drive a commercial motor vehicle for one year. If a person who has been disqualified for a year is subsequently convicted of one of the above offenses, he or she is to be disqualified for life, except that the Division of Motor Vehicles (DMV) may, in the case of some offenses, adopt guidelines under which

7. G.S. 20-4.01(3d)c.
8. G.S. 20-37.16(c).
9. G.S. 20-138.2A.

the disqualification can be reduced to ten years. In cases where drivers use a commercial vehicle in the commission of a felony involving the manufacture and distribution of controlled substances, the disqualification is for life without the possibility of modification. A first conviction of violating G.S. 20-138.2A results in only a ten-day disqualification, but multiple convictions for driving after consuming alcohol require a lifetime disqualification.[10]

G.S. 20-17.4(d) provides that a person is disqualified from driving a commercial vehicle for sixty days if convicted of two serious traffic violations (or 120 days if convicted of three or more such violations) committed in a commercial motor vehicle and arising from separate incidents occurring during a three-year period. A *serious traffic violation* is defined by G.S. 20-4.01 (41a) to include

- traveling 15 mph or more over the speed limit,
- careless and reckless driving,
- a traffic violation involving a fatal accident,
- improper or erratic lane changes,
- following the vehicle ahead too closely.

A driver convicted of an offense that requires disqualification but not license revocation may keep any regular Class C driver's license that he or she had at the time the offense was committed. If the offender had a Class A or B regular license or any commercial license at the time of the offense, that license must be turned in to the court or (if the driver is not present) to the DMV. The driver may then apply for a regular Class C driver's license.[11] Driving while disqualified is a violation of G.S. 20-28(d).

Out of service orders are temporary prohibitions against driving a commercial motor vehicle.[12] They are for shorter periods than disqualifications and are not necessarily based on convictions. These orders are issued primarily for safety reasons and usually do not result in criminal action, unless the driver is charged with driving in violation of the out of service order.[13] DMV enforcement officers issue out of service orders. Violation of an out of service order results in a disqualification to drive a commercial vehicle under new G.S. 20-17.4(g).

A person violates G.S. 20-28(d), driving while disqualified, if he or she

1. drives
2. a commercial motor vehicle
3. on a highway
4. while that person's commercial driver's license is disqualified.

IMPAIRED DRIVING IN A COMMERCIAL VEHICLE

This offense is covered in Part Two, Impaired Driving Offenses.

ONE DRIVER—ONE LICENSE

G.S. 20-30(8) makes it unlawful for a driver to possess more than one commercial driver's license or to possess both a commercial license and a regular license. Any commercial license (other than the one most recently issued) is subject to immediate seizure by any law enforcement officer or judicial official; and any regular driver's license possessed while also holding a commercial li-

10. *See* G.S. 20-17.4(b1).
11. G.S. 20-17.5(a).
12. G.S. 20-4.01(25a).
13. G.S. 20-37.12; 49 C.F.R. §§ 392.5 and 395.13. *Also see* G.S. 20-17.7.

cense is subject to immediate seizure in a like manner. This offense is punishable as a Class 2 misdemeanor as provided in G.S. 20-35.

Penalties and Points

A driver convicted of a violation requiring both disqualification and revocation of the license who subsequently drives during the revocation period is subject to punishment as provided in G.S. 20-28. A driver who has been disqualified only and subsequently drives a commercial motor vehicle during the disqualification period is guilty of a Class 1 misdemeanor and is disqualified for additional periods as provided in G.S. 20-28(d). A third offense of driving while disqualified results in disqualification for life (though the DMV may reduce it to ten years). Driving a commercial motor vehicle while disqualified and revoked is punishable for both. (See Chapter 2 for penalties incurred for driving while a license is revoked.)

As noted above, it is unlawful to operate a commercial motor vehicle on the highways of North Carolina unless the driver possesses a commercial driver's license with applicable endorsements for the vehicle being driven. It is unlawful also to drive a commercial motor vehicle in violation of an out of service order.[14] Driving a commercial vehicle in violation of G.S. 20-37.12 is a Class 3 misdemeanor carrying a minimum fine of $250 for a first offense and $500 for a second or subsequent offense.[15] Four driver's license points are assigned for driving without a commercial driver's license.[16] Driver's license violations appear to carry only one insurance point (for any other moving violation). (See Chapter 21, "Auto Liability Insurance.")

As of December 1, 1999, more points are assigned for some violations if the driver was operating a commercial motor vehicle.[17] In addition, the driver may be "assessed double the fine or penalty usually authorized."[18] (See Appendix A, the Punishment Chart.)

---

14. G.S. 20-37.12.
15. G.S. 20-37.21(a).
16. G.S. 20-16(c).
17. G.S. 20-16(c).
18. G.S. 20-16A.

4 The Nonresident Violator Compact and Waiver Lists

North Carolina is a member of the Nonresident Violator Compact as authorized by Sections 20-4.18 through -4.20 of the North Carolina General Statutes (hereinafter G.S.). If a driver licensed in North Carolina receives a citation (or other charge) in another state in the compact and fails to appear in court (or to pay the fine), the North Carolina Division of Motor Vehicles (DMV) will suspend the driver's North Carolina license until the matter is settled with the state where the offense occurred. Similarly the home state of an out-of-state driver who fails to comply with a North Carolina citation will suspend that driver's license if the home state is a member of the compact. North Carolina originally joined the compact in the early 1970s, when only a few east coast states were members. Membership in the compact has since gradually expanded to include almost every state. Thus any North Carolinian who receives an out-of-state citation and does not satisfy it in some manner will almost certainly have his or her license revoked by the DMV.

In North Carolina a nonresident may be required to post bond if the offense is one that would result in revocation of the driver's license. Thus a Virginia motorist charged with impaired driving in North Carolina will probably be arrested rather than receive a citation that can be satisfied later.

In *Palmer v. Wilkins*,[1] the DMV was sued in superior court after revoking the license of a North Carolina motorist who had an unsatisfied speeding citation from South Carolina. The motorist appealed his revocation under the provisions of G.S. 20-25, which provides an appellate procedure when a person's license has been cancelled, suspended, or revoked by the Division. The North Carolina Court of Appeals, however, held that there was no right to appeal for revocation pursuant to provisions of G.S. 20-4.20(b).

WAIVER LISTS

As directed by statute, the state's chief district judges annually "prepare and adopt uniform schedules of offenses for which magistrates and clerks may accept written appearances, waivers of trial or hearing, and pleas of guilty or admissions of responsibility, and establish a schedule of penalties or fines therefore."[2] In other words, they prepare a list of offenses that can be "paid-off" without going to court. There are five such waiver lists, including ones for alcohol offenses, hunting and fishing, parks and recreation, and marine fisheries as well as traffic offenses.[3] The traffic waiver list has two categories of offenses, one containing offenses for which a court appearance is mandatory, another containing offenses that may be waived and satisfied without going to court. The traffic waiver list for Y2k (the Year 2000) follows.

1. 73 N.C. App. 171, 325 S.E.2d 697 (1985).
2. Section 7A-148 of the North Carolina General Statutes (hereinafter G.S.).
3. G.S. 7A-273.

UNIFORM POLICIES RELATING TO TRAFFIC OFFENSES

TRAFFIC OFFENSES FOR WHICH COURT APPEARANCE IS MANDATORY

(Adopted by the Conference of Chief District Judges, October 7, 1999 pursuant to N.C. G.S. 7A-148)

Applies To Offenses Committed On Or After
December 1, 1999

1. All pleas of **not** guilty.
2. All felonies.
3. Driving while subject to an impairing substance. [G.S. 20-138.1]
4. Driving a commercial vehicle while subject to an impairing substance. [G.S. 20-138.2]
5. Careless and reckless driving. [G.S. 20-140]
6. Exceeding the applicable speed limit by over 15 mph while driving over 55 mph.
7. Driving in excess of 80 mph. [G.S. 20-141]
8. Violations of motor carrier safety and hazardous material regulations. [G.S. 20-396]
9. Passing stopped school bus. [G.S. 20-217]
10. Failure to stop for emergency vehicles. [G.S. 20-157(a)]
11. Failure to obey directions of a traffic officer, or of a fireman at the scene of a fire. [G.S. 20-114.1]
12. Failure to stop, etc., at the scene of an accident, or failure to report such an accident. [G.S. 20-166; G.S. 20-166.1]
13. Driving while (license) suspended, revoked or disqualified, or permitting an owned vehicle to be so operated. [G.S. 20-28; G.S. 20-34]
14. Driving a commercial motor vehicle without being licensed to do so, or driving a commercial motor vehicle while license suspended, revoked, or subject to a disqualification or out of service order. [G.S. 20-28(c); G.S. 20-37.12]
15. Possess fictitious, canceled, revoked, suspended or altered license, or counterfeit, sell, lend, or permit use of license by another or any other violation of G.S. 20-30.
16. Any violation of the financial responsibility laws. [Chapter 20, Articles 9A and 13]
17. Any violation of the vehicle registration laws involving stolen or altered registration plates or certificates.
18. Selling handicapped parking placards. [G.S. 20-37.6(c3)]
19. Any violation involving a false affidavit, or false statement under oath, or perjury. [G.S. 20-17(5); G.S. 20-31; G.S. 20-112; G.S. 20-313.1]
20. Any violation charged in the same citation, warrant, magistrate's order, or summons with a mandatory court appearance violation.
21. Death by vehicle. [G.S. 20-141.4]
22. Impaired instruction. [G.S. 20-12.1]
23. Transporting spent nuclear fuel without notifying Highway Patrol. [G.S. 20-167.1]
24. Driving by a person under 21 while drinking or after having consumed alcohol or controlled substance. [G.S. 20-138.3]
25. Racing (prearranged, spontaneous, permitting such use of an owned vehicle, betting on prearranged racing). [G.S. 20-141.3]
26. Unlawful use of red or blue lights on vehicle. [G S. 20-130.1]
27. Failure to give way to the right when being passed. [G.S. 20-149(b)]
28. Driving with open container after drinking. [G.S. 20-138.7]
29. Driving to elude arrest. [G.S. 20-141.5]
30. Operating commercial vehicle after consuming alcohol. [G.S. 20-138.2A]
31. Operating school bus, school activity bus, or child care vehicle after consuming alcohol. [G.S. 20-138.2B]

Source: Administrative Office of the Courts (1999).

TRAFFIC OFFENSES FOR WHICH COURT APPEARANCE MAY BE WAIVED

(on execution of written waiver of appearance and trial, and plea of guilty/responsible)
(Adopted by the Conference of Chief District Judges, October 7, 1999 pursuant to N.C. G.S. 7A-148)

**Applies To Offenses Committed On Or After
December 1, 1999**

A. Speeding Violations:

1. Speed over the applicable limit and over 55 mph but not over 80 mph	0–5	6–10	11–15	
Costs plus fine of	$0	$10	$25	
2. Speed over the applicable limit but 55 mph or under	0–5	6–10	11–15	16 & Over
Costs plus fine of	$0	$10	$25	$50

B. Other Violations:

1. Driving without, or with expired non-commercial driver's license (except when revoked or suspended), or operating motorcycle without proper license endorsement, or knowingly permitting an owned vehicle to be so operated .... $50 and Costs
2. Failure to yield right of way to emergency vehicles, except as provided in No. 10 of mandatory appearances. [G.S. 20-156, -157] .... $25 and Costs
3. Failure to use seat belts. [G.S. 20-135.2A] $25
4. Failure to wear helmet, or having too many passengers, on motorcycle or moped. [G.S. 20-140.4] $25
5. Driving the wrong way on a dual-lane highway .... $25 and Costs
6. Improper passing .... $25 and Costs
7. Failure to dim lights .... $10 and Costs
8. Height, length and width violations .... $10 and Costs
9. Failure to use child restraint systems. [G.S. 20-137.1] .... $25 and Costs
10. Driving too slowly .... $5 and Costs
11. Illegal parking in handicapped space .... $100 and Costs
12. Any other parking violation .... Costs
13. Violation of vehicle inspection law .... Costs
14. Exceeding a safe speed .... $25 and Costs
15. Following too closely .... $25 and Costs
16. Failure to stop for a red light or stop sign or flashing red light .... $25 and Costs
17. Failure to yield right-of-way .... $25 and Costs
18. Improper turn and/or improper signal .... $10 and Costs
19. Driving the wrong way on a one-way city street .... $25 and Costs
20. Improper vehicle equipment .... Costs
21. Use of darkened windows in motor vehicle. [G.S. 20-127(b)–(d)] .... $50 and Costs
22. Failure to reduce speed to avoid accident .... $25 and Costs
23. Violation of the vehicle registration laws, except as in No. 17 of mandatory appearances .... $25 and Costs
24. Failure to use headlights when wipers on $5
25. Speeding in a work zone. [G.S. 20-141(j2)] .... $250 and Costs
26. Any other traffic violation for which court appearance is not mandatory .... $10 and Costs
27. Littering [under G.S. 14-399(c) only] .... $250 and Costs
28. Operating vehicle with improper dealer plates. [G.S. 20-79(e)(1)] .... $50 and Costs
29. Transporting child under 12 in open bed or open cargo area. [G.S. 20-135.2B] $25
30. Speeding in school zone or on school property. [G.S. 20-141.1, -141(e1)] .... $25 and Costs
31. Transporting alcohol in commercial vehicle. [G.S. 20-138.2C] .... $50 and Costs

OTHER POLICIES RELATING TO TRAFFIC OFFENSES:

1. G.S. 7A-148 provides that the Conference of Chief District Judges shall prepare a "uniform schedule" of waivable traffic offenses and otherwise promote the "uniform administration of justice." In accordance with the statutory mandate, all judicial districts will adhere to the schedule provided herein and individual judicial district policies deviating from this schedule are prohibited.
2. Where more than one charge is made on a uniform traffic citation, the defendant shall be fined only for the offense carrying the highest fine. Only one bill of costs will be assessed.
3. When a defendant is charged with two traffic offenses arising out of the same transaction, only one citation should be used. If an additional one or two offenses arising out of the same transaction are charged, they should be placed on a separate citation.
4. This schedule does not apply to littering charges under G.S. 14-399(c) if the defendant is charged with a second offense under that subsection.

Source: Administrative Office of the Courts (1999).

5 Registration, Inspection, and Insurance Violations

REGISTRATION

Section 20-50 of the North Carolina General Statutes (hereinafter G.S.) requires vehicles operated on North Carolina highways to have registration, plates, and a certificate of title. A person violates G.S. 20-50 if he or she owns a vehicle that

1. is required to be registered and
2. is intended to be operated on a highway but
3. the owner fails to apply for and obtain
   (a) registration card,
   (b) registration plate, and
   (c) certificate of title.

Once obtained, the registration plate must be attached to the registered vehicle. G.S. 20-51 contains numerous exemptions from registration. Among these are

- vehicles driven in conformance with laws relating to manufacturers, dealers, or nonresidents;
- vehicles moved only for the purpose of crossing a highway from one property to another;
- farm tractors, road construction machinery, or other vehicles that are *not* self-propelled and are designed for work off the highway;
- any U.S. government vehicle;
- various tractors, trailers, and other equipment used by farmers;
- mopeds;
- motorized wheelchairs;
- a vehicle registered in another state and operated temporarily in North Carolina by a public utility.

Penalties and Points

Violation of G.S. 20-50 is a Class 2 misdemeanor under the provisions of G.S. 20-176(c). No driver's license points are assessed for an improper plate (or its improper display), improper registration, or failure to display a current inspection certificate. Neither do insurance points result from failure to display a registration card, a license plate, or an inspection certificate.[1]

1. *See* Section 20-16(c) of the North Carolina General Statutes (hereinafter G.S.) and Chapter 21, "Auto Liability Insurance."

REGISTRATION PLATE REQUIREMENTS

G.S. 20-63 sets forth requirements for the use of a license plate. Subsection (d) provides that when only one registration plate is issued, it must be attached to the rear of the vehicle, except in the case of truck-tractors, wherein it should be placed on the front. G.S. 20-63(e) requires a vehicle owner to keep the registration plate clean and free of dirt and dust and (when requested by an officer) to clean the registration plate. Concealing license numbers is expressly prohibited, as is operating a vehicle with false numbers.[2]

A person is guilty of operating with false numbers, if he or she

1. willfully operates
2. a motor vehicle
3. with a registration plate that has been
   (a) repainted
   (b) altered
   (c) forged.

Penalties and Points

Violations of G.S. 20-63 are Class 2 misdemeanors, except for failure to clean a plate, which is a Class 3 misdemeanor.[3] An improper license plate carries no driver license points, and failure to display a license plate carries no insurance points.[4]

OTHER REGISTRATION OFFENSES

G.S. 20-111 covers several miscellaneous registration offenses. Among these is driving an unregistered vehicle.[5] A person is guilty of this offense, if that person

1. drives (or for a vehicle owner to permit another to drive)
2. a vehicle
3. on a highway
4. when the vehicle
   (a) is not registered or
   (b) does not display a current registration plate.

Subdivision (2) of G.S. 20-111 makes it unlawful to display or possess a registration card, certificate of title, or registration plate knowing it to be fictitious, canceled, revoked, suspended, or altered. Subdivision (3) prohibits the giving, lending, or borrowing of a license plate for the purpose of using it on a motor vehicle other than the one for which it was issued. Other prohibitions of G.S. 20-111 include failure to surrender to the Division any title, registration card, or plate that has been suspended, canceled, or revoked; use of a fictitious name or address in an application for registration; giving, lending, selling, or obtaining a certificate of title for any purpose other than the registration, sale, or other legitimate use in connection with the vehicle for which it was issued.[6]

---

2. G.S. 20-63(f) and (g).
3. G.S. 20-63, 20-176(c).
4. *See* G.S. 20-16(c) and Chapter 21, "Auto Liability Insurance."
5. G.S. 20-111(1).
6. *See* G.S. 20-111(4), (5), and (6).

Penalties and Points

Giving, lending, or borrowing a license plate for an improper purpose[7] is a Class 3 misdemeanor. Use of a fictitious name or address on an application is a Class 1 misdemeanor (Subdivision 5). Other violations of G.S. 20-111 are punishable under G.S. 20-176(c), a Class 2 misdemeanor.

As a general rule improper plates and registration do not carry either driver's license or insurance points[8] and at the most would be considered as any other moving violation.

VEHICLE INSPECTIONS

G.S. 20-183.3 and -183.8 require annual safety inspections of motor vehicles to include the following equipment: brakes, lights, horn, steering mechanism, windows and windshield wipers, directional signals, tires, mirrors, and exhaust systems. A person violates G.S. 20-183.8 if that person

1. operates
2. a motor vehicle subject to inspection
3. on a highway or public vehicular area
4. when the vehicle has not been inspected.

Violation of this section is evidenced by the vehicle's lack of a current inspection sticker.

Penalties and Points

G.S. 20-183.8 provides for an infraction with a penalty of up to $50 for operating a motor vehicle that has not been inspected; allowing an inspection sticker to be put on the vehicle, knowing that it has not been inspected; or putting an inspection certificate on a vehicle knowing (or having reasonable grounds to know) that inspection of the vehicle was not performed or was performed improperly.

G.S. 20-183.8(c) makes it is a Class I felony to forge an inspection sticker; to buy, sell, or possess a forged inspection certificate; or to otherwise improperly possess an inspection certificate.

Failure to display a current inspection certificate apparently does not carry either driver's license or insurance points.[9]

OPERATING A VEHICLE WITHOUT INSURANCE

G.S. 20-309 provides that no self-propelled motor vehicle may be registered in North Carolina unless the owner has financial responsibility for operation of the vehicle. Usually this means a liability insurance policy as described in Article 9A of Chapter 20. G.S. 20-313 requires the owner of a motor vehicle to have financial responsibility. A person commits this offense if that person

1. owns
2. a motor vehicle
3. registered (or required to be registered) in North Carolina and
4. operates the vehicle (or permits its operation)
5. without the required financial responsibility.

---

7. G.S. 20-111(3)
8. *See* G.S. 20-16(c) and Chapter 21, "Auto Liability Insurance."
9. *See* G.S. 20-16(c) and Chapter 21, "Auto Liability Insurance."

Evidence that an owner operated (or permitted the operation) of a motor vehicle, coupled with Division records indicating that he or she had no financial responsibility, is prima facie evidence of a violation of G.S. 20-313.

Penalties and Points

A violation of G.S. 20-313 (no financial responsibility, i.e., no liability insurance) is a Class 1 misdemeanor resulting in three driver's license points. If there are insurance points, one is assigned for any other moving violation.[10]

10. *See* G.S. 20-16(c) and Chapter 21, "Auto Liability Insurance."

6 Reckless Driving

G.S. 20-140(a) and (b) divide reckless driving into a *careless and heedless* offense (a) and an *endangering persons or property* offense (b).

A person commits the offense of reckless driving if that person

1. drives
2. a vehicle
3. on a highway or a public vehicular area
4. carelessly and heedlessly
5. in willful or wanton disregard
6. of the rights and safety of others

or

1. drives
2. a vehicle
3. on a highway or a public vehicular area
4. without due caution and circumspection and
5. at a speed or in a manner
6. that could or does endanger other people or property.

This offense applies to all vehicles, not just motor vehicles; thus a person driving a moped or riding a bicycle may be charged with reckless driving. Also the offense applies in public vehicular areas, so a defendant might be guilty of this offense even if the vehicle was not operated on a public street or highway.

It is not possible to list the acts or the combination of acts that would at all times and places constitute a type of reckless driving. In *State v. Lewis*,[1] the defendant drove on a highway at 70 mph and in attempting to outrun a law enforcement officer, traveled down a dirt road at 45 mph with the vehicle lights turned off. A jury found him guilty of violating both subsections (a) and (b) of G.S. 20-140, and a four-month sentence was imposed. (On appeal the state supreme court affirmed the conviction but ruled that when a person violates both subsections during one continuous operation of a vehicle, he or she is guilty of one offense of reckless driving, not two separate offenses.) Another example of what might constitute reckless driving occurred in *State v. Floyd*.[2] In that case the court upheld a conviction under G.S. 20-140(b) based on evidence that the

1. 256 N.C. 430, 124 S.E.2d 115 (1962).
2. 15 N.C. App. 438, 190 S.E.2d 353 (1972).

defendant was traveling 70 mph in a 45 mph zone and that his car was fishtailing. The defendant in *State v. Dupree*,[3] however, was improperly convicted of a violation of G.S. 20-140(b) when his sole violation was being left of center.

At one time, reckless driving was a lesser included offense of driving while impaired (DWI) (as defined in G.S. 20-138, the predecessor of G.S. 20-138.1). However, the Safe Roads Act of 1983 created a new DWI law that made reckless driving and impaired driving separate offenses. Thus courts may not now treat reckless driving as a lesser included offense of impaired driving.[4]

Penalties and Points

A violation of Subsection (a) or (b) of G.S. 20-140 is a Class 2 misdemeanor. A conviction of reckless driving results in four driver's license points and four insurance points.[5] Two reckless driving offenses within twelve months require revocation of the driver's license for one year pursuant to G.S. 20-17(6) and 2-19(f).

3. 264 N.C. 463, 142 S.E.2d 5 (1965).

4. *In re* Martin, 333 N.C. 242, 424 S.E.2d 118 (1993).

5. G.S. 20-16(c) of the North Carolina General Statutes. See Chapter 21, "Auto Liability Insurance."

7 Speeding Offenses

VIOLATIONS OF SPEED LIMITS

North Carolina has historically regulated the speed of vehicles by means of two general statutory standards. First, the statutes set specific maximum (and sometimes minimum) speed limits. Second, Chapter 20 of the North Carolina General Statutes (hereinafter G.S.) provides that no motorist shall drive "at a speed that is greater than reasonable and prudent under the conditions then existing."[1] A person commits this offense if that person

1. drives
2. a vehicle
3. on a highway or public vehicular area
4. at a speed greater than is reasonable and prudent under the conditions then existing.

Subsection (m) of G.S. 20-141, which appears to be similar in intent to Subsection (a), provides that the fact that a vehicle's speed is lower than posted limits does not relieve the operator of the duty to decrease speed as necessary in order to avoid a collision with a person or vehicle. In *State v. Stroud*,[2] the North Carolina Court of Appeals held that construed together, these two subsections establish the duty to reduce speed if necessary to avoid a collision, irrespective of the local speed limit or the speed being driven.

G.S. 20-141(b) sets specific speed limits at 35 mph inside municipal corporate limits and 55 mph outside these limits. As a general rule, these are the speed limits throughout the state *except as otherwise posted.* However, both the State Department of Transportation and local authorities may adopt and post different speed limits, except that no legal limit may be set higher than 70 mph. Minimum speed limits also may be adopted, posted, and enforced by the state and local governments.[3] Unlike Subsection (a), provisions of G.S. 20-141(b) do not appear to apply in public vehicular areas.

Very few speeding convictions are appealed beyond the trial court level; thus there is not a great deal of case law with respect to these offenses. Among the criminal cases, at least one indicates that excessive speed may be established by a law enforcement officer's opinion as to the vehicle's speed as well as by clocking the defendant.[4]

---

1. G.S. 20-141(a).
2. 78 N.C. App. 599, 337 S.E.2d 873 (1985).
3. G.S. 20-141(c) and (g).
4. State v. Willis, 285 N.C. 195, 204 S.E.2d 33 (1973).

Penalties and Points

Subsections (a), (b), and (m) and most other provisions of G.S. 20-141 are infractions punishable by not more than $100.[5] However, a person who drives a vehicle on a highway at a speed that is either greater than 15 mph over the speed limit or more than 80 mph is guilty of a Class 2 misdemeanor.[6]

Three driver's license points are assigned for conviction of speeding in excess of 55 mph; two, for conviction of speeding 55 mph or less (assigned as any other moving violation).[7] The Division *may* suspend the license of a driver in the following instances:

- if convicted of two or more charges of speeding in excess of 55 mph but not more than 80 mph within a twelve-month period;
- if convicted of operating a motor vehicle at a speed in excess of 75 mph where the maximum speed is less than 70 mph;
- if convicted of operating a motor vehicle at a speed in excess of 80 mph where the maximum speed is 70 mph.[8]

A person convicted of exceeding the speed limit by more than 15 mph if also driving faster than 55 mph, or if speeding in excess of 80 mph, receives a mandatory thirty-day suspension for a first offense and a sixty-day suspension for a second offense that occurs within one year of the prior offense.[9] Thus a person who drove 71 mph in a 55 mph zone would have his or her license suspended, as would a person who traveled 56 mph in a 35 mph zone; both would be going more than 55 mph and exceeding the limit by more than 15 mph. When the suspension is pursuant to the provisions of G.S. 20-16.1, the trial judge may, when feasible, issue a limited driving privilege on a first conviction only.[10] Also when the Division suspends a license pursuant to G.S. 20-16(a)(9), (a)(10), or (a)(10a), the district court judge may grant a limited driving privilege or license for a period not to exceed twelve months, provided the licensee has not been convicted of any other moving violation within the past twelve months.[11]

Four insurance points are assigned for a conviction of speeding in excess of 75 mph when the limit is less than 70 mph, or speeding in excess of 80 mph when the limit is 70 mph or greater. Two insurance points are assigned for speeding *more* than 10 mph over the posted limit, provided that the total speed was in excess of 55 mph but less than 76 mph, or for speeding 10 mph *or less* in excess of a limit of 55 mph or greater. Only one insurance point is assigned for speeding 10 mph or less when the speed limit is less than 55 mph. *Insurance points are not assigned for speeding 10 mph or less over the limit unless the same driver has been convicted of at least one other moving violation during the last three years.* (See Chapter 21, "Auto Liability Insurance.")

---

5. G.S. 20-176(a) and (b).
6. G.S. 20-141(j1).
7. G.S. 20-16(c).
8. *See* G.S. 20-16(a), (9) through (10a). It would appear that the date of the conviction, not the date of the offense, is relevant for the purpose of suspending under the provisions of G.S. 20-16(a)(9) (two convictions of speeding in excess of 55 mph).
9. G.S. 20-16.1(a) and (c).
10. G.S. 20-16.1(b)(1).
11. G.S. 20-16(e)(1).

SPEEDING IN SCHOOL AND WORK ZONES

G.S. 20-141.1 provides that the state Board of Transportation or local authorities may by ordinance set speed limits lower than those designated by G.S. 20-141 for streets near a public, private, or parochial school. These lower limits are effective when signs are erected giving notice of the zone, the authorized limit, and the days and hours when the lower limit is effective. Subsection (e1) of G.S. 20-141 authorizes local authorities to set lower speed limits on the grounds of a public or private school, and these lower limits also are effective when appropriate signs are erected.

Speeding in a highway work zone is prohibited by G.S. 20-141(j2). A highway work zone is the area between the sign that designates the beginning of the work zone and the sign that marks the end of the work zone.

Penalties and Points

A driver violating a school zone speed limit under either G.S. 20-141 or -141.1 has committed an infraction that carries a penalty of not less than $25.[12] Speeding through a work zone also is an infraction and results in a penalty of $250.[13] A school zone speeding violation results in three driver's license points; a work zone violation also would carry three points if the speed was in excess of 55 mph but only two points if below that speed (any other moving violation). As with any other speeding violation, the number of insurance points would depend on the vehicle speed, but the exemption that usually is available to those going 10 mph (or less) over the limit may not apply to school zones.[14]

SPEEDING TO ELUDE ARREST

The 1997 General Assembly passed a new speeding to elude arrest law, which as contained in new G.S. 20-141.5, divides this charge into misdemeanor and felony offenses. A person commits the misdemeanor offense if that person

1. operates
2. a motor vehicle
3. on a highway or public vehicular area
4. while fleeing or attempting to elude
5. a law enforcement officer
6. who is lawfully performing his or her duty.

Although G.S. 20-141.5 is entitled Speeding to Elude Arrest, in fact speeding is not actually required for the misdemeanor offense or for some felony convictions. A person commits felony speeding to elude arrest if that person

1. operates
2. a motor vehicle
3. on a highway or public vehicular area

---

12. G.S. 20-141(e1).
13. G.S. 20-141(j2).
14. *See* G.S. 20-16(c) and Chapter 21, "Auto Liability Insurance."

4. while fleeing or attempting to elude
5. a law enforcement officer
6. who is lawfully performing his or her duties and when
7. two or more of the following aggravating factors are present at the time the violation occurs
   (a) speeding in excess of 15 mph over the legal limit;
   (b) gross impairment of the person's faculties while driving due to
      (1) consumption of an impairing substance or
      (2) blood alcohol concentration of 0.14 or more within a relevant time after the driving;
   (c) reckless driving in violation of G.S. 20-140;
   (d) negligent driving leading to an accident causing
      (1) property damage in excess of $1,000 or
      (2) personal injury;
   (e) driving when the person's driver's license is revoked;
   (f) driving in excess of the posted speed limit, during the days and hours when it is in effect, on school property or in an area designated as a school zone pursuant to G.S. 20-141.1, or in a highway work zone as defined in G.S. 20-141(j2);
   (g) passing a stopped school bus in violation of G.S. 20-217;
   (h) driving with a child under twelve years of age in the vehicle.

When a vehicle is operated in violation of G.S. 20-141.5 it is prima facie evidence that it is so operated by the registered owner. In the case of a rental vehicle, proof of who rented it constitutes such prima facie evidence.[15]

Penalties and Points

Felony speeding to elude arrest is a Class H felony; the misdemeanor offense is Class 1. The Division must suspend for up to one year, the driver's license of any person convicted of a misdemeanor under G.S. 20-141.5. For a felony the Division must revoke for two years the license of any person convicted on the basis of two of the aggravating factors listed in G.S. 20-141.5(b). Revocation is for three years for a felony conviction based on the presence of three or more of the aggravating factors. However, in the case of a first felony conviction involving only two aggravating factors, the licensee may apply to the sentencing court for a limited driving privilege after a period of twelve months of revocation. Ten insurance points are assigned for speeding to elude arrest (felony or misdemeanor).[16]

---

15. G.S. 20-141.5(c).
16. *See* G.S. 20-141.5(d) and Chapter 21, "Auto Liability Insurance."

8 Racing

Under the provisions of Section 20-141.3 of the North Carolina General Statutes (hereinafter G.S.), *racing* may be either prearranged or willful. A person is guilty of *prearranged racing* if that person

1. operates
2. a motor vehicle
3. on a highway
4. willfully
5. in prearranged speed competition with another motor vehicle.

A person is guilty of *willful racing* if that person

1. drives
2. a motor vehicle
3. on a highway
4. willfully
5. in speed competition with another motor vehicle.

As noted above, racing a motor vehicle on a public street or highway is classified into two separate offenses (neither of which applies in a public vehicular area). The more serious of the two is set out in G.S. 20-141.3(a), which makes it unlawful for a driver to engage in prearranged speed competition with another motor vehicle. A law enforcement officer who discovers a prearranged speed competition is required by G.S. 20-141.3(g) to seize any motor vehicles used in the race. The vehicles are then put in the actual or constructive possession of the sheriff of the county where the offense was committed. If the owner is convicted of prearranged speed competition, the court must order that the vehicle be sold at public auction. After all fees, expenses, liens, and other costs are paid, the proceeds of the sale go to the county school fund. If the person charged with operating the vehicle in prearranged racing is acquitted, then the sheriff returns the vehicle to its owner. Prearranged racing is considered such a serious offense that penalties are imposed on those other than the actual drivers. Any person who knowingly permits a motor vehicle owned by him or her, or under his or her control, to be used in the race violates G.S. 20-141.3(c), as does any person who places a bet or wager on the outcome of the race.

Willfully engaging in speed competition that is not prearranged is considered a less serious offense, and vehicles involved in the race are not seized by the arresting officer.[1] Although convictions

1. Section 20-141.3(b) of the North Carolina General Statutes (hereinafter G.S.).

for racing are more difficult to obtain than convictions for speeding or driving while impaired (DWI), successful prosecutions are not uncommon. An example is *State v. Turner*,[2] wherein the defendant was convicted of violating G.S. 20-141.3(b) after he and another driver accelerated rapidly from a traffic light. The race lasted for more than one-tenth of a mile, and the vehicles reached a speed of approximately 90 mph. It should be noted that G.S. 20-141.3 applies only to motor vehicles, not to all vehicles, and may be enforced only on a highway, not in a public vehicular area or on other private property.

Penalties and Points

Prearranged speed competition is a Class 1 misdemeanor; willful racing, a Class 2 misdemeanor. Lending a car for a race or betting on the outcome also is a Class 1 misdemeanor.[3]

A conviction of G.S. 20-141.3(a) or (c) (prearranged competition or lending a vehicle for or betting on a prearranged race) results in a mandatory license revocation of three years. The defendant may, however, apply for a new license after eighteen months from the date of revocation. The Division may suspend a license for up to one year for willful racing.[4]

Ten insurance points are assigned for highway racing or for knowingly lending a motor vehicle to be used in a highway race. Apparently a distinction is not made between prearranged and willful racing.

2. 13 N.C. App. 603, 186 S.E.2d 681 (1972).
3. G.S. 20-141.3(a), (b), and (c).
4. G.S. 20-141.3(d) and (e).

9 Driving on the Right

Section 20-146 of the North Carolina General Statutes (hereinafter G.S.) provides that vehicles must be driven on the right half of any street or highway of sufficient width, except when

1. passing another vehicle proceeding in the same direction,
2. an obstruction exists on the right side of the road,
3. the road is divided into three marked lanes, or
4. the street is designed for one-way traffic pursuant to G.S. 20-165.1 or -169.

On four-lane streets a vehicle may not be driven to the left of the center line unless permitted to do so by a traffic control device.[1] A motorist crossing an intersection or a railroad right of way must travel on the right half of the street.[2] Any vehicle that is traveling at less than the legal maximum speed must be driven in the right-hand lane or as close as possible to the right-hand curb or edge of the highway, except when passing or turning left.[3]

The rule requiring a vehicle to be driven to the right of center has been interpreted to mean that the entire vehicle must be on the right side of the road. In *Gladden v. Setzer*,[4] the state supreme court held that it was a violation of G.S. 20-146 for the tanker part of a tractor-trailer to be left of center.

While G.S. 20-146 does not expressly so state, apparently there are other exceptions to the driving left of center prohibition; among these are sudden emergencies. In *Ingram v. Smoky Mountain Stages, Inc.*,[5] a bus driver was held not to be negligent when he cut to the left and crossed the center line in an effort to avoid a collision with a vehicle that had driven directly in front of him. And in *Wade v. Grooms*,[6] the court held that a law enforcement officer was not necessarily negligent by being left of center while engaged in a high-speed chase.

Penalties and Points

A violation of G.S. 20-146, -147, or -165.1 is an infraction punishable by a penalty of not more than $100.[7] A person convicted of driving on the wrong side of the road is assigned four driver's license points[8] and two insurance points.[9]

---

1. Section 20-146(c) of the North Carolina General Statutes (hereinafter G.S.).
2. G.S. 20-147.
3. G.S. 20-146(b).
4. 230 N.C. 269, 52 S.E.2d 804 (1949).
5. 225 N.C. 444, 35 S.E.2d 337 (1945).
6. 37 N.C. App. 428, 246 S.E.2d 17 (1978).
7. G.S. 20-176(b).
8. G.S. 20-16(c).
9. See Chapter 21, "Auto Liability Insurance."

10 Passing and Being Passed

Drivers of vehicles that are approaching each other from opposite directions must pass each other while both are traveling on the right, each driver giving the other at least one half of the main-traveled portion of the road if possible.[1] Ordinarily a driver is not required to yield more than half of the roadway and may proceed straight ahead even if a vehicle is approaching head-on. The theory is that a driver traveling lawfully on the right side of the road is entitled to assume that the driver of an approaching vehicle also will obey the law and return to the proper side.[2] This rule does not apply if the driver of the approaching vehicle is obviously unable to turn back to the right.[3] A person violates Section 20-148 of the North Carolina General Statutes (hereinafter G.S.) (failure to pass approaching vehicle to right) if that person

1. while driving in the opposite direction
2. from another vehicle,
3. fails to pass the other vehicle while traveling on the right and
4. while giving (as nearly as possible) the other vehicle at least half of the main-traveled portion of roadway.

G.S. 20-149 requires the driver of a vehicle that is overtaking another vehicle that is proceeding in the same direction to pass while at least two feet to the left of the vehicle and not return to the right side of the highway until safely clear of the overtaken vehicle. (This requirement does not apply when the overtaking and passing is on the right as allowed by G.S. 20-150.1.) Except when the passing takes place on the right, the driver of the overtaken vehicle must, on audible signal, give way to the right in favor of the overtaking vehicle and not increase speed until completely passed. It should be noted that the duty to sound the horn when passing is not mandatory; at one time North Carolina law did require a passing driver to sound the horn, but such is no longer the case.[4]

G.S. 20-150.1 allows passing on the right in four instances:

1. when the overtaken vehicle is in a left-turn-only lane,
2. when the street has two or more unobstructed lanes for traffic moving in each direction (in other words, on four-lane roads),
3. on one-way streets, and
4. in a lane that allows a right turn on red.

---

1. Section 20-148 of the North Carolina General Statutes (hereinafter G.S.).
2. Morgan v. Saunders, 236 N.C. 162, 72 S.E.2d 411 (1952).
3. Brown v. Southern Prods. Co., 222 N.C. 626, 24 S.E.2d 334 (1943).
4. Perry v. Aycock, 68 N.C. App. 705, 315 S.E.2d 791 (1984).

Passing on the right legally is limited to these four instances. Thus in *Almond v. Bolton,*[5] a motorcyclist who passed another vehicle on the right while traveling on a two-lane highway violated G.S. 20-149(a), which requires overtaking drivers to pass at least two feet to the left of the vehicle being passed.

A motorist, in overtaking and passing, is not permitted to drive to the left of the center of the highway unless the left side is clearly visible and free of oncoming traffic for a sufficient distance to permit passing safely.[6] A driver probably would violate this rule if he or she passed in a manner that required an oncoming motorist to leave the road or come to a stop in order to avoid a collision; even if the left lane was completely free of traffic, the driver would still violate the rule unless the road was visible for a considerable distance ahead. A specific distance is not required for passing, except when the passing movement is made near the top of a hill or curve; in those situations the driver must have a view of at least 500 feet of highway.[7] A driver violates G.S. 20-150(b) (passing on hill or curve) if he or she

1. overtakes and passes
2. another vehicle proceeding in the same direction
3. upon the crest of a grade or curve in the highway
4. where the driver's view along the highway is obstructed within a distance of 500 feet.

Passing is prohibited also at railroad grade crossings, intersections in municipalities, and at other intersections marked with signs by the State Department of Transportation.[8] The rule against passing at an intersection in a city applies even if the driver is not aware that he or she is inside the city limits.[9]

Most motorists assume it is unlawful to pass another vehicle while driving on sections of a road or highway that are marked along the center by a solid yellow line, but in fact, the words *yellow line* do not appear in North Carolina motor vehicle law. The statute relevant to this issue is G.S. 20-150(e), which prohibits passing on any portion of a street or highway that is marked by "signs, markers, or markings" placed by the Department of Transportation to indicate that passing should not be attempted. Although there have been trial court convictions for passing on a yellow line, no appellate court has clearly stated that passing on a solid yellow line violates G.S. 20-150(e), except when the yellow line is accompanied by signs indicating that passing is not allowed on the yellow line.[10]

Penalties and Points

As a general rule any violation of G.S. 20-148, -149, or -150 is an infraction punishable by a penalty of not more than $100.[11] However, there is an exception in the case of G.S. 20-149(b), which requires the driver of an overtaken vehicle to give way to the right. A violation of this subsection is a Class 1 misdemeanor when the violation is the proximate cause of a collision resulting in serious bodily injury and a Class 2 misdemeanor when the violation is the proximate cause of a collision resulting in *any* bodily injury or property damage. Four driver's license points and two insurance points are assigned for illegal passing.[12]

---

5. 272 N.C. 78, 157 S.E.2d 709 (1967).
6. G.S. 20-150(a).
7. G.S. 20-150(b).
8. G.S. 20-150(c).
9. Poultry Co. v. Thomas, 289 N.C. 7, 220 S.E.2d 536 (1975).
10. Farmers Oil Co. v. Miller, 264 N.C. 101, 141 S.E.2d 41 (1965).
11. G.S. 20-176.
12. *See* G.S. 20-16(c) and Chapter 21, "Auto Liability Insurance."

11 Railroad Crossings

The point at which a street crosses a railroad track is probably not an intersection as defined in Section 20-4.01(16) of the North Carolina General Statutes (hereinafter G.S.). Nevertheless the street and the track do intersect, and certain duties are imposed by law on a driver who is approaching a railroad right-of-way. As a general rule, the manner in which a railroad crossing is marked governs the action required of motorists who approach the crossing. Under certain circumstances the driver must come to a complete stop, whereas under other circumstances the motorist may not even be required to slow down. The statutes regarding railroad crossings were reorganized and to some extent rewritten in 1991, and since then there have been no significant appellate court decisions interpreting them.

New G.S. 20-142.1 makes stops at railroad crossings mandatory in four situations:

1. when an electrical or mechanical signal gives warning of the immediate approach of a train;
2. when a crossing gate is lowered or a flagman signals that the train is approaching;
3. when a train approaching within fifteen hundred feet of the crossing emits an audible signal indicating that crossing is a hazard; and
4. when an approaching train is plainly visible and is in hazardous proximity to the crossing.

In any of these cases the driver must stop within 50 feet (but not less than 15 feet) from the nearest rail and not proceed until it can be done safely. Subsection (b) of 20-142.1 makes it unlawful to drive any vehicle through, around, or under any crossing gate or barrier while the barrier is closed or is being opened or closed.

G.S. 20-142.2 authorizes the state Department of Transportation to designate dangerous railroad crossings and then to erect signs at those crossings. Where a sign has been erected, all drivers must stop within 50 feet (but not less than 15 feet) of the nearest rail and then may proceed only by exercising due care. G.S. 20-142.3 requires certain categories of vehicles to stop at all railroad grade crossings regardless of whether there are gates or lights or the crossings are completely unmarked. Among these vehicles are school buses, activity buses, any motor vehicle carrying passengers for compensation, certain vehicles carrying hazardous materials, and any motor vehicle with a capacity of sixteen or more persons. While the vehicle is stopped, the driver must listen and look in both directions for any approaching train and may not proceed until it can be done safely. G.S. 20-142.3(b) makes exceptions to these rules for vehicles other than school buses, which apparently must stop before crossing *any* railroad track.

Special rules are set out with respect to moving crawler-type tractors (or other equipment with a customary operating speed of less than 5 mph) across railroad tracks. Notice of the crossing must be given to the railroad a reasonable time in advance; and the operator of the equipment must stop, check both directions, and not proceed until it can be done safely.[1] Drivers are prohibited from entering the railroad grade crossing unless there is sufficient space on the other side to accommodate the vehicle without obstructing the passage of other vehicles, pedestrians, or trains; this requirement applies even if there is a traffic control signal indicating that it is permissible to cross or proceed.[2]

Penalties and Points

A violation of any of the above-cited statutes concerning railroad grade crossings is an infraction punishable by a $100 penalty as provided by G.S. 20-176. A particular number of driver's license points is not designated for these violations, so apparently two points are assigned for any other moving violation. Also apparently only one insurance point for a moving traffic violation is assigned for any of these offenses.[3]

1. Section 20-142.4 of the North Carolina General Statutes (hereinafter G.S.).
2. G.S. 20-142.5.
3. G.S. 20-16(c). See Chapter 21, "Auto Liability Insurance."

12 Rules Regarding Intersections and Right-of-Way

The term *right-of-way* is used to describe many interactions between vehicles on streets and highways, but in the legal sense the term usually applies only at intersections or pedestrian crosswalks, and a charge of *failure to yield right-of-way* normally is appropriate only in regard to those two places. Section 20-4.01(16) of the North Carolina General Statutes (hereinafter G.S.) defines *intersection* as the "area embraced within the prolongation of the lateral curb lines" or, if there are no curb lines, "the lateral edge of roadway lines of streets that join one another at any angle." A *roadway* is defined by G.S. 20-4.01(38) as that part of a highway "designed, or ordinarily used for vehicular travel, exclusive of the shoulder." A "T" intersection, where one road meets another but does not cross it, is subject to all the rules governing other intersections. In *Dawson v. Jennette*,[1] the North Carolina Supreme Court ruled that the law makes no distinction between a "T" intersection and one at which the two highways cross each other completely.

G.S. 20-153 requires that a right turn be made as close as is practical to the right-hand curb or edge of the roadway. The driver of a vehicle intending to turn left at an intersection must approach the intersection in the extreme left-hand lane available to traffic moving in the direction of travel; after the vehicle enters the intersection, the driver must turn left such that the vehicle leaves the intersection along a course that is lawfully available to traffic moving in the direction of the lane being entered. In 1997 the General Assembly deleted wording from G.S. 20-153(b) suggesting that left turns "be made in that portion of the intersection to the left of the center of the intersection." This phrasing was found to encourage cars that were turning left to cut in front of oncoming traffic. Since left-turning vehicles customarily cut in front of approaching vehicles, the reason for this amendment was not apparent on its face. The turning rules set forth in G.S. 20-153 may be altered by local authorities or the State Department of Transportation by clearly indicating by markers or other directional signals the course to be followed.

When two vehicles approach, at approximately the same time, an intersection without traffic signs or lights, the driver on the left must yield the right-of-way to the vehicle on his or her right.[2] Also a left-turning vehicle must yield the right-of-way to a vehicle that is proceeding straight ahead.[3]

G.S. 20-156(a) requires that a vehicle entering a public street from an alley, building entrance, or driveway yield the right-of-way to vehicles on the street or highway. However, the statutes do not require that a vehicle coming from a private drive stop before it enters the public highway; yielding is all that is required.

---

1. 278 N.C. 438, 180 S.E.2d 121 (1971).
2. Section 20-155(a) of the North Carolina General Statutes (hereinafter G.S.).
3. G.S. 20-155(b).

VEHICLE CONTROL SIGNS AND SIGNALS

G.S. 20-158 sets forth the rules regarding stop signs and traffic lights. When a stop sign is in place, drivers are required to stop and yield the right-of-way; failure to do either is a punishable offense. Vehicles facing a steady red light may not enter the intersection except to make a right turn and then only after coming to a complete stop and yielding the right-of-way to pedestrians and other traffic in the intersection. Vehicles facing a yellow light are put on notice that a red light will be immediately forthcoming, but going through an intersection on a yellow light apparently is not a violation. A flashing red light has the same legal effect as a stop sign; vehicles that face a flashing red light must stop and yield the right-of-way. Vehicles facing a flashing yellow light may proceed through the intersection with caution, yielding the right-of-way to vehicles already in the intersection.

When a motorist is required to stop because of a stop sign, a red light, or other such signal, the vehicle should be stopped at a marked stop line, if there is one; if there is none, before entering a marked crosswalk. If there is neither a marked stop line nor a marked crosswalk, the stop should be made before entering the intersection, at the point nearest the intersecting street where the driver has a view of approaching traffic. The Department of Transportation, as well as cities and towns, are authorized to erect *yield right-of-way* signs. A driver approaching one of these signs is required to slow down (not stop) and yield the right-of-way to any vehicle on the main-traveled or through highway.[4]

EMERGENCY VEHICLES

Certain emergency service vehicles have the right-of-way at intersections even when facing a red light or stop sign. Among these are police or fire department vehicles, public and private ambulances, rescue squad vehicles, and vehicles operated by county fire marshals. To exercise this right-of-way, the emergency vehicle must give a warning by flashing an appropriate light (blue or red) as well as by an audible signal that can be heard under normal conditions for a distance of not less than 1,000 feet. Even while giving the required signals, however, the emergency service vehicle operator has the duty to drive with due regard for the safety of others who are using the highway.[5] A person violates this statute by

1. driving
2. a vehicle
3. on a highway
4. and failing to yield the right-of-way
5. to a police, fire department, or rescue squad vehicle; an ambulance; a vehicle responding to a call to recover or transport human tissue or organs for transplantation; or a vehicle operated by a county fire marshal or a civil preparedness coordinator that
6. is giving warning signals by appropriate light (red or blue) and bell, sirens, or exhaust whistle.

In addition to yielding the right-of-way, drivers are required to pull as close to the right-hand curb as possible and stop when a police or fire department vehicle (or certain other listed emergency vehicles) is approaching and giving warning by light as well as by audible signal that can be

4. G.S. 20-158.1.
5. G.S. 20-156(b).

heard from a distance of at least 1,000 feet. However, a violation of this section is referred to in G.S. 20-16(c) as "failure to stop for siren" rather than "failure to yield right-of-way."[6]

Other provisions of G.S. 20-157 make it unlawful to follow a fire department vehicle closer than one block (or 400 feet outside cities), to drive over a fire hose or other equipment being used to fight a fire, or to park a vehicle or leave it standing within 100 feet of police, fire, or rescue squad vehicles at the scene of an accident.[7]

Penalties and Points

A violation of G.S. 20-153, -155, -156, -157(b through e), -158, or -158.1 is an infraction punishable by a penalty of not more than $100.[8] Failure to pull over for an emergency vehicle[9] is a Class 2 misdemeanor. Three driver's license points are assigned for running through a stop sign, failing to yield right-of-way, running through a red light, or failing to stop for a siren.[10] Only one insurance point (for any other moving violation) is assigned for a conviction of any of the above-cited provisions. (See Chapter 21, "Auto Liability Insurance.")

6. G.S. 20-157(a).
7. G.S. 20-157(b), (c), (d), and (e).
8. G.S. 20-176(b).
9. G.S. 20-157(a).
10. G.S. 20-16(c).

13 Signals, Following, and Backing

Section 20-154(a) of the North Carolina General Statutes (hereinafter G.S.) provides that before starting, stopping, or turning from a direct line, a driver must first see that it is possible to do so safely. If a pedestrian may be affected by the pending action, the motorist must signal to the pedestrian by hitting the horn; if another vehicle may be affected, a mechanical, electrical, or hand signal must be given. The requirement to signal is not absolute; it applies only when another vehicle could be involved. (But changing lanes is a turn requiring a signal.[1])

As amended in 1985, G.S. 20-154(a) applies in public vehicular areas as well as on streets and highways. In areas where the speed limit is 45 mph or higher a signal to turn from a direct line of travel must be given continuously during the last 200 feet before making a turn; otherwise the signal must be given for the last 100 feet prior to stopping or making a turn.[2]

G.S. 20-152(a) prohibits a driver from following another vehicle more closely than is reasonable and prudent under the conditions. Outside of business and residential districts a driver should leave sufficient space between his or her vehicle and the vehicle ahead so that an overtaking vehicle would be able to enter and occupy the space without danger.[3] There is case law to the effect that a "collision with the vehicle ahead furnishes some evidence that the motorist to the rear was not keeping a proper lookout or that he was following too closely."[4]

Although an accident involving a rear-end collision often results in a following-too-close charge, such an accident could result also from a violation of G.S. 20-141(m), failure to decrease speed in order to avoid a collision. Except on interstate and other controlled-access highways, backing a vehicle down a street is not illegal as long as it can be done without interfering with other traffic.[5]

Penalties and Points

A violation of G.S. 20-152 or -154 is an infraction punishable by a penalty of not more than $100.[6] The offense of following too close results in four driver's license points;[7] however, failing to signal, or giving an improper signal, apparently carry only two driver's license points (for any other moving violation). Two insurance points are assigned for following too closely, but improper signals or failing to signal are treated as any other moving violation and result in only one insurance point.

---

1. Sass v. Thomas, 90 N.C. App. 719, 370 S.E.2d 73 (1988).
2. Section 20-154(b) of the North Carolina General Statutes (hereinafter G.S.).
3. G.S. 20-152(b).
4. Scher v. Antonucci, 77 N.C. App. 810, 812, 336 S.E.2d 434, 435 (1985), *quoting* Burnett v. Corbett, 264 N.C. 341, 343, 141 S.E.2d 468, 469 (1965).
5. G.S. 20-154(a).
6. G.S. 20-176(b).
7. G.S. 20-16(c).

14 Stopping and Parking

The words *stop*, *park*, and *leave standing* are not defined by statute, but their meanings have been interpreted in numerous appellate court decisions. These decisions indicate that as far as the rules of the road are concerned, *park* and *leave standing* are synonymous and neither includes the connotation of a mere temporary stop when a driver does not intend to break the continuity of travel.[1] The dividing line between *stopping* (which is temporary and usually legal) and *parking* (which breaks the continuity of travel and often is illegal) is necessarily vague and will depend on the circumstances of each case. It has been held, for example, that a bus that had stopped to take on a passenger was not parked[2] and that a driver who had stopped to avoid a collision was not parked.[3]

Section 20-161(a) of the North Carolina General Statutes (hereinafter G.S.) makes it unlawful to park (or leave standing) any vehicle on the paved or main-traveled portion of a street or highway outside cities, unless the vehicle is so disabled that it cannot be moved. Outside of cities, parking is prohibited also on the shoulder of the highway, unless the vehicle can be seen by approaching drivers from at least 200 feet in both directions and does not obstruct the normal movement of traffic.[4]

In addition to the general prohibitions outlined in the preceding paragraph, parking is prohibited in several specific places as follows:

- in front of a private driveway,
- within 15 feet in either direction of a fire hydrant or entrance to a fire station,
- within 25 feet of an intersection of curb lines or, if there are no curb lines, within 15 feet of the intersection of property lines, and
- in any area designated as a fire lane, except that persons who are loading or unloading supplies may park temporarily in a fire lane located in a shopping center or mall parking lot as long as their vehicle is not left unattended.[5]

Except for the restrictions noted above, no statutory prohibition exists against parking on a street or highway. For example, no statewide law makes it unlawful to park on the left side of the road.[6] Of course parking on the left may be prohibited by local ordinance and many cities have done so.

1. Wilson v. Miller, 20 N.C. App. 156, 201 S.E.2d 55 (1973).
2. Peoples v. Fulk, 220 N.C. 635, 18 S.E.2d 147 (1942).
3. Royal v. McClure, 244 N.C. 186, 92 S.E.2d 762 (1956).
4. Section 20-161(a) and (b) of the North Carolina General Statutes (hereinafter G.S.).
5. G.S. 20-162.
6. Webb v. Hutchins, 228 N.C. 1, 44 S.E.2d 350 (1947).

Law enforcement officers are authorized to move illegally parked vehicles to the shoulder of the highway; if such a vehicle is interfering with the flow of traffic or if it constitutes a hazard, it may be towed and stored at the owner's expense. In addition a vehicle left parked illegally anywhere on the right-of-way for forty-eight hours or more may be towed, even if it is not interfering with traffic.[7] However, the owner of a towed vehicle is entitled to an immediate hearing on the legality of the towing. (See the next section on towed motor vehicles.)

G.S. 20-163 provides that a motor vehicle shall not be left unattended on a highway or public vehicular area without the operator stopping the engine, setting the brake, and (on a grade) turning the front wheels to the curb or side of the highway. A person who parks a vehicle at night must dim the lights so that they will not blind oncoming traffic.[8]

That a vehicle is parked illegally is in itself prima facie evidence that it was so parked by its registered owner.[9]

TOWED MOTOR VEHICLES

Article 7A (G.S. 20-219.9, -219.14) allows a person whose vehicle has been towed pursuant to G.S. 20-219.10 to have a prompt hearing before a magistrate to determine whether there was probable cause for the towing. If there was not, then the owner is not responsible for the towing charges. This act was passed as a result of a concern that allowing vehicles to be towed without the opportunity for a prompt hearing would be an unconstitutional taking of property without due process of law. The new law grants the right of a hearing to the registered owner or other person entitled to claim possession of the vehicle that has been towed.[10]

After a vehicle has been towed, the owner (or other claimant who contests the towing) may make a written request for a hearing before a magistrate in the county where the vehicle was towed. The magistrate must set the hearing within seventy-two hours of receiving the request. The officer who ordered the towing and the tower may submit an affidavit rather than personally appearing at the hearing. Any aggrieved party may appeal the magistrate's decision to district court.[11]

Penalties and Points

A violation of G.S. 20-161, -161.1, -162, or -163 is an infraction punishable by a penalty of not more than $100 pursuant to G.S. 20-176. However, if the infraction is based on the prima facie rule of evidence set forth in G.S. 20-162.1 (that is, if the driver cannot be identified), the penalty for a parking violation is limited to $5. Neither driver's license nor insurance points are assigned for parking violations.

7. G.S. 20-161(d) and (e).
8. G.S. 20-161.1.
9. G.S. 20-162.1.
10. G.S. 20-219.11.
11. G.S. 20-219.11.

15 Motorcycles and Mopeds

Motorcycles are defined by Section 20-4.01(27)(d) of the North Carolina General Statutes (hereinafter G.S.) to include motor scooters and motor bikes but not mopeds. As a general rule the same laws that apply to automobiles govern the use of motorcycles. However, a few special provisions apply to the latter, including the following list. Motorcycles must

1. be operated by persons who have either a motorcycle learner's permit (and the required license) or a motorcycle endorsement on their regular driver's license;[1]
2. have their headlights and taillights on at all times when in operation on a highway or public vehicular area;[2]
3. be driven on a highway or public vehicular area only when the operator and all passengers wear helmets as required by G.S. 20-140.4(a);
4. not exceed the number of passengers for which the vehicle is designed to carry;[3]
5. not be operated more than two abreast in a single lane.[4]

Mopeds, though far less numerous on North Carolina roads than they were a decade ago, are still popular in some areas. They are defined by G.S. 20-4.01(27)(d1) as a vehicle that has two or three wheels with a motor that does not exceed 50 cubic centimeters (and cannot propel the vehicle at more than 20 mph on a level surface). While North Carolina law treats motorcycles just about the same as it does the family automobile, mopeds are treated more like bicycles. For example, the definition of motor vehicle contained in G.S. 20-4.01(23) expressly excludes mopeds (as does the definition of motorcycles). Thus any person who has reached age sixteen may operate a moped on a public street without a driver's license,[5] registration, or plates.[6] However, moped operators and passengers are required to wear safety helmets just as if they were riding a motorcycle.[7] Although mopeds are not motor vehicles, they are vehicles and must obey all parts of Chapter 20 that apply to *all* vehicles: They are required to drive on the right, stop for red lights, obey speed limits, and so on. The major distinguishing difference in the law between mopeds and bicycles is that it is unlawful for a person under sixteen to operate a moped on any highway or public vehicular area, and no such restriction applies to those riding bicycles.[8]

---

1. Section 20-7(a1) of the North Carolina General Statutes (hereinafter G.S.).
2. G.S. 20-129(c) and (d).
3. G.S. 20-140.4(a).
4. G.S. 20-146.1.
5. G.S. 20-8(7).
6. G.S. 20-51(9).
7. G.S. 20-140.4.
8. G.S. 20-10.1.

Penalties and Points

A violation of G.S. 20-10.1 (operation of a moped by a person under age sixteen) would be a Class 2 misdemeanor,[9] except than a person under age sixteen is punished as a juvenile. A violation of G.S. 20-129 (required lighting) is an infraction punishable under G.S. 20-176 by a penalty of up to $100. A violation of G.S. 20-140.4 (helmets required) also is an infraction but is punishable under G.S. 20-135.2A(e) and (f) by a penalty of $25. (However, no court costs, driver's license points, or insurance points are assessed.) A violation of G.S. 20-146.1 (motorcycles; more than two abreast) is an infraction punishable under G.S. 20-176 by a penalty of up to $100. For purposes of driver's license points and insurance points, a violation of G.S. 20-129 and -146.1 is treated as any other moving violation, which results in two driver's license points and one insurance point.[10]

9. G.S. 20-35.
10. G.S. 20-16(c). See Chapter 21, "Auto Liability Insurance."

16 School Buses

Section 20-218 of the North Carolina General Statutes (hereinafter G.S.) sets the maximum lawful speed for a school bus loaded with children at 45 mph. A school activity bus used to transport students or others to and from events other than regular classroom work may travel at a maximum speed of 55 mph. Thus, for example, an activity bus carrying students to a football game may travel at up to 55 mph on the highway, unless a lower limit is posted. G.S. 20-218.2 limits the speed of activity buses owned by a nonprofit organization to 55 mph.

Any driver who approaches a school bus from either direction (on the same street, highway, or public vehicular) is required to stop if the bus is displaying its mechanical stop signal or flashing red stop lights and is stopped for the purpose of receiving or discharging passengers. The motorist must remain stopped until the mechanical stop signal has been withdrawn, the flashing red stop lights have been turned off, and the bus has moved on. This requirement does not apply to vehicles approaching a school bus on an intersecting street or to vehicles traveling in the opposite direction on a street divided into two roadways separated by an intervening space or physical barrier (intervening space includes a center left-turn lane if the roadway consists of at least four more lanes).[1]

A person commits this offense if

1. while driving a vehicle
2. on a highway or public vehicular area, that person
3. passes *or* attempts to pass from any direction *on the same highway* or public vehicular area
4. a school bus
5. that is
   (a) displaying its mechanical stop signal or flashing red stoplights and
   (b) is stopped for the purpose of receiving or discharging passengers.

Few cases involving passing a stopped school bus have reached the appellate courts; the most recent may be *State v. Williams*.[2] In that 1988 case, the state had a witness who had recorded the license number of the passing vehicle and was able to describe its driver. In addition, at that time G.S. 20-217 still had a provision that made it prima facie evidence that the registered owner of a vehicle was driving it at the time of a passing violation. That prima facie evidence provision has since expired, making it more difficult now to get such a conviction.

---

1. Section 20-217 of the North Carolina General Statutes (hereinafter G.S.).
2. 90 N.C. App. 120, 367 S.E.2d 345 (1988).

The driver's license requirements for those operating school buses have become somewhat more strict in recent years. Currently the driver of a school bus must be at least eighteen years of age and hold a Class A, B, or C commercial license as well as a school bus driver's certificate. The driver of a school activity bus must meet the same qualifications as a school bus driver or have a license appropriate to the class of vehicle being driven.[3]

Penalties and Points

Passing a stopped school bus in violation of G.S. 20-217 is a Class 2 misdemeanor.[4] Violating the speed limit while operating a school bus, school activity bus, or nonprofit organization bus is a Class 3 misdemeanor.[5]

Passing a stopped school bus results in five driver's license points—more than any other single offense.[6] A special number of driver's license points is not assigned for a school bus driver who exceeds the speed limit. The driver receives the same number of points as if he or she were driving the family car, which depends on the speed of the vehicle at the time of the violation. Conviction of passing a stopped school bus carries four insurance points. A violation of G.S. 20-218 or -218.2 and the assignment of insurance points depend on the ticketed speed of the bus. (See Chapter 21, "Auto Liability Insurance.")

---

3. G.S. 20-218(a).
4. G.S. 20-217(e).
5. G.S. 20-218(c) and -218.2.
6. G.S. 20-16(c).

17 Pedestrians

The word *pedestrian* is not defined by Chapter 20 of the North Carolina General Statutes, but its usual meaning is *one who goes on foot.* The state supreme court has held that a person pushing a handcart on a highway is a pedestrian because the handcart, being propelled solely by human power, is not a vehicle.[1]

G.S. 20-172 authorizes the State Department of Transportation, as well as local authorities, to install WALK or DON'T WALK traffic control signals. Pedestrians facing the WALK signal have the right-of-way over vehicles. Where these special signals are not in operation, pedestrians apparently go or stop according to green or red lights, just as vehicles do.

At places where there are no traffic control signals, a motorist is required to yield the right-of-way to a pedestrian who is crossing the road within either a marked crosswalk or an unmarked crosswalk at or near an intersection.[2] In *Tucker v. Bruton,*[3] the North Carolina Court of Appeals noted that *unmarked crosswalk* is not defined by statute. However, citing earlier precedent, the court defined unmarked crosswalk to mean "an area within an intersection which also lies within the lateral boundaries of a sidewalk projected across the intersection." The court went on to hold that the plaintiff who had been hit by an automobile while crossing a highway was not within an unmarked crosswalk because there was no evidence that there was a "sidewalk-like area" on either side of the intersection (the result might have been different if there had been a sidewalk on just one side of the intersection). When a vehicle is stopped at a marked or unmarked crosswalk to permit a pedestrian to cross, it is unlawful for any driver approaching from the rear to pass the stopped vehicle.[4]

A pedestrian crossing a roadway any place other than within a marked or unmarked crosswalk must yield the right-of-way to vehicles.[5] A pedestrian may not walk along a roadway if sidewalks are provided. Where there are not sidewalks, pedestrians (where practical) must walk on the extreme left, facing traffic, and are required to yield the right-of-way to approaching vehicles.[6]

G.S. 20-174.1 makes it unlawful to stand, sit, or lie on a street in a manner that impedes the regular flow of traffic. Although this provision was probably aimed at demonstrators of various kinds, it might also apply when traffic is blocked by spectators at the scene of a fire or accident. There are very few appellate cases interpreting the wording of G.S. 20-174.1, and thus the law's

1. Lewis v. Watson, 229 N.C. 20, 47 S.E.2d 484 (1948).
2. Section 20-173(a) of the North Carolina General Statutes (hereinafter G.S.).
3. 102 N.C. App. 117, 401 S.E.2d 130 (1991).
4. G.S. 20-173(b).
5. G.S. 20-174(a).
6. G.S. 20-174(d).

exact scope cannot be determined. However, in *Haas v. Clayton*,[7] the court of appeals ruled that a North Carolina man who was injured while helping a motorist push his car off the highway did not violate this section. The court said there must be an intent to impede traffic in order to violate the statute.

G.S. 20-175(a) apparently permits hitchhiking as long as the hitchhiker remains on the shoulder of the road. Standing on the median or on any part of the main-traveled portion of the road to solicit a ride is not allowed.

Penalties and Points

A violation of G.S. 20-172, -173, -174, or -175 is an infraction punishable by a penalty of not more than $100.[8] A violation of 20-174.1 (impeding traffic) is a Class 2 misdemeanor.

A driver who is convicted of failing to yield the right-of-way to a pedestrian is probably assessed three driver's license points, just as for any other situation involving a failure to yield.[9] G.S. 20-172, -174, -174.1, and -175 for the most part describe duties of pedestrians, and no driver's license points—or insurance points—are assigned a pedestrian who violates the law. Failure to yield the right-of-way to a pedestrian probably results in only one insurance point (for any other moving violation). (See Chapter 21, "Auto Liability Insurance.")

7. 125 N.C. App. 200, 479 S.E.2d 805 (1997).
8. G.S. 20-176.
9. G.S. 20-16(c).

18 Hit-and-Run

Although the term *hit-and-run* does not appear in the North Carolina Statutes (hereinafter G.S.), G.S. 20-166 and -166.1 make hit-and-run conduct unlawful. There are at least four kinds of such violations, as follows:

1. failure to stop or to remain at the scene of personal injury or death;[1]
2. failure to give information or assistance where injury or death has occurred;[2]
3. failure to stop or to give information at the scene of property damage only;[3]
4. failure to notify authorities of a reportable accident.[4]

FAILURE TO STOP

A person commits this offense if that person

1. drives
2. a vehicle that is
3. involved in an accident or collision
4. causing personal injury or death and
5. he or she knows or reasonably should have known that the vehicle was involved in an accident or collision and
6. he or she
   (a) willfully fails to stop at the scene of the accident or collision; or
   (b) willfully fails to remain at the scene until authorized to leave by a law enforcement officer; or
   (c) willfully fails to return to the scene after temporarily leaving to call for an officer or medical assistance.

---

1. Section 20-166(a) of the North Carolina General Statutes (hereinafter G.S.).
2. G.S. 20-166(b).
3. G.S. 20-166(c) and (c1).
4. G.S. 20-166.1 and -4.01(33b).

FAILURE TO GIVE INFORMATION OR ASSISTANCE (INJURY OR DEATH INVOLVED)

A person commits this offense if that person

1. drives
2. a vehicle that is
3. involved in an accident or collision
4. causing personal injury or death and
5. he or she knows or reasonably should have known that the vehicle was involved in an accident or collision and
6. he or she
   (a) fails to give his or her name, address, and driver's license and license plate numbers to any person struck and to the driver or any occupants collided with or
   (b) fails to render reasonable assistance to any person injured in the accident or collision.

FAILURE TO STOP OR GIVE INFORMATION (PROPERTY DAMAGE ONLY)

A person commits this offense if that person

1. drives
2. a vehicle that is
3. involved in an accident or collision
4. causing
   (a) only property damage or
   (b) personal injury or death that is not apparent, and
5. he or she knows or reasonably should have known that the vehicle was involved in an accident or collision and
6. he or she fails to
   (a) stop at the scene of the accident or
   (b) give his or her name, address, and driver's license and license plate numbers to any person in any other vehicle involved in the accident and to any person whose property is damaged in the accident or collision.

FAILURE TO NOTIFY AUTHORITIES

A person commits this offense if that person

1. drives
2. a vehicle that is
3. involved in an accident or collision resulting in personal injury or death, or property damage of $1,000 or more, and
4. he or she fails to immediately notify a law enforcement agency
5. by the quickest means of communication.

An unusual feature of North Carolina hit-and-run law, as contained in G.S. 20-166, is that it applies *both on and off* public streets and highways, even though Chapter 20 does not specifically so state. Apparently a driver who is involved in an accident or collision on private property (even if the private property does not constitute a public vehicular area) has the same duty to stop, render aid, and so forth, as the motorist who is involved in an accident on a public highway. Nor is fault a factor; the requirements of G.S. 20-166 apply to the innocent and guilty alike.[5] The word *property* as used in G.S. 20-166 apparently includes any property, whether it be a vehicle, fire hydrant, house, tree, or some other object. Thus a driver who strikes a domestic animal, such as a dog or cat (or livestock), apparently must comply with the provisions of G.S. 20-166 or be guilty of hit-and-run.

A driver involved in a collision as described in G.S. 20-166(a) must render assistance to any injured person. This duty includes calling for medical assistance when it is apparent that medical assistance is necessary or when requested to do so by the injured person.[6] The North Carolina Supreme Court has held that a driver must *personally* give the information and render the assistance required by G.S. 20-166. Thus a driver who stopped 200 yards from the scene of an accident and sent another person back to render aid was found guilty of violating this section.[7] The state supreme court has also held that the law does not require useless acts. Thus a driver need not attempt to impart the information required by G.S. 20-166 to an unconscious person.[8]

The driver of a motor vehicle involved in a collision that results in death, personal injury, or total property damage of $1,000 or more has been involved in a *reportable accident* (crash) as that term is defined in G.S. 20-4.01(33b). G.S. 20-166.1 requires such a driver to report the accident to the state Highway Patrol or the county sheriff's office if the accident occurred outside of municipal limits and to the city police if the accident occurred inside a city or town. In addition G.S. 20-166.1(b) requires the driver of a vehicle involved in a reportable accident to furnish proof of financial responsibility upon request of the Division. Finally G.S. 20-166.1(c) requires a motorist whose vehicle collides with a motor vehicle parked on a street or highway to report the collision to the owner of the unattended vehicle. This report must be made within forty-eight hours of the accident. Usually the report must be sent to the owner by certified mail (return receipt requested) with a copy sent to the Division.

Penalties and Points

A violation of G.S. 20-166(a) (failure to stop in event of injury or death) is a Class H felony, one of the few felonies in the North Carolina motor vehicle law. A violation of Subsection (b) (failure to give information or to render assistance in the event of death or injury) is a Class 1 misdemeanor. A violation of Subsections (c) or (c1) (usually property damage only) also is punishable as a Class 1 misdemeanor. When a required report is not made pursuant to any provision G.S. 20-166.1, the offense is punishable as a Class 2 misdemeanor pursuant to G.S. 20-176.

Failure to stop and render aid in violation of G.S. 20-166(a) or (b) requires revocation of the driver's license.[9] Hit-and-run involving property damage only results in four driver's license points pursuant to G.S. 20-16(c); failure to report an accident, three driver's license points.

Twelve insurance points are assigned for failure to stop and render aid when involved in an accident resulting in bodily injury or death, whereas only four are assigned for failure to stop and report if the accident results in property damage only. (See Chapter 21, "Auto Liability Insurance.")

5. State v. Smith, 264 N.C. 575, 142 S.E.2d 149 (1965).
6. G.S. 20-166(b).
7. State v. Brown, 226 N.C. 681, 40 S.E.2d 34 (1946).
8. State v. Coggin, 263 N.C. 457, 139 S.E.2d 701 (1965).
9. G.S. 20-17(4).

19 Other Statutory Offenses

Several other violations of motor vehicle law as set forth in the North Carolina General Statutes (hereinafter G.S.), while not necessarily related and not fitting under any particular category, are committed often enough to deserve mention. The following is a discussion of the most important such statutory offenses.

Interstates and controlled-access highways. G.S. 20-140.3 sets forth special and additional rules with respect to the use of interstates and other controlled-access highways. Subdivision (2), for example, makes it unlawful to make a "U-turn" except through an opening provided for that purpose. (As a general rule, "U-turns" are not illegal, absent a local ordinance to the contrary.)

Driving on sidewalks. G.S. 20-160 makes it unlawful to drive a motor vehicle on a sidewalk. Because this statute uses the term *motor vehicle* rather than *vehicle*, bicycles and mopeds apparently may be legally driven on a sidewalk (unless prohibited by a local ordinance).

Animal riding. G.S. 20-171 provides that a person who is riding an animal (or driving an animal-drawn vehicle) is "subject to the provisions of this article applicable to the driver of a vehicle, except those provisions of the article which by their nature can have no application." For the most part, this means that a person riding an animal must follow the rules of the road, that is, travel on the right side of the street, stop for red lights, and otherwise obey the same traffic rules of the road as followed by the drivers of vehicles.

In *State v. Dellinger*,[1] for example, the North Carolina Court of Appeals found that the defendant, who was riding a horse while impaired, was guilty of driving while impaired (DWI) because horses were vehicles within the meaning of G.S. 20-138.1. Subsequent to that decision the General Assembly amended the statute to provide that the word *vehicle* does not include a horse, bicycle, or lawnmower. However, the court's reasoning in *Dellinger* should still apply to other rules-of-the-road violations.

Mandatory seatbelt use. G.S. 20-135.2A makes seatbelt use mandatory for those on the front seat of a passenger motor vehicle.

Child passenger restraints. G.S. 20-137.1 requires that children under age sixteen be properly secured in a child passenger restraint system (or seat belt) that meets federal standards. A child less than five (and under 40 pounds) must be in a child passenger restraint system.

Blue lights. G.S. 20-130.1 makes it unlawful to use a blue light except for law enforcement purposes.

1. 73 N.C. App. 685, 327 S.E.2d 609 (1985).

In addition to the miscellaneous Chapter 20 offenses mentioned above, a few motor vehicle offenses are contained in other chapters of the General Statutes. Two of those offenses are discussed below.

Joyriding. G.S. 14-72.2 (North Carolina's joyriding statute) makes it unlawful for a person (without permission) to take another's car for a drive, even if there is no intent to steal it. A person violates this statute if he or she

1. willfully takes or operates
2. a motor-propelled conveyance
3. of another person
4. without the consent of the owner or person in lawful possession of it.

Several cases have held a violation of this section to be a lesser included offense of larceny. It should be noted, however, that if there is intent on the part of the defendant to permanently deprive the vehicle's owner of the vehicle, larceny would be the proper charge.[2]

With very few exceptions, Chapter 20 of the General Statutes cannot be enforced on strictly private property that is located beyond the right-of-way and does not constitute a public vehicular area. Also Chapter 20 probably does not apply to streets or highways that are closed or under construction because such roads would not be open to the public "as a matter of right," as required by G.S. 20-4.01(13). Thus a person who is speeding, driving while impaired, or committing another such offense on a closed highway probably should be charged with a violation of G.S. 136-26 (closing of state highways during construction) rather than be cited for a Chapter 20 offense. (Section 136-26 apparently does not apply to city streets, however.)

Penalties and Points

A violation of G.S. 20-140.3 or -160 is an infraction punishable by a penalty of not more than $100 pursuant to G.S. 20-176(b). A violation of 20-135.2A (seat belt law) is an infraction punishable by a fine of $25, but court costs may not be assessed.[3] A violation of the child passenger restraint law, as contained in G.S. 20-137.1, can result in a penalty of $25, but a driver violating this section with regard to a child under five years of age will not be convicted if he or she produces in court proof that a child passenger restraint system has been acquired since the violation occurred. A violation of G.S. 14-72.2 (joyriding) is a Class 1 misdemeanor. Driving on a closed state highway in violation of G.S. 136-26 also is a Class 1 misdemeanor.

A conviction of violating G.S. 20-140.3 or -160 usually results in the assignment of two driver's license points (for any other moving violation). However, failure to yield the right-of-way and driving through a safety zone are three-point violations pursuant to G.S. 20-16(c). Driving on the wrong side of the road results in four driver's license points.

One insurance point (for any other moving violation) usually is assigned for a violation of G.S. 20-140.3 (interstate highways) or -160, but two insurance points might be assigned for a violation of G.S. 140.3(3) for driving on the wrong side of the road. No driver's license points or insurance points are assigned for a violation of the regular seat belt law or for the child passenger restraint law as contained in G.S. 20-135.2A and -137.1. Driver's license points and insurance points usually are not assigned for offenses in Chapter 14 or Chapter 136 of the General Statutes, although such offenses could involve a motor vehicle.

---

2. State v. McRae, 58 N.C. App. 225, 292 S.E.2d 778 (1982).
3. Section 20-135.2A(e) of the North Carolina General Statutes.

20 Vehicular Homicide

When injury or death results from the violation of a motor vehicle law, the violator may be guilty of an offense somewhat more serious than those outlined in Chapter 20 of the North Carolina General Statutes (hereinafter G.S.). North Carolina courts have consistently held that if a person's culpable (that is, criminal) negligence in the operation of a motor vehicle is the proximate cause of death, he or she may be guilty of involuntary manslaughter. When malice also is found, prosecution for second-degree murder also is a possibility.

FIRST-DEGREE MURDER

See Chapter 2 of Part Two (beginning on page 103).

SECOND-DEGREE MURDER

Murder in the second degree[1] is the unlawful killing of a human being *with malice but without premeditation*. Malice does not necessarily mean an actual intent to take human life; it may be inferred or implied, as when an action is taken so recklessly or wantonly as to manifest depravity of mind and disregard for human life. Thus in *State v. Trott*,[2] an early impaired driving case involving death, the state supreme court upheld a second-degree murder conviction occasioned by a vehicle driven by a highly intoxicated person hitting another car and killing one of its occupants. This principle was reiterated in *State v. Peterson*,[3] wherein the driver of a lumber truck was convicted of second-degree murder after it was shown that (1) while intoxicated and (2) traveling at an excessive speed, he (3) lost control of his vehicle and (4) fatally injured a woman who was standing completely off the road. There was absolutely no evidence that the defendant intentionally harmed the woman or anyone else. More recently, in *State v. Snyder*,[4] the state supreme court upheld a second-degree murder conviction because the driver's conduct was found to be reckless and "in total disregard for human life."

1. Section 14-17 of the North Carolina General Statutes (hereinafter G.S.).
2. 190 N.C. 674, 130 S.E. 627 (1925).
3. 212 N.C. 758, 194 S.E. 498 (1938).
4. 311 N.C. 391, 317 S.E.2d 394 (1984).

A person commits second-degree murder by

1. killing
2. another living human being
3. with malice.

INVOLUNTARY MANSLAUGHTER

The reported cases indicate that to be found guilty of involuntary manslaughter, a defendant must have committed an act of culpable negligence proximately resulting in death. It is not possible to list or outline *exactly* what acts on a motorist's part constitute the culpable negligence necessary for a manslaughter conviction because the facts and circumstances of the cases tend to vary widely, but the following examples are illustrative.

The defendant in *State v. McKenzie*[5] had struck and killed a bicycle rider who was proceeding lawfully in his own lane of traffic—after dark but with a rear reflector on the bicycle. The defendant admitted to consuming four beers and exceeding the speed limit. A chemical test of his blood showed that he registered an alcohol concentration of 0.10 and thus that he also was driving while impaired (DWI). The defendant's conviction for involuntary manslaughter was upheld by the appellate courts. A more recent state supreme court decision, *State v. McGill*,[6] indicates that an involuntary manslaughter conviction can be based on DWI alone without any proof whatsoever that there was any additional rule-of-the-road violation.

Another typical involuntary manslaughter case is *State v. Gainey*,[7] wherein the defendant was found to have violated G.S. 20-158(a) by failing to yield the right-of-way and G.S. 20-141(a) by driving at a speed greater than what was reasonable and prudent. The North Carolina Supreme Court concluded that the evidence was entirely adequate to support a finding that the defendant's violations constituted culpable negligence. In cases where death does not result, striking a person with a vehicle might be found to be assault with a deadly weapon.[8]

A person commits this offense by

1. killing
2. another living human being
3. unlawfully by
   (a) committing an unlawful act that does not amount to a predicate felony for felony murder or is not inherently dangerous to life; or
   (b) engaging in any other conduct in such a reckless and careless manner as to show a thoughtless disregard for the consequences or a heedless indifference to the rights and safety of others; or
   (c) culpably failing to perform a legal duty.

---

5. 292 N.C. 170, 232 S.E.2d 424 (1977).
6. 314 N.C. 633, 336 S.E.2d 90 (1985).
7. 292 N.C. 627, 234 S.E.2d 610 (1977).
8. State v. Ferguson, 261 N.C. 558, 135 S.E.2d 626 (1964).

DEATH BY VEHICLE

Death by vehicle is an appropriate charge when death results from the violation of a traffic law or ordinance but the element of culpable (that is, criminal) negligence necessary for a successful manslaughter prosecution is missing.[9] In fact the difficulty of establishing culpable negligence in manslaughter cases probably was the reason this offense was put into the motor vehicle law. A person is guilty of *felony* death by vehicle if that person

1. kills
2. another living human being
3. unintentionally
4. while engaged in
   (a) the offense of impaired driving under G.S. 20-138.1 or
   (b) the offense of impaired driving in a commercial vehicle under G.S. 20-138.2 and
5. commission of the impaired driving offense is the proximate cause of death.

There have not been many appellate court cases involving G.S. 20-141.4, but in one, the North Carolina Court of Appeals held that *felony* death by vehicle is not a lesser included offense of involuntary manslaughter but that *misdemeanor* death by vehicle is.[10]

A person is guilty of *misdemeanor* death by vehicle if that person

1. kills
2. another living human being
3. unintentionally
4. while committing a violation of any state law or local ordinance applying to the operation and use of a vehicle or to the regulation of traffic (other than those related to impaired driving) and
5. commission of that offense is the proximate cause of death.

In *State v. Thompson*,[11] the North Carolina Court of Appeals, in distinguishing death by vehicle from involuntary manslaughter, noted that criminal responsibility for death by vehicle is not dependent on culpable (criminal) negligence. It would appear then that if a driver's negligence is found to be culpable that the proper charge is involuntary manslaughter.

Penalties and Points

Assault with a deadly weapon (including a vehicle) is a Class A1 misdemeanor, whereas involuntary manslaughter is a Class F felony.[12] Second-degree murder is punished as a Class B2 felony.[13] Felony death by vehicle is a Class G felony, and misdemeanor death by vehicle is a Class 1 misdemeanor.[14]

G.S. 20-17 and -19(f) provide for a one-year license revocation for persons convicted of manslaughter (or negligent homicide) resulting from the operation of a motor vehicle, death by vehicle, and assault with a motor vehicle. However, when the person's license is revoked for manslaughter

9. G.S. 20-141.4.
10. State v. Williams, 90 N.C. App. 614, 369 S.E.2d 832 (1988).
11. 37 N.C. App. 444, 246 S.E.2d 81 (1978).
12. G.S. 14-18 and -33.
13. G.S. 14-17.
14. G.S. 20-141.4.

(negligent homicide) or death by vehicle and the offense involves impaired driving, G.S. 20-19(i) makes the license revocation permanent.

Twelve insurance points are assigned for manslaughter (or negligent homicide) resulting from the operation of a motor vehicle. Negligent homicide probably includes second-degree murder and death by vehicle.

21 Auto Liability Insurance

Fred, a Raleigh motorist, had been carrying a fairly standard automobile insurance package: $100,000 per person/$300,000 per accident bodily injury coverage, at a cost of $228 per year, and $50,000 property damage coverage, at a cost of $147 per year, for a total of $375 annually. Last New Year's Eve he was arrested and convicted of driving while impaired. His policy was transferred (ceded) to the Reinsurance Facility (an entity he had never heard of before) so that for the next three years, Fred's liability insurance will be calculated as follows: (1) bodily injury coverage will rise to $325, property damage coverage to $219, for a total of $544; and (2) this $544 will be surcharged by 400 percent (twelve insurance points) because of the driving-while-impaired conviction, for a total of $2,720.[1] *This constitutes more than a 700 percent increase for the one conviction.*

The rates that North Carolinians pay for automobile liability insurance coverage depend on several factors: the basic premium rates found in the *North Carolina Personal Auto Manual*; insurance points they have accumulated in the past three years for moving violations and accidents;[2] whether their insurance company has transferred their coverage to the Reinsurance Facility; where in the state they live; and whether the policy covers a driver with less than three years of experience. This chapter explains how insurance rates are set for North Carolina motor vehicle owners.[3]

THE SAFE DRIVER INSURANCE PLAN

All insurance companies approved to provide automobile liability insurance coverage in North Carolina must be members of the North Carolina Rate Bureau.[4] The Rate Bureau is required by law to develop and recommend to the North Carolina commissioner of insurance the components of the Safe Driver Insurance Plan (SDIP), which establishes classifications of drivers based on their

---

This chapter is an updated version of Ben F. Loeb, Jr., "Rate Plan for Automobile Liability Insurance: An Update," *Popular Government* 60 (Winter 1995): 34–42.

1. The 400 percent surcharge of $2,176 is added to the Reinsurance Facility rate of $544 for a total of $2,720.

2. The Safe Driver Insurance Plan (SDIP), which is contained in the *North Carolina Personal Auto Manual*, applies not only to premiums for bodily injury and property damage liability insurance but also to premiums for medical payments, fire, theft, and various other coverages. This chapter is devoted to liability insurance because that coverage is required by North Carolina law. *North Carolina Personal Auto Manual* (Raleigh, N.C.: Insurance Services Office, Inc., published yearly) (hereinafter *Auto Manual*).

3. Auto insurance rules and rates are under almost constant revision; these data are effective as of January 1999. Except as otherwise indicated, all information in this chapter was derived from the *Auto Manual*.

4. Section 58-36 of the North Carolina General Statutes (hereinafter G.S.).

Table 1
Surcharge per Insurance Point

Points	Surcharge (%)	Points	Surcharge (%)
One	25	Seven	180
Two	45	Eight	220
Three	65	Nine	260
Four	90	Ten	300
Five	120	Eleven	350
Six	150	Twelve	400

histories of accidents and convictions for violations.[5] The SDIP, once approved—and then as modified over time—sets the basic automobile insurance rates. The SDIP is most conveniently found in the *North Carolina Personal Auto Manual.*

INSURANCE POINTS

A major factor in determining how much a motor vehicle owner pays for liability insurance coverage under the SDIP is the number of insurance points on his or her driving record (or on the record of members of the household covered by the same insurance policy). The number of points on the driving record determines the percentage surcharge to be added under the SDIP to the owner's insurance costs. Table 1 shows how points determine the surcharge.

Points are assessed according to a schedule for convictions of various moving violations and for accidents in which the insured was at fault. For points to be assessed, the conviction or accident must have occurred during the *experience period,* which is defined as the three years immediately preceding the date of application or the preparation of the renewal of the insured's policy. SDIP points are applied to a policy for a period of not less nor more than three policy years; the surcharge is, in effect, added to the cost of insurance on the car on which the owner already pays the highest total for liability, comprehensive, and collision coverages combined.[6] Note that *insurance points are completely different from driver's license points,* which are used by the North Carolina Division of Motor Vehicles for the purpose of revoking licenses.

Points for Convictions

Table 2 shows the convictions that will result in points and insurance surcharges.[7] For purposes of the SDIP, the word conviction includes a plea of guilty or *nolo contendere.* It also includes a determination of guilt by a jury or by a court even when no sentence is imposed (which is a prayer for judgment continued, or PJC) or, when a sentence is imposed, if it has been suspended. It also includes a forfeiture of bail or collateral deposited to secure appearance in court, unless the forfeiture has been vacated. The SDIP provides that a conviction does not include PJC if it is the first PJC for all licensed operators in the insured's household. (This provision is commonly interpreted to mean the first PJC within the three-year experience period. Apparently each household can receive one PJC every three years without it counting as a conviction, with the resulting insurance points.) The term *moving traffic violation* includes infractions as described in Section 14-3.1 of the North Carolina General Statutes (hereinafter G.S.): noncriminal violations of law not punishable by imprisonment.[8]

5. G.S. 58-36-65.
6. *Auto Manual,* NC-GR-7, 8, 11.
7. As contained at NC-GR-5, 6 of the *Auto Manual.*
8. *See* G.S. 58-36-75(f), (g).

Table 2
Number of Insurance Points per Moving Violation or Accident

Twelve Points

- manslaughter (or negligent homicide) resulting from the operation of a motor vehicle
- prearranged highway racing or knowingly lending a motor vehicle to be used in a prearranged race
- failure to stop and render aid when involved in an accident resulting in bodily injury or death (hit-and-run driving)
- impaired driving, including driving a vehicle while under the influence of an impairing substance; driving a vehicle with an alcohol concentration of 0.08 percent or more; and driving a commercial vehicle with an alcohol concentration of 0.04 percent or more (a revocation pursuant to G.S. 20-16.5 is not a conviction)
- Transportation of intoxicating liquors for the purpose of sale

Ten Points

- highway racing (not prearranged) or knowingly lending a motor vehicle to be used in a race
- speeding to elude arrest

Eight Points

- operating a motor vehicle during a period of revocation or suspension of either the driver's license or vehicle registration

Four Points

- failure to stop and report when involved in a motor vehicle accident resulting in property damage only (hit-and-run)
- reckless driving
- passing a stopped school bus
- speeding in excess of 75 mph when posted limit is less than 70 mph
- speeding in excess of 80 mph when limit is 70 mph or greater
- driving by person under age twenty-one after consuming alcohol or drugs

Two Points

- illegal passing
- speeding more than 10 mph over the limit, provided total speed was in excess of 55 mph but less than 76 mph
- speeding 10 mph or less in excess of limit in speed zone of 55 mph or greater[a]
- following too closely
- driving on the wrong side of the road

One Point

- speeding 10 mph or less in excess of speed limit of less than 55 mph[a]
- any other moving violation

No Points

- Points are not assigned for equipment violations (except brakes) or for failure to display a registration card, license plate, current inspection certificate, or driver's license (as long as a valid one exists).

a. Points are not assigned for these violations unless the same driver has been convicted of at least one other moving violation during the experience period (the last three years).

Points for Accidents (On or after January 1, 1998)

Points are assigned for each accident that occurs during a three-year experience period as follows:

- Three points are assigned for an at-fault accident that results in bodily injury (damages in excess of $1,500) or death or total property damage—including that of the insured—of $2,500 or more.
- Two points are assigned for an at-fault accident that results in total property damage in excess of $1,500 but less than $2,500.
- One point is assigned for each at-fault accident that results in total property damage of $1,500 or less or personal injuries of $1,500 or less.

At-fault means negligent; no points are assigned for accidents when the operator of the insured vehicle is free of negligence. The initial determination of negligence is made by the insurance company, which usually will pay under the liability coverage only if the operator is negligent. If the company pays, it probably will assess at-fault points. In addition the SDIP specifically provides that no points are assigned under the following circumstances:

- The auto was lawfully parked when damaged.
- The vehicle owner was reimbursed by the person who was responsible for the accident or a judgment was rendered against the person responsible for the accident.
- The auto was struck in the rear and the operator of the struck vehicle was not convicted of a moving violation in connection with the accident.
- The operator of the other auto was convicted of a moving traffic violation and the insured was not convicted of a moving traffic violation in connection with the accident.
- The auto was struck by a hit-and-run vehicle and the insured reported the accident to the proper authority within twenty-four hours of the accident.
- The accident involved damage from contact with animals or fowl.
- The accident involved physical damage caused by flying gravel, missiles, or falling objects.
- The accident occurred as a result of the operation of a fire-fighting, rescue, or law enforcement vehicle responding to an emergency, if the operator was a paid or volunteer member of any fire department, rescue squad, or law enforcement agency.

In the case of one-point accidents, a surcharge is not assigned if (1) the operator was not convicted of a moving traffic violation in connection with the accident and (2) the vehicle owner, principal operator, and all licensed operators in the owner's household had no convictions for moving traffic violations and no other at-fault accidents during the three-year period immediately preceding the date of application or the date of preparation of renewal of the policy. In the event of a moving violation in connection with an accident, only the higher surcharge points are assigned (a driver will not get points for both).[9]

THE REINSURANCE FACILITY

After points, the second major factor affecting the cost of liability insurance is whether a motor vehicle owner has been transferred (through a process known as *ceding*) to the North Carolina Motor Vehicle Reinsurance Facility, a nonprofit legal entity consisting of all insurers engaged in writing motor vehicle insurance in North Carolina. The purpose of the Reinsurance Facility is to make liability insurance available to drivers or vehicle owners whom companies do not wish to insure as part of their regular voluntary business. In brief, it is a method of transferring the risk of loss from the individual insurance company to all insurance companies.[10]

North Carolina law makes no provision regarding which individuals are to be ceded to the Reinsurance Facility. The decision belongs entirely to each particular insurance company. If an applicant for motor vehicle liability insurance is, for any reason, considered an undesirable risk by a company, it may cede the applicant to the Reinsurance Facility, even if the person has a clean driving record. In other words, it is possible for a person who has never received a traffic citation, or had an accident, to be ceded to the Reinsurance Facility. Obviously those with bad driving records are prime candidates, but a company may transfer for any reason anyone it considers a bad risk. Reportedly young and elderly drivers, as well as drivers in certain occupational groups, often fall

9. *Auto Manual*, NC-GR-6, 7, 8.
10. G.S. 58-37.

Table 3
Regular (Voluntary) Business[a]

	Bodily Injury Limit				Property Damage Limit			Medical Payments Limit				
Territory	25/ 50/	50/ 100	100/ 300	300/ 300	15,000	25,000	50,000	500	750	1,000	2,000	5,000
11	$118	$144	$170	$183	$120	$122	$125	$11	$15	$18	$26	$37
13	177	216	255	274	135	138	140	16	21	26	37	54
14	150	183	216	233	137	140	142	14	19	22	33	47
15	164	200	236	254	126	129	131	15	20	24	35	51
16	158	193	228	245	141	144	147	14	19	22	33	47
17	190	232	274	295	137	140	142	17	23	27	40	57
18	121	148	174	188	115	117	120	11	15	18	26	37
24	126	154	181	195	110	112	114	12	16	19	28	41
25	169	206	243	262	139	142	145	15	20	24	35	51
26	195	238	281	302	116	118	121	18	24	29	42	61
31	177	216	255	274	122	124	127	16	21	26	37	54
32	129	157	186	200	115	117	120	12	16	19	28	41
33	163	199	235	253	105	107	109	15	20	24	35	51
40	200	244	288	310	141	144	147	18	24	29	42	61
41	155	189	223	240	121	123	126	14	19	22	33	47
43	144	176	207	223	104	106	108	13	17	21	30	44
47	140	171	202	217	108	110	112	13	17	21	30	44
51	147	179	212	228	132	135	137	13	17	21	30	44
52	216	264	311	335	158	161	164	20	27	32	47	68

a. Including "clean risks" ceded to the North Carolina Reinsurance Facility.

Table 4
Ceded Business[a]

	Bodily Injury Limit			Property Damage Limit			Medical Payments Limit			
Territory	25/ 50/	50/ 100	100/ 300	15,000	25,000	50,000	500	750	1,000	2,000
11	$156	$190	$225	$160	$163	$166	$18	$24	$29	$42
13	252	307	363	190	194	198	29	39	46	68
14	225	275	324	198	202	206	25	33	40	59
15	244	298	351	197	201	205	28	37	45	66
16	226	276	325	211	215	219	26	35	42	61
17	288	351	415	212	216	220	33	44	53	77
18	187	228	269	177	181	184	21	28	34	49
24	183	223	264	152	155	158	21	28	34	49
25	249	304	359	222	226	231	28	37	45	66
26	314	383	452	165	168	172	36	48	58	84
31	251	316	376	178	182	185	30	40	48	70
32	190	232	274	165	168	172	21	28	34	49
33	231	282	333	142	145	148	26	35	42	61
40	281	343	405	186	190	193	32	43	51	75
41	252	307	363	180	184	187	29	39	46	68
43	219	267	315	149	152	155	25	33	40	59
47	247	301	356	155	158	161	28	37	45	66
51	193	235	278	175	179	182	22	29	35	51
52	284	346	409	226	231	235	32	43	51	75

a. Excluding "clean risks."

within this category. There is no appeal process, but applicants may seek coverage with another company that would not cede them to the Reinsurance Facility.

Because the Reinsurance Facility has many high-risk drivers, the SDIP provides that it may charge a higher base rate than is allowed in the voluntary market. But insureds ceded to the Reinsurance Facility who are *clean risks*—meaning, for this purpose, that no one on the policy has any points and no driver on the policy has less than two years of driving experience—pay the same as other policyholders with clean driving records who have not been ceded.[11] However, a driver in the Reinsurance Facility who has *any points at all* pays the higher base rate. In the 1970s this rate was only slightly higher, but by the mid-1990s rates for drivers in the Reinsurance Facility who had insurance points were more than 50 percent higher. And those drivers pay the surcharge for their points on top of that higher rate.

Table 3 shows the base cost for insurance before any surcharge for points is added when the insurance is handled as voluntary business (that is, not ceded to the Reinsurance Facility). Table 4 shows the comparable base cost for an owner with points whose policy has been ceded to the Reinsurance Facility.

TERRITORY

The third factor determining a North Carolinian's automobile liability insurance costs is where the person lives in the state. North Carolina is divided into nineteen territories, each with its own base rate. The cost of insurance varies considerably from territory to territory. For example, the base cost for $100,000/$300,000 bodily injury coverage for a motor vehicle owner with no points is $170 in Asheville (Territory 11), whereas the identical coverage in Charlotte (Territory 52) is $311. For a vehicle owner whose policy has been ceded to the Reinsurance Facility (and who has even one point, therefore paying the higher Reinsurance Facility base rate), the cost for the same coverage would be $225 in Asheville and $409 in Charlotte (plus, in each case, the surcharge for the points). Table 5 lists the areas covered in the nineteen territories.[12]

INEXPERIENCED DRIVER SURCHARGE

A fourth factor that can raise an insured's liability insurance cost is inexperience as a driver, which usually correlates closely with age. The 1975 Session of the North Carolina General Assembly enacted legislation intended to prohibit insurance rates from being based on the age or sex of the insured. Specifically G.S. 58-3-25 provides: "No insurer shall . . . base any standard or rating plan for private passenger automobiles or motorcycles, in whole or in part, directly or indirectly, upon the age or sex of the persons insured." But the youngest drivers typically pay higher insurance rates (or have their parents pay the higher rates for them) because the surcharge is added to policies that cover drivers who have fewer than three years of driving experience as a licensed driver. (The surcharge is not added when a member of the household begins driving under a learner's permit; and time spent driving on a learner's permit does not count toward the three years.) For most drivers the surcharge is applied from age sixteen to nineteen, causing its impact to be felt most by young people and those who pay the insurance for young people, but the same rule would be applicable to a fifty-year-old if that person had no previous driving experience. This surcharge approximately doubles the cost of liability insurance on the car that the inexperienced driver "principally operates."[13]

11. *Auto Manual*, NC-GR-2.
12. *Auto Manual*, NC-T-1 to NC-T-3 and PA-R-001,002.
13. *Auto Manual*, NC-GR-4.

Table 5
North Carolina Territories for Automobile Liability Insurance Coverage

Alamance County—*see Burlington-Graham and remainder of state.*

Asheville (Territory 11) comprises the entire city of Asheville and all territory in Buncombe County included in the townships of Asheville, Limestone and Lower Hominy, including all of the following towns, cities, or places: Acton, Arden, Asheville School, Biltmore Forest, Boswell, Buena Vista, Busbee, Craggy, Emma, Enka, Haw Creek, Hominy, Luthers, New Bridge, Oakley, Oteen, Shiloh, Skyland, Woodfin

Beaufort County (Territory 33) comprises all territory in Beaufort County

Bertie County (Territory 33) comprises all territory in Bertie County

Bladen County (Territory 33) comprises all territory in Bladen County

Brunswick County (Territory 26) comprises all territory in Brunswick County not included in Wilmington territory

Buncombe County (Territory 32) comprises all territory in Buncombe County not included in Asheville territory

Burlington-Graham (Territory 32) comprises the entire city of Burlington; the entire town of Graham; all territory in Alamance County included in townships 3 (Boon Station), 6 (Graham), 10 (Melville), 12 (Burlington), and 13 (Haw River); the entire town of Mebane in Alamance and Orange counties, and all of the following towns, cities, or places: Elon College, Gibsonville, Glen Raven, Haw River, Kirkpatrick Heights, Lake Latham, Ossipee, Richmond Hill

Cabarrus County—*see Concord-Kannapolis-Salisbury and remainder of state.*

Camden County (Territory 33) comprises all territory in Camden County

Carteret County (Territory 33) comprises all territory in Carteret County

Charlotte (Territory 52) comprises the entire city of Charlotte and all areas in Mecklenburg County except those areas with U.S. postal ZIP codes 28025, 28026, 28031, 28036, 28075, 28078 and 28115

Chowan County (Territory 33) comprises all territory in Chowan County

Columbus County (Territory 26) comprises all territory in Columbus County

Concord-Kannapolis-Salisbury (Territory 32) comprises the entire cities of Concord, Kannapolis, and Salisbury; all territory in Cabarrus County included in townships 1 (Rocky River), 2 (Poplar Tent), 4 (Kannapolis), 5 (Mount Gilead), 11 (Baptist Church), and 12 (Concord); and all territory in Rowan County included in the townships of China Grove, Franklin, Litaka, and Salisbury, including all of the following towns, cities, or places: Brown-Norcott Mills, China Grove, Cooks Crossing, East Spencer, Faggarts Crossroads, Faith, Franklin, Glass, Harrisburg, Jackson Park, Landis, Majolica, Mount Gilead, Pharrs Mills, Pioneer Mills, Roberta Mills, Rocky Ridge, Rocky River, South River, Spencer, Yadkin Junction, Yost

Craven County (Territory 43) comprises all territory in Craven County

Cumberland County (Territory 26) comprises all territory in Cumberland County not included in Fayetteville territory

Currituck County (Territory 33) comprises all territory in Currituck County

Dare County (Territory 33) comprises all territory in Dare County

Davidson County—*see Lexington-Thomasville and remainder of state.*

Duplin County (Territory 33) comprises all territory in Duplin County

Durham (Territory 13) comprises the entire city of Durham and all territory in Durham County included in the townships of Durham, Oak Grove, and Patterson, including all of the following towns, cities, or places: Bethesda, Bilboa, Few, Gorman, Hope Valley, Joyland, North Durham, Oak Grove, Redwood

Durham County (Territory 32) comprises all territory in Durham County not included in Durham territory

Edgecombe County (Territory 33) comprises all territory in Edgecombe County not included in Rocky Mount territory

Fayetteville (Territory 40) comprises the entire city of Fayetteville; all territory in the Fort Bragg and Pope Air Force Base Military Reservations in Cumberland County; and all territory in Cumberland County included in the townships of Carvers Creek, Cross Creek, Eastover, Manchester, Pearces Mill, Rockfish, and Seventy First, including all of the following towns, cities, or places:

Continued on next page.

Table 5, *continued*
North Carolina Territories for Automobile Liability Insurance Coverage

Beard, Bonnie Doone, Cliffdale, Cumberland, Fenix, Gardners Chapel, Hope Mills, Lakedale, Linden, Manchester, Milan, Myrtle Hill, Owens, Roslin, Shaws, Slocomb, South Fayetteville, Spring Lake, Tokay, Victory Wade

Forsyth County (Territory 32) comprises all territory in Forsyth County not included in Winston-Salem territory

Franklin County (Territory 33) comprises all territory in Franklin County

Gaston County (Territory 25) comprises all territory in Gaston County

Gates County (Territory 33) comprises all territory in Gates County

Greene County (Territory 33) comprises all territory in Greene County

Greensboro–Hamilton Lakes (Territory 14) comprises the entire city of Greensboro; the entire town of Hamilton Lakes; and all territory in Guilford County included in the townships of Morehead and Gilmer, including all of the following towns, cities, and places: Battle Ground, Bessemer, Four Mile, Hamtown, Hill Top, Pomona

Greeneville (Territory 31) comprises the entire town of Greenville and all territory in Pitt County included in Greenville townships, including the following towns, cities, or places: House, James Mill, Staton

Guilford County (Territory 32) comprises all territory in Guilford County not included in either Greensboro–Hamilton Lakes territory or High Point territory

Halifax County (Territory 33) comprises all territory in Halifax County

Harnett County (Territory 26) comprises all territory in Harnett County

Hertford County (Territory 33) comprises all territory in Hertford County

High Point (Territory 15) comprises the entire city of High Point, the town of Westend, and all territory in Guilford County included in High Point township

Hoke County (Territory 26) comprises all territory in Hoke County

Hyde County (Territory 33) comprises all territory in Hyde County

Johnston County (Territory 26) comprises all territory in Johnston County

Jones County (Territory 33) comprises all territory in Jones County

Kinston (Territory 31) comprises the entire city of Kinston and all territory in Lenoir County included in Kinston townships, including the following towns, cities, or places: Georgetown, Hines Junction

Lee County (Territory 26) comprises all territory in Lee County

Lenoir County (Territory 33) comprises all territory in Lenoir County not included in Kinston territory

Lexington–Thomasville (Territory 32) comprises the entire cities of Lexington and Thomasville; all territory in Davidson County included in the townships of Lexington and Thomasville; and all territory in Randolph County included in Trinity township, including all of the following towns, cities, or places: Archdale, Arnold, Cedar Lodge, Fraziers, Glen Anna, Lake, Trinity, Welcome

Martin County (Territory 33) comprises all territory in Martin County

Mecklenburg County (Territory 51) comprises all territory in Mecklenburg County not included in Charlotte territory

Nash County (Territory 33) comprises all territory in Nash County not included in Rocky Mount territory

New Hanover County—*see Wilmington.*

Northampton County (Territory 33) comprises all territory in Northampton County

Onslow County (Territory 41) comprises all territory in Onslow County

Orange County—*see Burlington–Graham and remainder of state.*

Pamlico County (Territory 33) comprises all territory in Pamlico County

Pasquotank County (Territory 33) comprises all territory in Pasquotank County

Pender County (Territory 33) comprises all territory in Pender County

Perquimans County (Territory 33) comprises all territory in Perquimans County

Pitt County (Territory 33) comprises all territory in Pitt County not included in Greenville territory

Raleigh (Territory 16) comprises the entire city of Raleigh; all territory in Wake County included in the townships of Cary, House Creek, Meredith, Neuse River, Raleigh, St. Mary's, St. Matthews, and Swift Creek; and the entire town of Knightdale in St. Matthews and Marks Creek townships, in-

Continued on next page.

Table 5, *continued*
North Carolina Territories for Automobile Liability Insurance Coverage

cluding all of the following towns, cities, or places: Asbury, Auburn, Boushell, Camp Polk, Caraleigh, Carolina Pines, Cary, College View, Edgeton, Fetner, Garner, Macedonia, McCullers, Method, Milburnie, Milbrook, Neuse, Oakdale, South Raleigh, Westover, Wilders Grove

Randolph County—*see Lexington–Thomasville and remainder of state.*

Robeson County (Territory 26) comprises all territory in Robeson County

Rocky Mount (Territory 31) comprises the entire city of Rocky Mount; all territory in Nash County included in Rocky Mount and Stony Creek townships; all territory in Edgecombe County included in Township 12 (Rocky Mount); and the entire town of Sharpsburg in Edgecombe, Nash, and Wilson counties, including all of the following towns, cities, or places: Armstrong, Brake, Dortches, Winsteads Chapel

Rowan County—*see Concord–Kannapolis–Salisbury and remainder of state.*

Sampson County (Territory 33) comprises all territory in Sampson County

Scotland County (Territory 26) comprises all territory in Scotland County

Tyrrell County (Territory 33) comprises all territory in Tyrrell County

Vance County (Territory 33) comprises all territory in Vance County

Wake County (Territory 31) comprises all territory in Wake County not included in Raleigh territory

Warren County (Territory 33) comprises all territory in Warren County

Washington County (Territory 33) comprises all territory in Washington County

Wayne County (Territory 47) comprises all territory in Wayne County

Wilmington (Territory 17) comprises all of New Hanover County and the following towns, cities, or places: Belville, Clairmont, El Paso, Lanvale, Leland, Navassa, Woodburn

Wilson (Territory 31) comprises the entire town of Wilson and all territory in Wilson County included in the township of Wilson

Wilson County (Territory 33) comprises all territory in Wilson County not included in the Rocky Mount or Wilson territories

Winston-Salem (Territory 18) comprises the entire city of Winston-Salem and all territory in Forsyth County included in the townships of Broadbay, Middle Fork, Old Town, South Fork, and Winston, including all of the following towns, cities, or places: Alspaugh, Atwood, Daisy, Fisherville, Frontis, Hanes, Ogburntown, Oldtown, Reynolda, Tiretown, Walkertown

Remainder of State (Territory 24)

OTHER SURCHARGES

Other add-ons include a recoupment surcharge (to help finance the Reinsurance Facility) and a use surcharge (which is based on miles driven to and from work). These surcharges do not depend on convictions or accidents and therefore are beyond the scope of this chapter.[14]

CALCULATION OF RATE INCREASE

An insured who has received insurance points—like Fred from Raleigh, whose situation was described at the beginning of this chapter—can calculate the cost of his or her liability insurance in the following manner:

1. Determine the territory from Table 5. (Fred lives in Raleigh, Territory 16.)
2. Using the territory number, determine the basic cost of liability insurance from Table 3 (for those who are not in the Reinsurance Facility) or Table 4 (for those who have been

14. G.S. 58-37-75.

ceded). (Fred's ceded business in Territory 16 for $100,000/$300,000 bodily injury coverage and $50,000 property damage coverage totals $544 per year.)

3. Determine the total number of insurance points for the driver's offense (or offenses) and accidents for the past three years from Table 2. (Fred's one driving while impaired conviction results in twelve insurance points.)
4. Determine the surcharge from Table 1. (Fred's twelve points result in a 400 percent surcharge.)
5. Add the cost of the surcharge to the basic cost of the insurance from Step 2 above to get the total cost. (Fred's ceded basic cost is $544. The 400 percent surcharge totals $2,176. The resulting total insurance cost is $2,720.)

As the above calculations illustrate, Fred paid fairly low automobile liability insurance bills while he was a clean risk, but his one driving while impaired conviction caused him to pay the higher Reinsurance Facility base rate and the surcharge for his points. His case thus exemplifies the high cost of convictions or negligently caused accidents. North Carolina still has reasonably priced automobile insurance for clean-risk drivers, but the cost of liability insurance for those who have accumulated insurance points can be devastating. Also it should be remembered that these points and rates apply to almost all forms of vehicle insurance and not just to liability coverage. The North Carolina rate system creates a strong incentive for the prudent operation of a motor vehicle.

Part Two
Impaired Driving Offenses

by James C. Drennan

This part discusses criminal offenses, driver's license revocations, and other statutory provisions that apply to impaired driving offenses. Chapter 1 discusses the elements, punishments, license revocations, and limited-driving-privilege statutes applicable to the offense of impaired driving. Chapter 2 discusses other criminal offenses regulating driving and drinking. Chapter 3 discusses special procedural statutes applicable to some or all of the criminal offenses discussed in Chapters 1 and 2.

1 Impaired Driving Offenses, License Sanctions, and Punishments

This chapter discusses the elements of the North Carolina General Statutes (hereinafter G.S.) applicable to the offense of impaired driving, including punishments, license revocations, and limited driving privileges.

THE OFFENSE OF IMPAIRED DRIVING

A person is guilty of the offense of impaired driving (G.S. 20-138.1) if that person:

1. drives
2. a vehicle other than a riding lawn mower, bicycle, or horse
3. on a highway, a street, or a public vehicular area
4. while:
   (a) under the influence of an impairing substance or
   (b) with an alcohol concentration of 0.08 or more at any relevant time after the driving.

The definitions of *driver, vehicle, highway, street,* and *public vehicular area* are discussed in detail in Chapter 1 of Part One and are equally applicable to this offense. G.S. 20-138.1 specifically provides that drivers of riding lawn mowers or bicycles and riders of horses are not subject to this offense. Riders of horses are subject to all other provisions regulating the operation of vehicles except those that by their nature can have no application to horses.[1]

This offense is a single offense that may be proved in one of two ways:[2] either by showing that the defendant's faculties have been impaired by an impairing substance or by showing the presence of an alcohol concentration of 0.08 or more. In many cases both ways of proving the offense are involved. The state need not elect to proceed on a single theory. Both may be submitted to the fact finder; if the case is being heard by a jury, the judge is not required to instruct the jury to indicate in their verdict which theory or theories they relied on.[3] In factually appropriate cases, only one theory may be involved; for example, if no chemical analysis has been conducted, only the impairment theory may be considered.[4]

---

1. Section 20-171 of the North Carolina General Statutes (hereinafter G.S.).
2. State v. Oliver, 343 N.C. 202, 470 S.E.2d 16 (1996); State v. McCaslin, 132 N.C. App. 352, 511 S.E.2d 347 (1999).
3. State v. Garvick, 98 N.C. App. 556, 392 S.E.2d 115, *aff'd per curiam*, 327 N.C. 627, 398 S.E.2d 330 (1990).
4. State v. O'Rourke, 114 N.C. App. 435, 442 S.E.2d 137 (1994).

Related impaired driving offenses are discussed in Chapter 2. The offenses discussed are impaired driving in a commercial vehicle; driving a commercial vehicle after consuming alcohol (zero tolerance offense); driving a school bus or child-care vehicle after consuming alcohol (zero tolerance offense): driving by a person under twenty-one after consuming alcohol; habitual impaired driving; impaired instruction; and transporting an open container of alcohol after consuming alcohol.

Some issues that arise in impaired driving cases, in particular those involving the application of criminal procedure laws to impaired driving cases, are not discussed in this book. Those issues include whether a law enforcement officer has a legal basis to stop a vehicle and whether an interrogation at the scene of an arrest violates state or federal constitutional rights or a defendant's rights under the state and federal constitutions to be free from unreasonable searches or seizures.[5]

Conviction under Impairment Theory

The *impairment* element uses several terms of art that have legislatively prescribed meanings. They are discussed below.

Impairing substance means alcohol, a controlled substance under G.S. Chapter 90, any other drug or psychoactive substance capable of impairing a person's physical or mental faculties, or any combination of these substances.[6] *Alcohol* means any substance that contains alcohol, including ethanol, methanol, propanol, and isopropanol.[7] *Drug* means any substance recognized in the official United States Pharmacopeia, official Homeopathic Pharmacopeia of the United States, or official National Formulary; any substance intended for the diagnosis, cure, mitigation, prevention or treatment of disease in humans or animals; any substance (other than food) intended to affect the structure or the function of humans or animals; and any component parts of these substances.[8]

A person who drinks alcoholic beverages and ingests drugs has taken two different impairing substances. Both may contribute to the person's impairment, and the effects of either or both may be considered in determining if the statute has been violated.

Impairing substance also includes substances that are neither alcohol nor drugs if the substance is capable of impairing the person's faculties. An example of such a substance is the vapor from certain types of glue. *Under the influence* means the state of a person whose physical or mental faculties, or both, are appreciably impaired by such a substance.[9]

To convict a person under this theory, no particular form of evidence is required. Evidence of alcohol concentration is useful but not necessary. An alcohol concentration of less than 0.08 does not raise a presumption that a person is not under the influence.[10] Evidence of some impairing substance is essential, however, by some means. Opinion testimony by law enforcement officers is admissible. In *State v. Lindley*,[11] a police officer was allowed to testify as to his opinion that the defendant was under the influence and that he was under the influence of some drug instead of alcohol. The officer based his opinion on the following facts: the erratic manner in which the defendant operated his vehicle, his personal demeanor, a white substance on his lips, his pinpoint pupils, the absence of alcohol on his breath, a lack of muscular coordination, and a mental stupor. A negative or low result in an alcohol screening test conducted pursuant to G.S. 20-16.3 also

---

5. Another Institute of Government publication, *Arrest, Search, and Investigation in North Carolina,* by Robert Farb (2d ed. 1992; supplement 1998), addresses those issues in detail and is an excellent reference for those interested in the subject matter.

6. G.S. 20-4.01(14a).

7. G.S. 20-4.01(1a).

8. G.S. 90-87(12).

9. G.S. 20-4.01(48a); State v. Harrington, 78 N.C. App. 39, 336 S.E.2d 852 (1985).

10. State v. Sigmon, 74 N.C. App. 479, 328 S.E.2d 843 (1985).

11. 286 N.C. 255, 210 S.E.2d 207 (1974).

may be considered to determine if an alleged impairment is caused by an impairing substance other than alcohol.[12]

The results of the field sobriety test known as the Horizontal Gaze Nystagmus (HGN) test are sometimes used as a form of evidence. HGN evidence is obtained by persons trained in the proper evaluation technique observing the manner in which the eye follows an object in the person's peripheral vision. In *State v. Helms*,[13] the North Carolina Supreme Court held that such evidence is based on a "scientific" test and is not admissible unless accompanied by expert testimony relating to the correlation between intoxication and the nystagmus effects as well as evidence showing that the method employed is sufficiently reliable to be admitted under the North Carolina Rules of Evidence. The court also noted that in appropriate cases a court could take judicial notice of the facts necessary to establish admissibility. In *Helms*, the evidence was not admitted.

If a drug other than alcohol is involved, the fact that the drug that caused the impairment is a prescription drug that was lawfully taken within the prescribed dosage is not a defense, but it can be grounds for a mitigated punishment.[14]

Conviction under *Per Se* Theory

To convict under the alcohol-concentration prong of the statute, the level of impairment is not relevant. An outwardly sober person commits the crime if his or her alcohol concentration exceeds the stated level and the statutory elements and the provisions governing the use of chemical analyses are otherwise satisfied. Provisions like this are called *per se* laws. Again several terms used in describing the elements have specific statutory meanings.

Alcohol concentration means the concentration of alcohol in a person, expressed either as grams of alcohol per 100 milliliters of blood or per 210 liters of breath.[15] This formulation is different from that found in many *per se* statutes. Those statutes make it a crime only to have a specified *blood* alcohol content. They then often use *breath* alcohol content as an indirect measure of the alcohol in the person's blood. The intoxilyzer and other instruments designed to test breath alcohol content are constructed to report the results of their tests using a blood-to-breath ratio that is considered by scientists to be accurate for the vast majority of people. The ratio is 2,100 to 1 blood to breath; that is, it assumes there is twenty-one hundred times as much alcohol in one milliliter of blood as in one milliliter of breath. In fact, in most people in whom there is a deviation from the 2,100 to 1 ratio, the deviation is on the high side, and this causes the breath test results to be lower than the blood test results would be. In a small percentage of people the ratio is lower. In states that use only blood alcohol levels as the element of the criminal offense, the fact that a particular person's ratio is different may be highly relevant to whether his or her blood alcohol content is accurately measured by a breath-testing instrument.

North Carolina's statute, in contrast, makes the amount of alcohol in a person's breath an element of the offense, and it does not require a conversion to blood alcohol content.[16] The instrument, if working properly, will accurately indicate the number of grams of alcohol that would be in 210 liters of the breath of the person being tested, and that is all that is required. It does not matter for purposes of applying the impaired driving statute that a particular person's blood alcohol content may be slightly higher or lower than his or her breath content. As a result, evidence about a person's blood-breath ratio is inadmissible.[17]

12. G.S. 20-16.3(d).
13. 345 N.C. 578, 504 S.E.2d 293 (1998).
14. G.S. 20-138.1(b); -179(e)(5).
15. G.S. 20-4.01(1b).
16. *See* State v. Midgett, 78 N.C. App. 387, 337 S.E.2d 117 (1985).
17. State v. Cothran, 120 N.C. App. 633, 463 S.E.2d 423 (1995).

Any results of a defendant's alcohol concentration as determined by a chemical analysis of a person's breath or blood must be reported in hundreths. Any result between hundreths must be rounded down.[18]

Apparently analyses other than the chemical analyses under G.S. 20-16.2 may be used to establish a violation of the *per se* prong. In *State v. Cardwell,*[19] a defendant involved in an accident was charged with impaired driving. As part of her medical care, the treating physician ordered an alcohol blood test using a DuPont ACA Star Analyzer. That instrument analyzes plasma to determine blood alcohol content. The trial court and the appellate court approved the use of that particular instrument and the conversion ratio adopted by the hospital to convert the alcohol concentration in the plasma to the alcohol concentration in the blood. The trial judge submitted the converted reading to the jury as evidence that the defendant had violated the *per se* prong of this offense. The North Carolina Court of Appeals affirmed the use of the results in these circumstances.

As noted in the listing of elements, to be valid, a chemical analysis must reflect a person's alcohol concentration at a "relevant time after the driving."[20] This formulation is unusual in impaired driving statutes. The problem it addresses is this: Breath tests do not measure alcohol content at the time of driving; they measure it at the time of the test. Alcohol content is constantly changing as alcohol is absorbed into or eliminated from the body. Depending on the length of time between the test and the most recent consumption of alcohol, one's alcohol concentration may be rising or falling. Determining the direction in which the alcohol concentration is moving is important if the crime is keyed to the alcohol content at the time of the driving. For example, if a person's alcohol concentration at the time of the test is 0.08 and the alcohol concentration is still on the increase (because of the recent consumption of alcohol), it could reasonably be argued that the person's alcohol concentration at the time of the driving was less than 0.08. In North Carolina that argument is not relevant to the issue of whether this element is satisfied because it does not define the crime in terms of the alcohol concentration at the time of the driving. Instead the crime is defined by using the concentration at the time of the test.

Many states address this problem by specifying that the alcohol concentration must exceed their *per se* level within a specified time after the driving. Others deem the test result to be the same as if it were taken at the time of the driving if the analysis is taken within a specified time after the driving. North Carolina's statute takes a different approach. It rejects the idea of using a specified time (two hours is a common limit) and uses in its place the concept of *relevant time after the driving.* A test is conducted within a relevant time after the driving if it is measuring alcohol that was in the person's body at the time he or she stopped driving. As long as some of the alcohol being measured by the test was in the body at that time, the test is taken at a relevant time and is admissible.

One effect of this provision is that drivers who have extremely high alcohol concentrations may commit the offense even though long periods of time pass between the driving and the test. For example, in *State v. George,*[21] the test was taken 3 hours and 45 minutes after the arrest. The court held that a delay of that length did not make the test inadmissible but that the jury could consider the delay in determining if the test results should be believed. Another effect is that the person whose alcohol concentration is less than 0.08 at the time of the driving commits the offense if his or her concentration is 0.08 or higher when the test is taken later. Both effects are consistent with the concept that a person should not drive if he or she drinks enough to have an alcohol concentration of 0.08 or more at any later time. The driver who does that takes the risk of reaching the

18. G.S. 20-4.01(1b).

19. WL 387050 (N.C. App. June 15, 1999).

20 G.S. 20-4.01(33a).

21. 77 N.C. App. 470, 336 S.E.2d 93 (1985).

statutory limit at a later time; if he or she takes that risk and loses, he or she commits the crime. This portion of the statute is constitutional.[22]

What happens if a person has alcohol in his or her body that was consumed after the driving? If there is also alcohol that was present during the driving, it is still a "relevant time after the driving."[23] However, to convict, the crime requires that a person have consumed "sufficient alcohol" to have an alcohol concentration of 0.08 or more, so the state must be able to prove that at least 0.08 of the person's alcohol concentration was caused by alcohol consumed *before or during* the driving. In discussing a related issue, the North Carolina Supreme Court, in *State v. Cummings*, noted that a driver who had an accident was not "likely to hurry off for more intoxicants to make his or her condition more noticeable and his or her breath more 'odoriferous.'"[24]

SENTENCING OF IMPAIRED DRIVERS

The sentencing scheme for the impaired driving statute is unique. Except for death penalty cases, no sentence requires more documentation. G.S. 20-138.1 and capital murder cases are the most prominent of the very few criminal offenses not covered by the structured sentencing statutes in Article 81B of G.S. Chapter 15A. The basic punishment statute is G.S. 20-179. Table 1 (see page 100) summarizes the maximum and minimum punishments required by that statute.

There are five possible levels of punishment. Upon conviction, a judge must determine the appropriate level and impose a judgment. A judge may not enter a *prayer for judgment continued* in these cases.[25] A prayer for judgment continued is a court order continuing, either indefinitely or to a future date, a case in which a finding of guilt has been made. In such cases it often happens that neither a sentence nor a judgment is ever entered, and the person charged is treated as if the case were dismissed. *In re Tucker*[26] makes it clear that this practice is not allowed in impaired driving cases arising under G.S. 20-138.1 and punished under G.S. 20-179. *In re Tucker* does not prohibit a judge from delaying the imposition of a sentence to a *definite* date in the future, and a prayer for judgment continued to a *specific date* is one way to do that.[27]

To determine the proper punishment level, the sentencing judge must first determine, in writing, if certain *grossly aggravating factors* are present. If more than one grossly aggravating factor is present, a sentence at level one is required. If one is present, a sentence at level two is required. If none is present, the judge must determine, in writing, if any *aggravating* or *mitigating factors* are present and then balance those factors to determine if level three, four, or five is appropriate. Each level comprises mandatory minimum amounts and kinds of punishment, and in some cases the judge cannot go higher or lower than the amount prescribed in the statute.[28] To determine the proper sentence, the judge must hold a sentencing hearing.[29] The statute places certain mandatory duties on the prosecutor. He or she must make an effort to obtain the defendant's driving record and must present it to the court. A properly certified copy of a person's driving record is admissible and is prima facie evidence of any prior offense involving impaired driving.[30] The copy may

---

22. State v. Rose, 312 N.C. 441, 323 S.E.2d 339 (1984).
23. State v. Ferrell, 75 N.C. App. 156, 330 S.E.2d 225 (1985).
24. 267 N.C. 300, 148 S.E.2d 97 (1966); *see also* State v. Snead, 295 N.C. 615, 247 S.E.2d 893 (1978).
25. *In re* Tucker, 348 N.C. 677, 501 S.E.2d 67 (1998).
26. *Id.*
27. *See* State v. Absher, 335 N.C. 155, 436 S.E.2d 365 (1993).
28. *See* State v. Magee, 75 N.C. App. 357, 330 S.E.2d 357 (1985).
29. G.S. 20-179(a).
30. G.S. 8-35.1; 20-179(o).

be transmitted over the Division of Criminal Information Network.[31] The prosecutor must present to the court all evidence of which he or she is aware that would aggravate the sentence. If a chemical analysis was performed, he or she must attempt to introduce the results of that analysis into evidence. The defendant is entitled to introduce any evidence that may be of mitigating value.

The burden is on the prosecutor to prove by the greater weight of the evidence that grossly aggravating and aggravating factors are present.[32] The defendant bears a similar burden with respect to mitigating factors. Formal rules of evidence do not apply at the sentencing hearing,[33] but statements by counsel are not sufficient absent a stipulation.[34]

Grossly Aggravating Factors

There are five grossly aggravating factors:

1. A single conviction for an offense involving impaired driving if the conviction occurred within seven years before the date of the offense for which the person is being sentenced. Unlike the old driving-under-the-influence statutes in effect until 1983, previous convictions are not elements of the offense but are factors in punishment.[35] As is true with any statute in which prior convictions are used to enhance a punishment or to extend a license revocation, it is important to review the specific statutes. This use of prior convictions to enhance punishment for impaired driving is just one of many uses. Others are limited privilege eligibility, length of revocation, and elements of the offense of habitual impaired driving under G.S. 20-138.5. Each uses prior convictions but has a different purpose and a different method of determining if a conviction is eligible for consideration.

Offense involving impaired driving is a phrase defined in G.S. 20-4.01(24a). It is used in several places in the impaired driving statutes, including the vehicle forfeiture statutes. It includes the most serious drinking-and-driving offenses, but there are several offenses involving the consumption of alcohol that are not included in this definition. The included offenses are impaired driving under G.S. 20 138.1, homicides when the conviction is based on impaired driving, impaired driving in a commercial vehicle under G.S. 20-138.2, habitual impaired driving under G.S. 20-138.5, offenses under former driving-under-the-influence and *per se* laws, and offenses involving similar conduct in other jurisdictions.[36]

This factor is not present unless the subsequent offense occurs after a previous conviction (not after a previous offense). Each prior conviction constitutes a separate grossly aggravating factor. For purposes of determining the applicability of the seven-year period, the beginning date is the date of *conviction* of the prior offense; the ending date, the date of the current offense. If the gap between these two dates is more than seven years, the grossly aggravating factor is not present. However, a conviction that is more than seven years old using that method of calculation may be used as an aggravating factor (described later).

Prior convictions listed on state computer systems, such as the Division of Motor Vehicles (DMV) driving records or the Division of Criminal Information records, must be given prima facie effect by the judge. If as a result of a prior conviction, the judge imposes an active sentence that

31. G.S. 20-26(b).

32. State v. Denning, 316 N.C. 523, 342 S.E.2d 855 (1986); State v. Harrington, 78 N.C. App. 39, 336 S.E.2d 852 (1985).

33. G.S. 15A-1334(b).

34. State v. Haislip, 79 N.C. App. 656, 339 S.E.2d 832 (1986).

35. Denning, 316 N.C. 523, 342 S.E.2d 855.

36. G.S. 20-4.01(24a). State v. Parisi, ___ N.C. App. ___, 519 S.E.2d 531 (1999) held that a New York statute requiring "impairment to any extent" was "substantially equivalent to" G.S. 20-138.1, which requires appreciable impairment.

he or she would otherwise not impose, that conviction may not be used if it was obtained in violation of the defendant's right to counsel.[37] On this issue the defendant has the burden of proving by the preponderance of the evidence that in the prior case, he or she (1) was indigent, (2) had no counsel, and (3) did not waive the right to counsel. If he or she proves all three things, the state may not use the conviction to require an active sentence or to enhance it,[38] but the conviction may still be used for other purposes, such as determining eligibility for a limited driving privilege or determining the length of a revocation.

Conviction for purposes of impaired driving sentencing includes the following actions occurring in North Carolina: A final conviction of an offense, including those obtained by no contest pleas, an unvacated forfeiture of cash in the full amount of a bond required by Article 26 of G.S. Chapter 15A, and a third or subsequent prayer for judgment continued entered in a five-year period.[39] A determination that a person is responsible for an infraction is also a conviction, but an infraction cannot constitute a grossly aggravating factor. If the factor is based on an out-of-state conviction, the following actions constitute convictions: an unvacated adjudication of guilt, a determination in a court or administrative tribunal that a person has violated or failed to comply with the law, an unvacated forfeiture of bail, or a violation of a condition of release without bail.[40]

2. A single conviction of an offense involving impaired driving occurring after the date of the offense for which the defendant is being sentenced but prior to or contemporaneously with that sentencing. This factor applies any time a person charged with impaired driving commits a second offense before he or she is convicted of the first offense. Each such conviction is a separate grossly aggravating factor. *Contemporaneously* is not defined in the statute but likely is to be construed to mean that it occurs when sentencing for two offenses at or very nearly at the same time. And, unlike factor number one above, the finding is based on the time of conviction; the offense date is not relevant.

An example may help to illustrate the point. A defendant is charged on March 1 with impaired driving. On April 15, in a separate incident, he is charged again with impaired driving. On May 1, both cases are heard in the district court. He pleads guilty to the March 1 offense. For that offense the April 15 offense is not a grossly aggravating factor because at the time of sentencing, the defendant does not have a conviction. If the defendant immediately thereafter pleads guilty to the April 15 offense, he has a grossly aggravating factor because previous to this sentencing he had received a conviction for another (the March 1) offense. The same result would pertain if the order of sentencing is reversed and the guilty plea for the April 15 offense is received first. That offense would have no grossly aggravating factor under this factor, but the conviction for the March 1 offense would have a grossly aggravating factor for the April 15 conviction.

If instead both pleas are part of a negotiated plea and both pleas are taken before final judgment is entered in each case, the convictions will be obtained contemporaneously and each will serve as a grossly aggravating factor in the other conviction.

The statute does not expressly deal with the treatment of multiple convictions for which notice of appeal has been entered in district court. The question would be posed if the defendant immediately noted an appeal of the first conviction in the scenario described above. G.S. 15A-1431 provides for *de novo* appeals to superior court of misdemeanors heard in district court. GS 20-4.01(4a)a.1. defines *conviction* as "a *final* conviction of a criminal offense." Those statutes, read together, suggest that a conviction is not *final* if an entry of appeal has been noted and thus is not a *conviction* under this grossly aggravating factor. By analogy, the structured sentencing statutes

37. G.S. 20-179(o); Baldasar v. Illinois, 446 U.S. 222 (1980).
38. *Haislip*, 79 N.C. App. 656, 339 S.E.2d 832.
39. G.S. 20-4.01(4a)a.
40. G.S. 20-4.01(4a)b.

define *prior conviction* similarly. G.S. 15A-1340.11(7) does not treat district court convictions on appeal as prior convictions, but it does treat superior court convictions on appeal to the appellate division as prior convictions, even though they are being appealed. However, if the appeal is withdrawn and the subsequent case is still "*in fieri*" (i.e., the session or term of court has not concluded), the second case could apparently be reopened for sentencing based on the existence of the conviction in which the appeal has been withdrawn.

3. At the time of the offense, the defendant was driving while his or her license was revoked under G.S. 20-28 for previous impaired driving conduct. Revocations included for this purpose are listed in G.S. 20-28.2(a) and are imposed under the authority of the following statutes: G.S. 20-13.2 (provisional licensee offenses); G.S. 20-16(a)(8b) (impaired driving on a military base); G.S. 20-16.2 (refusing a chemical analysis of breath or blood); G.S. 20-16.5 (immediate, pretrial thirty-day revocation); G.S. 20-17(a)(2) and -17.2 (conviction of impaired driving); G.S. 20-17(a)(12) (second or subsequent conviction of transporting an opened container of alcoholic beverage under G.S. 20-138.7); G.S. 20-138.5 (conviction of habitual impaired driving); G.S. 20-16(a)(7) (out-of-state impaired driving conviction); G.S. 20-17(a)(1), (a)(3), or (a)(9) (conviction of felony death by vehicle, manslaughter, or any other felony while driving impaired) and G.S. 20-17(a)(11) (conviction of assault in a motor vehicle while driving impaired).

The conduct has to be sufficient to establish the offense of *driving while license revoked* under G.S. 20-28, but that offense does not have to be charged for the grossly aggravating factor to be applicable. That offense can only occur on a street or highway, so driving on a public vehicular area is not conduct that would support a finding that this factor is present. Also the conduct must occur in a motor vehicle, since that is an element of the offense under G.S. 20-28. Thus driving on a moped or bicycle will not support a finding that this factor is present.

G.S. 20-28 also includes as *impaired driving revocations* any revocations imposed by other states for conduct substantially similar to conduct that would support any of the listed revocations if the conduct occurred in North Carolina. However, since this aggravating factor also requires the driving to be in violation of G.S. 20-28 (the crime of driving while license revoked), it is not clear whether driving while one's license is revoked pursuant to an out-of-state revocation would satisfy this factor. The offense of driving while license revoked has generally been interpreted to require that one's license be revoked by the State of North Carolina and that notice of that fact be provided by the state. It is likely that in including out-of-state revocations the legislature was not intending to change that rule. Including the out-of-state revocations in the definitions of impaired driving revocations would insure that those revocations were included in applying the vehicle forfeiture laws discussed in Chapter 3 of this part. The act in which this amendment is contained includes several other amendments to that forfeiture law, which tends to support the view that the amendment is intended to affect the operation of that law and not of the criminal offense of driving while license revoked.[41] If that is correct, then driving subject to one of these out-of-state revocations would not satisfy the elements of this grossly aggravating factor, since the driving would not be in violation of G.S. 20-28.

4. Serious injury to another person caused by the defendant's impaired driving at the time of the offense. *Serious injury* is defined in other contexts to mean physical injury that falls short of causing death. Whether an injury is serious is "to be determined according to the particular facts of each case."[42] In the impaired driving context a broken leg and a compressed vertebra were held to constitute serious injury, but much less dramatic injuries would also constitute serious injury.[43]

41. SL 1999-406.
42. State v. Ferguson, 261 N.C. 558, 135 S.E.2d 626 (1964).
43. State v. Barber, 93 N.C. App. 42, 376 S.E.2d 497 (1989).

5. At the time of the offense a child under sixteen was in the vehicle. The statute does not specify whether driving with more than one child constitutes a separate factor for each child. However, the absence of language clearly establishing that each child's transportation constitutes a separate factor (as is true with the factors dealing with prior convictions) makes it likely that the statute will be construed to find that only one factor is present if more than one child is present in the vehicle.

There is no right to a jury trial on the issue of whether a grossly aggravating factor is present.[44]

Aggravating Factors

There are nine aggravating factors, some of which have more than one part:

1. Gross impairment of the defendant's faculties while driving or an alcohol concentration of 0.16 or more at any relevant time after the driving. *Gross impairment* is "a high level of impairment, higher than the level of impairment which must be shown to prove the offense of DWI." No minimum alcohol concentration is required; an alcohol concentration of 0.14 has been held to be sufficient to support a finding of gross impairment when combined with erratic driving, poor performance on field sobriety tests, a slurring of speech, and an unsteadiness in walking.[45] In one case, the court properly found the factor to be present because the defendant had a 0.27 alcohol concentration, smelled of alcohol, had trouble standing, had slurred speech, and kept asking the whereabouts of a woman who was not at the scene.[46] The same rules used to determine admissibility of a chemical analysis for proof of a *per se* violation apply to determining if the results may be used to establish that the driver had an alcohol concentration of 0.16 or more.

2. Especially reckless or dangerous driving. Both *especially reckless* and *especially dangerous* driving may be proved in the same offense, and if so, two factors are present. To prove both, however, at least one item of evidence not used to support an element of the offense or the other aggravating factor must be present.[47] The level of dangerousness or recklessness must be greater than the amount inherent in the most unaggravated form of impaired driving. Falling asleep at the wheel while driving, as a result of an impairing substance, has been found to be especially dangerous.[48] Driving into a telephone pole without applying brakes while speeding also has been found to be especially reckless.[49] In one case, however, because no evidence was presented to prove the allegation that the defendant had passed illegally through a red light, the factor could not be found to be present.[50] This factor may be present without the person's having been charged and convicted of the described conduct, as is required in factors six and seven (discussed on page 86).

3. Negligent driving that led to an accident that is required by law to be reported to law enforcement authorities. G.S. 20-4.01(33b) defines reportable accident as one in which death, personal injury, or property damage totaling more than $1,000 occurs. For this factor to be present, the accident must have occurred during the same act of driving as the impaired driving offense for which the defendant is being sentenced. In *State v. Gunter*,[51] the court of appeals held that photographs of the damaged vehicle were sufficient proof to demonstrate that damage over $500 had occurred.

---

44. State v. Denning, 316 N.C. 523, 342 S.E.2d 855 (1986); Field v. Sheriff of Wake County, 831 F.2d 530 (4th Cir. 1987).
45. State v. Harrington, 78 N.C. App. 39, 336 S.E.2d 852 (1985).
46. State v. Gunter, 111 N.C. App. 621, 433 S.E.2d 191 (1993).
47. State v. Mack, 81 N.C. App. 578, 345 S.E.2d 223 (1986).
48. *Id.* at 578, 345 S.E.2d at 227.
49. *Gunter*, 111 N.C. App. 621, 433 S.E.2d 191.
50. State v. Lockwood, 78 N.C. App. 205, 336 S.E.2d 678 (1985).
51. 111 N.C. App. 621, 433 S.E.2d 191.

4. Driving with a revoked driver's license at the time of the offense. If the revocation is an impaired driving revocation, grossly aggravating factor number three above is present instead. As in the grossly aggravating factor, the status of a person's license may be proved by the driving records maintained by the DMV. A certified copy of such records is prima facie evidence of a revoked license, and certified copies may be transmitted over the Division of Criminal Information Network.[52] Unlike grossly aggravating factor three above, this factor does not specifically refer to G.S. 20-28 in establishing the elements of the factor. It is not clear whether that distinction makes any substantive difference, but it is clear that this factor may be present without the person's having been charged and convicted under G.S. 20-28.

5. A driving record consisting of:

(a) two or more convictions of a motor vehicle offense not involving impaired driving that require the assessment of three driver's license points;
(b) two or more convictions not involving impaired driving that, standing alone, would require or authorize the DMV to revoke the person's license;
(c) one conviction as described in (a) and one conviction as described in (b); or
(d) one or more prior convictions of an offense involving impaired driving that are too old to use as grossly aggravating factors.

For purposes of subsections (a), (b), or (c), the final conviction date must have been in the five years immediately preceding the date of the impaired driving offense. *Conviction* is defined in G.S. 20-4.01(4a).

6. Conviction of speeding while fleeing or attempting to elude apprehension under G.S. 20-141.5 if the conduct occurred at the same time as the impaired driving offense. The elements of the offense cited in this factor do not literally require that the driver be speeding, although *speeding* appears in both the caption to that statute and in this aggravating factor. They simply require that the driver attempt to elude apprehension by a law enforcement officer. That statute also establishes several aggravating factors that can elevate the offense to a felony when two or more of them are present. Speeding over 15 mph or in a school or work zone are among those aggravating factors. It is likely that the legislative intent in using the word "speeding" in the aggravating factor was to refer to G.S. 20-141.5 by the words used in the caption to that offense and not to add an additional requirement that the defendant be found to have committed one of the aggravating factors involving speeding.

7. Conviction of speeding under G.S. 20-141 by at least 30 mph over the speed limit if the speeding occurred at the same time as the impaired driving offense.

8. Passing a stopped school bus under G.S. 20-217 if the conduct occurred at the same time as the impaired driving offense. Unlike factors six and seven (discussed above), this factor may be present without the person's having been charged and convicted.

9. Any other factor that aggravates the seriousness of the offense. This catchall must involve conduct that occurred at the time of the offense. Accordingly its use is relatively limited but probably is permissible if the driver does not cooperate with the charging officer, refuses to identify himself or herself, or engages in other similar conduct.

Mitigating Factors

The factors in mitigation are as follows:

1. Slight impairment of the defendant's faculties resulting solely from alcohol and an alcohol concentration that does not exceed 0.09. In some ways this is analogous to the first aggra-

---

52. G.S. 20-26(b).

vating factor, but it varies in one significant way. Unlike the aggravating factor, which is present if a judge determines a person to be grossly impaired even if his or her alcohol concentration is under 0.16, this factor may not be found if the person's alcohol concentration is over 0.09. Put another way, the 0.16 concentration *is not a minimum level for aggravation*, but the 0.09 concentration *is a maximum level for mitigation*. No one with an alcohol concentration above 0.09 can be slightly impaired.

The impairment must be solely from alcohol for this factor to be present.

2. Slight impairment of the defendant's faculties resulting solely from alcohol, when no chemical analysis was available to the defendant. This factor and factor one (above) are mutually exclusive; if one is present, the other may not be. For this factor to be present, no chemical analysis must be available to the defendant. A defendant who willfully refuses a chemical analysis offered to him or her may not claim the benefit of this factor. If drug impairment is present, this factor may not be found, no matter how slight the impairment.

No cases have construed either of these provisions dealing with slight impairment. Because they are considered only after a finding of guilt, however, the level of impairment may not be lower than that required to prove the elements of the offense.

3. Driving that was safe and lawful except for the impairment of the defendant's faculties. There are no cases construing this provision. In roadblocks, license checks, or inspection or registration violations, in which the cause for stopping the driver does not depend on overt signs of poor driving, this factor may be used. Because *lawful* driving is required, this factor apparently may not be found when a violation of the rules of the road other than impaired driving has been proved.

4. A safe driving record, defined as:

(a) no conviction for any offense requiring the assessment of four or more driver's license points or

(b) no conviction that standing alone would require or authorize the DMV to revoke the person's license.

The offenses carrying four or more points are passing a stopped school bus, reckless driving, hit-and-run (property damage only), following too closely, driving on the wrong side of the road, and illegal passing.[53] Only offenses that have a final conviction date occurring in the five years immediately preceding the date of the impaired driving offense may be considered in determining if this factor is present.

This is an analogous provision to aggravating factor five (page 86), but they are not mutually exclusive. For example, a person may have two convictions of speeding 65 mph in a 55 mph zone. That offense requires the assessment of three driver's license points. It does not authorize or require a driver's license revocation. Because it is not a four-point offense, the mitigating factor is present and would still be present if the person had a dozen such convictions. However, because both convictions are three-point violations, the aggravating factor also is satisfied. The weight to be given to each is left to the trial judge's discretion.

For revocation offenses the division between the factors is cleaner. No such convictions means that prong of the mitigating factor is satisfied. One such conviction means that neither factor is present. Two or more such convictions means that the aggravating factor is present.

Conviction is defined in G.S. 20-4.01(4a).

5. Impairment caused by a lawfully prescribed drug taken for an existing medical condition in the prescribed dosage. This provision must be read in conjunction with G.S. 20-138.1(b), which specifies that the fact that the substance causing one's impairment is a drug lawfully taken is not a defense. This factor softens the effect of that provision. The conduct, impaired driving, is a danger

---

53. G.S. 20-16.

to others regardless of the cause of the impairment. However, this provision makes it clear that the degree of fault ascribed to those who become impaired after taking prescription drugs is less than that ascribed to those who ingest other substances for different reasons.

6. Voluntary submission to a substance abuse assessment and treatment. This assessment must be conducted by a mental health *facility*. It is not clear from the text whether an individual conducting assessments qualifies as a facility; nor is it clear whether the assessing party must be a certified alcoholism counselor. If a defendant wants to use the *voluntary* assessment as a replacement for the *mandatory* assessment required after conviction as a condition of both probation and restoration of a driver's license, the voluntary assessment should be performed under the supervision of a certified counselor because assessments for probation and license restoration require the involvement of a certified counselor.[54]

Although the law does not grant them specific authority to do so, many courts interpret the law to allow a pretrial assessment to satisfy the need for a postconviction assessment. For that to happen, the pretrial assessment should be performed in a manner that satisfies the legal requirements for a postconviction assessment. If the assessment serves both purposes, the pretrial assessing agency should be notified of the court's action. Failure to so notify may delay the reporting of the assessment and any subsequent treatment or the completion of alcohol and drug education traffic school to the DMV and thereby result in an extension of the defendant's license revocation and a delay in the restoration of the defendant's license.

The fee for pretrial assessments is not specified by statute, but the legislature probably intended that the same fee that is charged for postconviction assessments ($50) be charged for pretrial assessments.[55] Area mental health authorities generally charge $50, but private assessors are not regulated in this regard, and some of them apparently charge much more than $50.

As noted above, the law requires a substance abuse assessment if the defendant is placed on probation. In addition, in all cases, even those in which the defendant is not on probation, G.S. 20-17.6 requires an assessment and appropriate treatment or education before the driver's license revocation that is imposed as a result of the conviction can be terminated and the person's license can be restored. (See Chapter 2 of this part for more detail on this statute.)

To qualify for the mitigating factor, the defendant must also participate in any recommended treatment or education required up to the time of the conviction and sentencing.[56] Unless the recommended treatment or education is completed, the fact that a defendant has been assessed will not be reported to the DMV, and the defendant's license revocation for the conviction may be extended until the assessment and treatment is completed and notice of that fact is sent to the DMV.

7. Any other factor that mitigates the seriousness of the offense. This factor is similar to the catchall aggravating factor, with one major exception. It is not limited to conduct that occurred at the time of the offense for which the defendant is being sentenced. However, to be found, the factor must in some way mitigate the seriousness of the offense.

Limitations on the Judge's Sentencing Discretion

A distinguishing characteristic of the impaired driving statutes is the extent to which they limit prosecutorial and judicial discretion. Nowhere is that limitation more evident than in the restrictions on sentencing. Each of the five levels of punishment has its own set of specific restrictions, and additional requirements are applicable to all levels of punishment. The general requirements are discussed in this section, followed by a discussion of each level of punishment.

---

54. *See* G.S. 20-17.6.
55. *See* G.S. 122C-142.1.
56. State v. Gunter, 111 N.C. App. 621, 433 S.E.2d 193 (1993).

Consolidation of Judgments

In many instances in which a single defendant is convicted of multiple offenses, judges consolidate the convictions into a single judgment. The impaired driving statutes authorize consolidation of judgments in some impaired driving cases, but in most such circumstances, significant practical and legal issues arise.

G.S. 20-179(f2) provides that consolidation of judgments is possible, subject to two limitations. First, if the impaired driving charge is *not* the lesser offense, the court must determine which sentencing factors are applicable to the impaired driving case. (If impaired driving *is* the lesser offense, that determination need not be made.) Second, the consolidation of two impaired driving judgments is flatly prohibited.

When the consolidation of judgments statute was passed in 1984, the sentencing systems for impaired driving and other criminal offenses were fairly similar. However, in 1993 a *structured* sentencing system was enacted for all crimes except for first-degree murder, impaired driving, and a public health offense. The structured sentencing system requires the judge to make a finding in each case as to the appropriate prior record level in which a defendant falls, and the punishment level authorized is in part determined by that finding. G.S. 15A-1340.15 and -1340.22 require that consolidated judgments for structured sentencing offenses be consistent with the prior record level for the highest class of offense that is being disposed of in the consolidated judgment. That can never be the case if the consolidated judgment is an impaired driving judgment, because it does not use prior record levels. Therefore a structured sentencing judgment should be prepared in every case in which a structured sentencing offense is being disposed of.

If impaired driving is the lesser offense, it is permissible to consolidate the impaired driving case with the greater offense and not prepare a separate impaired driving judgment. In *State v. Santon*,[57] the court of appeals ruled that impaired driving, because it is potentially punishable by as much as two years of imprisonment in some circumstances, was a two-year misdemeanor for purposes of determining if the offense constituted an aggravating factor under the Fair Sentencing Act. There is no case analyzing how the determination of whether the impaired driving offense is the "lesser" offense should be made, but if the *Santon* analysis is applied in this context, impaired driving would always be a two-year offense, regardless of the facts of the case. If that logic is applied to the offense in which the impaired driving offense is being compared under the structured sentencing law, the maximum sentence for the structured sentencing offense would be the most aggravated sentence for the most serious prior record level offender. Using that analysis, no misdemeanors and Class I felonies would be treated as lesser offenses than impaired driving for purposes of applying this statutory provision.

Regardless of the manner in which this provision on consolidation is interpreted, there is another practical consideration that suggests that consolidation is not appropriate when impaired driving and structured sentencing offenses are combined in a single judgment. Under Article 85B of G.S. Chapter 15A, impaired driving defendants may be paroled. Structured sentencing defendants may not be paroled. Often in cases where one judgment must be interpreted under both sentencing schemes, the court's intention is not clear. Applying both sets of laws to the same judgment is very difficult, and it often leads to results that the courts did not intend. To avoid problems in interpretation, the better practice is not to consolidate structured sentencing and impaired driving cases.

There is one circumstance in which consolidation would not create those problems. Impaired driving charges are commonly accompanied by other motor vehicle charges that are infractions instead of misdemeanors. Infractions are punishable by monetary penalties only. There is no problem with a consolidation of judgment for an infraction and an impaired driving offense, if the required sentencing determinations are made and recorded.

---

57. 101 N.C. App. 710, 401 S.E.2d 117 (1991).

Aider and Abettor Punishment

A person who aids and abets another to drive while impaired is guilty of the principal offense. However, because the sentencing factors are all focused on the conduct of the driver, it is difficult to determine the level of punishment for aiders and abettors using those factors. Accordingly G.S. 20-179(f1) provides that all aiders and abettors are to be punished at level five, regardless of their previous record. For example, a person convicted of impaired driving by aiding and abetting who has five previous impaired driving convictions would still be punished at level five.

Most consequences involving driver's licenses (i.e., revocations or points) apply to an aider and abettor because for the most part, the DMV is concerned only with whether one has been convicted, not with whether one has been convicted as a principal or as an aider and abettor. However, an aider and abettor is not subject to the immediate, pretrial revocation provided for by G.S. 20-16.5 because this revocation requires that an individual have an alcohol concentration of 0.08 or more or have refused a chemical analysis.

Substance Abuse Assessments

Every person convicted of impaired driving under G.S. 20-138.1 has their driver's license revoked in North Carolina for at least a year.[58] G.S. 20-17.6, as a condition to being relicensed under that revocation, requires all persons convicted of impaired driving to obtain a substance abuse assessment and to complete any treatment or education recommended as a result of that assessment. Failure to obtain the assessment or to complete the treatment or education will extend the period of revocation until the person does so. If the person has a limited driving privilege (only available in first offenses in which the period of revocation is one year), that limited driving privilege is not valid past the one-year revocation period originally imposed by the DMV. (A more complete discussion of the statutes regulating substance abuse assessments is presented in the next chapter.)

For persons placed on probation for convictions of impaired driving, the judge must require as a condition of probation that the person obtain an assessment and complete any treatment or education recommended as a result of the assessment. A similar requirement is not imposed on the judge in cases in which an active sentence is imposed, but the same relicensing requirements apply.

Limits on Credit for Imprisonment

Convicted impaired drivers may go to jail (unless noted otherwise, *jail* includes sentences to prison) in one of two ways: on an active sentence or as a condition of *special probation* pursuant to G.S. 15A-1351(a). If a defendant is sentenced to jail as a condition of special probation, a judge may give the defendant credit for time spent as an inpatient in a treatment facility licensed or operated by the state or may order the defendant to enroll in such an inpatient treatment program.[59] If the credit is for time spent in treatment before trial, the treatment must have occurred after the charge. This credit may also be used to replace an active sentence of imprisonment (as opposed to one served on special probation).

No treatment facility may be required to take a defendant pursuant to this statute, and the defendant must pay for the treatment, unless the judge orders that the costs be absorbed by the state. The statute provides no further guidance on *which state entity* must absorb those costs. If the treatment is provided by a state facility, the sliding scale of G.S. 122C-146 applies. But no such rule applies to

58. G.S. 20-17(a)(2).
59. G.S. 20-179(k1).

private facilities, so absorbing of the cost of the treatment delivered by a private entity would likely require the use of state funds by some state agency. The statute is silent on this point.

A defendant must receive credit for time spent in jail awaiting trial, subject to two limitations.[60] First, no credit may be given for the first twenty-four hours of time spent in jail awaiting trial.[61] If the defendant is ordered to jail as a condition of special probation, the judge may credit any pretrial detention after the first twenty-four hours either to the special probation jail time or to the suspended sentence that will be activated if the special probation is revoked.[62] Second, credit for good time and gain time may not be given in such a manner as to reduce a defendant's actual time served to less than the appropriate mandatory minimum sentence.

Limits on Use of Supervised Probation

G.S. 20-179(r) provides that any person convicted of impaired driving and placed on probation be placed on unsupervised probation if he or she is sentenced at levels three through five, has no impaired driving convictions in the seven years preceding the current offense date, and has been assessed and completed any recommended treatment unless the judge makes specific findings in the record about the need for probation supervision.[63] If a judge places a convicted impaired driver on supervised probation, either because of prior convictions, level one or level two punishment, because treatment has not been completed or because of specific findings of the need for such supervision, the judge must also authorize the probation officer to transfer the defendant to unsupervised probation after he or she completes any ordered community service and pays any fines.

Limits on Parole

Impaired driving offenses under G.S. 20-138.1 are the only offenses still covered by parole rules. In 1994 parole was eliminated for all structured sentencing offenses. There are three separate parole rules applicable to impaired driving convictions. The general rule, which applies if neither of the two exceptions described below do not, allows for parole after service of a minimum sentence or up to one-fifth the statutory maximum.[64] (If no minimum is imposed it is treated as a minimum sentence of zero. As noted later, however, G.S. 20-138.1 requires minimum sentences for each level of punishment.) In addition, if the sentence is between thirty days and eighteen months, parole is presumptive after completion of one-third of the maximum sentence regardless of whether the person is otherwise eligible for parole. In these cases the offender must be paroled unless the Parole and Post-Release Supervision Commission finds that it would be inappropriate to do so.[65] Finally, after service of one-half the minimum sentence, the Commission may release an offender on community service parole.[66]

For any of these parole rules to apply, however, G.S. 20-179(p)(3) requires that the person obtain a substance abuse assessment,[67] serve any mandatory minimum, and complete any treatment recommended. The completion of treatment is not required if the offender is paroled to a residential treatment facility. In many cases in which offenders are sentenced to jail or prison immediately, completion of treatment will not be possible unless it can be done while the offender

60. G.S. 15-196.1–4.
61. G.S. 20-179(p).
62. G.S. 15A-1371.
63. *See* State v. Gunter, 111 N.C. App. 621, 433 S.E.2d 191 (1993).
64. G.S. 15A-1371(a).
65. G.S. 15A-1371(g).
66. G.S. 15A-1371(h).
67. *See* G.S. 122C-142.1.

is incarcerated. The effect of this requirement in those cases is to require that the maximum sentence be served, less any good time.

Levels of Punishment

Level One

Level one punishment is the most severe and is required only when at least two grossly aggravating factors are present. The maximum punishment that may be imposed for each offense is two years of imprisonment, a $4,000 fine, or both. The minimum term of imprisonment that may be imposed is thirty days. That term may be suspended only if a condition of probation requiring at least thirty days of imprisonment is imposed. The judge also may impose any other reasonable condition of probation and must include a condition requiring assessment and treatment. The factor distinguishing this punishment from other levels of punishment is the irreducible minimum sentence of thirty days in jail.

Level Two

Level two punishment is required when only one grossly aggravating factor is present. The maximum punishment that may be imposed for each offense is one year of imprisonment, a $2,000 fine, or both. The minimum term of imprisonment that may be imposed is seven days. That term may be suspended only if a condition of probation requiring at least seven days of imprisonment is imposed. The judge also may impose any other reasonable condition of probation and must include a condition requiring assessment and treatment. The factor distinguishing this punishment from other levels of punishment is the irreducible minimum sentence of seven days in jail.

Level Three

Level three punishment is required when no grossly aggravating factors are present and the regular aggravating factors present outweigh any mitigating factors. The maximum punishment that may be imposed is six months of imprisonment, a $1,000 fine, or both. The minimum term is seventy-two hours of incarceration. The sentence of imprisonment may be suspended. If it is suspended, the judge *must* impose at least *one* of the following probation conditions:

1. At least seventy-two hours in jail;
2. At least seventy-two hours of community service;
3. At least ninety days of not driving;
4. Any combination of (1), (2), and (3).

The use of mandatory conditions of probation is unusual, but it expresses a legislative intent to have mandatory minimum punishments that involve community service, imprisonment, or license revocations for impaired driving. The judge also may impose any other reasonable condition of probation and must include a condition requiring assessment and treatment.[68]

Community service requirements must be served under the supervision of community service coordinators appointed pursuant to G.S. 20-179.4. That statute imposes a supervision fee of $100. If the requirement is seventy-two or more hours under this punishment level, the probation judgment must require the work to be performed within ninety days, but the court may extend those time limits for good cause upon the defendant's motion.[69] In practice, coordinators routinely make

68. G.S. 20-179(i).
69. G.S. 20-1

such requests if justified, and the courts routinely grant them. A defendant also may at any time seek an extension on his or her own. Failure to successfully complete community service may lead to a revocation of the defendant's driver's license until he or she completes the community service.[70] It may lead also to the revocation of any limited privilege, if one has been issued.[71]

The period of nonoperation ordered as a condition of probation is the basis for an additional driver's license revocation.[72] The revocation based on the period of nonoperation is authorized by G.S. 20-17.2 and lasts for the period specified in the judgment. It runs concurrently with the revocation under G.S. 20-17(a)(2). Since the defendant is already revoked under G.S. 20-17(a)(2) because of the conviction, the chief effect of this revocation is that no limited driving privilege is valid during the period specified in the judgment.

Level Four

Level four punishment is required when no grossly aggravating factors are present and either no other factors are present or the factors that are present are substantially balanced by other factors. The maximum punishment that may be imposed is 120 days of imprisonment, a $500 fine, or both. The minimum term is forty-eight hours of incarceration. The sentence of imprisonment may be suspended. If it is suspended, the judge *must* impose at least *one* of the following conditions of probation:

1. forty-eight hours in jail;
2. forty-eight hours of community service;
3. sixty days of not driving;
4. any combination of (1), (2), and (3).

The remarks explaining level three apply to this level of punishment, with two exceptions: First, the number of hours or days for each condition is specified by statute; *it may not be raised or lowered by the judge*.[73] Second, the judgment must give the defendant sixty days to complete the community service requirement.[74]

Level Five

Level five punishment is required when no grossly aggravating factors are present and the mitigating factors outweigh any regular aggravating factors that are present. The maximum punishment that may be imposed is sixty days of imprisonment, a $200 fine, or both. The minimum term is twenty-four hours of incarceration. The sentence of imprisonment may be suspended. If it is suspended the judge *must* impose at least *one* of the following conditions of probation:

1. twenty-four hours in jail;
2. twenty-four hours of community service;
3. thirty days of not driving;
4. any combination of (1), (2), and (3).

---

70. G.S. 20-17(b)(2).
71. G.S.20-179.4(e).
72. All convicted impaired drivers face a revocation of at least one year because of the conviction, pursuant to G.S. 20-17(a)(2).
73. *See* State v. Magee, 75 N.C. App. 357, 330 S.E.2d 357 (1985).
74. G.S. 20-179(n)(2).

The remarks explaining level three apply to this level of punishment, with two exceptions: First, the number of hours or days for each condition is specified by statute; *it may not be raised or lowered by the judge.* Second, the judgment must give the defendant thirty days to complete the community service requirement.[75]

Conditions of Probation

Any reasonable condition of probation may be imposed as part of the punishment under any level of punishment for impaired driving.[76] Common conditions imposed in impaired driving cases that have been approved by appellate courts are that the defendant not be present at an establishment licensed to sell alcoholic beverages[77] and that the defendant attend Alcoholics Anonymous sessions.[78]

INSURANCE POINTS

A conviction of impaired driving will add twelve insurance points to a driver's record. (See Chapter 21 of Part One for more information about insurance consequences of these convictions.)

REVOCATIONS BASED ON CONVICTION OF IMPAIRED DRIVING

There are two potential revocations based on conviction of impaired driving. Under G.S. 20-17.2, revocation may be part of the court-ordered punishment. (See the earlier section on Sentencing of Impaired Drivers.) In addition the DMV will revoke the license of every person convicted of impaired driving for at least one year under G.S. 20-17(a)(2). The length of the revocation is determined by G.S. 20-19(c1), (d), or (e). Eligibility for a limited driving privilege is determined by G.S. 20-179.3. The length of revocation is as follows:

One year for a first offender or for persons with no other offense involving impaired driving, as defined in G.S. 20-4.01(24a), occurring in the three years immediately preceding the date of the current offense. For this statute the time period runs from offense date to offense date.[79]

Four years for an offender who has one other offense involving impaired driving, as defined in G.S. 20-4.01(24a), occurring in the three years immediately preceding the date of the current offense. After two years a person may apply for a conditional restoration of his or her license. The Division may grant the request upon a showing by the defendant that he or she is not an excessive user of alcohol or drugs and has no motor vehicle, drug, or alcohol convictions during the period of revocation.[80] The defendant must demonstrate also that he or she has insurance or is exempt from the requirement of insurance.[81]

For offenses committed on or after July 1, 2000, a first restoration under this section carries with it two mandatory conditions. The defendant must agree not to drive any vehicle while he or she has an alcohol concentration of 0.04 or more at any relevant time after the driving. The defendant must also agree to submit to a chemical analysis to determine if the condition has been violated upon request of a law enforcement officer who has reasonable grounds to believe that the condition has been violated. The defendant must agree to be transported to the test site as necessary. These conditions are in effect for three years from the date the license is restored.[82]

---

75. G.S. 20-179(n)(3).
76. G.S.15A-1343.
77. State v. Harrington, 78 N.C. App. 39, 336 S.E.2d 852 (1985).
78. State v. McGill, 114 N.C. App. 479, 442 S.E.2d 166 (1994).
79. *See* G.S. 20-19(d).
80. G.S. 20-19(d).
81. G.S. 20-19(k).
82. G.S. 20-19(c3). The provisions of this statute become effective July 1, 2000.

Violation of this *per se* condition is not a criminal offense but will result in a reactivation of the original revocation and an additional one-year revocation of the driver's license. For a more thorough discussion of this provision, see Chapter 3 of this part.

If the conviction for the second offense occurs after the conviction of the first offense, the second offense will nonetheless result in a four-year revocation, even if a one-year revocation order was initially issued. G.S. 20-19(j) authorizes the DMV to issue amended orders to provide the correct duration of the revocation.[83]

Permanent revocation for an offender who has at least two other offenses involving impaired driving, the most recent one occurring in the five years immediately preceding the date of the current offense. After three years a person may apply for a conditional restoration of his or her license. The Division may grant the request upon a showing by the defendant that he or she is not an excessive user of alcohol or drugs and has no motor vehicle, drug, or alcohol convictions during the period of revocation.[84]

For offenses committed on or after July 1, 2000, a second or subsequent restoration under this section carries with it two mandatory conditions. The defendant must agree not to drive any vehicle while he or she has any alcohol concentration at any relevant time after the driving. The defendant must also agree to submit to a chemical analysis to determine if the condition has been violated upon request of a law enforcement officer who has reasonable grounds to believe that the condition has been violated. The defendant must agree to be transported to the test site as necessary. These conditions are in effect for three years from the date the license is restored.[85]

Violation of the *per se* condition is not a criminal offense, but the DMV, upon being notified of the violation by a law enforcement officer, must reactivate the original revocation and, in addition, impose an additional one-year revocation. For a more thorough discussion of this provision, see Chapter 3 of this part.

In addition to the lower *per se* levels imposed when licenses are restored to impaired drivers, G.S. 20-17.8, effective July 1, 2000, for offenses committed on or after that date, also conditions some restorations on the use of ignition interlock devices.[86] Those requirements are that the defendant had an alcohol concentration of 0.16 or more, or had a conviction of an offense involving impaired driving in the seven years preceding the date of the offense for which the defendant is seeking to have his or her license restored. A person subject to this requirement must only use a vehicle with an approved interlock system, must personally activate the system before driving, and must not drive with an alcohol concentration of 0.04 or greater. The interlock requirement is in effect for one year if the original period of revocation was one year, for three years if the period was four years, and for seven years if the original revocation was permanent. If the defendant was subject to an interlock requirement while using a limited driving privilege, the time the defendant spent driving with the limited privilege applies toward that period.[87]

If a defendant drives in violation of any of the conditions related to the use of the interlock system, that conduct constitutes the crime of driving while license revoked under G.S. 20-28. The judicial official reviewing the charge, upon finding that there is probable cause, must suspend the defendant's license pending the resolution of the criminal charge.[88] (Note that this is different from the treatment accorded a violation of the lower *per se* rules imposed on restorations, discussed above). In addition, the violation is an implied consent offense under G.S. 20-16.2. (For a more

83. Wagoner v. Hiatt, 111 N.C. 448, 432 S.E.2d 417 (1993).
84. G.S. 20-19(e).
85. G.S. 20-19(c3). The provisions of this statute become effective July 1, 2000.
86. G.S. 20-17.8 becomes effective July 1, 2000.
87. G.S. 20-17.8(b), (c), effective July 1, 2000.
88. G.S. 20-17.8(f), effective July 1, 2000.

complete discussion of implied consent offenses and the procedures applicable to chemical testing for alcohol, see Chapter 3 of this part.) If there is a violation but no criminal charge is lodged, the DMV must, if it is informed of the violation, impose an additional one-year revocation. A defendant may seek a review of the DMV action in an administrative hearing. The hearing is limited to whether the defendant was subject to the interlock requirement and whether he or she drove a vehicle that was not equipped with an interlock system or failed to personally activate the system or violated the *per se* level imposed on him or her. The defendant receives credit toward the service of a revocation for any time in which the person's license was surrendered to the court pending resolution of any criminal charge, if the person's license was not also revoked under G.S. 20-16.5.[89] (For more information on this immediate pretrial revocation, see Chapter 3 of this part.)

In all cases, if the person had been restored before serving the maximum period of revocation under G.S. 20-19, the remaining period of the revocation is activated before any additional revocation periods begin.

In some cases, it is possible that the interlock conditions will impose a *per se* level at 0.04, while the provisions of G.S. 20-19 (discussed above) impose a zero *per se* level. In those cases, since there are separate enforcement mechanisms, the enforcement provisions of G.S. 20-19 will apply.

Since both the reduced *per se* level provisions of G.S. 20-19 and the *per se* levels imposed in the interlock provisions of G.S. 20-17.8 can be violated by the same conduct, it is not clear from the statute whether revocations will be imposed separately for both violations. If they are, and the interlock violation is treated as a violation of the driving-while-license-revoked statute, the revocations will run consecutive to each other because G.S. 20-28 imposes a revocation that is "additional" to any other revocations in effect.

LIMITED DRIVING PRIVILEGES

For some first offenders whose licenses were revoked under G.S. 20-17(a)(2), a judge may issue a limited driving privilege authorizing the driver to do some driving during the revocation period. If a person is eligible, the judge does not have to grant the privilege but must consider a request that one be granted.[90]

Limited privileges are valid to negate specific driver's license revocations. Only the DMV may license a person to drive.[91] Unless there is specific authority to issue such a privilege, it is invalid. For example, there are numerous ways in which a convicted impaired driver may lose his or her license, but only two of them may be negated by a limited privilege.[92]

Eligibility

To be eligible for a limited driving privilege in a case in which the defendant did not willfully refuse a chemical analysis, a defendant must:

Have been validly licensed at the time of the offense or have a license that has been expired for less than one year. For this purpose the license need not be a North Carolina license but must be recognized as valid to allow the person to drive in this state. Thus a nonresident possessing a license

89. G.S. 20-17.8(g), (j), (k), effective July 1, 2000.

90. State v. Sigmon, 74 N.C. App. 479, 328 S.E.2d 843 (1985); State v. Bailey, 93 N.C. App. 721, 379 S.E.2d 266 (1989).

91. Fox v. Scheidt, 241 N.C. 31, 84 S.E.2d 259 (1954); Honeycutt v. Scheidt, 254 N.C. 607, 119 S.E.2d 777 (1961); Smith v. Walsh, 34 N.C. App. 287, 238 S.E.2d 157 (1977); *see* State v. Warren, 230 N.C. 299, 52 S.E.2d 879 (1949).

92. G.S. 20-179.3(e), -16.2(e1).

issued by his or her home state would satisfy this requirement if the driving would be authorized in the home state.[93]

Although not listed as a specific requirement for eligibility, the person's license must, at the time of the issuance of the limited privilege, be revoked solely under G.S. 20-17(a)(2) as a result of a conviction for impaired driving.[94]

Be a first offender. For this purpose a first offender is one who has no convictions for offenses involving impaired driving in the previous seven years. *Conviction* is defined in G.S. 20-4.01(4a). G.S. 20-179(o), which limits the use of certain uncounseled convictions to enhance punishment, is not applicable to this issue. The definition of *offense involving impaired driving* is contained in G.S. 20-4.01(24a) and includes impaired driving under G.S. 20-138.1, previous DUI statutes, homicides involving impaired driving, habitual impaired driving under G.S. 20-138.5, impaired driving in a commercial vehicle under G.S. 20-138.2, and substantially similar offenses in other states. The seven-year period used in this statute runs from the prior conviction date to the current offense date.

Have been sentenced to punishment levels three, four, or five.

Have not been convicted of, or not have another charge pending for, an offense involving impaired driving after the date of the current offense.

Have obtained and filed with the court a substance abuse assessment of the type required by G.S. 20-17.6. (See the section on assessments in Chapter 2 of this part.)

Have liability insurance or other forms of suitable financial responsibility valid and in effect at the time of the issuance of the privilege.

In some instances a defendant may be convicted of impaired driving and also have his or her license revoked for refusing a chemical analysis under G.S. 20-16.2. In those cases, eligibility for limited privilege is governed by G.S. 20-16.2(e1). That provision is discussed in Chapter 3 of this part.

Purposes

Limited driving privileges may allow driving only for the following purposes:

1. **Employment.** Driving related to employment is regulated by G.S. 20-179.3(g) and (g1). If all of a defendant's employment-related driving is done during standard working hours (6 A.M. to 8 P.M., Monday through Friday), the privilege must limit the driving to employment-related driving during those hours. The judge may impose additional restrictions as to time and routes to be driven. The judge must require that the privilege contain the name and address of the defendant's place of work or employer.

If any employment-related driving is done during nonstandard working hours, the statute requires more specificity. If the driving is predictable as to routes, the privilege must limit the driving to those routes. If the driving is predictable as to times, the privilege must limit the driving to those times. If neither time nor route can be predicted, the privilege must contain a geographic limitation so that driving will be allowed only in the necessary minimum area. For any employment-related driving during nonstandard hours, the defendant must first present to the judge documentation of his or her need to drive then, and the limited privilege must contain the name and the address of the employer. If the defendant is self-employed, the documentation of the need to drive must be attached to the privilege.

2. **Maintenance of the household.** This is the broadest category of the allowable purposes. Driving for this purpose may not be allowed except during standard working hours, and the judge may limit it further as he or she sees fit.[95]

93. G.S. 20-8(3).
94. G.S. 20-179.3(e).
95. G.S. 20-179.3(g2).

3. Education. Driving for education (other than drug and alcohol education ordered by the court) is subject to the same restrictions as work-related driving, including the judge's power to deny such driving altogether. However, it is much less likely that routes and, to a lesser degree, times of educational driving cannot be predicted. Driving for alcohol and drug schools established pursuant to G.S. 20-179.2 must be allowed in the privilege. However, it must be limited in the same way as work-related driving if done during nonstandard working hours, and the name and the address of the school must be included in the privilege.

4. Court-ordered treatment or assessment. Driving for these purposes must be allowed but must be limited in the same way as work-related driving if done during nonstandard working hours. The name and the address of the treating agency must be included in the privilege.

5. Community service ordered as a condition of probation. Driving for this purpose must be allowed but must be limited in the same way as work-related driving if done during nonstandard working hours. The name and the address of the treating agency must be included in the privilege.

6. Emergency medical care. The need to drive for this purpose cannot, by definition, be predicted in advance. The driving must be authorized without limitation as to time or route, but to be authorized, it must be for an emergency. Driving related to routine medical care would be authorized under the maintenance-of-the-household purpose, subject to the judge's restrictions on that driving contained in the privilege.

To be valid, driving pursuant to a limited driving privilege must meet two criteria: It must be for a purpose authorized by the privilege, and it must be at a time and a place that is authorized by the privilege.

Conditions Not Related to the Purpose of the Driving

The limited privilege must also contain a *zero per se provision.* A *zero per se provision* makes it a violation to drive while there is any alcohol or any nontherapeutic amounts of a drug in a person's body or blood. Thus any alcohol concentration over 0.00 violates this provision.[96] An alcohol screening test (roadside breath test) conducted pursuant to G.S. 20-16.3 may be used to establish the presence of alcohol in a charge of driving while license revoked based on a failure to comply with this section.[97]

The limited privilege must require the defendant to *maintain insurance or other financial responsibility* throughout the period of the privilege.[98]

Finally, *the judge may impose any other restrictions he or she finds necessary or desirable*, such as limiting the defendant to driving specified vehicles or requiring the defendant to submit to a chemical analysis upon request of a law enforcement officer. A condition that a defendant not drive within three days after consuming an alcoholic beverage was accepted without discussion as valid in *State v. Cooney*.[99]

The limited privilege may require the defendant to operate a specified motor vehicle and, in addition, may require that the vehicle be equipped with a functioning ignition interlock system of a type approved by the DMV.[100] If the defendant had an alcohol concentration of 0.16, the limited privilege *must* require the defendant to drive only a vehicle equipped with an ignition inter-

---

96. G.S. 20-179.3(h).

97. G.S. 20-179.3(j). A 1999 amendment to this statute in SL 199-406 effectively overruled *State v. Bartlett* [130 N.C. App. 79, 502 S.E.2d 53 (1998)].

98. G.S. 20-179.3(1).

99. 72 N.C. App. 649, 325 S.E.2d 15 (1985).

100. G.S. 20-179.3(g3).

lock system.[101] The statute mandating this requirement does not specify the kind of proof necessary to establish a particular alcohol concentration at or above 0.16.

The privilege may not allow the defendant to operate a commercial motor vehicle, even if the offense occurs in a noncommercial vehicle. G.S. 20-17.4(f) provides that a person is disqualified from operating a commercial vehicle for the period during which the person's license is revoked. There is no authority in G.S. 20-179.3 to negate or override a disqualification.[102] Thus the disqualification prevents the defendant from legally operating a commercial vehicle pursuant to a limited driving privilege.

Procedure for Granting and Modifying the Privilege

Most privileges are applied for at the time of sentencing. There is no specified procedure for applications at that time, but because the district attorney is present at the time of sentencing, he or she need not be given special notice of the defendant's intent to apply for a privilege.

Less common, and more complicated, are applications made subsequent to sentencing and applications made by residents of North Carolina who have been convicted in another state.[103] The application for a privilege made subsequent to sentencing must be filed with the clerk, and the clerk must file a copy with the district attorney. No hearing on the application may be held until the district attorney has had a reasonable time to review the application. The application must be heard by the sentencing judge if he or she is still holding court in the district. For this purpose it does not matter whether the judge is conducting civil or juvenile court; he or she is still conducting court in the district. If the judge is not still in the district (e.g., because of rotation out of the district; retirement; death; defeat at election; or, for retired district and superior court judges and active superior court judges, expiration of their commission to act in the district), the privilege may be granted only by the chief district judge for cases disposed of finally in the district court and by the senior resident superior court judge for cases disposed of in the superior court.

Out-of-state convictions. The application for a privilege to negate a revocation for an out-of-state conviction must also be filed with the clerk, and notice must be given to the district attorney. Only the chief district judge may consider such an application. If the jurisdiction in which the defendant was convicted requires a period of nonoperation before a limited privilege or a similar limited license may be effective (e.g., an occupational license limited to work-related driving), the privilege may not be effective until the defendant's license is revoked for sixty days as a result of the conviction.

If a limited privilege may not legally be effective at the time of sentencing, may a judge issue the privilege at the time of sentencing, to be effective at a date in the future, and request that the clerk maintain custody until the effective date? That practice is not specifically prohibited by the statute. However, the statute does contemplate the judge's determining at the time of issuance that the defendant has insurance coverage, and it is not possible to do that with certainty in advance. In addition the statute implicitly directs the judge to be sure that the defendant's license is not otherwise revoked, and that too cannot be done with certainty in advance. Accordingly the safest practice is to require the defendant to make application when or very shortly before he or she is eligible in order to allow the judge to be certain that all the eligibility criteria have been met.

Text continues on page 102.

---

101. G.S. 20-179.3(g5). The provisions of this statute become effective July 1, 2000.
102. *See* G.S. 20-179.3(e).
103. G.S. 20-179.3(d).

Table 1
DWI Punishment Summary Offenses Committed before December 1, 1997[a, b, c]

General Statutes Section	Offense	Punishment: Imprisonment and Mandatory Probation Conditions	Punishment: Fine
G.S. 20-138.1, -179(g)	Impaired driving (Level One)	14 days minimum to 24 months maximum imprisonment or special probation for: (i) a minimum term of imprisonment of 14 days or (ii) at least 4 consecutive days imprisonment and electronic house arrest for twice the length of time remaining under (i)	Up to $2,000
G.S. 20-138.1, -179(h)	Impaired driving (Level Two)	7 days minimum to 12 months maximum imprisonment or special probation for: (i) a minimum term of imprisonment of 7 days or (ii) at least 2 consecutive days imprisonment and electronic house arrest for twice the length of time remaining under (i)	Up to $1,000
G.S. 20-138.1, -179(i)	Impaired driving (Level Three)	72 hours minimum to 6 months maximum imprisonment but *must* be suspended on one or more of the following conditions: • no driving for at least 90 days • at least 72 hours of community service within 90 days or • serve at least 72 hours imprisonment on special probation	Up to $500
G.S. 20-138.1, -179(j)	Impaired driving (Level Four).	48 hours minimum to 120 days maximum imprisonment but *must* be suspended on one or more of the following conditions: • no driving for 60 days • 48 hours of community service within 60 days or • serve at least 48 hours imprisonment on special probation	Up to $250
G.S. 20-138.1, -179(k)	Impaired driving (Level Five)	24 hours minimum to 60 days maximum imprisonment but *must* be suspended on one or more of the following conditions: • no driving for 30 days • 24 hours of community service within 30 days or • serve 24 hours imprisonment as special probation	Up to $100

a. Defendants sentenced for these impaired driving convictions are eligible for parole under Article 85 of Chapter 15A of the North Carolina General Statutes (hereinafter G.S.).

b. If defendant is placed on probation for these offenses, the court may, as a condition of that probation, require the defendant to obtain a substance abuse assessment and the education or treatment required by G.S. 20-17-6 for the restoration of a driver's license. The defendant must obtain the assessment and complete any recommended treatment or education to be eligible for license restoration, even if the court does not make it a condition of probation, or if the defendant gets an active sentence.

c. Under the version of G.S. 20-179(k1) in effect for these offenses, the term of imprisonment imposed as a special probation condition may, in the court's discretion, be served as an inpatient in a facility owned or licensed by the state to treat alcoholism and substance abuse; the defendant must bear the cost of the treatment. The court may restrict the defendant's ability to leave the facility. The court may, once every seven years, give credit against any active sentence for any time spent in an inpatient facility if the treatment occurs after the offense was committed.

Table 1
DWI Punishment Summary Offenses Committed after December 1, 1997[d, e, f]

General Statutes Section	Offense	Punishment: Imprisonment and Mandatory Probation Conditions	Punishment: Fine[g]
G.S. 20-138.1, -179(g)	Impaired driving (Level One)	30 days minimum to 24 months maximum imprisonment or special probation term if imprisonment of at least 30 days	Up to $4,000
G.S. 20-138.1, -179(h)	Impaired driving (Level Two)	7 days minimum to 12 months maximum imprisonment or special probation term if imprisonment of at least 7 days	Up to $2,000
G.S. 20-138.1, -179(i)	Impaired driving (Level Three)	72 hours minimum to 6 months maximum imprisonment; *may* be suspended on one or more of the following conditions: • no driving for at least 90 days • at least 72 hours of community service within 90 days or • serve at least 72 hours imprisonment on special probation	Up to $1,000
G.S. 20-138.1, -179(j)	Impaired driving (Level Four)	48 hours minimum to 120 days maximum imprisonment; *may* be suspended on one or more of the following conditions: • no driving for 60 days • 48 hours of community service within 60 days or • serve 48 hours imprisonment on special probation	Up to $500
G.S. 20-138.1, -179(k)	Impaired driving (Level Five)	24 hours minimum to 60 days maximum imprisonment; may be suspended on one or more of the following conditions: • no driving for 30 days • 24 hours of community service within 30 days or • serve 24 hours imprisonment on special probation	Up to $200

d. Defendants sentenced for these impaired driving convictions are eligible for parole under Article 85 of G.S. Chapter 15A. Defendants otherwise eligible under that statute may not be paroled for these offenses until they obtain an assessment and either complete any recommended treatment or education or are paroled to a residential treatment program. G.S. 20-179(p)(3).

e. If defendant is placed on probation for these offenses, the court must impose a condition requiring the defendant to obtain a substance abuse assessment and the education or treatment required by G.S. 20-17.6 for the restoration of a driver's license. Even if the defendant is not placed on probation, obtaining an assessment and completing recommended treatment or education is a requirement to be eligible for restoration.

f. Under the version of G.S. 20-179(k1) in effect for these offenses, the term of imprisonment imposed as a special probation condition may, in the court's discretion, be served as an inpatient in a facility owned or licensed by the state to treat alcoholism and substance abuse. The defendant must bear the cost of the treatment, "unless the trial judge orders that the costs be absorbed by the state." The court may restrict the defendant's ability to leave the facility. The court may also give credit against any active sentence for any time spent in an inpatient facility if the treatment occurs after the offense was committed.

g. For offenses committed between December 1, 1997, and December 1, 1998, the maximum fines are 50 percent of the amounts listed in this chart.

Violations—Criminal Conviction

Because a limited privilege operates only to negate a specific revocation, a person who operates a vehicle in violation of a condition of the privilege commits the offense of driving while his or her license is revoked.[104] If the violation is based on a violation of the zero *per se* condition, the defendant is subject to a requirement that he or she take a breath or blood test upon request or risk further loss of his or her license under G.S. 20-16.2 if he or she refuses.[105] Roadside breath test results are admissible to prove a violation of the zero *per se* condition if the test is conducted in accordance with the applicable regulations of the commission as to the manner of its use.[106]

Violations—Revocation of the Privilege

A limited driving privilege may be revoked for several reasons: First, if a defendant is charged with, and a judicial official finds probable cause for, a violation of G.S. 20-28 (by violating a condition of the privilege), the judicial official must revoke the privilege at that time and notify the defendant of the revocation. The revocation lasts until the disposition of the charge.[107]

Second, if a defendant fails to pay any community service fee or fails to complete the work as ordered by the community service coordinator, the court must revoke the person's limited privilege, in addition to imposing any other sanctions for violation of probation. However, the community service coordinator is instructed by the statute to report only significant violations to the court for its consideration.[108]

Third, the judge who issued the privilege, if he or she is presiding over the court in which the privilege was issued, or any other judge presiding over the court in which the privilege was issued, may modify or revoke the privilege "upon a showing that the circumstances have changed sufficiently to justify the modification or revocation."[109] There are no cases elaborating on this standard, but the judge must enter a written order giving the reasons for the modification or the revocation.

---

104. G.S. 20-28.
105. G.S. 20-179.3(j).
106. G.S. 20-179.3(j). A 1999 amendment to this statute in SL 1999-406 effectively overruled *State* v. *Bartlett* [130 N.C. App. 79, 502 S.E.2d 53 (1998)].
107. G.S. 20-179.3(j).
108. G.S. 20-179.4(e).
109. G.S. 20-179.3(i).

2 Other Impaired Driving Offenses

First-degree murder, second-degree murder, and involuntary manslaughter may involve impaired driving as the conduct leading to death, and felony death by vehicle is always an offense involving impaired driving. *First-degree murder* is appropriate only when the felony murder rule is applicable.[1] *Second-degree murder*, in this context, is applicable only when the driving shows recklessness of such a level that it constitutes malice.[2] *Involuntary manslaughter*, in this context, is applicable when a homicide occurs as the result of a willful, intentional, or reckless violation of a motor vehicle law designed to protect the safety of others. When that happens, culpable or criminal negligence is present, and that is necessary to support a conviction of involuntary manslaughter. Driving while impaired is *per se* culpable negligence.[3] *Felony death by vehicle* results when an unintentional killing results in tandem with an impaired driving violation. While the terms used to define the elements are different from those used in involuntary manslaughter, there is no material difference between the two. Felony death by vehicle carries a lesser punishment and is most often used in plea negotiations. It is not, however, a lesser-included offense of involuntary manslaughter.[4] (See Chapter 20 in Part One for additional discussion of these offenses.[5])

In addition to homicides, impaired driving under Section 20-138.1 of the North Carolina General Statutes (hereinafter G.S.), and the charge of driving while a driver's license is revoked (for driving, under the authority of a limited driving privilege, with alcohol in one's body), there are seven other state criminal offenses that involve the consumption of alcohol or drugs and subsequent driving. Every one of those offenses is an implied consent offense for which the person charged may be requested to submit to a chemical analysis or risk a license revocation. Only two are offenses involving impaired driving as defined in G.S. 20-4.01(24a). Those two are described below, followed in line by the other five offenses.

---

1. State v. Jones, ___ N.C. App. ___, 516 S.E.2d 405 (June 15, 1999).

2. State v. Snyder, 311 N.C. 391, 317 S.E.2d 394 (1984); State v. McBride, 109 N.C. 64, 425 S.E.2d 731 (1993).

3. State v. McGill, 314 N.C. 633, 336 S.E.2d 90 (1985).

4. State v. Williams, 90 N.C. App. 614, 369 S.E.2d 872 (1988); State v. Byers, 105 N.C. App. 377, 413 S.E.2d 586 (1992).

5. These offenses are discussed in more detail in the Institute of Government's basic criminal law text, *North Carolina Crimes*, 4th ed., ed. & rev. Thomas Thornburg (1995).

HABITUAL IMPAIRED DRIVING—G.S. 20-138.5

A person is guilty of this offense if that person:

1. drives
2. a vehicle, other than a lawnmower, bicycle, or horse,
3. on a highway or public vehicular area
4. while
   (a) under the influence of an impairing substance or
   (b) with an alcohol concentration of 0.08 or more at any relevant time after the driving, and
5. at the time of the offense, has been convicted of three or more offenses involving impaired driving in the seven years immediately preceding the date of the offense.

The first four elements of this offense are the elements of the offense of impaired driving under G.S. 20-138.1. This is a separate offense from impaired driving under G.S. 20-138.1, not an enhanced punishment for that offense.[6] This is an offense involving impaired driving under G.S. 20-4.01(24a). It is an implied consent offense under G.S. 20-16.2. A conviction of this offense is a covered charge under the vehicle forfeiture laws applicable to impaired driving offenses.

These convictions may occur at any time within the seven years. For example, they could all occur on the same date. It is not required that each of the three convictions must occur consecutively to each other—which is required by other laws, such as the habitual felon law (*see* G.S. 14-7.1). Records maintained on the Administrative Office of the Courts computer of prior convictions may be used to prove prior convictions under this section.[7]

Since habitual impaired driving is an offense involving impaired driving,[8] a previous conviction of habitual impaired driving apparently may serve as one of the three previous convictions necessary to satisfy element five. The convictions used to satisfy element five may not also be used in determining the defendant's prior record level under G.S. 15A-1340.14.[9]

G.S. 15A-928(b) requires that an indictment or information for this offense must allege the prior convictions in either (1) a separate count of the indictment or information charging the substantive offense or (2) a separate indictment or information. Under G.S. 15A-928(c), the defendant is arraigned during the superior court trial before the close of the state's case in the jury's absence. If the defendant admits the prior convictions, this element is satisfied and proof of the convictions and jury instructions about this element are not permitted (this provision does not bar evidence of a prior conviction under other rules of evidence).

If the defendant denies the prior conviction or a particular conviction, then the state has the burden of proving the convictions before the jury. However, the defendant has the burden of proving that a conviction was obtained in violation of right to counsel and may not collaterally attack a conviction on grounds other than a right-to-counsel violation.[10]

The provisions of G.S. 20-138.4 apparently apply to this new offense. Thus a prosecutor who enters a voluntary dismissal, accepts a plea to a lesser offense, substitutes another charge, and so forth, must enter detailed facts in the record to explain that action.

Impaired driving is a lesser included offense of habitual impaired driving.

---

6. State v. Priddy, 115 N.C. App. 547, 445 S.E.2d 610 (1994).
7. State v. Ellis, ___ N.C. App. ___, 504 S.E.2d 787 (1998).
8. G.S. 20-4.01(24a)g.
9. State v. Gentry, ___ N.C. App. ___, 519 S.E.2d 68 (1999).
10. G.S. 15A-980; Custis v. United States, 511 U.S. 485 (1994); State v. Stafford, 114 N.C. App. 101, 440 S.E.2d 846 (1994); State v. Muscia, 115 N.C. App. 498, 445 S.E.2d 86 (1994).

Penalties and Points

Habitual driving while impaired is a Class F felony. It carries a mandatory minimum twelve-month active term of imprisonment, even though the first three prior record levels of punishment for that class of offense otherwise allow an intermediate punishment. If the prior record level requires a minimum sentence of more than twelve months, the prior record level minimum governs.

Following conviction, the motor vehicle driven by the defendant at the time of the offense may be property subject to forfeiture according to the procedures set out in G.S. 20-28.2.[11] (That statute and the sections that follow it are discussed extensively in Chapter 3 of this part.) However, G.S. 20-138.5 contains language that also addresses the forfeiture issue. It provides that in applying the forfeiture procedures, an owner or holder of a security interest is considered an innocent party in relation to the motor vehicle subject for forfeiture if (1) the owner or holder of the security interest did not know and had no reason to know that the defendant had been convicted, within the prior seven years, of three or more offenses involving impaired driving or (2) the defendant drove the motor vehicle without the consent of the owner or the holder of the security interest. These provisions are largely duplicated by provisions in G.S. 20-28.2–28.9, and the language in G.S. 20-138.5 appears to be redundant.

A conviction of this offense results in permanent driver's license revocation and assignment of twelve insurance points.

IMPAIRED DRIVING IN A COMMERCIAL VEHICLE—G.S. 20-138.2

A person is guilty of this offense if that person:

1. drives
2. a commercial motor vehicle
3. on a highway or public vehicular area
4. while
    (a) under the influence of an impairing substance or
    (b) after having consumed sufficient alcohol that he or she has, at any relevant time after the driving, an alcohol concentration of 0.04 or more.

This offense has the same elements as impaired driving with two major exceptions. First, it must be committed in a commercial motor vehicle. G.S. 20-4.01(3d) defines *commercial motor vehicle* as a single vehicle that has a Gross Vehicle Weight Rating (GVWR) of at least 26,001 pounds; a combination of vehicles that has a GVWR of at least 26,001 pounds and includes a trailer or other towed unit with a GVWR of 10,001 or more pounds; a passenger vehicle designed to transport at least sixteen passengers; or a vehicle that transports hazardous materials and is required by federal law to display a placard to that effect.[12] (These definitions are discussed in Chapter 3 of Part One.)

Second, the *per se* level at which one commits this offense is 0.04, which is lower than the traditional impaired driving level of 0.08. The remainder of the elements are the same as the elements of impaired driving. The terms common to all motor vehicle offenses—*drive, vehicle, motor vehicle, highway,* and *public vehicular area*—are discussed in Chapter 1 of Part One. Other terms common to all or most impaired driving offenses—*under the influence, impairing substance, alcohol, alcohol concentration,* and *relevant time after the driving*—are discussed in Chapter 1 of this part.

11. G.S.20-138.5(e).
12. G.S. 2-4.01(2a), (2b), and (3d).

Like impaired driving under G.S. 20-138.1, it is not a defense to this charge that the defendant is legally entitled to use the drug that led to the impairment; in some circumstances, that can be a mitigating factor.

This is an offense involving impaired driving, which means that it can be the basis for a vehicle seizure, is a grossly aggravating factor under G.S. 20-179, and is a prior conviction for purposes of determining the length of revocation under G.S. 20-17(a)(2).[13]

The provisions of G.S. 20-138.4 apparently apply to this new offense. Thus a prosecutor who enters a voluntary dismissal, accepts a plea to a lesser offense, substitutes another charge, and so forth, must enter detailed facts in the record to explain that action.

This offense is subject to the assessment requirement in G.S. 20-17.6. The offense described below, *operating a commercial vehicle after consuming alcohol*, is a lesser included offense of this offense.

Penalties and Points

A person convicted of this offense is punished as though he or she were convicted of impaired driving under G.S. 20-179. That statute is discussed extensively in Chapter 1 of this part, and that discussion is applicable here. There is one possible exception: G.S. 20-179(e) provides that it is a mitigating factor in a regular impaired driving offense if the defendant has slight impairment and an alcohol concentration of no more than 0.09. Given the *per se* level of 0.04, instead of 0.08, it is less likely that an alcohol concentration of 0.05 or higher will be found to constitute *slight impairment* when a commercial motor vehicle is being driven, even though it might well support such a finding if a noncommercial motor vehicle is being driven.

The license consequences for a charge and conviction of this offense are complex since they involve actions taken against the person's entire license as well as some actions taken to affect only the ability to drive a commercial vehicle. At least four separate actions are triggered. First, under G.S. 20-16.5, a person charged with this offense may have his or her license revoked for at least thirty days at the time of the charge. Second, a person convicted of this offense has his or her license revoked for one year for a first offense, four years for a second conviction within three years of the first, and permanently for a third conviction within five years of the second.[14] The four-year and permanent revocations may be reduced by the DMV. Limited driving privileges are authorized for revocations for convictions of this offense "to the extent the law would allow limited driving privileges if the person had been driving a noncommercial motor vehicle when the offense occurred."[15] This provision apparently would authorize a judge to issue a limited privilege consistent with the eligibility requirements, procedure, and mandatory conditions in G.S. 20-179.3. That limited privilege may not include authorization to drive a commercial vehicle. (For a discussion of that statute see Chapter 1 of this part.) Third, a person convicted of this offense is disqualified from driving a commercial motor vehicle for one year for a first offense.[16] For a second offense, the disqualification is for life, but the license may be restored after ten years.[17] For a third or subsequent offense, the disqualification is for life and may not be reduced.[18] If the disqualification extends past

13. G.S. 20-4.01(24a).
14. G.S. 20-17(a)(2)b.; -19(c1), (d), and (e).
15. G.S. 20-17.5(b)(2).
16. G.S. 20-17.4(a).
17. G.S. 20-17.4(b).
18. G.S. 20-17.4(b1).

a parallel revocation, the person may apply for a Class C noncommercial license.[19] Fourth, G.S. 20-17.6 applies to the revocation imposed by G.S. 20-17(a)(2) for conviction of this offense, so the person must obtain a substance abuse assessment and any recommended treatment or education. Failure to do so will result in an extension of the revocation under G.S. 20-17(a)(2) until those conditions are satisfied.

In addition to the revocations discussed above, for offenses committed on and after July 1, 2000, the restoration of the license carries with it special conditions in some instances. A restoration under G.S. 20-17(a)(2)b (the second revocation discussed above) carries with it two mandatory conditions. The defendant must agree not to drive any vehicle while he or she has an alcohol concentration greater than 0.00 at any relevant time after the driving. The defendant must also agree, upon request of a law enforcement officer who has reasonable grounds to believe that the condition has been violated, to submit to a chemical analysis to determine if the condition has been violated. The defendant must agree to be transported to the test site as necessary. These conditions are in effect for three years from the date the license is restored unless the underlying revocation is permanent, in which case the conditions last for seven years.[20]

Violation of this *per se* condition is not a criminal offense but will result in a reactivation of the original revocation and an additional one-year revocation of the driver's license. For a more thorough discussion of this provision, see Chapter 3 of this part.

A conviction of this offense carries twelve insurance points. See Chapter 21 of Part One for more information about the insurance consequences of these convictions

OPERATING A COMMERCIAL VEHICLE AFTER CONSUMING ALCOHOL—G.S. 20-138.2A

A person is guilty of this offense if that person:

1. drives
2. a commercial motor vehicle
3. on a highway or public vehicular area
4. while consuming alcohol or while alcohol remains in his or her body.

This offense is a lesser included offense of impaired driving in a commercial vehicle under G.S. 20-138.2. This is an implied consent offense under G.S. 20-16.2, but it is not an offense involving impaired driving under G.S. 20-4.01(24a). It is subject to the assessment requirement in G.S. 20-17.6.

Elements one, two, and three are the same as for the offense of *impaired driving in a commercial vehicle under G.S. 20-138.2* (discussed on pages 105 and 106.)

To establish element four, a specific alcohol concentration is not required to be proved, which means that a chemical analysis under G.S. 20-16.2 and -139.1 is not required. Alcohol screening tests, while they do not establish a specific alcohol concentration, may be used if the tests used instruments approved by the Commission for Health Services and the test is conducted in accordance with the regulations of the commission.[21] The odor of alcoholic beverages is insufficient evidence to establish proof beyond a reasonable doubt that this element has been satisfied unless the defendant was offered an alcohol screening test or a chemical analysis under G.S. 20-16.2.

19. G.S. 20-17.5(b)(3).
20. G.S. 20-19(c3). The provisions of this statute become effective July 1, 2000.
21. G.S. 20-138.2A(b1).

Other evidence, such as the result of field sobriety tests, may also be used to help establish the presence of alcohol in the defendant.

Penalties and Points

A first offense under this section is a Class 3 misdemeanor, punishable by a fine of $100.[22] One hundred dollars is apparently not a maximum fine but the only amount a judge may fine someone. Second and subsequent offenses are punishable under G.S. 20-179 in the same manner as impaired driving convictions.[23] (For a discussion of the provisions of G.S. 20-179 see Chapter 1 of this part.) A conviction is a second or subsequent conviction if it occurs within the seven years immediately preceding the date of the current offense.[24]

For a first offense under this section, the person is disqualified from driving a commercial motor vehicle for ten days.[25] For a second or subsequent conviction, the disqualification is one year and, in addition, the person's driver's license is revoked for one year.[26] A person whose license is revoked for a second or subsequent conviction under G.S. 20-17(a)(13) must obtain a substance abuse assessment and complete any recommended treatment or education. Failure to do so before the end of the revocation period will extend the revocation until the treatment or education is completed.[27]

A violation of this section apparently is a moving violation for which one insurance point is assessed. See Chapter 21 of Part One for more information about the insurance consequences of these convictions.

OPERATING A SCHOOL BUS OR CHILD-CARE VEHICLE AFTER CONSUMING ALCOHOL—G.S. 20-138.2B

A person is guilty of this offense if that person:

1. drives
2. a school bus, a school activity bus, or a child-care vehicle
3. on a highway or public vehicular area
4. while consuming alcohol or while alcohol remains in his or her body.

This is an implied consent offense under G.S. 20-16.2, but it is not an offense involving impaired driving under G.S. 20-4.01(24a). It is subject to the assessment requirement in G.S. 20-17.6.

A *child-care vehicle* is one under the direction and control of a *child-care facility*, as that term is defined in G.S. 110-86(3). The vehicle must be driven by the owner or an employee or agent of the facility and must be actually transporting children to or from the facility or to an event or activity in connection with the facility.[28] A *school bus* is a vehicle whose primary purpose is to transport students on an established route to or from a school. It must be equipped with flashing red lights and a mechanical stop signal and must have the words SCHOOL BUS on the front and rear of the vehicle in letters at least eight inches high. Public, private, or parochial schools may have buses

22. G.S. 20-138.2A(c).
23. G.S. 20-138.2A(c).
24. G.S. 20-138.2A(d).
25. G.S. 20-17.4(a1).
26. G.S. 20-17.4(a)(6); -7(a)(13).
27. G.S. 20-17.6.
28. G.S. 20-4.01(27)c1.

that meet this definition.[29] A *school activity bus* is a vehicle (often painted a different color from a school bus) whose primary purpose is to transport students to events other than regular classroom work.[30] There is no requirement that children actually be in a school bus or school activity bus for this offense to be committed. The definition of child-care vehicle, however, has the effect of requiring that children be in the vehicle for this offense to be committed.

To establish element four, a specific alcohol concentration is not required to be proved, which means that a chemical analysis under G.S. 20-16.2 and -139.1 is not required. Alcohol screening tests, while they do not establish a specific alcohol concentration, may be used if the tests used instruments approved by the Commission for Health Services and the test is conducted in accordance with the regulations of the commission.[31] The odor of alcoholic beverages is insufficient evidence to establish proof beyond a reasonable doubt that this element has been satisfied unless the defendant was offered an alcohol screening test or a chemical analysis under G.S. 20-16.2. Other evidence, such as the result of field sobriety tests, may also be used to help establish the presence of alcohol in the defendant.

Penalties and Points

A first offense under this section is a Class 3 misdemeanor, punishable by a maximum fine of $100.[32] One hundred dollars is apparently not a maximum fine but the only amount that a judge may fine someone. Second and subsequent offenses are punishable under G.S. 20-179 in the same manner as impaired driving convictions.[33] (For a discussion of the provisions of G.S. 20-179, see Chapter 1 of this part.) A conviction is a second or subsequent conviction if it occurs within the seven years immediately preceding the date of the current offense.[34]

For a first offense under this section, the person's license is revoked for ten days.[35] For a second or subsequent conviction occurring within seven years of the date of the current offense, the revocation is for one year.[36] A person whose license is revoked for a conviction under G.S. 20-17(a)(14) must obtain a substance abuse assessment and complete any recommended treatment or education. Failure to do so before the end of the revocation period will extend the revocation until the treatment or education is completed.[37]

A violation of this section apparently is a moving violation for which one insurance point is assessed. See Chapter 21 of Part One for more information about the insurance consequences of these convictions.

29. G.S. 20-4.01(27)d4.
30. G.S. 20-4.01(27)d3.
31. G.S. 20-138.2B(b2).
32. G.S. 20-138.2B(c).
33. G.S. 20-138.2B(c).
34. G.S. 20-138.2B(d).
35. G.S. 20-17(a)(14).
36. G.S. 20-17(a)(14); -19(c2); -138.2B(d).
37. G.S. 20-17.6.

UNDERAGE DRIVER ZERO *PER SE* OFFENSE—G.S. 20-138.3

A person is guilty of this offense if that person:

1. while under the age of twenty-one,
2. drives
3. a motor vehicle
4. on a highway or a public vehicular area
5. while
   (a) consuming alcohol or
   (b) has remaining in his or her body
      (1) any alcohol previously consumed or
      (2) any controlled substance previously consumed unless the controlled substance was lawfully obtained and has been taken in therapeutic doses.[38]

Elements two, three, and four are defined in the definitions chapter in Part One.

This offense is a *per se* offense: It is committed when the underage person has *any* detectable amount of alcohol or drugs in his or her body, regardless of the level of impairment being experienced. Unlike impaired driving, which sets the *per se* level at a 0.08 alcohol concentration, this offense in effect sets the *per se* level at 0.01, since driving with any alcohol or illegal drugs is a violation.

This is not an offense involving impaired driving under G.S. 20-4.01(24a). It is an implied consent offense under G.S. 20-16.2.[39] G.S. 20-138.3(b1) provides that an odor of alcoholic beverage on the breath of the driver is insufficient, by itself, to prove beyond a reasonable doubt that alcohol was present in the driver's body. That rule does not apply, however, if the driver refused to provide a breath or blood sample to an officer making a valid request for an alcohol screening test or a chemical analysis. Alcohol screening tests may be used to establish guilt under this offense if they follow the procedures in G.S. 20-16.3 and the regulations adopted to implement that statute.

This offense is subject to the assessment requirement in G.S. 20-17.6.

Penalties and Points

A violation of this offense is a Class 2 misdemeanor punishable under G.S. 15A-1340.23. The maximum imprisonment is sixty days. The maximum fine is $1,000. This offense is not a lesser included offense of impaired driving, but if a person is convicted of this offense and an offense involving impaired driving arising out of the same transaction, the maximum aggregate punishment may not exceed the maximum punishment for the impaired driving offense.[40]

A person convicted of this offense has no driver's license points assigned as a result of the conviction, but his or her driver's license is revoked for one year.[41] This revocation does not begin until the person is finally convicted, although a person charged under this section may also be subject to the immediate pretrial revocation imposed under G.S. 20-16.5. Apparently a conviction of this offense carries one insurance point as a nonspecified moving violation.

A judge may issue a limited driving privilege to partially negate the revocation imposed for a conviction of this offense, if the person (1) is eighteen, nineteen, or twenty years old at the time of the offense, (2) has no previous convictions under this offense, (3) had a valid license at the time of the offense or had one that had not been expired for more than one year, (4) had no impaired

38. G.S. 20-138.3.
39. G.S. 20-138.3(b).
40. G.S. 20-138.3(c).
41. G.S. 20-13.2(a) and (d).

driving convictions in the preceding seven years, (5) has no pending charges or convictions occurring since the instant offense occurred for an offense involving impaired driving, and (6) has obtained and filed with the court a substance abuse assessment since the offense occurred. If the privilege is issued, the mandatory and permissible conditions, and the procedure for applying for a privilege in G.S. 20-179.3, apply.[42]

If the person is convicted of both this offense and G.S. 20-138.1, G.S. 20-138.3(d) provides that the provisions of G.S. 20-179.3 govern the person's eligibility for a limited privilege. Since G.S. 20-179.3 prohibits the issuance of a limited privilege when the person's license is revoked for any other reason,[43] it is likely that the existence of the two revocations is a bar to the issuance of a limited privilege for the conviction of impaired driving.

G.S. 20-13.2, the statute revoking a person's license for a conviction under this offense, also applies to two other situations: First, it applies when a person who is under twenty-one is charged with an implied consent offense and willfully refuses a chemical analysis. The revocation under G.S. 20-13.2 lasts for one year and is in addition to revocations under G.S. 20-16.2 or -16.5 for the same refusal, although it runs concurrently with those revocations.[44]

Second, it applies when a person is convicted of impaired driving under G.S. 20-138.1 or any other offense involving impaired driving under G.S. 20-4.01(24a) that occurs while he or she is under twenty-one. Again the revocation under G.S. 20-13.2 lasts for one year. The revocation under G.S. 20-13.2 is in addition to any other revocation imposed as a result of the conviction, although it runs concurrently with those revocations.[45]

Finally when the person convicted of this offense has his or her license restored for a revocation based on a conviction of this offense, the restoration comes with two mandatory conditions if the underlying offense is committed on or after July 1, 2000. The defendant must agree not to drive any vehicle while he or she has an alcohol concentration of greater than 0.00 at any relevant time after the driving. The defendant must also agree to submit to a chemical analysis to determine if the condition has been violated upon request of a law enforcement officer with reasonable grounds to believe that the condition has been violated. The defendant must agree to be transported to the test site as necessary. These conditions are in effect until the defendant reaches twenty-one years of age.[46] Apparently the condition is not applied if the defendant is over twenty-one at the time the license is restored.

Violation of this *per se* condition is not a criminal offense but will result in an additional one-year revocation of the driver's license. For a more thorough discussion of this provision, see Chapter 3 of this part.

If a person's license is revoked under G.S. 20-13.2, a limited driving privilege is not valid and should not be issued except as described above for some convictions under G.S. 20-138.3. Limited privileges are not authorized for the other two kinds of revocations under G.S. 20-13.2.

---

42. G.S. 20-138.3(d).
43. G.S. 20-179.3(e).
44. G.S. 20-13.2(c) and (d).
45. G.S. 20-13.2(b) and (d).
46. G.S. 20-19(c3). The provisions of this statute become effective July 1, 2000.

IMPAIRED INSTRUCTION—G.S. 20-12.1

A person is guilty of this offense if that person:

1. serves as a supervising driver under G.S. 20-7(l) or -11, or as an approved instructor under G.S. 20-7(m),
2. while the person
   (a) is under the influence of an impairing substance or
   (b) has an alcohol concentration of 0.08 at any relevant time after the driving.[47]

Element two of this offense is the same as the corresponding element of impaired driving, and the discussion of that element in Chapter One of this part applies to it.

This offense applies to the person accompanying or instructing a person with a learner's permit or supervising a holder of a Level 1 or 2 graduated provisional license under G.S. 20-11. It is irrelevant whether the permittee is under the influence; only the teacher's degree of impairment matters.

This offense is not subject to the assessment requirements in G.S. 20-17.6.

This is an implied consent offense.[48] It is the only implied consent offense in which a person other than the driver is authorized to be tested under the implied consent law. It is not an offense involving impaired driving.

A person charged under this section is probably subject to the chemical analysis requirements of G.S.20-16.2 and -139.1 and to immediate, pretrial revocation under G.S. 20-16.5, since those laws apply to persons charged with an implied consent offense and this is an implied consent offense. However, some of the words used to define the conditions under which the license is to be revoked clearly imply that driving is required—for example, relevant time after the *driving*. In addition, the statute under which a chemical analysis is obtained states that "any person who *drives* a vehicle . . . gives consent to a chemical analysis.[49] The legislative intent is thus not entirely clear, but it seems reasonable to interpret the specific statement in G.S. 20-12.1 to mean that this offense is an implied consent offense as an exception to any provisions of G.S. 20-16.2 or 16.5, which require the person charged to be a driver.

Penalties and Points

A violation of this offense is a Class 2 misdemeanor punishable under G.S. 15A-1340.23. The maximum imprisonment allowed is sixty days. The maximum fine allowed is $1,000.[50] A person convicted of this offense may have his or her license revoked for up to one year, at the discretion of the DMV.[51]

No driver's license points are assessed for convictions of this offense, and it is likely that no insurance points are assessed, since the defendant was not the vehicle driver. See Chapter 21 of Part One for more information about the insurance consequences of these convictions.

---

47. G.S. 20-12.1.
48. G.S. 20-12.1(b).
49. G.S. 20-16.2(a).
50. G.S. 20-35.
51. G.S. 20-16(a)(8a); -19(c).

TRANSPORTING AN OPEN CONTAINER OF AN ALCOHOLIC BEVERAGE AFTER CONSUMING ALCOHOL—G.S. 20-138.7

A person is guilty of this offense if that person:

1. drives
2. a motor vehicle
3. on a highway or public vehicular area
4. while
   (a) an alcoholic beverage in an opened container is in the passenger area and
   (b) the driver is consuming alcohol or has previously consumed alcohol remaining in his or her body.

This is not an offense involving impaired driving under G.S. 20-4.01(24a). It is an implied consent offense under G.S. 20-16.2. It is not covered by the assessment requirements of G.S. 20-17.6. It is not a lesser included offense of impaired driving under G.S. 20-138.1.[52]

Elements one, two, and three are discussed in Chapter 1 of Part One.

The phrase *alcoholic beverage* is not defined in G.S. Chapter 20. G.S. 18B-101(4) defines it as any beverage containing at least 0.5 percent alcohol by volume, including malt beverages, unfortified wine, fortified wine, spirituous liquors, and mixed beverages. Those specific beverages also are defined in G.S. 18B-101. The *passenger area* is the area designed to seat the driver and passengers and any area within the reach of a driver or passenger, including the glove compartment. The trunk or the area behind the last seat in a station wagon, van, or hatchback is not the passenger area.[53] A container with an alcoholic beverage is open if the seal has been broken, even if the cap or lid has been replaced.[54] A glass or cup containing an alcoholic beverage constitutes an open container.

The results of an alcohol screening test are admissible to establish the presence of alcohol, if the test is performed in a manner consistent with the regulations promulgated pursuant to G.S. 20-16.3.[55] The odor of alcohol is insufficient to establish the presence of alcoholic beverages, unless the driver refused to submit to an alcohol screening test or a chemical analysis.[56]

Penalties and Points

This is a Class 3 misdemeanor, punishable by a maximum of twenty days of imprisonment and a maximum fine of $200. A second or subsequent offense is a Class 2 misdemeanor, punishable by a maximum of sixty days of imprisonment and a fine of $1,000.[57] A violation of this section is a moving violation under G.S. 20-16(c), for which two driver's license points are assessed.[58] A second or subsequent conviction under this section carries a one-year license revocation.[59] A judge may issue a limited driving privilege to authorize driving during the period a person's license is revoked for a conviction under this section; the privilege may only negate this specific revocation.[60] To be eligible for this limited privilege the person must not have been convicted of an offense involving impaired driving in the preceding seven years, must have had a license that was valid or had been expired for

52. G.S. 20-138.7(e).
53. G.S. 20-138.7(f).
54. G.S. 20-138.7(f).
55. G.S. 20-138.7(d).
56. G.S. 20-138.7(c).
57. G.S. 20-138.7(e); 15A-1340.23.
58. G.S. 20-138.7(e).
59. G.S. 20-17(a)(12); -19(f).
60. G.S. 20-138.7(h).

less than one year at the time of the offense, have no cases pending involving offenses involving impaired driving under G.S. 20-4.01(24a), and have obtained and filed a substance abuse assessment with the court.[61] Apparently the traditional limitation that the applicant be a first offender under the relevant offense is not included in this statute; as a result, a judge may grant a limited privilege regardless of how many previous convictions the person has under this section.

Two related offenses are contained in G.S. 18B-401(a). That section makes it a Class 3 misdemeanor to transport fortified wine or spiritous liquor in an open container in the passenger area of a motor vehicle. This offense does not require that the driver be drinking or have alcohol remaining in his or her body. It is a Class 3 misdemeanor also under that section for a driver to consume any malt beverage or unfortified wine while driving. This offense does not require that any alcohol be transported, as does G.S. 20-138.7. There is no driver's license revocation required for conviction of either offense, although G.S. 20-16(a)(8) authorizes the Division of Motor Vehicles to revoke the license of a person convicted of "illegal transportation of alcoholic beverages."

A violation of this section (G.S. 20-138.7) apparently is a moving violation for which one insurance point is assessed. See Chapter 21 of Part One for more information about the insurance consequences of these convictions. The related offenses in Chapter 18B of the General Statutes do not carry insurance points.

POSSESSION OF ALCOHOLIC BEVERAGES WHILE OPERATING A COMMERCIAL VEHICLE—G.S. 20-138.2C

A person is guilty of this offense if that person:

1. drives
2. a commercial motor vehicle
3. on a highway, street, or public vehicular area
4. while having an open or closed alcoholic beverage in the passenger area of the motor vehicle.

This offense is not an implied consent offense under G.S. 20-16.2, nor is it an offense involving impaired driving under G.S. 20-4.01(24a). It is not covered by the assessment requirements of G.S. 20-17.6.

Elements one, two, and three are the same as for the offense of *impaired driving in a commercial vehicle* under G.S. 20-138.2, discussed earlier in this chapter. The phrases *alcoholic beverage* and *passenger area* are discussed in the commentary to the offense of *Transporting an Open Container of an Alcoholic Beverage after Consuming Alcohol* (see previous section). Unlike similar other offenses dealing with the transportation of alcohol,[62] this offense is committed when beverages in the manufacturer's original, unopened container are transported. The offense does not apply to drivers of commercial vehicles that are excursion passenger vehicles, for-hire passenger vehicles, common carriers of passengers, or motor homes if the beverage is in the possession of a passenger or is in the passenger area of the motor vehicle.

Penalties and Points

This is an infraction, punishable by a maximum penalty of $100. A violation of this section apparently carries four drivers license points. It apparently carries one insurance point.

---

61. G.S. 20-138.7(h); -179.3(b).

62. *See* G.S. 18B-401(a), (c); G.S. 20-138.7.

3 Special Provisions Applicable to Impaired Drivers

North Carolina motor vehicle law contains several provisions applicable to impaired driving cases under Section 20-138.1 of the North Carolina General Statutes (hereinafter G.S.) as well as to some or all of the other offenses related to impaired driving discussed in Chapter 2 of this part. These provisions include the implied consent testing provisions to determine impairment, vehicle forfeiture procedures, pretrial revocations of persons charged with some offenses, limitations on the dismissal of charges, and substance abuse assessment and treatment requirements. This chapter discusses each of those procedures in the context of the offenses to which each applies.

CHEMICAL TESTS FOR ALCOHOL

Definitions

To understand the laws regulating the chemical testing of drivers to determine alcohol concentration, certain terms need to be defined, in addition such terms as *alcohol, alcohol concentration,* and *relevant time after the driving*, which were discussed in Chapter 1 of this part.

Chemical Analysis. A test of the breath, blood, or other bodily substance of a person to determine his or her alcohol concentration or the presence of an impairing substance, performed in accordance with G.S. 20-139.1, including any necessary duplicate or sequential breath tests.[1] This definition is important because it does not limit the analysis to testing for alcohol; testing for *any* impairing substance is authorized. It also does not limit the analysis to testing of breath or blood; *any* bodily fluid or substance can be tested. This definition provides the legal authority to use the implied consent laws to test for drugs, but the statutes do not provide the degree of guidance for blood testing that they do for alcohol testing. For example, they establish no *per se* levels for any drugs, nor do they deal with the relationship between the presence of a drug and the impairment of a person's faculties. These problems and the practical problems of expense and delay in testing for drugs make it likely that the implied consent statutes will, with rare exceptions, be used to test only for the presence of alcohol.

Chemical analyst. A person granted a permit by the Department of Health and Human Services to perform chemical analyses.[2]

1. Section 20-4.01(3a) of the North Carolina General Statutes (hereinafter G.S.).
2. G.S. 20-4.01(3b).

Implied consent offense. An offense involving impaired driving or an offense involving alcohol consumption declared by statute to be an implied consent offense.[3]

Implied consent offenses are: impaired driving; the provisional licensee *per se* offense (G.S. 20-138.3); impaired instruction of a learner's permittee (G.S. 20-12.1); homicides involving impaired driving; habitual impaired driving (G.S. 20-138.5); impaired driving in a commercial vehicle (G.S. 201-138.2); driving a commercial vehicle after drinking (zero tolerance) (G.S. 20-138.2A); driving a school bus or child-care vehicle after drinking (zero tolerance) (G.S. 20-138.2B); transporting an open container of alcohol after drinking (G.S. 20-138.7); and driving while license revoked by violating a condition in a limited driving privilege by driving after drinking (G.S. 20-179.3[j]). Effective July 1, 2000, driving while license revoked by violating the conditions related to the use of interlock ignition devices imposed on the restoration of a license after a revocation for a conviction of driving while impaired also will be an implied consent offense.[4] A person charged with any of these offenses is subject to the implied consent laws. (See Table 2.)

Charged. Being arrested for an offense or being served with a criminal process charging one with an offense.[5] The kinds of processes that satisfy this requirement and that do not involve an arrest include the *criminal summons* and the *citation*.[6]

Charging officer. The law enforcement officer who arrests a person charged or lodges a charge against him or her by issuing a citation or requesting that a criminal summons be issued; in addition to the initial charging officer, any officer who assists that person by assuming custody to request that the person submit to a chemical analysis or to present the person to a judicial official for an initial appearance. This definition in essence codifies the holding of *Oldham v. Miller*.[7] That the defendant is ultimately tried on a different pleading than the one initially obtained by a charging officer does not render invalid the actions taken by the initial charging officer.[8]

Conditions Invoking Implied Consent Laws

North Carolina's chemical testing statute is an implied consent statute; that is, the consent necessary to request that a person take the test is implied in the act of driving. In many ways, to speak of implied consent is misleading. Being asked to take a chemical test of one's breath or blood is more appropriately viewed as a condition of driving, much the same as being required to have a driver's license or being required to refrain from driving while impaired. Several conditions must be present before a person may properly be requested to take a test, but if those conditions are present, no consent is necessary to subject the person to a request to take the test, and no consent is necessary to support a license revocation for a person who refuses to take a test when validly requested to do so. In fact two courts have held that the state may validly require certain drivers to submit to tests without the option to refuse.[9]

The cases cited in this discussion of implied consent statutes arise in two contexts. Either they contest the validity of a revocation or they seek to suppress evidence in a criminal case involving

---

3. G.S. 20-16.2(al).

4. G.S. 20-17.8(f), as enacted by SL 1999-406. Ignition interlock devices require a person to activate the device using an assigned code and to provide a breath sample that falls below a specified alcohol concentration before the person may start a vehicle.

5. G.S. 20-16.2(al).

6. G.S. 15A-302 and -303.

7. 38 N.C. App. 178, 247 S.E.2d 767 (1978).

8. State v. Gunter, 111 N.C. App. 621, 433 S.E.2d 191 (1993).

9. Montgomery v. Department of Motor Vehicles, 455 F. Supp. 338 (W.D.N.C. 1978), *aff'd*, 599 F.2d 1048 (4th Cir. 1979); Etheridge v. Peters, 45 N.C. App. 358, 263 S.E.2d 308, *aff'd*, 301 N.C. 76, 269 S.E.2d 133 (1980).

Table 2
Implied Consent Offenses

1. Impaired instruction—G.S. 20-12.1
2. Driving while impaired—G.S. 20-138.1
3. Driving while impaired in a commercial vehicle—G.S. 20-138.2
4. Driving a commercial vehicle after consuming alcohol or drugs—G.S. 20-138.2A
5. Driving a school bus or child care vehicle after consuming alcohol or drugs—G.S. 20-138.2B
6. Driving while less than twenty-one years of age after consuming alcohol or drugs—G.S. 20-138.3
7. Habitual impaired driving—G.S. 20-138.5
8. Transporting alcohol beverage after consuming alcohol—G.S. 20-138.7
9. Vehicular homicides involving impaired driving—G.S. 20-16.2(a1), G.S. 20-4.01(24a)
10. Driving while license revoked based on violation of zero tolerance provision of DWI limited privilege—G.S. 20-179.3(j)
11. Driving while license revoked based on violation of ignition interlock conditions on DWI limited privilege—G.S. 20-179.3; G.S. 20-17.8(f) (effective July 1, 2000)

the offense of impaired driving. Both kinds of cases provide precedents for understanding the legal principles applicable to these proceedings.

The standard for the suppression of evidence obtained in an implied consent chemical analysis, if it is based on a violation of the statute, is that it must be a substantial violation of the statute under G.S. 15A-974, and the motion to suppress must be consistent with the procedure of G.S. Chapter 15A.[10]

What are the conditions that make one subject to the implied consent law? The first is that the person be charged with an implied consent offense or otherwise made subject to this requirement by statute. As previously noted, this means that the person has either been arrested or been served with a citation or a criminal summons. If the person has been charged by being arrested (which is the norm), the arrest does not have to be legal to support a valid request, although an unconstitutional arrest will not support such a request.[11] Further, in *Quick v. DMV*,[12] the North Carolina Court of Appeals reaffirmed that condition in light of the legislative changes that triggered the implied consent laws if a person is *charged* (instead of being *arrested*, as was required by the law in effect until 1983).

Effective July 1, 2000, G.S. 20-19 imposes as a condition to restore the driver's license of certain offenders a lower alcohol *per se* level than is applicable to the general public. This condition applies to persons whose licenses are revoked for some alcohol driving offenses. Those people are subject also to the implied consent statutes, even though they will not be charged with an implied consent offense for violating the lower *per se* levels.[13]

The second condition is that there be reasonable grounds to believe that the person charged committed an implied consent offense. *Reasonable grounds* and *probable cause* are generally used interchangeably by North Carolina's appellate courts.[14] In applying this law, courts determine whether there were reasonable grounds based on the evidence known to the officer *at the time of the charge* or the arrest and not *after the chemical analysis*.

10. State v. Pearson, 131 N.C. App. 315, 507 S.E.2d 301 (1998).

11. State v. Eubanks, 283 N.C. 556, 196 S.E.2d 706 (1973); State v. Stewardson, 32 N.C. App. 344, 232 S.E.2d 308 (1977); *In re* Pinyatello, 36 N.C. App. 542, 245 S.E.2d 185 (1978).

12. 125 N.C. App. 123, 479 S.E.2d 226 (1997).

13. G.S. 20-19(c3), as enacted by SL 1999-406. The provisions of this statute are discussed in more detail later in this chapter.

14. *See, e.g.,* Church v. Powell, 40 N.C. App. 254, 252 S.E.2d 229 (1979).

Church v. Howell[15] gives some guidance as to what is required to show reasonable grounds. The driver in that case had been drinking heavily on the day before the wreck. He testified that he had last had a drink at 4:00 P.M. and wrecked his automobile at 7:30 P.M. The patrolman saw him less than one hour later, although the defendant testified that he had consumed an additional nine to twelve ounces of liquor since the accident, and he then told the patrolman he was driving the car when it wrecked. The patrolman arrested him at 8:20 P.M. Despite the long delay between the accident and the arrest and the alleged consumption of alcohol after the accident, the court found that the officer had had reasonable grounds to believe that the defendant had been driving under the influence of an intoxicating liquor. Other cases discussing this issue include *Richardson v. Hiatt*[16] and *Moore v. Hodges*.[17]

The third condition is that the charging officer designate the type of chemical analysis to be administered. This requirement gives the officer control over the type of test and makes the "I will take a blood test but not a breath test" response a willful refusal when the officer has designated a breath test as the appropriate kind. Officers almost universally designate the breath test unless no instrument is available or the defendant is hospitalized or otherwise unable to give an adequate breath sample.

The fourth condition is that the defendant be informed of his or her implied consent rights and the consequences of his or her choice, in the manner prescribed by G.S. 20-16.2(a). The statute requires a chemical analyst authorized to administer a test of the person's breath to give this notice, even if the analysis is to be a blood or other test. If the charging officer is also a chemical analyst, the charging officer may give the person charged the oral and written rights required by G.S. 20-16.2(a). The results of a chemical analysis are inadmissible in a criminal trial if the chemical analyst fails to notify a defendant of his or her rights as provided in the statute.[18] The notification must be both oral and written. It is sufficient to provide the written notice by attaching it to a defendant's hospital chart, in an instance in which the defendant could not receive the notice because his or her hands were strapped to a medical table.[19] The state is not required to show that the defendant has read the rights listed on the form[20] or that the defendant has understood them.[21] If the defendant is so unruly and boisterous that the analyst is "drowned out" by the defendant's talking, the analyst need not complete the oral notification required by the statute before determining that the defendant's actions constitute willful refusal to submit to the analysis.[22] The defendant's rights and the consequences of his or her choices are as follows:

One, the defendant has a right to refuse to be tested. This is not a constitutional right but one granted solely by statute.[23] G.S. 20-16.2(c) specifically provides that if a refusal occurs, no test may be given pursuant to that section, but "the refusal does not preclude testing under other applicable procedures of law." This language enables the state to obtain a test without the defendant's consent, as authorized by *Schmerber v. California*[24] and G.S. 15A-231.[25]

---

15. *Id.*

16. 95 N.C. App. 196, 381 S.E.2d 866 (1989) (single-car accident on clear day, odor of alcohol about driver, and defendant's statement that he fell asleep constituted reasonable grounds).

17. 116 N.C. 727, 449 S.E.2d 218 (1994) (one-car accident, positive Alcosensor test, defendant first seen while in hospital forty-five minutes after accident).

18. State v. Shadding, 17 N.C. App. 279, 194 S.E.2d 55 (1973).

19. State v. Lovett, 119 N.C. App. 689, 460 S.E.2d 177 (1995).

20. State v. Carpenter, 34 N.C. App. 742, 239 S.E.2d 596 (1977).

21. Sermons v. Peters, 51 N.C. App. 147, 275 S.E.2d 218 (1981).

22. Rice v. Peters, 48 N.C. App. 697, 269 S.E.2d 740 (1980).

23. Montgomery v. Department of Motor Vehicles, 455 F. Supp. 338 (W.D.N.C.), *aff'd*, 599 F.2d 1048 (4th Cir. 1979).

24. 384 U.S. 757 (1966).

25. *See also* State v. Drdak, 330 N.C. 587, 411 S.E.2d 604 (1992); State v. Byers, 105 N.C. App. 377, 413 S.E.2d 586 (1992).

Two, refusal will result in an immediate revocation of the defendant's driving privilege for at least thirty days (under G.S. 20-16.5) and for an additional twelve months (under G.S. 20-16.2). The revocations are separate, although each is based on the same refusal. They do not run consecutively, but neither is credit given for one revocation on the other. If the two revocations are in effect at the same time, they run concurrently.

Three, the test results, or the fact of refusal, will be admissible in trial on the impaired driving or other charge. The use of a refusal to take a test as evidence of guilt has been upheld in *State v. Flannery*[26] and *South Dakota v. Neville*.[27] The refusal need not be willful to be admissible.[28]

Four, if the test results reveal an alcohol concentration of 0.08 or greater, or an alcohol concentration of 0.04 or greater and the defendant was driving a commercial motor vehicle, or any alcohol concentration and the defendant was under the age of twenty-one at the time of the offense, the defendant's driver's license will be revoked under G.S. 20-16.5 for at least thirty days.

Five, the defendant may have a qualified person of his or her choosing administer a test in addition to those administered by the state. Failure to notify a defendant of this right will make the test results inadmissible in the criminal trial.[29] (The legal duties of the charging officer and the chemical analyst in the implementation of this right are discussed later in this chapter.)

Six, the defendant has the right to call an attorney and select a witness to view the testing procedures, but the testing may not be delayed for these purposes for more than thirty minutes from the time the defendant is notified of his or her rights. (The legal duties of the charging officer and the chemical analyst in the implementation of this right are discussed later in this chapter.)

The fifth condition that the state must satisfy in order to subject a person to a request to submit to a chemical analysis is that the charging officer request the defendant to submit to a chemical analysis. G.S. 20-16.2(c) provides that the "charging officer, in the presence of the chemical analyst who has notified the person of his or her rights . . . , must request the person charged" to submit to the test. The clear implication of the word *notified* is that the request is intended to follow and not precede the notification of rights. However, in cases interpreting an earlier, similar version of this statute, the court of appeals declined to find any problem with the timing of the request as long as the times of both the request and the notification of rights preceded the time at which the defendant's decision to take the test had to be made. *Mathis v. Department of Motor Vehicles*[30] affirmed a case in which the request followed the notification of rights, and *Rice v. Peters*[31] affirmed a case in which the request apparently preceded the notification. In both cases the court indicated that the legislature did not intend to prescribe a "rigid sequence of events" necessary to obtain a valid chemical analysis. In most instances there will be, in effect, two requests: the formal request by the charging officer that the defendant submit and the directions from the chemical analyst telling the defendant what to do to take the test.[32]

The cited cases deal with situations in which there is a charging officer and a separate chemical analyst. That is not always the case, however. If the charging officer is also a chemical analyst, special rules apply. G.S. 20-139.1(b1) authorizes a charging officer to also perform a chemical analysis of a person's breath if (1) the officer possesses a valid permit for the type of chemical analysis being performed and (2) the analysis is performed on an automated instrument that prints the results of the analysis. The Intoxilyzer 5000, the only instrument currently being used in the state to perform chemical analyses, is such an instrument. The Breathalyzer, some models of which are

26. 31 N.C. App. 617, 230 S.E.2d 603 (1976).
27. 459 U.S. 553 (1983).
28. State v. Pyatt, 125 N.C. App. 147, 479 S.E.2d 218 (1997).
29. State v. Gilbert, 85 N.C. App. 594, 355 S.E.2d 261 (1987) (dictum).
30. 71 N.C. App. 413, 322 S.E.2d 426 (1984).
31. 48 N.C. App. 697, 269 S.E.2d 740 (1980).
32. *See also In re* Vallender, 81 N.C. App. 291, 344 S.E.2d 62 (1986).

not automated, is no longer used in North Carolina. This provision allowing a charging officer to also serve as chemical analyst in effect overrules several cases that construed an earlier statute that prohibited charging officers from performing the analysis.[33]

In *Nicholson v. Killens*,[34] the North Carolina Court of Appeals held that the statute did not authorize the charging officer to provide the notice required by G.S. 20-16.2(a) and (c), unless the test designated is a blood test. The result was to make the provision of G.S. 20-139.1(b1) ineffective in cases of refusals. In 1995 the General Assembly effectively overruled *Nicholson* by specifying that the charging officer may provide the required notices if he or she is an authorized chemical analyst, regardless of the type of test designated.[35]

Another condition necessary to a valid request for a chemical analysis is that the defendant be given an opportunity to exercise the right to communicate with his or her attorney and the right to communicate with friends. (The relationship between the thirty-minute time limit mentioned in the rights, and the defendant's waiver of or attempt to exercise those rights, is discussed later in this chapter.)

Finally, this discussion has focused on the use of breath or blood tests to determine alcohol concentration. It should be noted, however, that in 1997 the General Assembly amended the implied consent statutes to include tests of urine or other bodily fluids or substances to determine the presence of impairing substances other than alcohol.[36] At present no tests to determine the presence of drugs or other controlled substances are readily available, except for those that can be conducted in forensic or similarly equipped labs. There also are no legislatively established levels at which the presence of a particular substance is considered to constitute impairment. If the request to test for substances other than alcohol comes after a test for alcohol, the notice of rights specified under G.S. 20-16.2(a) must be repeated.[37]

Administration of the Chemical Analysis

G.S.20-139.1 and regulations adopted by the Commission for Health Services pursuant to that section specify the manner in which a chemical analysis must be performed. The basic rule is from G.S. 20-139.1(b): A chemical analysis, to be valid, "shall be performed in accordance with the provisions of this section . . . according to methods approved by the Commission for Health Services by an individual possessing a current permit issued by the Department of Health and Human Services for that type of chemical analysis."

Analyses performed consistent with this rule are admissible in evidence pursuant to G.S. 20-139.1(a) without the need for further evidence as to the scientific reliability of the instrument used or the validity of the underlying scientific principles.[38]

Proof that the operator has a valid permit may be given in three ways: (1) by stipulation, (2) by introduction into evidence of a certified copy of the analyst's permit, or (3) by presentation of any other relevant evidence that proves the fact. This other evidence is typically an oral statement by the analyst.[39] If the state fails to provide proof that an analyst had a permit valid at the time

---

33. State v. Stauffer, 266 N.C. 358, 145 S.E.2d 917 (1966); State v. Spencer, 46 N.C. App. 507, 265 S.E.2d 451 (1980); State v. Jordan, 35 N.C. App. 652, 242 S.E.2d 192 (1978); State v. Dail, 25 N.C. App. 552, 214 S.E.2d 219 (1975).

34. 116 N.C. App. 473, 448 S.E.2d 542 (1994), *superseding opinion* at 115 N.C. App. 552, 445 S.E.2d 608 (1994).

35. G.S. 20-16.2(a).

36. G.S. 20-4.01(3a).

37. G.S. 20-139.1(b5).

38. *See* State v. Powell, 279 N.C. 608, 184 S.E.2d 243 (1971); State v. George, 77 N.C. App. 470, 336 S.E.2d 93 (1985).

39. State v. Mullis, 38 N.C. App. 40, 247 S.E.2d 265 (1978).

of the test, the test results may not be admitted.[40] Failure to mention that the permit was issued by the State Board of Health (now the Department of Health and Human Services) has been ruled to be prejudicial error.[41] The kind of evidence needed to prove that the analyst followed the approved methods is similar to that needed to prove that the analyst had a permit: either a stipulation, a copy of the rules and the checklist used, or oral testimony to that effect.[42]

In testifying, analysts have been permitted to express the results as ".11" without specifying whether the results are from breath or blood or even that the number represents "alcohol concentration" as long as the term is defined for the jury.[43]

The rules for the administration of all chemical analyses are found in Title 15A, Chapter 19B, of the *North Carolina Administrative Code,* which spells out in detail the steps that are required to obtain a permit and to conduct a chemical test.

After the test or tests are completed, if the analysis is a breath analysis, the analyst must note the *time of the collection* of the samples and the *results of the analysis.* The defendant or his or her attorney must be given a copy of the results before any trial or other proceeding in which the analysis is sought to be used.[44]

It is not a substantial violation sufficient under G.S. 15A-934 to suppress the results of a chemical analysis that the chemical analyst took the defendant outside of the officer's territorial jurisdiction to administer the analysis.[45]

Sequential Breath Testing

G.S. 20-139.1 (b3) requires sequential testing to obtain a valid breath test result of a defendant's particular alcohol concentration. To obtain a valid result, the analyst must take at least two breath samples, although as noted below, there are important exceptions to that rule. The samples must be within 0.02 of each other and must be obtained consecutively. If the first two samples are not within 0.02 of each other a third test "shall be administered as soon as feasible by repeating steps [in the regulations governing the use of the testing instrument], as applicable."[46] When the automated Intoxilyzer is used, the only steps that are required in administering a third test are the steps required by the instrument to collect a breath sample and record the results. No instrument calibration is necessary.[47]

If both of these conditions are met on two tests, the lower breath sample may be used to establish a defendant's particular alcohol concentration. To illustrate, if a first breath sample is 0.12, a second is 0.09, and a third is 0.10, the last two may be used because on two consecutive tests the results do not differ by 0.02. The defendant's alcohol concentration used in this case will be 0.09. Courts in interpreting this provision have held that it is not error to: (1) introduce documents showing both test results when both tests had the same reading and the defendant did not specifically object at trial to the introduction of that portion of the documents[48] and (2) introduce testimony of a defendant's refusal to take a second test and/or to mention that he or she took a

40. *See* State v. Gray, 28 N.C. App. 506, 221 S.E.2d 765 (1976).

41. State v. Franks, 87 N.C. App. 265, 360 S.E.2d 473 (1987); State v. Caviness, 7 N.C. App. 541, 173 S.E.2d 12 (1970).

42. *See Powell,* 279 N.C. at 608, 184 S.E.2d at 245.

43. State v. Jones, 76 N.C. App. 160, 332 S.E.2d 494 (1985); *see also* State v. Midgett, 78 N.C. App. 387, 337 S.E.2d 117 (1985).

44. G.S. 20-139.1(e).

45. State v. Pearson, ___ N.C. App. ___, 507 S.E.2d 301 (1998) (court assumed, but did not formally decide, that the officer's conduct was a statutory violation in this case).

46. 15A NCAC 19B.0320 (June 1998).

47. State v. Moore, ___ N.C. App. ___, 513 S.E.2d 346 (1999).

48. State v. Harper, 82 N.C. App. 398, 346 S.E.2d 226 (1986).

first test if there is no mention of the results of the first test.[49] The significance of the second holding[50] is limited by a subsequent statutory amendment (discussed later) that allows the introduction of that first test result.

A 1998 amendment to G.S. 20-4.01(1b) requires that all alcohol concentrations be reported to hundredths. That amendment in essence codifies the holding of *State v. Tew*.[51]

If more than two tests are needed to obtain a valid result, the analyst is authorized to request that the defendant submit to additional tests, and failure to submit to a third or subsequent test is specified by the statute to be a willful refusal.[52] That failure to submit may include the failure to submit to a test of urine or other bodily substance for the presence of impairing substances other than alcohol.[53] In that case, however, the defendant must be rewarned of the rights and responsibilities to which he or she is subject under G.S. 20-16.2(a) after submitting to the test for alcohol.

In addition, if the defendant provides a breath test sample, but fails to provide a second or subsequent sample as requested, the first (or if there is more than one sample, the lowest) reading is nonetheless admissible for any purpose in a judicial or administrative hearing.[54] Thus a defendant who provides one sample that reveals a concentration of 0.11, and who then refuses to provide a second sample will have his or her license revoked for refusing and may have the test results admitted to establish a violation of the *per se* prong of impaired driving under G.S. 20-138.1. That the defendant refused to provide the second sample also would be admissible in the criminal trial.

Preventive Maintenance

G.S. 20-139.1(b2) provides that no breath test result is admissible if the defendant proves that preventive maintenance was not performed on the instrument within the time limits specified in the regulations. The obligation to object as well as the burden of proof is on the defendant. The form affidavit used by breath analysts to report test results in district court criminal cases, to report refusals to the Division of Motor Vehicles (DMV), and to report either test results or refusals in pretrial revocations under G.S. 20-16.5[55] contains a statement by the analyst referring to the date on which the most recent preventive maintenance procedures were reported to have been performed. That statement is not required by statute, and failure to include it on the affidavit should have no effect on the admissibility of the affidavit.

Time Limits in Breath Test Administration

Two time limits can have an impact on the validity of a test result or on the willfulness of a refusal. The first is the *observation period* applicable to breath tests. It is not specified by statute, although G.S. 20-139.1(b3) states that the regulations must specify both a minimum observation period before a breath test may be given and the time requirements applicable to subsequent breath tests.

Section 19B.0101(6) of Title 15A of the *North Carolina Administrative Code* specifies that the initial observation period is fifteen minutes. The fifteen-minute period is intended to ensure that the breath sample collected is free of mouth alcohol and other foreign substances that could interfere with an accurate breath analysis. To that end the test may not be given unless in the fif-

---

49. State v. Wike, 85 N.C. App. 516, 355 S.E.2d 221 (1987).

50. *Id.*

51. 326 N.C. 732, 392 S.E.2d 603 (1990).

52. G.S. 20-139.1(b3); Watson v. Hiatt, 78 N.C. App. 609, 337 S.E.2d 871 (1985); Gibson v. Faulkner, ___ N.C. App. ___, 515 S.E.2d 452 (Apr. 6, 1999).

53. G.S. 20-139.1(b5).

54. G.S. 20-139.1(b3).

55. Form AOC-CVR-1/DHHS 3907.

teen minutes immediately preceding it, the defendant has not ingested alcohol or other fluids, regurgitated, vomited, eaten, or smoked. It is immaterial whether the analyst observed the defendant for much more than fifteen minutes if any of the prohibited acts occurred in the fifteen minutes preceding the test. The regulation requires the analyst to *observe* the defendant; it does not say that observing the defendant is *all* the analyst may do. If the analyst continuously has the defendant in his or her immediate sight and range of hearing as he or she prepares the instrument, the analyst is complying with the regulation. If one of the prohibited acts (for example, regurgitation) occurs between the taking of breath samples, at least fifteen minutes must pass before the second sample can be taken. If the person refuses to obey the analyst's instructions and places a foreign substance in, or refuses to remove a foreign substance from, his or her mouth so that the observation period can be adhered to, that action constitutes a refusal.[56]

As noted, G.S. 20-139.1(b3) also requires that regulations governing the use of testing equipment specify the intervals that are necessary between the collection of the first and any subsequent samples. The regulations for use of the Intoxilyzer 5000 (the only instrument used in this state) address that requirement by directing the analyst to collect the first breath sample when the words PLEASE BLOW appear on the instrument display panel and to collect the second or subsequent samples when the same phrase appears again on the display panel.[57] Thus the time specified in the regulations is the amount of time it takes for the testing instrument to recycle and ready itself to take the next sample. This satisfies the requirement of G.S. 20-139.1(b3) even though it does not spell out a time in minutes that must separate the two breath samples.[58]

G.S. 20-16.2(a) also includes a *statutory time limit.* It is thirty minutes, and it begins immediately after the defendant has been notified of his or her rights by the chemical analyst. This period is provided so the defendant can call an attorney or select a witness to view the testing procedures. It is not a constitutional right, either in a criminal prosecution or in an administrative proceeding to revoke a license.[59] The period begins at the time the defendant is notified of his or her rights under the statute, not at the time the defendant is requested to take the test by the charging officer.[60] The defendant is entitled to delay the test only if he or she has indicated a desire to exercise the right to call an attorney or a witness or both.[61] The forms recommended for use by breath analysts contain a specific set of questions designed to determine if a defendant wishes to exercise this right, and, if applicable, it is wise to obtain a specific waiver of this right. If a defendant indicates a desire to exercise this right, the test must be delayed until the thirty minutes have expired or the rights have been exercised, whichever occurs first.

This section raises several procedural issues:

One, if a defendant indicates a desire to call an attorney or select a witness, may the defendant delay the test for more than thirty minutes while attempting to contact an attorney or while waiting for a witness? No. The North Carolina Court of Appeals, in *Creech v. Alexander*,[62] held that a defendant who is informed once of the existence of the time limit may have his or her license revoked for refusing even if he or she is not specifically notified again at the expiration of the thirty minutes that the time has expired.[63]

---

56. Tolbert v. Hiatt, 95 N.C. App. 380, 382 S.E.2d 453 (1989).

57. 15A NCAC 19B.0320(6) and (7).

58. State v. Lockwood, 78 N.C. App. 205, 336 S.E.2d 678 (1985); State v. Garvick, 98 N.C. App. 556, 392 S.E.2d 115 (1990).

59. State v. Howren, 312 N.C. 454, 323 S.E.2d 335 (1984); Seders v. Powell, 298 N.C. 453, 259 S.E.2d 544 (1979).

60. *In re* Vallender, 81 N.C. App. 291, 344 S.E.2d 62 (1986).

61. McDaniel v. Division of Motor Vehicles, 96 N.C. App. 495, 386 S.E.2d 173 (1989); State v. Buckner, 33 N.C. App. 447, 238 S.E.2d 635 (1977); State v. Lloyd, 33 N.C. App. 370, 235 S.E.2d 281 (1970).

62. 32 N.C. App. 139, 231 S.E.2d 36 (1977).

63. *See also* Etheridge v. Peters, 301 N.C. 76, 269 S.E.2d 133 (1980).

Two, if a defendant is not successful in obtaining a witness in the thirty-minute period, but is successful shortly thereafter, may the defendant be permitted to take the test if he or she so desires and the analyst is willing to offer the test? Yes.[64]

Three, if a defendant is successful in obtaining a witness, must the witness be allowed to view the entire testing procedure? No. The witness is only entitled to view the portion of the procedure remaining to be performed after he or she arrives.[65]

Four, if a defendant chooses to take the test before the expiration of the thirty-minute period, is the test admissible? Yes.[66]

Defendant's Right to a Test of His or Her Choosing

G.S. 20-139.1(d) entitles a defendant to a chemical test of his or her own choosing, in addition to the test administered at the officer's request.[67] To be eligible to obtain such a test, the defendant must submit to the analysis requested by the charging officer. It is the duty of the law enforcement officer in custody of the defendant to assist the defendant in contacting someone to administer the additional test. When that contact must be allowed to be made is not specified in the statute, but to be timely, it must be allowed as soon as possible. This usually means that the charging officer is responsible for assisting the defendant in contacting someone, but if the request comes after a defendant is in the custody of a jailer, then the jailer must assist the defendant. Complying with such a request would be a necessary delay for the purposes of meeting the statutory requirement that an arrested person be presented to a judicial official without unnecessary delay.[68]

There is no requirement that the state pay for the test, and the defendant is responsible for ensuring that payment is made. Having enough money is only one of a defendant's problems if he or she is in custody during the critical period. Because virtually no breath testing instruments are in use for additional tests requested by defendants, the kind of test usually available to a defendant is a blood test, and the persons most likely to perform a blood test are in local hospitals. Unless a defendant can get to a hospital or can get a local blood analyst to come to the jail, the right to an additional test is not of much use. If a defendant does get an analyst to come to the jail, the statute gives that person the right to access to the defendant.

The defendant has no right to be transported to the testing site.[69] Nor does the defendant have any right to compel the charging officer to sign any forms as may be requested by the testing authority.[70] Also, providing access to a phone is sufficient to satisfy this statute's requirements on allowing contact.[71]

Administration of Blood Tests

Most of the statutory provisions applicable to chemical analyses apply to breath and blood tests. A few, however, apply only to breath tests, and some apply only to blood tests. For example, the observation period of fifteen minutes applies only to breath tests, as does the statutory requirement

---

64. Pappas v. Department of Motor Vehicles, 42 N.C. App. 497, 256 S.E.2d 829 (1979).

65. State v. Martin, 46 N.C. App. 514, 265 S.E.2d 456 (1980).

66. *Buckner,* 33 N.C. App. 447, 238 S.E.2d 635; *Lloyd,* 33 N.C. App. 370, 235 S.E.2d 281.

67. *See* State v. Magee, 75 N.C. App. 357, 330 S.E.2d 825 (1985).

68. G.S. 15A-511.

69. State v. Bumgarner, 97 N.C. App. 567, 389 S.E.2d 425 (1990); State v. Bunton, 27 N.C. App. 704, 220 S.E.2d 354 (1975).

70. State v. Sawyer, 26 N.C. App. 728, 217 S.E.2d 116 (1975).

71. *Bumgarner,* 97 N.C. App. 567, 389 S.E.2d 425.

that the defendant be given a copy of the test results. The requirement that a chemical analyst administer the test is not applicable to the withdrawal of blood. However, under the implied consent statute, a chemical analyst authorized to administer breath tests must be present to inform a person requested to take a blood test of his or her rights.

G.S. 20-139.1(c) provides that only a physician, a nurse, or another qualified person may withdraw blood for this purpose. Blood technicians at a hospital,[72] a hospital laboratory technologist with a degree in medical laboratory technology,[73] and a hospital nurse[74] have all been approved as qualified persons. The state has the burden to prove compliance with the statute, but it does not have to "negate every possible flaw in the testing procedure."[75]

Some hospitals request that an officer asking for a blood sample do so in writing. G.S. 20-139.1(c) requires the officer to comply with such a request. That statute also provides limited immunity to health professionals drawing blood for actions based on lack of consent but not for the negligent drawing of blood or other acts or omissions amounting to negligence.

Analysis of a blood sample taken pursuant to the implied consent statute must still be done by an analyst who has a permit issued by the Department of Health and Human Services. Most blood analyses are done in the laboratory of the State Bureau of Investigation.

Unconscious Defendants

If a defendant is unconscious or is otherwise in a condition that makes him or her incapable of deciding whether to refuse the test, he or she may be given a blood test or any other kind of chemical analysis that may be effectively performed. It is highly unlikely that anything but a blood test will be possible for a person incapable of refusing, inasmuch as the level of cooperation necessary to obtain a breath test is not apt to be met by such a person. The same standards of probable cause to charge an implied consent offense are applicable to cases involving unconscious people, but the notification of rights and the formal request to submit to the test are not required, nor is the defendant required to be charged at the time the blood is extracted.[76] In *State v. Garcia-Lorenco*,[77] the North Carolina Court of Appeals, in applying this statute, held that officers did not violate the defendant's right under this statute when the injured, conscious defendant had to be sedated and rendered unconscious for valid medical reasons before officers had the opportunity to notify him of his rights, including the right to refuse a blood test.

Testing after Refusal or Pursuant to Authority Not in Implied Consent Law

If a person charged exercises the right to refuse a chemical analysis, G.S. 20-16.2(c) provides that "none may be given under the provisions of this section, but the refusal does not preclude testing under other applicable procedures of law." There are at least two other applicable provisions of law. The first is the power of a judge under G.S. Chapter 15A to issue search warrants; the second is the power of a law enforcement officer, under G.S. 15A-231 and *Schmerber v. California*,[78] to obtain a blood test without a warrant under certain circumstances.

---

72. State v. Watts, 72 N.C. App. 661, 325 S.E.2d 505 (1985).

73. State v. Bailey, 76 N.C. App. 610, 334 S.E.2d 266 (1985), *overruled on other grounds by* State v. Drdak, 330 N.C. 587, 411 S.E.2d 604 (1992).

74. Richardson v. Hiatt, 95 N.C. App.196, 381 S.E.2d 866 (1989).

75. *Bailey*, 76 N.C. App. at 613, 334 S.E.2d at 269.

76. State v. Hollingsworth, 77 N.C. App. 36, 334 S.E.2d 463 (1985).

77. 110 N.C. App. 319, 430 S.E.2d 290 (1993).

78. 384 U.S. 757 (1966).

Table 3
Revocations Eligible to Be Negated by Limited Driving Privilege

1. Driving while impaired—G.S. 20-138.1, G.S. 20-17(a)(2), G.S. 20-179.3
2. Refusal to take chemical analysis—G.S. 20-16.2 (e1)
3. Driving while impaired in a commercial vehicle—G.S. 20-138.1, G.S. 20-17(a)(2), G.S. 20-17.5(b)(2)
4. Driving while less than twenty-one years of age after consuming alcohol or drugs—G.S. 20-138.3 (d) (must be eighteen, nineteen, or twenty and not also convicted of DWI), G.S. 20-13.2
5. Transporting alcohol beverage after consuming alcohol—G.S. 20-138.7 (second offense), G.S. 20-27(a)(12)
6. Immediate pretrial revocation for consuming alcohol or refusing chemical analysis—G.S. 20-16.5

Several cases have dealt with blood tests taken in connection with impaired driving offenses in which the implied consent statutes were not used. In *State v. Drdak*,[79] the North Carolina Supreme Court held that if a blood alcohol test is performed in a hospital while the patient is being treated, hospital personnel are not required to follow the requirements of G.S. 20-139.1 because that statute permits "other competent evidence" of the defendant's alcohol concentration.[80] In *State v. Cardwell*,[81] a defendant involved in an accident was charged with impaired driving. As part of the defendant's medical care, the treating physician ordered an alcohol blood test using a DuPont ACA Star Analyzer. That instrument analyzes plasma to determine blood alcohol content. The trial court and the appellate court approved the use of that particular instrument as well as the conversion ratio adopted by the hospital to convert the alcohol concentration in the plasma to the alcohol concentration in the blood. In this case the converted reading was properly submitted to the jury as evidence that the defendant had violated the *per se* prong of this offense. Finally, in *Ferguson v. Killens*,[82] the defendant was involved in an accident and taken to a hospital. Before he was charged, the hospital took a blood test. He was then charged with impaired driving and was requested to take a blood test under the implied consent statutes. He refused. The court affirmed the DMV's decision to revoke the license for the refusal. In addition, the trial court allowed the state to use the hospital blood test as evidence. Based on these holdings, it is possible that a reversal of the sequence—a refusal followed by a subsequent test conducted outside the implied consent law—would render the same result. That result would also be that the license is revoked and the test result is admissible.

Refusal and Its Consequences

A defendant has a right to refuse to be tested under the implied consent law. A refusal is the "declination of a request or demand, or the omission to comply with some requirement of law, as the result of a positive intention to disobey."[83] The effects of a refusal are to cause the immediate revocation of the defendant's license for at least thirty days under G.S. 20-16.5 and for an additional twelve months under G.S. 20-16.2. For persons under age twenty-one at the time of the offense, there is an additional revocation under G.S.20-13.2, although it would run concurrently with either of the other two revocations if they were in effect at the same time. As noted in the

79. 330 N.C. 587, 411 S.E.2d 604 (1992).
80. *See also* State v. Byers, 105 N.C. App. 377, 413 S.E.2d 586 (1992).
81. ___ N.C. App. ____, 516 S.E.2d 388 (June 15, 1999).
82. 129 N.C. App. 131, 497 S.E.2d 722 (1998).
83. Joyner v. Garrett, 279 N.C. 226, 233, 182 S.E.2d 553, 558 (1971).

next section, in some circumstances a judge may issue a limited driving privilege to negate this revocation. If the refusal occurs in the course of breath testing and one sample has been obtained, the analysis of that sample is admissible and the revocation for the refusal stands.[84]

The fact that the defendant refused may also be used against him or her as evidence in any criminal charge for an implied consent offense.[85] The use of a refusal to take a test as evidence of guilt was upheld in *State v. Flannery*[86] and *South Dakota v. Neville.*[87] The refusal need not be willful to be admissible.[88]

Refusals may take many forms. The most common is probably an overt statement by the defendant that he or she will not submit to an analysis. Refusals also occur when a person does one or more of the following:

- provides one sample but refuses to provide a second[89]or provides two breath samples but refuses to provide a third upon request;[90]
- fails to provide an adequate breath sample, as determined by the chemical analyst;[91]
- puts fingers in mouth and as a result, does not provide an adequate breath sample;[92]
- fails to comply with the thirty-minute time limit allowed to call an attorney or to obtain a witness, thereby delaying the test impermissibly;[93]
- fails to comply with the chemical analyst's direction not to smoke during the observation and testing process;[94]
- is so boisterous during the period in which the chemical analyst is reading the person his or her rights that the analyst cannot complete the test;[95]
- refuses to remove paper from mouth at the request of the chemical analyst.[96]

A defendant who refuses and for that has his or her license revoked is entitled to a hearing on each refusal.[97] The hearing must be requested in a timely manner and is limited to the issues specified in the statute.[98] The most commonly contested issues are whether the refusal was willful and whether the charging officer had reasonable grounds to charge the person with an implied consent offense. At that hearing the defendant may not raise the issue of failure by the state to show compliance with the testing procedures as required for a valid analysis by G.S. 20-139.1.[99]

Limited Driving Privilege

G.S. 20-16.2(el), allows judges to issue limited driving privileges to negate the revocation under that section in some instances. (See Table 3.) The privilege may be valid only for the last six months of the revocation. If the refusal occurs in a case involving death or critical injury to some-

---

84. G.S. 20-139.1(b3).
85. G.S. 20 139.1(f).
86. 31 N.C. App. 617, 230 S.E.2d 603 (1976).
87. 459 U.S. 553 (1983).
88. State v. Pyatt, 125 N.C. App. 151, 479 S.E.2d 218 (1997).
89. Gibson v. Faulkner, ___ N.C. App. ____, 515 S.E.2d 452 (Apr. 6, 1999).
90. Watson v. Hiatt, 78 N.C. App. 609, 337 S.E.2d 871 (1985).
91. Poag v. Powell, 39 N.C. App. 363, 250 S.E.2d 93 (1979).
92. Tedder v. Hodges, 119 N.C. App. 169, 457 S.E.2d 881 (1995).
93. Etheridge v. Peters, 301 N.C. 76, 269 S.E.2d 133 (1980); Seders v. Powell, 298 N.C. 453, 259 S.E.2d 544 (1979); Creech v. Alexander, 32 N.C. App. 139, 231 S.E.2d 36 (1977).
94. Byrd v. Wilkins, 69 N.C. App. 516, 317 S.E.2d 108 (1984).
95. Rice v. Peters, 48 N.C. App. 697, 269 S.E.2d 740 (1980).
96. Tolbert v. Hiatt, 95 N.C. App. 380, 382 S.E.2d 453 (1989).
97. G.S. 20-16.5(g) and -16.2(d) and (e).
98. Gibson v. Faulkner, ___ N.C. App. ____, 515 S.E.2d 452 (Apr. 6, 1999).
99. *Id.*

one other than the defendant, the twelve-month revocation may not run concurrently with any other license revocation and no limited driving privilege may be issued.[100]

To be eligible for this limited privilege a defendant must:

- have a valid license or one that has been expired for less than one year;
- have no convictions of offenses involving impaired driving in the seven years preceding the refusal;
- have not willfully refused a chemical analysis in the seven years immediately preceding the date of the current refusal;
- not have critically injured or killed anyone in the course of the impaired driving offense;
- have disposed of the underlying charge other than by conviction, or by conviction and sentencing to levels three, four, or five; if the defendant has been convicted, he or she must also have completed at least one of the mandatory minimum conditions of probation (jail, community service, or nonoperation of a vehicle) before he or she is eligible;
- have no unresolved charges or additional convictions of an offense involving impaired driving since the underlying offense;
- have completed at least six months of the revocation under G.S. 20-16.2;
- have obtained a substance abuse assessment and successfully completed any treatment or education required by the assessment; and
- demonstrate that he or she has appropriate insurance or other financial responsibility or is exempt from this requirement.[101]

To be eligible for this privilege, the defendant must have had his or her license revoked solely under G.S. 20-16.2 and G.S. 20-17(a)(2).[102] The third criterion listed above applies only to willful refusals under G.S. 20-16.2. Thus a similar refusal occurring in another state would not disqualify a defendant from obtaining a limited privilege under this section. In contrast, convictions from other jurisdictions, if they are offenses involving impaired driving under G.S. 20-4.01(24a), disqualify a defendant under the second criterion listed above.

Affidavits in District Court

G.S. 20-139.1(el) authorizes the introduction of affidavits by chemical analysts in trials in district court. The affidavits are limited to the following information: (1) alcohol concentration of the person tested, (2) time of collection of samples, (3) type of analysis used and procedures followed, (4) type of permit held by the analyst; and (5) if the instrument is a breath testing one on which preventive maintenance is required to be performed, the date of performance of the most recent preventive maintenance. The North Carolina Supreme Court found this statute to be constitutional in *State v. Smith*.[103]

---

100. G.S. 20-16.2(d1).

101. G.S. 16.2(e1) requires a privilege issued under that section to contain the "restrictions required . . . to be included" in a limited privilege issued under G.S. 20-179.3 for an impaired driving revocation based on a conviction for DWI. That statute requires proof of financial responsibility as a precondition of granting the privilege, as well as a requirement that it be maintained throughout the duration of the privilege. While neither G.S. 20-16.2 nor G.S. 20-179.3 explicitly require proof of financial responsibility before the privilege can be issued under G.S. 20-16.2, the Administrative Office of the Courts form privilege (AOC CR 313) does, and since the financial responsibility must be maintained immediately upon issuance, it seems to be a reasonable interpretation of the statutes.

102. G.S. 20-16.2(e1).

103. 312 N.C. 361, 323 S.E.2d 316 (1984).

G.S. 20-139.1(el) is subject to widely varying interpretations in district courts. The statute makes the affidavit admissible, without qualification, if it meets the statutory standards ("affidavit by a chemical analyst sworn to and properly executed before an official authorized to administer oaths"). However, sometimes the affidavit may not contain all five types of information listed above. The information on preventive maintenance is sometimes left off, either inadvertently or intentionally. This does not seem to make the rest of the affidavit inadmissible because the statute does not require the affidavit to contain all the information; instead it says the affidavit is admissible "with respect to the following matters: . . . ." In addition the burden of raising the issue of preventive maintenance is on the defense, as is the burden of proof on the issue. It is anomalous to place the burden to object to the admissibility of evidence on this point on the defendant and then condition the admissibility of the analyst's affidavit on its having information that the state has no duty to provide unless the defendant raises the issue.

When blood tests are used, the information admissible by affidavit is possessed by two analysts: the breath analyst who informs the defendant of his or her rights and the blood analyst in the laboratory who analyzes the blood. In those cases two affidavits are used, neither of which contains all the information listed in the statute.

Finally, the defendant may subpoena the analyst and cross-examine him or her as though the analyst were an adverse witness. The issuance of a subpoena does not in itself render the affidavit inadmissible. However, difficult issues are presented when wholesale subpoenas are issued but analysts are seldom actually called as witnesses, or when analysts do not honor subpoenas.

Roadside and Precharge Breath Tests

There are two kinds of chemical tests given to defendants before they are charged. Preliminary alcohol screening (*roadside*) tests are governed by G.S. 20-16.3. They involve the use of portable instruments commonly used in the field by law enforcement officers for screening purposes. For most impaired driving offenses, they are not admissible in evidence except to establish probable cause or reasonable grounds or to support a claim that an impairment was caused by something other than alcohol.[104] For persons charged with violating the zero *per se* offenses—G.S. 20-138.3 (driving by person under age twenty-one after drinking), G.S. 20-138.7 (transporting an open container of alcohol while driving), G.S. 20-138.2A (operating a commercial vehicle after consuming alcohol), G.S. 20-138.2B (operating a school bus or child-care vehicle after consuming alcohol), and G.S. 20-179.3(j) (violating zero *per se* restriction on limited driving privilege)—test results may be admitted to help prove that the person charged has alcohol present in his or her body if the device used is approved by the Commission for Health Services and the test is conducted in accordance with regulations adopted by the commission for that purpose.[105] The only authority to issue such regulations is G.S. 20-16.3.

There is no requirement that the warnings required by G.S. 20-16.2 be provided to persons requested to submit to alcohol screening tests.

Precharge tests are governed by G.S. 20-16.2(i). They are admissible as evidence of a particular alcohol concentration, are offered only on request of the person being investigated, and in general must follow the procedures applicable to postcharge tests. These tests use the same instruments (Intoxilyzer) as the post-arrest tests under G.S. 20-16.2. An officer making a charge of impaired driving has no duty to inform the person to be charged of the availability of the precharge test.[106]

---

104. *See* State v. Bartlett, 130 N.C. App. 79, 502 S.E.2d 53 (1998); Moore v. Hodges, 116 N.C. App. 727, 449 S.E.2d 218 (1994).

105. G.S. 20-138.3(b2).

106. State v. McGill, 114 N.C. App. 479, 442 S.E.2d 166 (1994).

ISSUES IN IMPLIED CONSENT CASES

Collateral Estoppel

Common issues may arise in several impaired driving proceedings. A breath or blood test result may be considered in a revocation proceeding under G.S. 20-16.5 (an immediate, pretrial revocation) and in a criminal trial. A refusal may be at issue in a revocation under G.S. 20-16.5, a revocation under G.S. 20-16.2, and in a criminal trial. Probable cause determinations may be made in each proceeding. In each case, a separate forum makes the determination—typically a magistrate makes the determination under G.S. 20-16.5, a DMV hearing officer (or on appeal, a superior court judge) in a refusal hearing under G.S. 20-16.2, and a trial judge in a criminal proceeding. The relationship between the findings made in those various proceedings has been a point of discussion in several recent appellate cases.

In *State v. O'Rourke*,[107] an impaired driving defendant refused a chemical analysis, and the DMV revoked his license pursuant to G.S. 20-16.2. He contested that revocation, and at an administrative hearing the Division rescinded the revocation. At the criminal trial, the defendant argued that admission of evidence of the refusal should be barred because the Division had determined that there was no refusal and that that finding should not be subject to relitigation under the collateral estoppel doctrine. That doctrine provides that a party is bound by a previous finding on an issue if the issue has been determined previously in an appropriate forum, and the parties to the first action are the same as, or in privity with (sharing the same interest with), the parties in the first action. The court held that the parties in the two cases, the DMV and the district attorney, did not share a sufficiently common interest in the litigation of the issue to establish privity. The court also prohibited either party from introducing into evidence the conclusions reached by the DMV.

In *Brower v. Killens*,[108] the defendant was charged with impaired driving. He refused to submit to a chemical analysis, and the DMV revoked his license. His criminal case was heard first, and in that case, a district court judge determined that the arresting officer did not have probable cause to arrest the defendant. The DMV revoked the defendant's license for the refusal. The defendant appealed that decision to superior court. In that appeal, he argued that collateral estoppel prevented the DMV from relitigating the issue of the absence of probable cause (or its equivalent, *reasonable grounds*). The court concluded that the district attorney and the DMV are in privity for this purpose (on this point it reached the opposite result from *O'Rourke*) and ruled that the DMV, in the hearing in the superior court, was bound by the district court ruling on the issue of probable cause. It agreed with *O'Rourke* that the district attorney is not fully represented in a DMV hearing, so it limited its holding to a finding that the DMV was collaterally estopped by the determination made in the criminal case. The estoppel in this case goes only one way—the criminal court may bind the DMV, but the DMV may not bind a criminal court. In addition the court explicitly limited its ruling to the issue of probable cause determinations.

In *Ferguson v. Killens*,[109] the issue was whether the DMV was estopped from relitigating the issue of whether the defendant refused to submit to a chemical analysis. Apparently the defendant had been convicted in criminal court on an impaired driving charge. There is no indication in the case how the criminal court judge ruled on the issue of whether the defendant refused a chemical analysis. As a result, the court held that since the issue of whether a defendant refused an analysis is not necessary to determine if a person is guilty of impaired driving, the doctrine did not apply in that case.

107. 114 N.C. App. 435, 442 S.E.2d 137 (1994).
108. 122 N.C. App. 685, 472 S.E.2d 33 (1996).
109. 129 N.C. App. 131, 497 S.E.2d 722 (1998).

In *State v. Summers*,[110] a defendant arrested for impaired driving was requested to submit to a breath test. He gave an insufficient breath sample, followed by a sufficient breath sample (0.11 alcohol concentration) and a third insufficient sample. The chemical analyst determined that the defendant had willfully refused. The DMV revoked the defendant's license, and he appealed the revocation to superior court. The superior court ruled that he did not willfully refuse to submit to the analysis, and it rescinded the revocation. The defendant was then convicted on the criminal charge in district court; he appealed to the superior court. In that trial, the judge allowed into evidence the single test result pursuant to G.S. 20-139.1(b3), which allows the introduction of single breath test results when there is a subsequent "willful refusal." The court of appeals, in reviewing the criminal case, distinguished *O'Rourke*, noting that *Brower* had revisited the privity issue that was dispositive in *O'Rourke*. (Another difference, not specifically noted by the court, is that in *O'Rourke* the finding was made by an administrative agency, whereas in this case, it was made by a judge.) The court held that the DA and the DMV, as represented in the superior court by the attorney general, were in privity. It further held that the issue of willful refusal was the exact same issue in both proceedings. Accordingly it was error for the trial court to not collaterally estop the district attorney from introducing evidence of the single breath test and of the subsequent refusal by the defendant to submit to additional analyses. The court was careful to limit its holding to circumstances in which the interest of the state in revocation hearings under G.S. 20-16.2 is represented by the attorney general in superior court. Thus findings by DMV hearing officers are not binding on the state in criminal matters. (*Note: As of this writing, the North Carolina Supreme Court had agreed to review this case and had issued a stay of the ruling pending its review.*)

Finally, in *Gibson v. Faulkner*,[111] the DMV found the defendant in an impaired driving charge to have refused under G.S. 20-16.2. He was acquitted in district court of the criminal charge. He then appealed the DMV's determination in the revocation hearing. In that appeal, he argued that the finding of not guilty necessarily disposed of the issue of his willful refusal in his favor. The court rejected that argument, noting that the burden of proof in the two forums is different and that the acquittal could be based on failure to prove things other than a willful refusal.

These cases do not resolve all possible collateral estoppel issues. They do make it clear that collateral estoppel can apply with respect to the issues of whether the charge underlying the action was based on probable cause/reasonable grounds and whether the defendant refused to submit to a chemical analysis. It also appears to be the case that for collateral estoppel to apply, the determination that is asserted to have already been made must have been made by a trial court in which the interests of the state are represented by an attorney and not by an administrative agency.

These cases do not provide explicit guidance on issues such as whether the state may assert collateral estoppel to prevent a defendant from relitigating an issue resolved against him or her; what kind of record of the finding is necessary to provide the necessary formality to insure that the finding is known and understood by a subsequent court, or when the DMV in conducting its administrative review is bound by the criminal court's findings on these issues. Answers to these and other questions must await further legislation or appellate cases on the subject.

Double Jeopardy

The Double Jeopardy Clause of the United States Constitution prohibits the state from imposing multiple punishments for the same offense. Double jeopardy is a complex area of the law beyond the scope of this book, but two recent North Carolina cases raise issues in the impaired driv-

110. ___ N.C. App. ____, 513 S.E.2d 575 (1999).
111. ___ N.C. App. ____, 515 S.E.2d 452 (Apr. 6, 1999).

ing context that should be noted. The first is *State v. Oliver*,[112] in which the state supreme court held that the revocation of a person's license under G.S. 20-16.5 was not a punishment for purposes of applying the Double Jeopardy Clause.[113] The second is *Ferguson v. Killens*,[114] in which the North Carolina Court of Appeals held that a revocation under G.S. 20-16.2 for a willful refusal to submit to a chemical test is not the "same offense" for the purpose of applying the Double Jeopardy Clause. The appeals court did not find it necessary to determine if the revocation under G.S. 20-16.2 is a "punishment," but it is likely that *Oliver* supports a finding that it is not.

IMMEDIATE, PRETRIAL CIVIL REVOCATION (CVR)

This revocation is governed by G.S. 20-16.5. It applies to any person properly charged (i.e., with probable cause) with an implied consent offense who:

- has an alcohol concentration of 0.08 or more;
- has an alcohol concentration of 0.04 or more and is driving a commercial vehicle;
- has any alcohol concentration and is under the age of twenty-one at the time of the offense; or
- refuses a chemical analysis.[115]

This revocation requires the presence of an *alcohol concentration* that is at or above the various *per se* levels. G.S. 20-16.3(d) makes it clear that alcohol screening test results may not be used to establish a particular alcohol concentration, so they may not be used to support a revocation under this section. They may, however, be used to support a conviction of the underage driver zero *per se* offense under G.S. 20-138.3.

A person charged with committing an implied consent offense by aiding and abetting the driver is not subject to this revocation because the aider and abettor's guilt is not determined by his or her alcohol concentration but by that of the driver (in addition to the other elements necessary to establish guilt by aiding and abetting).

A person operating a moped, as that term is defined in G.S. 20-4.01(21a) and 105-164.3, would be subject to this revocation if the statutory criteria are met. That is true even though a person does not need a driver's license to operate a moped.

The revocation order is usually entered by a judicial official (typically a magistrate) at the time of the initial appearance, based on information contained in affidavits submitted by the charging officer and the chemical analyst. In such cases the person is served with the order before he or she is released pending trial. In other cases (such as when there is a blood test, when the person charged is not arrested, or when the paperwork cannot be prepared in time) the entry of a revocation order may be delayed until later.

A revocation under this section is effective on the date specified in the order.[116] If the person charged is present when the order is issued, the effective date is the date on which the order is issued. If the person is not present and the order has to be mailed, the effective date is four days after the order is mailed, as specified in the order.

---

112. 343 N.C. 202, 470 S.E.2d 16 (1996).
113. *See also* State v. Pyatt 125 N.C. App. 151, 479 S.E.2d 218 (1997).
114. 129 N.C. App. 131, 497 S.E.2d 722 (1998).
115. G.S. 20-16.5(b).
116. Eibergen v. Killens, 124 N.C. App. 534, 477 S.E.2d 684 (1996).

The period of revocation is never less than thirty days, but these revocations occur in two distinct situations, each of which has a revocation of a different duration. The two situations are:

1. For persons who have no other charge pending when the order is entered, the revocation lasts until three things have occurred:
   (a) the person has surrendered his or her driver's license or has demonstrated to the court that he or she either has no license or has lost it;
   (b) thirty days (forty-five in limited circumstances in which the person was not present when the order was issued) have passed since the surrender of the license; and
   (c) the person has paid the costs.[117]
2. For persons who commit one offense in which the license is revoked under this section and then, before that underlying criminal charge is disposed of, commit a second offense for which the license is revoked under this section, the revocation is indefinite and lasts until all the pending charges are disposed of and the applicable costs have been paid.[118] In no event may this revocation period be less than thirty days, however. This indefinite revocation applies even if the first revocation ends before the second becomes effective; the key is whether the underlying criminal charge is pending.

This revocation is treated as a special kind of civil case, civil license revocation (CVR), for which a special court cost is established in G.S. 20-16.5(j). That cost is currently $50. Half is returned to the county for its use, and half is used to support the chemical testing for alcohol program conducted by the Department of Health and Human Services.

Thus a revocation may continue indefinitely under this section if a person who never surrenders his or her license or if anyone whose license is revoked under the section never pays the costs. In that respect the revocation is unusual in North Carolina. It is also the only revocation for which the order is issued by the court instead of the DMV.[119]

Normally the minimum period of revocation is thirty days. In some cases, however, it is forty-five. These are cases in which the person is not present when the order of revocation is entered (and thus is notified by mail) and does not surrender his or her license or demonstrate that he or she does not have a license within five working days of the order's effective date.

A few more peculiarities about an already very unusual revocation procedure are as follows:

1. If a person has a license but has lost the card issued by the DMV or its equivalent in another state, the only way the person may satisfy the requirement of license surrender is to file an affidavit to that effect with the clerk of court. No other judicial official has the power to receive that affidavit.[120]
2. If a person, through inaction, causes the revocation to last longer than the minimum thirty- or forty-five-day period, the person's license continues to be revoked and the person, if he or she drives, is still subject to being charged with driving while his or her license is revoked. However, the punishment for driving after that minimum period is much less severe than for other driving-with-license-revoked offenses.[121] No additional license revocations are imposed under G.S. 20-28 for a person convicted under those circumstances, but additional license revocations are imposed under G.S. 20-28.1 for such convictions.

---

117. G.S. 20-16.5(e) and (f).
118. G.S. 20-16.5(e) and (f).
119. G.S. 20-16.5(e) and (f).
120. G.S. 20-16.5(a)(5).
121. G.S. 20-28(al).

3. To comply with this revocation, a person must surrender his or her license even if it was issued by another state.[122] For no other revocation is a person required by statute to surrender an out-of-state license.

A person who desires a hearing to review the decision of the official issuing the order is entitled to one if he or she requests it in time and specifies the grounds upon which the decision is challenged.[123] The request for a hearing does not prevent the revocation order from becoming effective. Inasmuch as the period of revocation is short, the cost of the action is relatively low, and the hearing does not delay the revocation, hearing requests are rare. In addition G.S. 20-16.5(m) provides that a judicial official "presiding over a proceeding under this section may issue a modified order if he or she determines that an inappropriate order has been issued." When serious errors have been made, this authority has been used to correct them even if the time for hearing has passed.

The original statute establishing the revocation (at ten days for most offenders) has been found to be constitutional.[124] In addition, imposing a revocation under this section and convicting a person for the same conduct has been found not to violate the double jeopardy clauses of the state and the federal constitution.[125]

Under certain circumstances a person whose driver's license is revoked under this section may obtain a limited driving privilege.[126] The first such circumstance is after the person's license has been revoked for thirty or at least forty-five days. In those cases, the defendant must:

- have had a valid license, or one that has been expired for no more than one year, at the time of the offense;
- have no other pending "charge involving impaired driving" or no convictions for an offense involving impaired driving since the time of the offense;
- have served at least ten days of a thirty-day, or thirty days of a forty-five-day, period of revocation imposed under G.S. 2-16.5; and
- have obtained a substance abuse assessment and agreed to participate in any recommended treatment or education.

The second circumstance is when the person's license is revoked indefinitely. In those cases, the defendant must:

- serve at least thirty days of the revocation (or forty-five days if that is the period that normally would be imposed if the revocation were not indefinite);
- demonstrate that the privilege is necessary to overcome undue hardship;
- have no convictions for offenses involving impaired driving in the seven years preceding the date of the current offense;
- have had a valid license or one that has been expired for no more than one year at the time of the offense;
- have no convictions or additional charges since the time of the current offense;
- have obtained and filed with the court a substance abuse assessment.

Both of these limited privileges are subject to the mandatory and permissive conditions specified in G.S. 20-179.3 for impaired driving limited privileges. Those conditions are discussed in Chapter 1 of this part, and they include the requirement that the person maintain motor vehicle liability insurance or other financial responsibility during the period in which the privilege is effective.

---

122. G.S. 20-16.5(a)(5).
123. G.S. 20-16.5(g).
124. Henry v. Edmisten, 315 N.C. 474, 340 S.E.2d 720 (1986).
125. State v. Oliver, 343 N.C. 202, 470 S.E.2d 343 (1996).
126. G.S. 20-16.5(p).

Table 4
Offenses Subject to Assessment and Treatment Requirement of G.S. 20-17.6

1. Driving while impaired—G.S. 20-138.1
2. Driving while impaired in a commercial vehicle—G.S. 20-138.2
3. Driving a commercial vehicle after consuming alcohol or drugs—G.S. 20-138.2A
4. Driving a school bus or child care vehicle after consuming alcohol or drugs—G.S. 20-138.2B
5. Driving while less than 21 years old after consuming alcohol or drugs—G.S. 20-138.3

Any district court judge authorized to hold court in the district in which the offense occurred may issue the privilege. The procedure for application is as provided in G.S. 20-179.3. In applying that statute to this situation, it appears that the application must be filed in writing with the clerk, and the clerk must provide a copy of the application to the district attorney. No hearing may be held until the district attorney has had a reasonable time to review the application.[127]

Apparently a person need not demonstrate that this is his or her first privilege under this section. Thus a person may obtain a limited privilege for two revocations under this section in effect at the same time. There is no minimum age for this limited privilege. A person under eighteen may obtain a limited privilege under this section, even though that person would be prohibited under G.S. 20-13.2 and 20-138.3 from obtaining a limited privilege after being convicted of an offense involving impaired driving or the underage zero tolerance offense.

A privilege issued under this section is valid only if the person's license is revoked solely under this section.[128] Thus if a person's license is revoked indefinitely under this section because he or she has a pending charge at the time the second charge is lodged, that person's limited privilege(s) would become invalid if he or she is convicted of either offense because the person would then be revoked also under G.S. 20-17(a)(2).

FAILURE TO OBTAIN ASSESSMENT OR TO COMPLETE TREATMENT OR SCHOOL

G.S. 20-17.6 provides that persons convicted of certain offenses, all of which require the DMV to revoke the license of persons so convicted, must obtain a substance abuse assessment and complete any treatment or education recommended as a result of the assessment. If the person fails to do so before the revocation period imposed by the DMV ends, the revocation is extended until this requirement has been satisfied. If the person has a limited driving privilege, that limited driving privilege is not valid past the revocation period originally imposed by the DMV.

The offenses subject to this requirement (see Table 4) are the following:

- impaired driving under G.S. 20-138.1
- impaired driving in a commercial vehicle under G.S. 20-138.2
- driving while under twenty-one years of age after consuming alcohol under G.S. 20-138.3
- driving a commercial vehicle, zero tolerance offense under G.S. 20-138.2A (second or subsequent offenses)
- driving a school bus, school activity bus, or child-care vehicle, zero tolerance offense under G.S. 20-138.2B

127. G.S. 20-16.5(p); -179.3(d).
128. G.S. 20-16.5(p).

The requirement applies regardless of the alcohol concentration of the defendant or the number of offenses with which he or she is charged. If a defendant is convicted of three offenses simultaneously, there is a literal requirement that he or she be assessed for each conviction, and because obtaining an assessment is a prerequisite to being relicensed as a driver, there is no effective alternative to obtaining multiple assessments in that situation.

For persons placed on probation, the judge may require as a condition of probation that the person obtain an assessment and complete any treatment or education recommended as a result of the assessment, but this requirement applies even if the judge does not include it as a condition of probation. The requirement also applies when an active sentence is imposed. The statute does not define *treatment*, so as a practical matter, the treatment regimen for a particular defendant is determined by the assessing and treating entities, subject to any orders entered by the court. Attendance at meetings of Alcoholics Anonymous is not treatment in and of itself and may be imposed independent of any treatment required to comply with this section.[129]

G.S. 122C-142.1 describes the procedures that are applicable to a substance abuse assessment. First, the assessment must be performed by an alcoholism, drug abuse, or substance abuse counselor certified by the North Carolina Substance Abuse Professional Certification Board; a physician licensed by the Board of Medical Examiners; a psychologist licensed by the North Carolina Psychology Board; a high school graduate with three years of supervised experience in the profession of alcohol and substance abuse counseling; a person with a bachelor's degree and two years of experience; or a person with a master's degree and one year of experience.[130]

Second, the assessment must include both a clinical interview and a standardized test approved by the Department of Health and Human Services (DHHS). Eight tests are approved for use at this time.

Third, the assessing agency must recommend that the defendant participate in treatment if the result of the assessment indicates that the person has a substance abuse disability, if the person had an alcohol concentration of 0.15 or more for the offense, or if the person has a prior conviction of an offense involving impaired driving under G.S. 20-4.01(24a). There is apparently no time limit on how far back the previous conviction may have occurred. If none of these conditions is present, the assessment must recommend that the person attend the Alcohol and Drug Education Traffic School.

The fees required are specified in the statute. The assessment fee is $50, and the fee for the school is $75. If treatment is ordered instead of the school, an initial fee of $75 is prescribed for the treatment service. If the treatment is provided by a public agency, subsequent fees vary according to the level of service provided and the defendant's ability to pay.[131] If the service is privately provided, there is no such limitation on the fees charged for treatment.

If the person convicted resides in another state, he or she may obtain the assessment and treatment services in that state if the service is substantially similar to the service provided in North Carolina. G.S. 122C-142.1(a) confers on DHHS the right to approve out-of-state services, and failure to obtain that approval may result in the license revocation remaining in effect.

The DMV may not terminate a revocation or reissue a license to a person convicted of an offense covered by this section until it has been notified that the person has obtained an assessment and completed any ordered treatment or education. The form used to notify the Division is Form 508 of the Division of Mental Health, Mental Retardation, and Substance Abuse Services. The assessing and treating agencies notify that division, which in turn notifies the DMV that the person has successfully completed the treatment or education.

---

129. State v. McGill, 114 N.C. 479, 442 S.E.2d 166 (1994).
130. 10 NCAC 18F.0316 (Aug. 1, 1997).
131. G.S. 122C-146.

A service provider may require that any applicable fees be paid before it submits a certificate of completion of the assessment, treatment, or education on behalf of the person convicted. For area mental health authorities, any action taken pursuant to this authority to withhold the certificate must be consistent with G.S. 122C-146. That statute provides that no person may be denied services because of an inability to pay a fee.

The legislature in 1995 repealed a statute that provided for court review of a treatment provider's failure to submit a certificate of completion. Thus there is no statutory procedure for review of that decision.

Finally, there is no specific statutory provision for using a pretrial assessment to comply with the provisions of this statute. However, the common interpretation of the two statutes is that a pretrial assessment complying with the requirements of G.S. 20-179(e) satisfies the requirements of G.S. 20-17.6 if the only reason it would not satisfy that statute is that it was obtained before the trial (but after the offense). Both the assessment manual of the Department of Health and Human Services and the judgment forms used by the Administrative Office of the Courts adopt that interpretation. Care must be taken, however, to ensure that Form 508 of the Division of Mental Health, Mental Retardation, and Substance Abuse Services is transmitted to the DMV so that the defendant will receive credit for the assessment and treatment or education program ordered by the court.

VEHICLE FORFEITURE

In 1997 and 1998 the General Assembly substantially revised the provisions of the statutes governing the seizure and forfeiture of motor vehicles driven by impaired drivers. The resulting statutes[132] provide much more procedural guidance, but vehicle forfeiture remains a complex enterprise involving multiple parties, procedures, rights, and duties.

Overview

The basic operation of the law is simple. A vehicle is subject to pretrial seizure and forfeiture if (1) it is driven by a person charged with one of the impaired driving offenses listed in the forfeiture law (a *covered offense*) and (2) the driver had a revoked driver's license based on one of a number of acts involving impaired driving (a *covered revocation*). With very narrow exceptions, the law enforcement officer lodging the charge must seize the vehicle, and the judicial official reviewing the charge must determine if there is probable cause to support the charge and seizure. Seized vehicles are placed in the custody of the county school board or its designated agents. The vehicle generally is held until the charge resulting in the seizure is resolved. If the person charged is not convicted of that charge, the vehicle is returned to its owner. If the person is convicted, the court must conduct a hearing to determine if the vehicle should be forfeited. If the court orders forfeiture, the school board can keep the vehicle or sell it. In some circumstances, the defendant, a nondriving owner, or a lienholder can obtain release of the vehicle before trial. These persons also may seek release of the vehicle at the forfeiture hearing after the trial.

The North Carolina Court of Appeals has ruled that the forfeiture statute, as it existed in 1998, is constitutional.[133]

---

132. G.S. 20-28.2 through -28.9.
133. State v. Chisholm, ____ N.C. ____, 521 S.E.2d 487 (1999).

Coverage of Law

The seizure and forfeiture requirement applies when two circumstances are present: (1) a driver is charged with a covered offense and (2) at the time of the offense, his or her license is revoked for a covered reason.[134] The categories of covered offenses and covered revocations are listed below.

Covered offenses are *offenses involving impaired driving* under G.S. 20-4.01(24a).[135] Those offenses (see Table 5) are:

- impaired driving under G.S. 20-138.1;
- habitual impaired driving under G.S. 20-138.5;
- impaired driving in a commercial vehicle under G.S. 20-138.2;
- felony death by vehicle under G.S. 20-141.4; and
- other homicides arising out of impaired driving (first- and second-degree murder and involuntary manslaughter).

Covered revocations are *impaired driving license revocations* as listed in G.S. 20-28.2(a). Those revocations are those based on:

- convictions of underage drivers (under age twenty-one) for offenses involving impaired driving or for violation of the zero tolerance offense for young drivers under G.S. 20-138.3 or for refusal to submit to a chemical analysis by an underage driver;[136]
- findings by a military commander that a person drove while impaired on a military base;[137]
- refusal to submit to a chemical analysis under the implied consent law;[138]
- failure to pass a breath or blood test, or refusal of a chemical analysis under the immediate pretrial civil revocation statute;[139]
- conviction of impaired driving or impaired driving of a commercial vehicle;[140]
- conviction of a second offense of transporting an open container of alcohol after drinking under G.S. 20-138.7;[141]
- probation conditions imposed on persons convicted under G.S. 20-138.1 forbidding them from driving;[142]
- convictions for habitual impaired driving;[143]
- convictions in another state of an offense involving impaired driving;[144]
- convictions for manslaughter or any other felony involving impaired driving;[145]
- conviction of felony death by vehicle;[146]
- conviction of assault with a motor vehicle involving impaired driving;[147] and
- revocations in other states for conduct that would support one of the other covered revocations if committed in North Carolina.[148]

---

134. G.S. 20-28.2(b).
135. G.S. 20-28.2(b); -28.2(a).
136. G.S. 20-13.2.
137. G.S. 20-16(a)(8b).
138. G.S. 20-16.2.
139. G.S. 20-16.5.
140. G.S. 20-17(a)(2).
141. G.S. 20-17(a)(12).
142. G.S. 20-17.2.
143. G.S. 20-138.5.
144. G.S. 20-16(a)(7).
145. G.S. 20-17(a)(1); -(a)(3).
146. G.S. 20-17(a)(9).
147. G.S. 20-17(a)(11).
148. G.S. 20-28.2(a)(3).

Table 5
Offenses Subject to Vehicle Forfeiture Statutes[a]

1. Driving while impaired—G.S. 20-138.1
2. Driving while impaired in a commercial vehicle—G.S. 20-138.2
3. Felony death by vehicle—G.S. 20-141.4
4. Murder or involuntary manslaughter involving impaired driving
5. Habitual impaired driving—G.S. 20-138.5

a. To be subject to the vehicle forfeiture statutes, these offenses must occur while there is an impaired driving revocation under G.S. 20-28.2.

A person who does not reside in North Carolina could be subject to these statutes if he or she had a covered revocation and was charged with a covered offense.

While it is necessary that the person charged have a covered revocation, it is not necessary that the person be charged with or commit the offense of driving with license revoked. Thus if a person whose license is revoked for a covered revocation commits a covered offense (e.g., driving while impaired) on a public vehicular area and is properly charged, the vehicle is subject to forfeiture pursuant to G.S. 20-28.2(b) and should be seized pursuant to G.S. 20-28.3(b). This is true even though the defendant could not be properly charged with the offense of driving with license revoked under G.S. 20-28 because that offense may only be committed on a street or highway and not on a public vehicular area, or because the revocation that supports the seizure is initiated by another state. In this respect the coverage of the forfeiture law is broader than the coverage of the grossly aggravating factor in G.S. 20-179(c)(2).

The statutes do not specify whether seizure and forfeiture are authorized when a person whose license is revoked under this statute is charged with one of the above offenses under the common law concept of aiding and abetting. However, G.S. 20-28.2(b) states that if the two prongs of the law's coverage are satisfied, "the motor vehicle that was *driven by the defendant* at the time the defendant committed the offense becomes property subject to forfeiture," which suggests that an aider and abettor who has a revoked license for a covered offense would *not* be subject to the forfeiture law. The vehicle driven in the offense would be subject to seizure and forfeiture only if the *driver* has a covered revocation.

There are two instances in which a vehicle is not subject to forfeiture even if the driver is charged with a covered offense and has a covered revocation. First if an officer determines prior to seizure that the vehicle has been reported stolen, the officer may not seize the vehicle at all. Second, an officer may not seize a vehicle if he or she determines before seizure that the vehicle is a rental vehicle driven by a person not listed as an authorized driver on the rental contract.[149]

If a vehicle is reported stolen *after* it has been seized, the owner may seek return of the vehicle on the ground that he or she is an *innocent* owner.[150] The procedures for obtaining release of a seized vehicle (before trial or at a forfeiture hearing after trial) are discussed later.

If a vehicle owner files a report of unauthorized use of a vehicle and agrees to support the prosecution of the unauthorized user, he or she also can get the vehicle back by following the procedures on release of seized vehicles, again on the ground that he or she is an *innocent* owner.[151] But, the filing of a report of unauthorized use, even before seizure, would not preclude an officer from seizing the vehicle.

149. G.S. 20-28.3(b).
150. G.S. 20-28.2(a1)(2)c.
151. G.S. 20-28.2(a1)(2)d.

There is no exception for vehicles that have titles and registration in other states or countries. Although practical issues may arise in securing transfers of titles to these forfeited vehicles, the statute applies to them in the same manner as it applies to vehicles titled and registered in North Carolina.

Seizure Procedures

If a person is properly charged with a covered offense, and at the time of the covered offense the person's license is revoked for a covered offense, the officer lodging the charge must seize the vehicle driven by the defendant[152] and prepare an affidavit indicating the basis for the seizure.[153] If the magistrate finds that seizure was appropriate, he or she must order that the vehicle be held. If the magistrate finds that seizure was not appropriate, he or she must order that the vehicle be released to its owner; the owner, however, must pay any towing and storage fees to recover the vehicle.[154]

Although the normal procedure is to seize the vehicle at the time of the charge and then appear before the magistrate, an officer may apply to the magistrate after the charge has been made for authority to seize a vehicle that the officer believes should be seized. This procedure might be used if the officer did not discover until after the arrest was completed that the person's license was revoked at the time of the offense.

The officer, if he or she has territorial and subject matter jurisdiction over Chapter 20 violations, may enter private property to execute a seizure order, but in some instances the officer may need a search warrant. Thus the statute provides that if an officer has probable cause to believe that a vehicle is located on property owned by someone other than the defendant, the officer may obtain a search warrant.[155] The statute apparently does not require an officer to obtain a search warrant before entering the defendant's property to seize a vehicle subject to a seizure order.

After the vehicle is seized, the officer must give notice within seventy-two hours of seizure to the Division of Motor Vehicles, the agency the governor has designated to handle those notices.[156] Within forty-eight hours of receipt of a seizure notice, the DMV must provide written notice to all vehicle owners and lienholders. If the vehicle was damaged, the DMV also must give written notice to the owner's insurance company.[157] The DMV may not permit the transfer of title to a motor vehicle seized pursuant to this law unless ordered by a court.[158] However, in some instances (to be discussed later) a school board is allowed to sell seized vehicles without a court order, an apparent exception to that prohibition on transfer of title without a court order.[159]

Pretrial Release of Vehicles

Vehicles that have been seized generally are impounded until a forfeiture hearing is held or the underlying criminal case is disposed of without a conviction. There are, however, a few instances in which the vehicle may be released before the case is disposed of. Each such instance is discussed below.

---

152. G.S. 20-28.3(b).
153. G.S. 20-28.3(c).
154. G.S. 20-28.3(c).
155. G.S. 20-28.3(c1); *see also* G.S. 15A-244 (as condition for issuance of search warrant, officer must establish probable cause that items subject to seizure may be found in described place).
156. G.S. 20-28.3(b1).
157. G.S. 20-28.3(b) and (b1).
158. G.S. 20-28.3(b1).
159. G.S. 20-28.3(i).

Nondriving Vehicle Owners

The first instance in which a vehicle can be released before the underlying criminal case is disposed of without a conviction is when the vehicle owner is not the driver. The term *motor vehicle owner* is defined in G.S. 20-28.2(a1)(3a) as a person in whose name a registration card or certificate of title is issued at the time of seizure. This latter definition may prove troublesome in some circumstances—for example, there may be a gap in time between the date a person obtains ownership of a vehicle and the date the DMV issues a new certificate of title. Whether such a person could seek relief as a nondriving owner upon producing sufficient evidence of ownership is unclear, as that action would not be in literal compliance with the statutory definition. A person who is a co-owner of a vehicle driven by the defendant may, however, qualify as a nondriving owner as that term is used in this discussion.[160]

Any nondriving owner may obtain *temporary* release of the vehicle pending trial if the owner:

- pays all towing and storage fees due;
- posts a bond equal to the fair market value of the vehicle, as defined in G.S. 20-28.2(a)(a1); and
- executes a document (an *acknowledgment*) acknowledging that the defendant was charged with conduct that could lead to forfeiture, that similar conduct in the future will result in forfeiture, and that a lack of knowledge or consent to the operation will not be a defense unless the owner takes precautions to prevent future driving by the defendant and reports any driving to the local authorities.[161]

The bond may be posted in cash, by deed of trust, or by a bail bond. It will be forfeited if the vehicle is not returned to the court on the date the owner is notified to do so, and the owner may be held in contempt of court as well. If the owner has previously forfeited a bond to secure the release of the vehicle in question, the vehicle may not be released.[162]

If the owner has previously executed an acknowledgment to release this motor vehicle as a result of impaired driving by this defendant, the vehicle may not be released.[163]

The clerk of court is the only official authorized to release a vehicle under this provision.

A nondriving owner may also seek *permanent* pretrial release of the vehicle. In that instance the owner must be *innocent*. An *innocent* owner is one who:

- did not know, and had no reason to know, that the driver had a revoked license;
- knew that he driver had a revoked license, but the driving occurred without his or her permission and the owner filed a police report for unauthorized use of the vehicle and agreed to prosecute the operator for that offense;
- reported the vehicle to be stolen;
- rents vehicles and the driver is not an authorized driver or
- leases motor vehicles, holds legal title to the vehicle, and had no knowledge of the driver's revocation at the time of the execution of the lease.[164]

To obtain permanent pretrial release the owner must file a formal petition with the court.[165] The petitioner must file the petition with the clerk of court, who must schedule a hearing within ten

160. *See* G.S. 20-28.2(a)(3a) and (e).
161. G.S. 20-28.2(a1)(1); 20-28.3(e).
162. G.S. 20-28.3(e).
163. G.S. 20-28.3(e).
164. G.S. 20-28.2(a)(2).
165. G.S. 20-28.3(e1).

business days of filing or as soon thereafter as feasible. The clerk has forms prepared by the Administrative Office of the Courts for this purpose. Notice must be provided to the defendant, the district attorney, and the school board. If the court finds that the petitioner is an innocent owner, the petitioner is entitled to return of the vehicle if he or she agrees to pay towing and storage fees, demonstrates financial responsibility (that is, insurance or its equivalent), and executes an acknowledgment. If the vehicle is registered in another state, proof of financial responsibility sufficient to satisfy that state's laws is sufficient.[166] The burden of proof is on the owner.[167] If the owner is a lessor, the owner must also agree not to transfer possession to the defendant.[168]

The court hearing may be avoided if the district attorney determines that the vehicle is "not subject to forfeiture" and consents to the release of the vehicle before the hearing by so noting on the petition and returning it to the clerk of court. In that case the clerk must enter an order releasing the vehicle subject to the same conditions. It is not clear from the statute whether the district attorney must conclude that at least one of the two conditions for seizure is absent (a covered charge and a covered revocation), or whether the presence of an innocent owner is sufficient to make the vehicle "not subject to forfeiture." Both seem likely to have been intended by the legislature.

If the court grants the petition or the district attorney consents to it, the vehicle is returned to the owner permanently upon payment of fees owed. The owner need not post any bond and need not return the vehicle for further proceedings. If the petition is denied, the ruling is preliminary only. The owner still may seek return of the vehicle at a forfeiture hearing after trial, at which point the issue is again whether the owner is legally innocent.[169]

Defendant Owners

A *defendant owner*—a person who owns the vehicle and is charged with an offense involving impaired driving—may seek permanent release of the vehicle before trial. These opportunities are more limited than those afforded to nondriving owners, however. The procedure is the same as that for petitions by nondriving owners. The statute provides, however, that the court is required only to decide whether the defendant's license was revoked for a covered reason at the time of the offense. The prosecution is not required to prove the underlying offense of impaired driving, and the defendant may not raise the issue. The prosecutor may consent to the release of the vehicle without a hearing if the prosecutor concludes that the vehicle is not subject to forfeiture. In this context, the determination by the district attorney seems to be limited to consideration of whether there is a covered revocation. If the prosecutor doubts that the underlying criminal charge can be proved, a dismissal of the criminal charge (which also terminates the seizure and forfeiture) is more appropriate. If the defendant fails to obtain release of the vehicle at the hearing, he or she may raise the issue of the revocation status at a later forfeiture hearing.[170]

The forfeiture law does not provide a defendant owner any other avenue to get a vehicle back before trial. Unlike a nondriving owner, a defendant owner may not obtain temporary possession of a vehicle before trial by posting a bond with the clerk of court.

---

166. G.S. 20-28.2(e).
167. *See* G.S. 20-28.2(e).
168. G.S. 20-28.2(e).
169. G.S. 20-28.2(e).
170. G.S. 20-28.3(e2).

Lienholders

A lienholder is a party who loans money to a person to purchase a vehicle and retains a perfected security interest in the vehicle until the loan is paid off.[171] Lienholders also are allowed to seek permanent pretrial release of a seized vehicle. They have no right to temporary pretrial release of a vehicle.

To obtain release, a lienholder must file a petition with the court seeking release. The lienholder must serve written notice on the registered owner, the titled owner, the district attorney, and the school board as well as the defendant. This statute does not specify who schedules the hearing, but it cannot be held sooner than ten days after notice is served on the interested parties. If all parties waive, in writing, their right to a hearing on this issue, the clerk may release the vehicle to the lienholder if the lienholder agrees not to allow the defendant or vehicle owner to retake possession of the vehicle. Absent that waiver, the court must hold a hearing to determine if the lienholder is entitled to possession.[172] The statute also does not specify who among the "parties" must waive their right to a hearing, but at a minimum the owner, prosecutor, and school board seem to be parties for this purpose.

The lienholder must show that the loan is in default and that the lienholder is entitled to possession of the vehicle. The lienholder also must agree to sell the vehicle and pay to the clerk of court the proceeds from the sale, less the amount of the lien and towing and storage costs paid by the lienholder. If the court ultimately orders forfeiture, any surplus proceeds go to the county school board.[173] If the court does not order forfeiture, the proceeds go to the vehicle owner.

If the vehicle has previously been released to the lienholder under this procedure, the vehicle may not be released to the same lienholder a second time.

A lienholder may also seek return of the vehicle at a forfeiture hearing held after the defendant is convicted, subject to the same conditions.[174] Lienholders also have the right to purchase vehicles, without tendering cash, after the vehicle is forfeited and ordered to be sold by the school board under G.S. 20-28.5(a), if they are the highest bidder and their bid is the amount of the lien. In that case they must pay the towing and storage fees.

Trials and Forfeiture Hearings

Although many vehicles are returned before trials and forfeiture hearings are held, many others are not. If a trial is not held promptly, fees for storage can accumulate quickly and surpass the value of the vehicle. To address that possible problem, the statute provides that if the case is in district court, the trial of the impaired driving offense must be scheduled on the arresting officer's next court date or within thirty days of the offense, whichever occurs first. Any party seeking to continue the case beyond that date must file a written motion, with notice to the opposing party, and the judge must find a compelling reason for the continuance. The motion and the judge's finding must be attached to the record of the case.[175] In addition, the forfeiture hearing must be held *immediately* or as soon thereafter as feasible. The statute provides no remedy if the state does not comply with either of these requirements.

These scheduling requirements do not apply to cases in superior court, although a party may seek permanent pretrial release of the vehicle if he or she has not already attempted to do so in

171. G.S. 20-28.2(a)(3).
172. G.S.20-28.3(e3).
173. G.S. 20-28.2(d)(2)a.
174. G.S. 20-28.2(f).
175. G.S. 20-28.3(m).

district court.[176] Presumably these requirements do not apply in district court also if a party has obtained permanent pretrial release of a vehicle, as the case would no longer involve the potential forfeiture of a vehicle.

If the defendant is acquitted of the underlying criminal charge, or if the charge is reduced to a noncovered charge or is dismissed, the forfeiture proceeding is terminated. If the vehicle has not been sold, the owner may reclaim the seized vehicle upon payment of any towing and storage fees. Failure to claim the vehicle within thirty days after a court orders its release allows the entity storing the vehicle to claim a lien under G.S. 44A-2(d) for all storage fees that have accrued.[177] Under G.S. 44A-2, the vehicle may be sold to pay the fees. If the clerk is holding proceeds from insurance or from an expedited sale of the vehicle (to be discussed later in this chapter) those proceeds are paid to the owner.

If the defendant is convicted of the charge supporting forfeiture, the court must conduct a forfeiture hearing either at the time of sentencing or at a separate hearing to be held as soon thereafter as feasible.[178] Possible issues to be resolved at the hearing include the status of the defendant's license at the time of the offense, the legal innocence of nondriving vehicle owners, and the right of a lienholder to repossess the vehicle.[179] At least ten days before the hearing, the prosecution must notify the defendant and each vehicle owner and lienholder of the hearing.[180] The forfeiture may be delayed to allow time for notice to be served, but sentencing may not be delayed for that purpose.[181]

The court may also hold a forfeiture hearing if the defendant has failed to appear (and the vehicle has not been permanently released to an owner or lienholder). This hearing is held even though there is not a conviction of the defendant. A person may not be tried for a criminal offense unless he or she is present, so the defendant's failure to appear would otherwise prevent the state from disposing of the state's forfeiture claim to the vehicle, at least until the point at which the fees accrued to a level that authorized the vehicle to be sold to satisfy the fees. To avoid that problem, the court may hold a forfeiture hearing sixty days after a defendant fails to appear if the order for arrest for failing to appear has not been set aside. At this hearing, the prosecution must prove by a preponderance of the evidence that the defendant committed a covered offense and that his or her license was revoked for a covered reason. If the prosecution meets this burden, the court may enter an order of forfeiture (unless a vehicle owner or lienholder is entitled to recover the vehicle).[182] This process does not result in a criminal conviction, however, which may be imposed only if the state locates and successfully prosecutes the defendant. As with forfeiture hearings after conviction, the prosecution must give at least ten days notice of the hearing.[183]

At a forfeiture hearing, the court must order the vehicle forfeited if the state demonstrates that the defendant committed the covered offense and had a covered revocation at the time, unless a lienholder or innocent owner establishes a valid claim for the vehicle.

The court must order the forfeited vehicle sold, unless the school board elects to retain it for its own use. The school board must satisfy any outstanding liens if it elects to retain the vehicle for itself. If there is more than one school system in a county, the proceeds must be shared in the same manner that fine and forfeitures are shared. Sale of a vehicle pursuant to court order extinguishes all liens on the vehicle.[184] Vehicle sales procedures are discussed in more detail later in this chapter.

---

176. G.S. 20-28.3(m).
177. G.S. 20-28.4.
178. G.S. 20-28.2(d); -28.3(m).
179. G.S. 20-28.2(d), (e), and (f).
180. G.S. 20-28.2(c).
181. G.S. 20-28.2(d).
182. G.S. 20-28.2(b) and (d).
183. G.S. 20-28.2(c).
184. G.S. 20-28.5(b) and (c).

Towing and Storage Fees

G.S. 20-28.9 authorizes the Department of Public Instruction to enter into a regional or statewide contract for the towing, storage, and sale of seized and forfeited vehicles. That department established such a contract on July 1, 1999. The contractor acts as the agent for the county school board. Without that contract, the school board would be responsible for insuring that the towing and storage of seized vehicles are administered properly.[185] Under the statewide contract, the contractor is responsible for towing and storage of the vehicles. In either case, the towing fee is not regulated by statute. The maximum authorized storage fee is $10 per day. The fee may be assessed regardless of whether the vehicle is stored on commercial or school board property.[186] In addition the state contractor collects a $10 per vehicle fee for the Department of Public Instruction on any vehicle it sells or returns to its owner.[187]

The current state contract gives the contractor the right either to tow vehicles or to contract with local commercial towing companies. (At the time of publication, the contractor was largely relying on local towing companies for the initial towing.) In the absence of a contract, the school board may contract with a designated towing company or leave the matter of towing to law enforcement officers. If neither a contract nor a local school board policy is in effect, the law enforcement officer lodging the charge may designate a towing company in the same manner as for any other law enforcement towing need. In that case, the school board must retrieve the vehicle from the towing company within ten days and must pay any applicable fees at the time the vehicle is retrieved.[188] The school board may not be held responsible for any damage to vehicles or to property in vehicles for which it is responsible, unless the damage is caused by the school system's gross negligence or intentional misconduct. Private entities towing or storing the vehicles do not have similar protection; presumably they are responsible for damages caused by their simple negligence.

Towing and storage fees can mount up quickly. They apply even if the vehicle should never have been seized, the owner is innocent, or the defendant is not guilty of the underlying offense. To recover a vehicle from a school board, a private storage entity, or a statewide or regional contractor, the owner or lienholder seeking recovery of the vehicle must pay the towing and accumulated storage fees, at least initially. Thus if the court finds that a vehicle owner is an innocent owner and is entitled to return of the vehicle, the owner must pay the fees.[189] The same is true of lienholders.[190] It is applicable also when the defendant prevails at his or her criminal trial, at a forfeiture hearing, or in a pretrial motion.[191] In no instance may an owner recover his or her vehicle under this statute without paying the applicable fees to the entity storing the vehicle. If the vehicle is towed under the DWI seizure statutes but the towing is completely without a legal basis, Article 7A of G.S. Chapter 20 provides a possible remedy and procedure for recovering the vehicle. G.S. 20-219.10 specifies that that article does not apply to DWI seizures, but if the seizure was not authorized by the DWI seizure statutes, then arguably those statutes were not the basis for the initial seizure. Under that interpretation, Article 7A would apply to such seizures.

If the owner fails to obtain release of the vehicle within thirty days of a court's order that it be released, the person or entity in possession of the vehicle obtains a lien for the full amount of the

185. G.S. 20-28.3(d).
186. G.S. 20-28.3(d); -28.9.
187. G.S. 20-28.9(c).
188. G.S. 20-28.3(d).
189. G.S. 20-28.2(e); -28.3(e1).
190. G.S. 20-28.2(f); -28.3(e3); -28.5(a).
191. G.S. 20-28.4(d); -28.3(e2).

towing and storage charges and may dispose of the vehicle to satisfy that lien (in accordance with Article 1 of Chapter 44A).[192]

If the defendant is convicted of a covered offense, an innocent owner or lienholder may be able to recoup from the defendant the fees paid to recover the vehicle. The court must order the defendant to pay as restitution to a vehicle owner or lienholder the amounts paid or owing for towing, storage, or sale of the vehicle "to the extent" that these costs are not covered by the proceeds from sale of the vehicle.[193] It is not clear whether this requirement applies only when the vehicle is sold or if it is applicable also when there is no sale. The statute also allows restitution to the school board for these costs. A school board has the power, however, to sell a vehicle before the towing and storage fees exceed the vehicle's value. If a school board unduly delays a sale, the defendant may have grounds to argue for limiting restitution. In any event, the court could order restitution using its authority to order restitution in any criminal case.

If a defendant is ordered to pay restitution under the mandatory provisions of G.S. 20-28.3(l), the clerk of court must docket a civil judgment in the amount of the restitution ordered under the authority of that section. If the defendant is sentenced to active imprisonment, the judgment is docketed and becomes effective when the conviction is final. If the defendant is placed on probation, the judge determines the amount still owing at the time of revocation or termination of the probation, and only then is a judgment docketed.

Vehicle Sales

As previously noted, if the vehicles seized have relatively little value and they are held until after a trial and a forfeiture hearing are held, in many cases the fees owed will exceed the value of the vehicle. By always imposing that fee liability on the vehicle owner, the statute recognizes that at some point any interest the owner or the school board has in a forfeited vehicle will be negated by the fees. As a result, in three instances the school board (or its agent under the statewide or regional contract to handle and dispose of these vehicles) is authorized to dispose of some vehicles before the criminal matter and the forfeiture hearing are concluded. The school board may sell the vehicle before trial if (1) all the motor vehicle owners consent, (2) the vehicle is worth $1,500 or less and has been held at least ninety days, or (3) the outstanding towing and storage fees exceed 85 percent of the value of the vehicle. In the second and third situations, the school board may sell the vehicle without the owner or owners' consent. The proceeds of any pretrial sale must be deposited with the superior court clerk. They go to the school board if the court orders forfeiture and to the vehicle owner if the court does not order forfeiture (less towing and storage fees, costs of sale, and outstanding liens).[194] G.S. 20-28.3 (b1) provides that the DMV "shall prohibit title to a seized motor vehicle from being transferred by a motor vehicle owner unless authorized by court order." It is likely that a school board is not a "motor vehicle owner" for this purpose, although as a matter of caution, some school boards may under these circumstances seek a court order approving the sale.

For sales after trial, the school boards or their agents must use the procedure they normally use in G.S. Chapter 160A to dispose of surplus property, but they must still give at least ten days notice to the vehicle owners and lienholders.[195] There is no statutory requirement that the defendant be notified (although a defendant who is the owner would get notice), since he or she cannot legally purchase the vehicle or have someone purchase it on his or her behalf.

---

192. G.S. 20-28.4.
193. G.S. 20-28.3(l).
194. G.S. 20-28.3(i).
195. G.S. 20-28.3(i); -28.5(a).

Appeals

Appeals of forfeiture matters can become quite complicated. The statutes answer some appeal issues directly, but others are not addressed. The following is a discussion of some issues that are addressed directly.

Innocent owners

When the owner is not the defendant, that owner's appeal rights from the district court appear to depend on whether the defendant appeals the conviction. If the owner seeks pretrial release and is denied by the clerk, the owner apparently has no right to have that decision reviewed. If the owner seeks permanent pretrial release and is found by the court not to be an innocent owner, the owner may seek to have that decision reviewed at a forfeiture hearing held after the defendant's conviction.[196] If the decision is reaffirmed at that hearing, the decision that the owner is not innocent may be immediately appealed to the court of appeals.[197] If the defendant does not appeal the criminal conviction to the superior court, that is the clear route of appeal for an owner.

If the owner raises his or her claim of innocence in a pretrial petition, but does not raise the issue at a forfeiture hearing, there is no clear statutory rule specifying if the matter can be appealed or the route it should take if there is an appeal.

If the defendant does appeal the conviction, G.S. 20-28.5(e) provides that "[w]hen the conviction of an offense that is the basis for an order of forfeiture is appealed from district court, the issue of forfeiture shall be heard in superior court de novo." That apparently would entitle an owner to raise again the issue of innocence in the superior court, although that would be inconsistent with the provision in G.S. 20-28.2(e) allowing a declaration of non-innocence to be appealed to the court of appeals as a final judgment. It is possible that these statutes give an owner the choice to contest the matter at the superior court or on appeal to the court of appeals.

A vehicle owner may apply for temporary pretrial release of a vehicle in a case appealed to the superior court from the district court once the case is in superior court.[198] If the owner posted a bond in district court for release of a vehicle, the bond would continue in effect in superior court.

If the criminal matter is appealed, the issue of forfeiture would not be before the superior court if the district court determines that the owner was innocent. G.S. 20-28.5(e) provides for a de novo forfeiture hearing in superior court when the defendant appeals a conviction that is the basis of an "order of forfeiture." Since the district court has not entered an order of forfeiture, this provision authorizing a de novo consideration of the forfeiture issue apparently does not apply.

Is a forfeiture order in which an owner asserts his or her innocence stayed pending appeal? G.S. 20-28.5(e) states that a forfeiture order is stayed if the defendant appeals the conviction underlying the order. But it does not specify what happens if the owner appeals the forfeiture order but the defendant does not appeal the conviction. Absent any clear automatic stay provision, the owner would need to apply to the appropriate court for a stay.

---

196. G.S. 20-28.3(e1).
197. G.S. 20-28.2(e); -28.5(e).
198. G.S. 20-28.3(m).

Defendant Owners

If a defendant seeks permanent pretrial release under G.S. 20-28.3(e2) and is denied relief, he or she may again raise the issue at a forfeiture hearing held after conviction. If the defendant appeals a conviction in district court, the forfeiture matter is heard de novo by the superior court.[199] If the defendant does not appeal the criminal conviction, an appeal of an order of forfeiture is to the court of appeals.[200]

If the defendant appeals the district court conviction before that court holds a forfeiture hearing, apparently no forfeiture hearing is held in district court. While the forfeiture law does not specifically address the question, the general rule that the district court loses jurisdiction when an appeal is filed seems to control. As a result any forfeiture hearing would have to be held in superior court at an appropriate time.

Lienholders

There are no provisions in the forfeiture statutes dealing with the rights of lienholders to appeal a determination that they are not entitled to possession of a vehicle.

District Attorney

There are no provisions in the forfeiture statutes authorizing a district attorney to appeal a finding of innocence or a finding that a defendant or lienholder is entitled to possession of a seized vehicle.

Miscellaneous Forfeiture Provisions

Insurance Proceeds

If a seized vehicle was damaged during seizure or while the defendant was committing the underlying impaired driving offense, the proceeds of any insurance must be paid to the clerk of court. The proceeds are subject to forfeiture or return to the vehicle owner in the same manner as a vehicle. A vehicle owner who objects to the amount paid to the clerk may file an independent claim with the insurance company.[201]

Revocation of Registration

If a defendant is convicted of a covered offense while his or her driver's license was revoked, he or she loses the right to register *any vehicle* until the defendant's license is restored. A nondriving owner loses the right to register the *seized vehicle* for the same time period unless he or she is found to be an innocent owner. This is an automatic administrative action taken by the DMV upon receiving notice of the conviction.[202]

199. G.S. 20-28.5(e).
200. G.S. 20-28.5(e).
201. G.S. 20-28.2(c1); -28.2(d)(2); -28.3(h).
202. G.S. 20-54.1.

Role of School Board Attorney

The attorney for the local school board has the right to appear and be heard at all proceedings related to forfeiture of seized vehicles. With the consent of the local school board, the district attorney may delegate to the school board's attorney any of the district attorney's duties concerning forfeiture proceedings.[203]

DETENTION OF IMPAIRED DRIVERS

Impaired drivers, like all who are arrested, have a right to have a judicial official promptly determine if conditions of pretrial release should be set and, if so, what the conditions should be. Impaired drivers, however, present peculiar problems for the official making that decision. One peculiar problem is that the driver has been found to be sufficiently impaired to be charged with an offense involving impaired driving (as defined in G.S. 20-4.01(24a), and immediate release may not be in the driver's or the public's interest. The statutes recognize that fact in several places: G.S. 15A-534(c), -534.2, and -511. However, the time at which the driver may benefit most from seeing potential witnesses is the time closest to his or her arrest.[204]

In balancing these interests G.S. 15A-534.2 authorizes judicial officials to hold an impaired driver without benefit of pretrial release upon a showing by clear and convincing evidence that the person presents a danger if released. The person may be held until:

- he or she is no longer impaired;
- a sober, responsible adult assumes responsibility for him or her; or
- twenty-four hours have passed, whichever is shorter.

If this authority is used, the judicial official making the decision must set the conditions of pretrial release at the time the person is ordered to be held, and the appropriate conditions must be met in addition to the conditions just listed. In addition, to be sure the person is not denied the opportunity to communicate with family, attorney, or friends during the period in which he or she is alleged to be impaired, the authorities with custody over the person must allow him or her access to such people as requested.

In a series of cases reported under *State v. Knoll*,[205] the North Carolina Supreme Court found violations of the pretrial release provisions in which access to friends or family was denied to the defendant or in which judicial officials declined to release a defendant to another adult. The court adopted a rule that requires dismissal of the charge when there is a violation of the statute and the defendant is prejudiced thereby. In each case the court found that the defendant had been prejudiced by the violation and ordered that the cases be dismissed. None of the magistrates had invoked the authority to hold impaired drivers under G.S. 15A-534.2, relying instead on their general authority under G.S. 15A-534. It is likely that a judicial official who complies with G.S. 15A-534.2 will not be found to be in violation of the *Knoll* ruling.[206] It is likely also that the existence of a valid chemical analysis that would support a conviction under the *per se* prong of the impaired driving statute would support a finding that no prejudice had been suffered by a violation of *Knoll*.

203. G.S. 20-28.3(k).

204. *See* State v. Hill, 277 N.C. 547, 178 S.E.2d 462 (1971).

205. 322 N.C. 535, 369 S.E.2d 558 (1988).

206. *See* State v. Bumgarner, 97 N.C. App. 567, 389 S.E.2d 425 (1990); State v. Eliason, 100 N.C. App. 313, 395 S.E.2d 702 (1990); State v. Ham, 105 N.C. App. 658, 414 S.E.2d 577 (1992); State v. Haas, 131 N.C. App. 113, 505 S.E.2d 311 (1998).

WRITTEN REASONS IN DISMISSALS

G.S. 20-138.4 requires a prosecutor, before dismissing a charge in an impaired driving case, to enter detailed facts in the record explaining the reasons for the action. The requirement applies to the taking of a voluntary dismissal, acceptance of a guilty or no contest plea to a lesser included offense, the substitution of a lesser charge, or the taking of any other action that reduces or dismisses the original charge. These requirements apply to "any case involving impaired driving." It is clear that charges of impaired driving under G.S. 20-138.1 and habitual impaired driving under G.S. 20-138.5 are included. It is likely that charges of impaired driving in a commercial vehicle under G.S. 20-138.2 also are included, since that section has language identical to the main impaired driving statute making it unlawful to drive while one's faculties are appreciably impaired. The other offenses involving drinking and driving are all zero tolerance offenses. While they involve consumption and driving, they do not involve "impairment," and this statute apparently does not apply to the dismissal of those charges.

General explanations such as *in the interest of justice* or *insufficient evidence* do not meet the standard of detail required by this statute. There is no remedy in the statute for failure by a prosecutor to comply with this statute.

LICENSE RESTORATION PROVISIONS

For revocations based on convictions of some impaired driving offenses, there are special conditions attached to the restoration of the defendant's driver's license. Those conditions require the defendant to drive with lower alcohol concentrations than are generally applicable to the public at large. These conditions apply to revocation based on offenses committed on or after July 1, 2000.

Table 6 outlines the offenses covered by this requirement along with the applicable alcohol level and the duration of the condition.[207]

The Division of Motor Vehicles must impose these conditions on any person whose license is revoked for a covered offense. In addition the person, in agreeing to accept the restored license must agree to submit to chemical analysis in accordance with G.S. 20-16.2 at the request of any law enforcement officer who has reasonable grounds to believe that the person is operating a motor vehicle on a highway with an alcohol concentration that is higher than the applicable *per se* level at any relevant time after the driving. This apparently means that this requirement does not apply on public vehicular areas, even though the underlying offenses that trigger the imposition of this offense may be committed on public vehicular areas. In addition the person must agree to be transported by the officer to the appropriate testing site. If a person subject to these conditions refuses to submit to the chemical analysis, his or her license is subject to revocation in the same manner as a person who refuses after being charged with an implied consent offense. It is not clear what happens if a person fails to cooperate with the officer; it may be a crime to resist the officer in the performance of his or her duties, but the statute does not authorize a revocation for that conduct. The revocation must be based on either a *per se* violation or a refusal to submit to a chemical analysis that occurs after the person has been notified of his or her rights and is offered the chance to submit to the analysis.

It is not a crime to fail to comply with these conditions of restoration, but the failure to comply with them will result in the person's losing his or her restored license, and the imposition of an additional one-year revocation. If the person's license was restored early, any remaining time on the original revocation is activated and must be served before the additional revocation period begins.

---

207. G.S. 20-19(c3), as enacted by SL 1999-406.

Table 6
License Restoration Conditions for Impaired Driving Offenses

Basis of Original Revocation	Number of Restorations	*Per Se* Level	Duration of Condition
Driving while impaired (G.S. 20-138.1)	First restoration	0.04	Three years from restoration date
Driving while impaired (G.S. 20-138.1)	Second or subsequent restoration	0.00	Three years from restoration date, if revocation not permanent; seven years if underlying revocation was permanent
Out-of-state DWI offense leading to revocation in this state (G.S. 20-23 and -23.2)	First restoration	0.04	Three years from restoration date
Out-of-state DWI offense leading to revocation in this state (G.S. 20-23 and -23.2)	Second or subsequent restoration	0.00	Three years from restoration date, if revocation not permanent; seven years if underlying revocation was permanent
Driving commercial vehicle while impaired (G.S. 20-138.2)	Any restoration	0.00	Three years, from restoration date, if revocation not permanent; seven years if underlying revocation was permanent
Driving with any alcohol in body by person under twenty-one (G.S. 20-138.3)	Any restoration	0.00	Until person is twenty-one
Felony death by vehicle	Any restoration	0.00	Seven years
Manslaughter involving impaired driving	Any restoration	0.00	Seven years
Out-of-state commercial DWI offense leading to revocation in this state (G.S. 20-23 and -23.2)	Any restoration	0.00	Three years, from restoration date, if revocation not permanent; seven years if underlying revocation was permanent
Out-of-state felony death by vehicle leading to revocation in this state (G.S. 20-23 and -23.2)	Any restoration	0.00	Seven years
Out-of-state manslaughter involving impaired driving leading to revocation in this state (G.S. 20-23 and -23.2)	Any restoration	0.00	Seven years

Table 7
Ignition Interlock License Restoration Conditions[a]

Basis of Original Revocation	Conditions	Length of Underlying Revocation	Duration of Conditions
DWI, G.S. 20-138.1	Vehicle must have interlock, driver must activate interlock, and AC must not exceed 0.04	One year	One year
DWI, G.S. 20-138.1	Vehicle must have interlock, driver must activate interlock, and AC must not exceed 0.04	Four years	Three years
DWI, G.S. 20-138.1	Vehicle must have interlock, driver must activate interlock, and AC must not exceed 0.04	Permanent	Seven years

These conditions, imposed by SL 1999-406, are effective July 1, 2000.

a. The interlock is required only if the person had an alcohol concentration of 0.16 or more or if the person had a conviction of an offense involving impaired driving in the seven years immediately preceding the date of the current offense. G.S. 20-17.7(a).

Law enforcement officers must report suspected violations of these conditions to the DMV. Officers may not base the reports on readings obtained from ignition interlock devices. It is not clear whether they may be based on roadside screening tests or on other evidence not using a chemical analysis. Upon receipt of the officer's information, the DMV must revoke the person's license if the information is sufficient to establish a violation. The person may apply to the DMV for a hearing before the revocation becomes effective, but the hearing is limited to the following issues:

- Did the officer have reasonable grounds to believe that a restoration condition was being violated?
- Was the person notified of his rights under G.S. 20-16.2?
- Did the person's license have an alcohol concentration restriction?
- Did the person submit to a chemical analysis and did it reveal an alcohol concentration in excess of the applicable *per se* level?

Apparently the DMV has no authority to consider any other issues. If other issues, such as whether the officer had a basis to stop the person initially, may be raised in civil actions against the officer, but not in this proceeding, as this statute is currently written.[208]

The DMV's decision may be reviewed by a superior court judge, but that judge's review is limited to a review of whether the DMV followed proper procedures and whether the DMV hearing officer made findings of fact sufficient to support the revocation.[209] It is a very narrow standard of review.

In addition, some offenders are also required to obtain and use an ignition interlock as a condition of obtaining a restoration. See Table 7 for a description of those provisions.

---

208. *See* G.S. 20-19(c5), as enacted by SL 1999-406: "The hearing must be conducted in the county where the charge was brought, and *must be limited to consideration of* [the listed issues]." (Italics added.)

209. G.S. 20-19(c6), as enacted by SL 1999-406, effective July 1, 2000.

Appendix A

Punishment Chart for North Carolina Motor Vehicle Offenses

Detailed Table of Contents

Description of Punishment Chart for Motor Vehicle Offenses / 157

Punishment Chart / 159

- Driver's License Violations / 159
  - Driving without License or Violating Restrictions / 159
  - Age Limits / 159
  - Learner's Permit / 160
  - Impaired Driving Instructor / 160
  - Driving with Suspended or Revoked License / 160
  - Illegal Activity Relating to License / 161
  - Parking Privileges for Handicapped Drivers / 162
  - Special I.D. Card / 162
- Commercial Licenses / 162
- Vehicle Registration / 163
- Salvage Titles / 164
- Transfer of Title or Interest / 164
- Dealer Plates / 164
- Car Theft and Related Offenses / 164
- Violation of Registration Provisions / 165
- Perjury / 165
- Failure to Obey Directions of Police or Firefighters / 165
- Equipment Violations / 166
  - Tires / 166
  - Steering Mechanism / 166
  - Speedometer / 166
  - Brakes / 166
  - Selling Unapproved Brake Fluid or Lining / 166
  - Horns and Warning Devices / 167
  - Mirrors / 167
  - Windshields / 167
  - Mufflers / 167
  - Lights / 168
  - Seat Belts / 169
  - Smoke Screens / 169
  - Child Restraint Systems / 169

Rules of the Road Violations / 170
- Impaired Driving Offenses / 170
- Reckless Driving / 172
- Use of Controlled-access Highways / 172
- Motorcycles and Mopeds / 172
- Speeding / 173
- School Zones / 174
- Racing, Death by Vehicle, and Eluding Arrest / 174
- Failing to Stop for Railroad Signal or Tracks / 175
- Driving on Wrong Side of Road / 175
- Improper Passing / 176
- Following Too Closely / 177
- Improper Turning / 177
- Failing to Yield Right-of-way / 178
- Actions Prohibited in Emergencies / 178
- Failing to Stop / 178
- Failure to Yield at Yield Signs / 179
- Driving through Safety Zones or on Sidewalks / 179
- Parking on Highway / 179
- Traveling Wrong Way on One-way Street / 180

Accident Responsibility Laws / 180
Transportation of Spent Nuclear Fuel / 181
Violations at Pedestrian Crosswalks / 181
Standing, Sitting, or Lying in Street / 181
Soliciting Rides, Employment, or Business on Highways / 181
Violating Limited Driving Privileges / 182
Failure to Dim Lights / 182
Equipment Inspection Laws / 182
Passing Stopped School Bus / 182
Bus Driver Rules / 182
Insurance Violations / 183

Index to Punishment Chart for North Carolina Motor Vehicle Offenses / 185

Description of Punishment Chart for Motor Vehicle Offenses

This chart lists (in numerical order by section number) the more common and/or more important motor vehicle offenses. The first column gives the section number that creates the offense, and an asterisk (*) beside the section number indicates that the court must require the defendant (if convicted) to surrender his or her driver's license pursuant to Chapter 20, Section 24(a), of the North Carolina General Statutes [hereinafter G.S.]; the clerk of court must then give the defendant a dated receipt. The second column briefly describes the offense; there is no attempt to cover all of the elements of a particular offense in this description. The third column gives the section number of the statute that contains the punishment, and the last column indicates whether the punishment is an infraction, misdemeanor, felony, etc.

Each year the chief district court judges adopt a "waiver list," designating those offenses that are waiverable and those where a mandatory court appearance is required; those requiring a mandatory court appearance are so indicated in the last column. All other offenses are waiverable—meaning that they can be paid off without going to court. (The 2000 waiver list is contained at the end of Chapter Four of Part One.)

Driver's license revocations and suspensions are indicated in the footnotes for many of the more serious offenses. The abbreviations DMV and CMV are used to refer to the Division of Motor Vehicles and the Commissioner of Motor Vehicles; DOT refers to the North Carolina Department of Transportation; app. stands for appearance. G.S. 20-16, "Authority of Division to suspend license," sets out the North Carolina driver's license point system. It can be found in its entirety in Appendix B, which contains the full text of statutes cited in this book. As of December 1, 1999, more points are assigned if the driver was operating a commercial vehicle; in those cases the fine or penalty may be double the amount "authorized by statute." These offenses are designated by "(comm.)" in the first column. (*See* G.S. 20-16A.) In addition to those offenses designated as involving a commercial vehicle, the fine or penalty may be doubled for "all other moving violations." [*See* G.S. 20-16(c).]

Punishment Chart for North Carolina Motor Vehicle Offenses

Offense Statute	Description of Offense	Punishment Statute	Punishment
Driver's License Violations			
Driving without License or Violating Restrictions			
20-7(a) (comm.)	Operating motor vehicle without N.C. license (see G.S. 20-8 for exceptions)	20-35	Class 2 misdemeanor
20-7(a) (comm.)	Driving class of motor vehicle which driver's license does not entitle a person to drive	20-35	Class 2 misdemeanor
20-7(a)	Failure to carry license while operating vehicle [production of license valid at time of charge is a good defense, G.S. 20-35(c)]	20-35	Class 2 misdemeanor
20-7(al)	Operating motorcycle without having proper driver's license endorsement	2-35	Class 2 misdemeanor
20-7(e) (comm.)	Operating vehicle in violation of restriction noted on license	20-35	Class 2 misdemeanor
20-7(l),(m)	Operating vehicle in violation of restriction noted on instruction or learner's permit	20-35	Class 2 misdemeanor
Age Limits			
20-10	Operating a public passenger vehicle if under age 18	20-35	Class 2 misdemeanor
20-10	Operating any road machine, tractor, etc., on state highway, age 14 or under	20-35	Class 2 misdemeanor
20-10.1	Unlawful for any person under age 16 to drive a moped on highway or public vehicular area	20-35	Class 2 misdemeanor

Offense Statute	Description of Offense	Punishment Statute	Punishment
Learner's Permit			
20-11(c), (e), (h)	Unlawful for any person to drive in violation of restriction of limited learner's permit, limited provisional license, or temporary permit.	20-11(l)	Class 2 misdemeanor
	Violation of time or supervising driver restriction is driving without license (NOL).	20-35	Infraction
	Any other restriction violation is an infraction[1]	20-176	
Impaired Driving Instructor			
20-12.1	Unlawful to instruct while impaired[2, 3]	20-35	Class 2 misdemeanor (mandatory app.)
Driving with Suspended or Revoked License			
20-16.1(b)*	Violating limited driving privilege for excessive speeding[4]	20-16.1(b)(4) 20-28(a)	Class 1 misdemeanor (mandatory app.)
20-28(a)*	Driving while license is suspended or revoked[5]	20-28(a)	Class 1 misdemeanor (mandatory app.)
20-28(a)	Driving of vehicle by a restoree of a suspended or revoked license without the requisite financial responsibility	20-28(a) 20-7 20-35	Class 2 misdemeanor (mandatory app.)
20-28(al)	Driving without reclaiming license revoked pursuant to G.S. 20-16.5. (Immediate Civil Revocation)[6]	20-28(a1) 20-35	Class 2 misdemeanor
20-28(d)*	Driving a vehicle while person is disqualified and revoked[7]	20-28(d) 20-28(a), (b)	Class 1 misdemeanor (mandatory app.)
20-28(d)	Driving a commercial motor vehicle during disqualification[8]	20-28(d)	Class 1 misdemeanor (mandatory app.)

*Pursuant to G.S. 20-24(a), the court must require the driver convicted of this offense to surrender his or her driver's license to the court.

1. *See* G.S. 20-11(m) for insurance status of permittee.

2. G.S. 20-16(8a) authorizes DMV to suspend a license for "impaired instruction under 20-12.1," for a period of up to 1 year pursuant to G.S. 20-19(c).

3. This is an implied consent offense under G.S. 20-16.2.

4. Under G.S. 20-16.1(b)(4) the punishment is the same as for driving while license suspended in violation of G.S. 20-28.

5. For a first offense under this section, the license is revoked for an additional year; for a second offense, 2 additional years; a third or subsequent offense brings permanent revocation. The licensee is entitled to apply for restoration of the license early according to schedule set forth in G.S. 20-28(c).

6. A person convicted of driving while license revoked under these circumstances is treated as if convicted of driving without a license (NOL) for purposes of punishment and points (G.S. 20-28(a1)).

7. Driver is treated as if revoked under 20-28(a).

8. G.S. 20-28(d) provides additional disqualification periods for this offense.

Offense Statute	Description of Offense	Punishment Statute	Punishment
Illegal Activity Relating to License			
20-29	Refusing to give uniformed officer information required by statute, such as name, address, or vehicle owner; or giving false information; or refusing to surrender or produce license upon demand of court or DMV	20-29	Class 2 misdemeanor
20-29	Driver of a car involved in an accident refusing to give information required by statute	20-29	Class 2 misdemeanor
20-29.1	Failure to observe restrictions imposed by DMV about the kinds of vehicles a licensee may operate	20-7 20-29.1 20-35	Class 2 misdemeanor
20-30(1)	Displaying or possessing any license or learner's permit known to be invalid[9]	20-35 20-16(a) (6) 20-19(c)	Class 2 misdemeanor (mandatory app.)
20-30(2)	Counterfeiting, selling, lending, or knowingly permitting the use of any driver's license or learner's permit by one not entitled thereto[9]	20-35 20-16(a) (6) 20-19(c)	Class 2 misdemeanor (mandatory app.)
20-30(3)	Displaying or representing as one's own a license not issued to the person displaying it[9]	20-35 20-16(a) (6) 20-19(c)	Class 2 misdemeanor (mandatory app.)
20-30(4)	Refusing to surrender to DMV a driver's license that has been revoked or suspended	20-35	Class 2 misdemeanor (mandatory app.)
20-30(5)*	Using or allowing others to use false names and addresses in license applications or renewals[10]	20-35 20-17(8) 20-19(f)	Class 2 misdemeanor (mandatory app.)
20-30(5)*	Making false statements, concealing material facts, or otherwise committing a fraud in applying for a license or permit[10]	20-35 20-17(8) 20-19(f)	Class 2 misdemeanor (mandatory app.)
20-30(6)	Reproducing or possessing a reproduced copy of a license or permit	20-35	Class 2 misdemeanor (mandatory app.)
20-30(7)	Offering simulated license for sale	20-30(7)	Class I felony (mandatory app.)
20-30(8)	To possess more than one commercial license, or to possess a commercial license and a regular license	20-35	Class 2 misdemeanor (mandatory app.)
20-30(9)	Use of license with false name in commission of a felony	20-30(9)	Class I felony

*Pursuant to G.S. 20-24(a), the court must require the driver convicted of this offense to surrender his or her driver's license to the court.

9. Under G.S. 20-16(a)(6) and -19(c), DMV may suspend a person's license for 1 year or less upon conviction of this offense.

10. Under G.S. 20-17(8) and -19(f), DMV must revoke a person's license for 1 year upon conviction of this offense.

Offense Statute	Description of Offense	Punishment Statute	Punishment
20-31*	Making a false affidavit or knowingly swearing or affirming falsely to any matter or thing required by the statutes to be sworn to[10]	20-31 20-17(5)	Class I felony (mandatory app.)
20-32	Causing or permitting an unlicensed minor to drive on a highway	20-35	Class 2 misdemeanor
20-34	Allowing motor vehicle to be driven in violation of license law	20-35	Class 2 misdemeanor (mandatory app.)
Parking Privileges for Handicapped Drivers			
20-37.6(c3)	Selling of a handicapped license plate or windshield placard	20-37.6(c3) 20-176(c)	Class 2 misdemeanor (mandatory app.)
20-37.6(e)(1)	Parking in a handicapped space without displaying a handicapped license tag or windshield placard[11]	20-37.6(f)(1)	Infraction
20-37.6(e)(2)	Using or attempting to use handicapped license tag or windshield placard when not entitled to do so[11]	20-37.6(f)(1)	Infraction
20-37.6(e)(3)	Parking in front of a handicapped ramp or curb cut[11]	20-37.6(f)(1)	Infraction
20-37.6(e)(4)	Those responsible for designating parking spaces as handicapped using signs not conforming to G.S. 30-37.6(d)[11]	20-37.6(f)(2)	Infraction
Special I.D. Card			
20-37.7	Engaging in fraud or misrepresentation in applying for and using a special identification card	20-37.7(e)	Class 2 misdemeanor (mandatory app.)
20-37.8(b)	Use of card with false name in commission of a felony	20-37.8(c)	Class I felony
Commercial Licenses			
20-37.12 (a) (comm.)	Driving a commercial vehicle without a valid ommercial driver's license with applicable endorsements[12]	20-37.21 (a)	Class 3 misdemeanor (mandatory app.)
20-37.12(b)	Driving a commercial vehicle in violation of an out-of-service order[12]	20-37.21 (a), 20-17.4	Class 3 misdemeanor (mandatory app.)

*Pursuant to G.S. 20-24(a), the court must require the driver convicted of this offense to surrender his or her driver's license to the court.

10. Under G.S. 20-17(8) and -19(f), DMV must revoke a person's license for 1 year upon conviction of this offense.

11. Penalty of $100 to $250.

12. Fined no less than $250 for first offense and no less than $500 for second or subsequent offense. Driving commercial vehicle in violation of "out-of-service order" results in disqualification to drive commercial vehicle for 90 days to 3 years.

Offense Statute	Description of Offense	Punishment Statute	Punishment
20-37.18(a)	Possessing a commercial driver's license and failing to notify DMV within 30 days of a traffic conviction[13]	20-37.21(b)	Infraction
20-37.18(b)	Possessing a commercial driver's license and failing to notify the employer within 30 days of a traffic conviction[13]	20-37.21(b)	Infraction
20-37.18(c)	Failing to notify the employer on the next business day that the commercial driver's license has been suspended, revoked, or canceled or that the privilege to drive a commercial vehicle has been lost[13]	20-37.21(b)	Infraction
20-37.19(a)	Failure to require an employee to notify the employer that commercial driver's license has been suspended, revoked, or canceled or the privilege lost[14]	20-37.21(c)	Infraction
20-37.19(b)(1)	Knowingly allowing, permitting, or authorizing a driver to drive a commercial vehicle while the commercial license has been suspended, revoked, or canceled, etc.[14]	20-37.21(c)	Infraction
20-37.19(b)(2)	Knowingly allowing, permitting, or authorizing a driver to drive a commercial vehicle when the driver has more than one driver's license[14]	20-37.21(c)	Infraction
Vehicle Registration			
20-50	Owning a vehicle which is not registered with DMV or which is not displaying current registration plates (unless vehicle is exempt from registration by statute)	20-176(a), (c)	Class 2 misdemeanor
20-57(c)	Failure to display registration card	20-176(a), (c)	Class 2 misdemeanor
20-63(a)	Willfully failing to surrender illegible registration plates upon request of DMV	20-63(a)	Class 2 misdemeanor
20-63(d)	Failing to place registration plate at proper place on vehicle	20-176(a), (c)	Class 2 misdemeanor
20-63(e)	Failing to clean registration plates after being requested to do so by an officer	20-63(e)	Class 3 misdemeanor
20-63(f)	Willfully operating vehicle with a registration plate which has been altered	20-63(f)	Class 2 misdemeanor (mandatory app.)
20-63(g)	Willfully altering, disguising, or concealing numbers on a registration plate	20-63(g)	Class 2 misdemeanor (mandatory app.)
20-71(a)	Altering certificate of title, registration card, or application for such with fraudulent intent	20-71(a) 20-177	Class I felony (mandatory app.)

13. Penalty of no less than $100 and no more than $500.

14. Penalty of no less than $500 and no more than $1,000.

Offense Statute	Description of Offense	Punishment Statute	Punishment
20-71(a)	Forging or counterfeiting certificate of title or registration card	20-71 (a) 20-177	Class I felony (mandatory app.)
20-71(a)	Knowingly using an altered, forged, or falsified certificate of title or registration card	20-71(a) 20-177	Class I felony (mandatory app.)
20-71(b)	Possessing a blank N.C. certificate of title or facsimile with fraudulent intent	20-71(b)	Class I felony (mandatory app.)
Salvage Titles			
20-71.4(a)	Failing to disclose that a vehicle was flooded, reconstructed, or salvaged or that it was damaged when repair cost was over 25% of fair market value	20-71.4(a)	Class 2 misdemeanor
20-71.4(b)	Removing the title or supporting documents to any vehicle to conceal damage	20-71.4(b)	Class 2 misdemeanor
Transfer of Title or Interest			
20-72(b)	Delivering or accepting a certificate of title assigned in blank	20-72(b)	Class 2 misdemeanor (mandatory app.)
20-73(a)	Failing to apply for certificate of title within required time[15]	20-73(c)	Class 2 misdemeanor
20-74	Knowingly making a false statement about the date a vehicle was sold or acquired	20-74	Class 3 misdemeanor
Dealer Plates			
20-79(e)(1)	Driving a vehicle with dealer license plates in violation of restrictions[16]	20-79(e)(1)	Infraction
Car Theft and Related Offenses			
20-102.1	Knowingly making false report of vehicle theft to DMV or officer	20-102.1	Class 2 misdemeanor
20-106	Receiving or transferring stolen vehicles	20-106	Class H felony (mandatory app.)
20-106.1	Failure to return a rented vehicle with intent to defraud	20-106.1	Class I felony (mandatory app.)
20-107(a)	Willfully tampering with or removing parts from a vehicle without owner's consent	20-107(a)	Class 2 misdemeanor
20-107(b)	Tampering with or attempting to steal vehicle	20-107(b)	Class 2 misdemeanor

15. Subject to a civil penalty of $10.

16. Subject to a penalty of $50.

Offense Statute	Description of Offense	Punishment Statute	Punishment
20-108(a)	Knowingly possessing, selling, receiving, etc., a vehicle that has had any identification or serial number altered or removed	20-108(a)	Class 2 misdemeanor
20-109(a)	Knowingly altering or removing any serial or identification numbers on parts of a vehicle, or knowingly placing an unauthorized number on any vehicle or part or allowing such actions	20-109(a)	Class I felony (mandatory app.)
20-109(b)	Intentionally concealing or misrepresenting true identity of a vehicle by altering or defacing a serial number, or allowing such actions on one's vehicle, or using or selling parts of a vehicle containing serial numbers with intent to conceal the identity of the vehicle	20-109(b)	Class I felony (mandatory app.)
Violation of Registration Provisions			
20-111(1)	Operating a vehicle which is not registered with DMV or which is not displaying current registration plates	20-176(a), (c)	Class 2 misdemeanor
20-111(2)	Knowingly displaying or possessing an altered, expired, or revoked registration card or plate	20-176(a), (c)	Class 2 misdemeanor (mandatory app.)
20-111(3)	Giving, lending, or borrowing a registration plate for use on another vehicle	20-111(3)	Class 3 misdemeanor
20-111(4)	Failing to surrender to DMV, upon demand, any title certificate, registration card, or plate which has been suspended or canceled	20-176(a), (c)	Class 2 misdemeanor
20-111(5)	Using false names or addresses or concealing or misrepresenting material facts in registration applications	20-111(5)	Class 1 misdemeanor
20-111(6)	Giving, lending, selling, or obtaining any title certificate for any purpose other than registration, sale, etc., of vehicle for which issued	20-111(6)	Class 2 misdemeanor
Perjury			
20-112*	Knowingly making any false affidavit or swearing or affirming falsely	20-112 20-17(5)	Class I felony (mandatory app.)
Failure to Obey Directions of Police or Firefighters			
20-114.1(a)	Willfully failing or refusing to comply with lawful orders of law-enforcement officer related to control of traffic	20-176(a), (c)	Class 2 misdemeanor (mandatory app.)

*Pursuant to G.S. 20-24(a), the court must require the driver convicted of this offense to surrender his or her driver's license to the court.

Offense Statute	Description of Offense	Punishment Statute	Punishment
20-114.1(b)	Willfully failing or refusing to comply with lawful orders of firefighters (at scene of fire) or rescue squads (at scene of an accident) related to traffic control	20-176(a), (c)	Class 2 misdemeanor (mandatory app.)

Equipment Violations

Tires

Offense Statute	Description of Offense	Punishment Statute	Punishment
20-122.1	Driving with unsafe tires	20-115 20-176(a), (b)	Infraction

Steering Mechanism

Offense Statute	Description of Offense	Punishment Statute	Punishment
20-123.1	Failing to maintain steering mechanism in good working order	20-115 20-176(a), (b)	Infraction

Speedometer

Offense Statute	Description of Offense	Punishment Statute	Punishment
20-123.2	Operating a vehicle without a working speedometer[17]	20-123.2(b)	Infraction

Brakes

Offense Statute	Description of Offense	Punishment Statute	Punishment
20-124(a)	Absence of brakes sufficient to stop and control vehicle	20-115 20-176(a), (b)	Infraction
20-124(a)	Failure to maintain brakes in conformity with regulations	20-115 20-176(a), (b)	Infraction
20-124(c)	Failure to maintain originally equipped brakes, including failure to maintain two separate means of applying brakes	20-115 20-176(a), (b)	Infraction
20-124(d)	Absence of at least one brake on motorcycle used on highway	20-115 20-176(a), (b)	Infraction
20-124(e)	Absence on trucks of brakes sufficient to stop vehicle within required distances	20-115 20-176(a), (b)	Infraction
20-124(el)	Absence of brakes acting on all wheels on specified trucks or tractor-trucks with trailers	20-115 20-176(a), (b)	Infraction

Selling Unapproved Brake Fluid or Lining

Offense Statute	Description of Offense	Punishment Statute	Punishment
20-124(h)	Selling any unapproved brake fluid or lining	20-124(h)	Class 2 misdemeanor

17. Penalty of no more than $25 and no license or insurance points.

Offense Statute	Description of Offense	Punishment Statute	Punishment
Horns and Warning Devices			
20-125(a)	Driving a vehicle without a horn audible up to 200 feet in normal conditions	20-115 20-176(a), (b)	Infraction
20-125(a)	Using a siren, compression, or spark plug whistle when not allowed	20-115 20-176(a), (b)	Infraction
20-125(a)	Using a horn for other than a reasonable warning or making any unnecessary loud or harsh sound by horn or other warning device	20-115 20-176(a), (b)	Infraction
Mirrors			
20-126(a)	Driving a vehicle on streets without a rearview mirror which provides unobstructed view (exempted vehicles in statute)	20-115 20-176(a), (b)	Infraction
20-126(a)	Driving a loaded vehicle which renders a rearview mirror ineffective without using a mirror that reflects the rear view	20-115 20-176(a), (b)	Infraction
20-126(b)	Operating a vehicle without an outside mirror on the driver's side (for vehicles assembled or sold after 1965)	20-115 20-176(a), (b)	Infraction
20-126(c)	Operating a motorcycle on streets without a rearview mirror that provides an unobstructed view of at least 200 feet	20-115 20-176(a), (b)	Infraction
Windshields			
20-127(a)	Operating a vehicle without a windshield wiper for cleaning snow, rain, moisture, etc., from the front windshield	20-115 20-176(a), (b)	Infraction
20-127(b)	Having tinted windows or windshield not meeting state standards	20-127(d) 20-176(a), (c)	Class 2 misdemeanor
Mufflers			
20-128(a)	Driving vehicle when muffler not in sufficiently good working order to prevent excessive noise or smoke	20-115 20-176(a), (b)	Infraction
20-128(b)	Using a muffler cut-out	20-115 20-176(a), (b)	Infraction
20-128(c)	Operating a motor vehicle without required emission control devices	20-115 20-176(a), (b)	Infraction
20-128.1(a)	Operating a gasoline-powered vehicle that emits visible air contaminants for longer than 5 seconds[18]	20-128.1(d) 20-176(a), (b)	Infraction

18. A person charged under this section has 30 days in which to repair the vehicle.

Offense Statute	Description of Offense	Punishment Statute	Punishment
20-128.1(a)	Operating a diesel-powered vehicle that emits visible contaminants of a specific shade or density for longer than 5 seconds[18]	20-128.1(d) 20-176 (a), (b)	Infraction

Lights

Offense Statute	Description of Offense	Punishment Statute	Punishment
20-129(a)(1)	Failing to have lights on from sunset to sunrise	20-115 20-176(a), (b)	Infraction
20-129(a)(2)	Failing to have lights on when a person cannot be seen clearly 400 feet ahead	20-115 20-176(a), (b)	Infraction
20-129(a)(4)	Failing to have lights on when windshield wipers are in use due to rain, fog, etc.[19]	20-129(a)(4)	Infraction
20-129(b)	Absence on vehicle of at least two headlamps (statute lists exceptions)	20-115 20-176(a), (b)	Infraction
20-129(c)	Absence on motorcycle of headlamp complying with requirements of statute	20-115 20-176(a), (b)	Infraction
20-129(c)	Failure to keep motorcycle lamps lighted while motorcycle in use on highway or public vehicular area	20-115 20-176(a), (b)	Infraction
20-129(d)	Absence of any of required rear lamps as listed in statute	20-115 20-176(a), (b)	Infraction
20-129(e)	Absence of required lamps or reflectors on bicycles used at night	20-115 20-176(a), (b)	Infraction
20-129(f)	Absence of required lights on other vehicles (farm tractors, etc.; see statute for details)	20-115 20-176(a), (b)	Infraction
20-129(g)	Selling or operating a vehicle or motorcycle without a stop lamp	20-115 20-176(a), (b)	Infraction
20-129.1(1)	Absence of two reflectors and one stop light on rear of bus or truck	20-115 20-176(a), (b)	Infraction
20-129.1(2)	Absence of additional specified lights and reflectors on certain trucks or buses	20-115 20-176(a), (b)	Infraction
20-129.1(3)	Absence of two clearance lamps on front, and one stop light at rear, on truck tractor	20-115 20-176(a), (b)	Infraction
20-129.1(4)	Absence of specified lights and reflectors on certain trailers or semi-trailers	20-115 20-176(a), (b)	Infraction
20-129.1(5)	Absence of specified lights and reflectors on certain large pole-trailers	20-115 20-176(a), (b)	Infraction
20-129.1(6)	Absence of required reflectors and stop lights on certain smaller trailers	20-115 20-176(a), (b)	Infraction
20-129.1(7),	Failure on vehicle of front-clearance lamps to reflect an amber color, or rear lamps and brake lights to reflect a red color	20-115 20-176(a), (b)	Infraction

18. A person charged under this section has 30 days in which to repair the vehicle.

19. Fined $5, but no court costs or license or insurance points.

Offense Statute	Description of Offense	Punishment Statute	Punishment
20-129.1(10)	Absence of combination marker lamp mounted on the bottom side rail at or near the center of each side of certain trailers showing amber color	20-115 20-176(a), (b)	Infraction
20-130.1(a)	Installing or using a red light on a vehicle (see 20-130.1(b) for vehicle exceptions)	20-130.1(e)	Class 1 misdemeanor (mandatory app.)
20-130.1(c)	Installing or using a blue light on a vehicle (see 20-130.1(d) for vehicle exceptions)	20-130.1(e)	Class 1 misdemeanor (mandatory app.)
20-130.3	Driving a vehicle in forward motion while displaying white or clear lights on the rear of the vehicle (does not apply to backup lights)	20-115 20-176(a), (b)	Infraction
20-134	Failing at required times to display certain lights on the front and rear of a vehicle parked or stopped on a highway (attended or unattended)	20-115 20-176(a), (b)	Infraction

Seat Belts

Offense Statute	Description of Offense	Punishment Statute	Punishment
20-135.2A	Failure of driver or front seat occupant to have seat safety belt properly fastened[20]	20-135.2A(e)	Infraction
20-135.2B	Transporting children in the open bed of a pickup truck[20]	20-135.2B(c)	Infraction

Smoke Screens

Offense Statute	Description of Offense	Punishment Statute	Punishment
20-136*	Driving, using, or possessing a vehicle with a mechanism capable of discharging an unusual amount of smoke or gas, or possessing such device	20-136(b) 20-17(a)(3)	Class I felony (mandatory app.)

Child Restraint Systems

Offense Statute	Description of Offense	Punishment Statute	Punishment
20-137.1	Transporting child less than 16 years of age without having him or her secured in passenger restraint system (or seat belt) meeting federal standards. Child under five (and weighing less than 40 pounds) must be in a child safety seat[21]	20-137.1(c)	Infraction

---

*Pursuant to G.S. 20-24(a), the court must require the driver convicted of this offense to surrender his or her driver's license to the court.

20. Penalty of $25; no court costs. Under G.S. 20-135.2A(f) and -135.2B(d), no license or insurance points are assessed.

21. Maximum $25 penalty but no license or insurance points. [*See* G.S. 20-137.1(d).]

Offense Statute	Description of Offense	Punishment Statute	Punishment

Rules of the Road Violations

Impaired Driving Offenses

Offense Statute	Description of Offense	Punishment Statute	Punishment
20-138.1*	Driving a vehicle while impaired or after consuming sufficient alcohol so that, at any relevant time after driving, the driver has a concentration of .08[22]	20-138.1(d) 20-179(g) 20-17(a)(2)	Level One: Up to $4,000 and 30 days to 24 months (mandatory app.)
20-138.1*	Driving a vehicle while impaired or after consuming sufficient alcohol so that, at any relevant time after driving, the driver has a concentration of .08[22]	20-138.1(d) 20-179(h) 20-17(a)(2)	Level Two: Up to $2,000 and 7 days (minimum) to 12 months (mandatory app.)
20-138.1*	Driving a vehicle while impaired or after consuming sufficient alcohol so that, at any relevant time after driving, the driver has a concentration of .08[22]	20-138.1(d) 20-179(i) 20-17(a)(2)	Level Three: Up to $1,000 and 72 hours (minimum) to 6 months (mandatory app.)

*Pursuant to G.S. 20-24(a), the court must require the driver convicted of this offense to surrender his or her driver's license to the court.

22. The driving-while-impaired sentencing statute (G.S. 20-179) contains several unique provisions. The punishments listed in this chart are the minimums and maximums allowable under the statute for each level of punishment, but for each level there are other relevant sentencing provisions.

Level One: 30 days to 24 months in jail. At least 30 days must be imposed, and this sentence cannot be suspended unless the defendant serves at least 30 days in jail. There is also a fine of up to $4,000.

Level Two: 7 days to 12 months in jail. At least 7 days must be imposed, and this sentence cannot be suspended unless the defendant serves at least 7 days in jail as a condition of special probation. There is also a fine of up to $2,000.

Level Three: 72 hours to 6 months in jail. A minimum of 72 hours must be imposed, and this sentence can be suspended only if the defendant meets certain conditions. The judge must require that the defendant do at least one of three things: 1) not drive for at least 90 days; 2) perform at least 72 hours of community service; or 3) serve at least 72 hours in jail under the special probation statute. There is also a fine of up to $1,000.

Level Four: 48 hours to 120 days in jail. A minimum of 48 hours must be imposed, and this sentence can be suspended only if the defendant meets certain conditions. The judge must require that the defendant do at least one of three things: 1) not drive for 60 days; 2) perform 48 hours of community service; or 3) serve 48 hours in jail under the special probation statute. There is also a fine of up to $500.

Level Five: 24 hours to 60 days in jail. A minimum of 24 hours must be imposed, and this sentence can be suspended only if the defendant meets certain conditions. The judge must require that the defendant do at least one of three things: 1) not drive for 30 days; 2) perform 24 hours of community service; or 3) serve 24 hours in jail under the special probation statute. There is also a fine of up to $200.

Under any level of punishment, if the defendant is placed on probation a substance abuse assessment is required, as is education or treatment as required by G.S. 20-17.6.

Under G.S. 20-17(a)(2), DMV must revoke a driver's license when it receives a record of the driver's final conviction of "impaired driving under G.S. 20-138.1."

A trial judge (under G.S. 20-179.3) may allow a limited driving privilege if punishment level 3, 4, or 5 was imposed and the criteria established by that statute are met.

Offense Statute	Description of Offense	Punishment Statute	Punishment
20-138.1*	Driving a vehicle while impaired or after consuming sufficient alcohol so that, at any relevant time after driving, the driver has a concentration of .08[22]	20-138.1(d) 20-179(j) 20-17(a)(2)	Level Four: Up to $500 and 48 hours (minimum) to 120 days (mandatory app.)
20-138.1*	Driving a vehicle while impaired or after consuming sufficient alcohol so that, at any relevant time after driving, the driver has a concentration of .08[22]	20-138.1(d) 20-179(k) 20-17(a)(2)	Level Five: Up to $200 and 24 hours (minimum) to 60 days
20-138.2(a)*	Impaired driving in a commercial vehicle or after consuming sufficient alcohol so that, at any relevant time after driving, the driver has a concentration of .04[23]	20-138.2(e) 20-17(a)(2)	Class 1 misdemeanor (mandatory app.)
20-138.2A	Operating commercial vehicle after consuming alcohol[23]	20-138.2A(c) 20-179 20-17(a)(13) 20-17.4	Class 3 misdemeanor $100 penalty for first offense (mandatory app.)
20-138.2B*	Driving school bus, school activity bus or child care vehicle after consuming alcohol[23]	20-138.2B(c) 20-17(a)(14) 20-179 20-19(c2)	Class 3 misdemeanor $100 penalty for first offense (mandatory app.)
20-138.2C (comm.)	Operating commercial vehicle while possessing alcoholic beverage	20-176(b)	Infraction
20-138.3(a)*	Driving by person under age 21 after consuming alcohol or drugs[24]	20-138.3(c) 20-13.2	Class 2 misdemeanor (mandatory app.)
20-138.5(a)*	Driving while impaired after being convicted of three or more offenses involving impaired driving within 7 years	20-138.5(b) 20-138.5(d)	Class F felony (mandatory app.)
20-138.7*	Transporting open container of alcoholic beverage after consuming alcohol[24]	20-138.7(e)	Class 3 misdemeanor for first offense (mandatory app.)

*Pursuant to G.S. 20-24(a), the court must require the driver convicted of this offense to surrender his or her driver's license to the court.

23. Under G.S. 20-17.4 a person convicted of violating G.S. 20-138.2A will be disqualified from driving a commercial vehicle. (*See* G.S. 20-17(a)(13) for revocation for driving commercial vehicle after consuming alcohol.) Violation of G.S. 20-138.2B results in revocation under G.S. 20-17(a)(14).

24. G.S. 20-13.2 requires revocation of the driver's license for a violation of G.S. 20-138.3. G.S. 20-17(a)(12) requires revocation for a second conviction under G.S. 20-138.7.

Offense Statute	Description of Offense	Punishment Statute	Punishment
Reckless Driving[25]			
20-140(a) (comm.)	Driving carelessly and heedlessly[25]	20-140(d)	Class 2 misdemeanor (mandatory app.)
20-140(b) (comm.)	Driving without due caution[25]	20-140(d)	Class 2 misdemeanor (mandatory app.)
Use of Controlled-access Highways[26]			
20-140.3(1)	Driving across a curb, dividing section, or dividing line on controlled-access highways	20-176(a), (b)	Infraction
20-140.3(2)	Making a left, semicircular, or U-turn when there is no opening provided for that purpose in the dividing curb, separation, or line on controlled-access highways	20-176(a), (b)	Infraction
20-140.3(3)	Driving in the wrong lane or wrong direction on controlled-access highways	20-176(a), (b)	Infraction
20-140.3(4)	Driving onto or from any controlled-access highway when such entrances and exits are not established by public authority	20-176(a), (b)	Infraction
20-140.3(5)	Stopping, parking, or leaving a vehicle (attended or unattended) on any part of the right-of-way	20-176(a), (b)	Infraction
20-140.3(6)	Failing to yield the right-of-way when entering the highway to a vehicle already traveling on highway	20-176(a), (b)	Infraction
Motorcycles and Mopeds			
20-140.4(a)(1)	Operating a motorcycle or moped with more persons than it is designated to carry[27]	20-140.4(c) 20-135.2A(e), (f)	Infraction
20-140.4(a)(2)	Operating a motorcycle or moped without an approved safety helmet[27]	20-140.4(c) 20-135.2A(e), (f)	Infraction

25. Reckless driving violations are subject to the following provisions for revocation or suspension of license: discretionary suspension under G.S. 20-16(a)(9) and -19(a) is not to exceed 6 months for conviction of one or more charges of reckless driving (and *one* or more charges of speeding in excess of 55 mph and not more than 80 mph) within a 12-month period. Mandatory revocation under G.S. 20-17(a)(6), (7), and -19(f) is for 1 year for conviction upon one charge of reckless driving while illegally transporting intoxicants for the purpose of sale or for *two* charges of reckless driving in 12 months.

26. G.S. 136-89.58 also creates certain controlled-access road offenses that roughly parallel those in G.S. 20-140.3 (but are Class 2 misdemeanors).

27. Fined according to G.S. 20-135.2A(e) and (f), which calls for $25 and no court costs or license or insurance points.

Offense Statute	Description of Offense	Punishment Statute	Punishment
Speeding[28]			
20-141(a)	Driving faster than is reasonable and prudent under conditions	20-176(a), (b)	Infraction
20-141(b) (comm. if going over 55 mph)	Operating vehicle in excess of following speeds (except where otherwise permitted in G.S. Ch. 20); 35 mph inside municipal corporate limits (for all vehicles); 55 mph outside municipal corporate limits (except as otherwise posted)	20-176(a), (b)	Infraction
20-141(e)	Violating speed limit set by local authority for streets *not* in state highway system (not to be more than 55 mph, and effective only if signs are posted)	20-176(a), (b)	Infraction
20-141(e1)	Violating speed limit on school property	20-141(e1)	Infraction (minimum $25)
20-141(f)	Violating speed limit set by local authority on streets in the state system and within corporate limits (effective when Department of Transportation passes concurring ordinance and signs are posted)	20-176(a), (b)	Infraction
20-141(g)	Violating minimum speed limit established on state highways or by local authorities (effective when appropriate signs giving notice are erected)	20-176(a), (b)	Infraction
20-141(j1)*	Driving more than 15 mph over speed limit[29]	20-141(j1) 20-16.1	Class 2 misdemeanor (mandatory app. if driver going over 55 mph)
20-141(j1)*	Driving over 80 mph[29]	20-141(j1) 20-16.1	Class 2 misdemeanor (mandatory app.)

*Pursuant to G.S. 20-24(a), the court must require the driver convicted of this offense to surrender his or her driver's license to the court.

28. All speeding violations are subject to the following provisions for suspension or revocation of license: discretionary suspension under G.S. 20-16(a)(10) and -19(b) is not to exceed 12 months if the person has been convicted of operating a motor vehicle over 75 mph where the maximum speed is less than 70 mph. Discretionary suspension under G.S. 20-16(a)(9) and -19(a) is not to exceed 6 months if the person has within a 12-month period been convicted of two or more charges of speeding over 55 mph and not more than 80 mph (or one or more charges of reckless driving and one or more charges of speeding in excess of 55 mph and not more than 80 mph). Mandatory suspension under G.S. 20-16.1 is for 30 days upon conviction of exceeding the speed limit by more than 15 mph if the person was also exceeding 55 mph at the time of the offense (or for 60 days upon conviction of a second or subsequent offense that occurred within 1 year of the first or prior offense). Same provisions apply if driver was exceeding 80 mph. A judge may grant limited driving privileges to a first offender under G.S. 20-16.1(a).

29. License suspended when speed is also over 55 mph. *See* G.S. 20-16.1. Mandatory app. required for more than 15 mph over limit while also over 55 mph.

Offense Statute	Description of Offense	Punishment Statute	Punishment
20-141(j2)	Driving in highway work zone in excess of posted speed[30]	20-141(j2)	Infraction
20-141(m)	Failing to reduce speed as necessary to avoid accident	20-176(a), (b)	Infraction

School Zones

Offense Statute	Description of Offense	Punishment Statute	Punishment
20-141.1 (comm.)	Violating speed limits set by the Board of Transportation or local authority for areas near schools (effective when signs are erected giving notice of school zone, speed limit, and days and hours)	20-176(a), (b)	Infraction (minimum penalty is $25)

Racing, Death by Vehicle, and Eluding Arrest

Offense Statute	Description of Offense	Punishment Statute	Punishment
20-141.3(a)*	Engaging in prearranged speed competition with another motor vehicle[31, 32]	20-141.3(a) 20-141.3(d)	Class 1 misdemeanor (mandatory app.)
20-141.3(b)	Willfully engaging in speed competition with another motor vehicle (not prearranged)[33]	20-141.3(b) 20-141.3(e)	Class 2 misdemeanor (mandatory app.)
20-141.3(c)*	Allowing or authorizing others to use one's motor vehicle in prearranged speed competition[31]	20-141.3(c) 20-141.3(d)	Class 1 misdemeanor (mandatory app.)
20-141.3(c)*	Placing or receiving a bet or wager on a prearranged speed competition[31]	20-141.3(c) 20-141.3(d)	Class 1 misdemeanor (mandatory app.)
20-141.4(al)*	Unintentionally causing death when driving while impaired[34]	20-141.4(b) 20-17(a)(9)	Class G felony (mandatory app.)
20-141.4(a2)*	Unintentionally causing death while engaged in violation other than DWI[34]	20-141.4(b) 20-17(a)(9)	Class 1 misdemeanor (mandatory app.)

*Pursuant to G.S. 20-24(a), the court must require the driver convicted of this offense to surrender his or her driver's license to the court.

30. Must pay $250 penalty.

31. Under G.S. 20-141.3(d) a driver convicted under this subsection has his or her license revoked for 3 years by the CMV; after 18 months DMV may issue a new license upon such terms and condition as it sees fit. G.S. 20-141.3(f) apparently makes the provisions of G.S. 20-24 applicable to this offense. Thus under G.S. 20-24(a), the court should pick up the defendant's driver's license.

32. Under G.S. 20-141.3(g) any vehicle used by a person convicted under this subsection is to be forfeited and sold at public auction. If the owner of the vehicle can show that it was used in prearranged racing without his or her consent and that there were no reasonable grounds to believe it would be so used, the vehicle may be recovered.

33. Under G.S. 20-141.3(e) the CMV may suspend for up to 1 year the license of a driver convicted under this subsection.

34. Under G.S. 20-17(a)(9) and -19(f), DMV must revoke for 1 year the license of a driver convicted of death by vehicle. If the offense involved impaired driving, then the revocation is permanent (G.S. 20-19(i)).

Offense Statute	Description of Offense	Punishment Statute	Punishment
20-141.5*	Speeding or otherwise attempting to elude arrest[35]	20-145.5	Class 1 misdemeanor or Class H felony (mandatory app.)

Failing to Stop for Railroad Signal or Tracks

Offense Statute	Description of Offense	Punishment Statute	Punishment
20-142.1(a) (comm.)	Failing to stop at railroad grade crossing for electrical signal, gate, audible signal, or train in hazardous proximity to crossing	20-142.1 (d) 20-176(a), (b)	Infraction
20-142.1(b) (comm.)	Driving through crossing gate while gate is closed, opening, or closing	20-142.1(d) 20-176(a), (b)	Infraction
20-142.2 (comm.)	Failure to stop at stop sign erected at dangerous railroad crossing by Department of Transportation	20-142.2 20-176(a), (b)	Infraction
20-142.3 (comm.)	Failing to stop; certain kinds of vehicles at all railroad crossings (exceptions noted in statute)	20-142.3(c) 20-176(a), (b)	Infraction
20-142.4(a),(b)	Crossing a railroad track with a tractor or with other equipment that normally has an operating speed of 5 mph or less without giving notice to a railroad superintendent	20-142.4(f) 20-176(a), (b)	Infraction
20-142.4(a),(c)	Crossing a railroad track with a tractor or with other equipment that normally has an operating speed of 5 mph or less without stopping first, listening and looking in both directions, and crossing when safe (doesn't apply to crossings where authorities have determined no trains are running)	20-142.4(f) 20-176(a), (b)	Infraction
20-142.4(a),(d)	Crossing a railroad track with a tractor or with other equipment that normally has an operating speed of 5 mph or less when signal, gates, or flagman are giving a warning	20-142.4(f) 20-176(a), (b)	Infraction
20-142.5 (comm.)	Driving into intersection, crosswalk, or railroad grade crossing in manner to obstruct vehicles, pedestrians, or trains	20-142.5 20-176(a), (b)	Infraction

Driving on Wrong Side of Road

Offense Statute	Description of Offense	Punishment Statute	Punishment
20-146(a) (comm.)	Failing to drive on right half of highway of sufficient width (exceptions noted in statute)	20-176(a), (b)	Infraction
20-146(b)	Failing to drive in the right lane when driving below speed limit (except when passing or turning left)	20-176(a), (b)	Infraction
20-146(c) (comm.)	Driving to left of center on a road with four or more lanes with two-way movement of traffic, except when authorized by signs or to avoid obstructions	20-176(a), (b)	Infraction

*Pursuant to G.S. 20-24(a), the court must require the driver convicted of this offense to surrender his or her driver's license to the court.

35. This offense is usually a misdemeanor, but it is a felony if any two of the aggravating factors in subsection (b) are present.

Offense Statute	Description of Offense	Punishment Statute	Punishment
20-146(d)(1)	Failure to: (a) drive within a single lane or (b) ascertain that a lane change can be made safely in a road with two lanes moving in same direction	20-176(a), (b)	Infraction
20-146(d)(2) (comm.)	Driving in center lane of road with three or more lanes and two-way traffic, unless passing a vehicle, turning left, or in accordance with traffic signs	20-176(a), (b)	Infraction
20-146(d)(3)	Failure to: (a) obey traffic control devices directing that specified traffic use a designated lane or (b) obey traffic control devices designating lanes for traffic moving in certain direction	20-176(a), (b)	Infraction
20-146(d)(4)	Failure to obey signals as to lane changes	20-176(a)(b)	Infraction
20-146(e)	Impeding traffic by using lane next to median of dual-lane highway, unless traveling at speed limit or preparing to turn left (road must be posted)	20-176(a), (b)	Infraction
20-146.1(a)	Depriving a motorcycle of full use of a lane (except when two motorcyles are abreast in a single lane)	20-176(a), (b)	Infraction
20-146.1(b)	Operating more than two motorcycles abreast in single lane	20-176(a), (b)	Infraction
20-147 (comm.)	Failing to drive vehicle on right half of highway in crossing an intersection of two highways or of a highway and railroad right-of-way, unless the right side is obstructed	20-176(a), (b)	Infraction
20-148	Failing to pass a vehicle going in the opposite direction to the right, and leaving at least half of the road, if possible, for vehicle going in opposite direction	20-176(a), (b)	Infraction

Improper Passing

Offense Statute	Description of Offense	Punishment Statute	Punishment
20-149(a) (comm.)	Passing another vehicle going in same direction without passing at least 2 feet to left of other vehicle (G.S. 20-150.1 permits passing on right in certain instances)	20-176(a), (b)	Infraction
20-149(a) (comm.)	When passing on the left, returning to right lane before being safely clear of the passed vehicle	20-176(a), (b)	Infraction
20-149(b)	When being passed by another vehicle on the left, failing to give way to the right on hearing an audible warning signal from passing vehicle (not applicable if being passed on right under G.S. 20-150.1)[36]	20-176(a), (b) 20-149(b)(1) 20-149(b)(2)	Infraction; or Class 1 misdemeanor; or Class 2 misdemeanor (mandatory app.)

36. This offense is usually an infraction, but it is a misdemeanor if a collision results (Class 1 in case of serious injury, and Class 2 when there is any personal injury or property damage).

Offense Statute	Description of Offense	Punishment Statute	Punishment
20-150(a) (comm.)	Passing on left when the left side of roadway is not clearly visible and free of traffic for sufficient distance to allow movement in safety	20-176(a), (b)	Infraction
20-150(b) (comm.)	Passing on the crest of a grade or on a curve when driver cannot see roadway ahead for at least 500 feet	20-176(a), (b)	Infraction
20-150(c) (comm.)	Passing at a railway grade crossing or at an intersection, unless allowed to do so by a police officer	20-176(a), (b)	Infraction
20-150(d) (comm.)	Driving to left of a visible center line on the crest of a hill or on a curve	20-176(a), (b)	Infraction
20-150(e) (comm.)	Passing another vehicle when signs or markings clearly indicate that passing should not be attempted	20-176(a), (b)	Infraction
20-150.1	Passing on right permitted	No violation	

Following Too Closely

Offense Statute	Description of Offense	Punishment Statute	Punishment
20-152(a) (comm.)	Following a vehicle more closely than is reasonable and prudent, with regard for speed of other vehicles, traffic, and road conditions	20-176(a), (b)	Infraction
20-152(b)	When following a vehicle and being passed by another, failing to allow passing vehicle enough space to reenter his original lane of traffic (subject to exceptions listed in statute)	20-176(a), (b)	Infraction

Improper Turning

Offense Statute	Description of Offense	Punishment Statute	Punishment
20-153(a)	When approaching or turning right at an intersection, failing to keep vehicle as close as practicable to the right curb	20-176(a), (b)	Infraction
20-153(b)	When approaching intersection to turn left, failing to use extreme left-hand lane lawfully available	20-176(a), (b)	Infraction
20-153(b)	When turning left, failing to turn into a lane lawfully available to traffic leaving the intersection	20-176(a), (b)	Infraction
20-153(c)	Failure to obey lawful traffic control devices modifying the general turning rules of G.S. 20-153	20-176(a), (b)	Infraction
20-154(a)	Starting, stopping, or turning without first seeing that the movement can be made safely	20-176(a), (b)	Infraction
20-154(a)	Failure to sound the horn before making a movement that may affect pedestrians	20-176(a), (b)	Infraction
20-154(a)	Failure to give a signal of intention when stopping, starting, or turning when another vehicle may be affected (requirements for signals set out in statute)	20-176(a), (b)	Infraction
20-154(a)	Backing a vehicle in unsafe manner or in a manner that interferes with other traffic	20-176(a), (b)	Infraction

Offense Statute	Description of Offense	Punishment Statute	Punishment
Failing to Yield Right-of-way			
20-155(a)	When two vehicles enter intersection at approximately the same time, failure by driver on left to yield right-of-way	20-176(a), (b)	Infraction
20-155(b)	Failure to yield to oncoming traffic when turning left	20-176(a), (b)	Infraction
20-155(c)	Failure to yield to pedestrian at clearly marked crosswalks or regular pedestrian crossing (exceptions noted in statute)	20-176(a), (b)	Infraction
20-155(d)	When approaching a traffic circle, failing to yield to vehicle already in circle	20-176(a), (b)	Infraction
20-156(a)	When entering a public highway from a private road, failing to yield to traffic on the highway	20-176(a), (b)	Infraction
20-156(b)	Failure to yield right-of-way to police, fire, and other emergency vehicles with sirens and lights on	20-176(a), (b)	Infraction
20-157(a) (comm.)	Upon approach of a fire, police, rescue vehicle, etc., with lights and siren on, failing to stop on right side of road until emergency vehicle passes	20-157(a)	Class 2 misdemeanor (mandatory app.)
Actions Prohibited in Emergencies			
20-157(b)	Following closer than one block any fire apparatus traveling in response to a fire alarm	20-176(a), (b)	Infraction
20-157(b)	Driving into or parking within one block where fire apparatus has stopped to answer an alarm	20-176(a), (b)	Infraction
20-157(c)	Outside of a city, following closer than 400 feet any fire apparatus traveling in response to a fire alarm	20-176(a), (b)	Infraction
20-157(c)	Outside of a city, driving into or parking within 400 feet of where fire apparatus has stopped to answer an alarm	20-176(a), (b)	Infraction
20-157(d)	Driving over a fire hose or any other equipment that is being used at a fire	20-176(a), (b)	Infraction
20-157(d)	Blocking firefighting apparatus from its source of supply	20-176(a), (b)	Infraction
20-157(e)	Parking or leaving a vehicle within 100 feet of police, fire, or rescue vehicles which are investigating or assisting at an accident	20-176(a), (b)	Infraction
Failing to Stop			
20-158(b)(1) (comm.)	Failure to stop at intersections in obedience to posted stop sign or failure to yield right-of-way after stopping at stop sign	20-176(a), (b)	Infraction

Offense Statute	Description of Offense	Punishment Statute	Punishment
20-158(b)(2) (comm.)	Failure to stop at intersection and yield right-of-way when traffic light emits a steady (or strobe) red light (also failure to enter intersection with due care when light is green)	20-176(a), (b)	Infraction
20-158(b)(3) (comm.)	Failure to stop at intersection and yield when a flashing red light controls traffic in driver's lane	20-176(a), (b)	Infraction
20-158(b)(4) (comm.)	Failure to proceed with caution and yield the right-of-way to vehicles in or approaching the intersection when a flashing yellow light controls the intersection	20-176(a), (b)	Infraction
20-158(b)(5)	When required to stop, (1) failing to stop at the appropriate marked line, (2) if no line, failing to stop before marked crosswalk, or (3) if no crosswalk, failing to stop at the point nearest the intersecting street where the driver has a view of approaching traffic	20-176(a), (b)	Infraction
20-158(c)(1) (comm.)	Failure to obey a stop sign and yield right-of-way at place other than at an intersection	20-176(a), (b)	Infraction
20-158(c)(2) (comm.)	Failure to obey a traffic light emitting a steady red light at place other than an intersection	20-176(a), (b)	Infraction
20-158(c)(3) (comm.)	Failure to stop and yield to pedestrians or other vehicles at a flashing red light at place other than an intersection	20-176(a), (b)	Infraction
20-158(c)(4) (comm.)	Failure to proceed with caution or yield at a yellow traffic light at place other than an intersection	20-176(a), (b)	Infraction
20-158(c)(5)	When required to stop, (1) failing to stop at the appropriate marked line, (2) if no line, failing to stop before marked crosswalk, or (3) if no crosswalk, failing to stop before proceeding past the signal device	20-176(a), (b)	Infraction

Failure to Yield at Yield Signs

Offense Statute	Description of Offense	Punishment Statute	Punishment
20-158.1	Failure to yield at intersections where yield signs have been erected	20-176(a), (b)	Infraction

Driving through Safety Zones or on Sidewalks

Offense Statute	Description of Offense	Punishment Statute	Punishment
20-160 (comm.)	Driving through or over a safety zone or driving on a sidewalk (except upon a driveway)	20-176(a), (b)	Infraction

Parking on Highway

Offense Statute	Description of Offense	Punishment Statute	Punishment
20-161(a)	Outside of the city limits, parking or leaving a vehicle (attended or unattended) on the paved or main-traveled portion of road or bridge (unless vehicle is so disabled that it was impossible to avoid stopping)	20-176(a), (b)	Infraction

Offense Statute	Description of Offense	Punishment Statute	Punishment
20-161(b)	Outside of the city limits, parking or leaving a vehicle on the shoulder of the road (unless the vehicle can be clearly seen 200 feet away and does not obstruct normal traffic)	20-176(a), (b)	Infraction
20-161(c)	Failing to display warning signals on any truck, truck tractor, trailer, or semi-trailer in a manner required by the U.S. Department of Transportation and DMV as long as the vehicle is disabled on any portion of the highway	20-176(a), (b)	Infraction
20-161.1	Parking or leaving a vehicle at night on a road or on a side road entering a highway while shining its bright lights when facing oncoming traffic	20-176(a), (b)	Infraction
20-162(a)	Parking or leaving a vehicle (attended or unattended) (1) in front of a private driveway, (2) within 15 feet of a fire hydrant, (3) within 15 feet of fire station entrance, or (4) within 25 feet from the intersection of curb lines or, if none, then within 15 feet of the intersection of property lines	20-176(a), (b)	Infraction
20-162(b)	Parking or leaving a vehicle (attended or unattended) in a public vehicular area, street, highway, or road designated as a fire lane	20-176(a), (b)	Infraction
20-163	Leaving a vehicle unattended on a highway or public vehicular area without stopping engine, setting the brake, properly parking the vehicle	20-176(a), (b)	Infraction

Traveling Wrong Way on One-way Street

Offense Statute	Description of Offense	Punishment Statute	Punishment
20-165.1	Willfully going wrong way on one-way street designated and marked as such	20-176(a), (b)	Infraction

Accident Responsibility Laws

Offense Statute	Description of Offense	Punishment Statute	Punishment
20-166(a)*	Failure to stop by driver who knew or should have known he or she was involved in accident and that accident caused death or injury to any person[37]	20-166(a) 20-17(a)(4)	Class H felony (mandatory app.)
20-166(b)*	Failure of driver, as set forth in G.S. 20-166(a), to give required information and render assistance[37]	20-166(b) 20-17(a)(4)	Class 1 misdemeanor (mandatory app.)
20-166(c)	Failure of driver involved in accident causing property damage or personal injury or death (if driver did not know of injury or death) to stop at scene of accident	20-166(c)	Class 1 misdemeanor (mandatory app.)

*Pursuant to G.S. 20-24(a), the court must require the driver convicted of this offense to surrender his or her driver's license to the court.

37. G.S. 20-17(a)(4) and -19(f) require license revocation for 1 year.

Offense Statute	Description of Offense	Punishment Statute	Punishment
20-166(c1) (comm.)	Failure of driver, as set forth in G.S. 20-166(c), to give required information	20-166(cl)	Class 1 misdemeanor (mandatory app.)
20-166.1(a) (comm.)	Failure by driver to make required reports, by quickest means, to police if accident involves personal injury, death, or $1,000 or more in property damage	20-166.1(k) 20-176(c) 20-4.01(33b)	Class 2 misdemeanor (mandatory app.)
20-166.1(b)	Failure by driver involved in accident to make report of financial responsibility to DMV if so requested by DMV	20-166.1(k) 20-176(c)	Class 2 misdemeanor (mandatory app.)
20-166.1(c) (comm.)	Failure by driver in collision with parked vehicle to make a timely report to owner and DMV	20-166.1(k) 20-176(c)	Class 2 misdemeanor (mandatory app.)
Transportation of Spent Nuclear Fuel			
20-167.1	Transporting spent nuclear fuel without notifying State Highway Patrol[38]	20-167.1(d)	Class 3 misdemeanor (mandatory app.)
Violations at Pedestrian Crosswalks			
20-173(a)	Where traffic control signals are not in operation, failing to yield to pedestrians at a marked crosswalk or at an unmarked crosswalk near an intersection	20-176(a), (b)	Infraction
20-173(b)	Passing a vehicle stopped at a pedestrian crosswalk	20-176(a), (b)	Infraction
20-173(c)	When entering highway from private road or driveway, failing to yield to pedestrians or bicyclists on sidewalk	20-176(a), (b3)	Infraction
Standing, Sitting, or Lying in Street			
20-174.1	Willfully standing, sitting, or lying on a highway in such a manner as to impede traffic	20-174.1(b)	Class 2 misdemeanor
Soliciting Rides, Employment, or Business on Highways			
20-175(a)	Standing in any portion of a state highway for purpose of soliciting a ride from a driver (except upon the shoulders of the highway)	20-176(a), (b)	Infraction
20-175(b)	Standing or loitering in the main traveled portion, including the shoulders and median, of a state highway or street, or stopping a vehicle for the purpose of soliciting employment, business, or contributions that impedes the movement of traffic	20-176(a), (b)	Infraction

38. Minimum fine is $500.

Offense Statute	Description of Offense	Punishment Statute	Punishment
Violating Limited Driving Privileges			
20-179.3(j)* 20-16.1(b)(4)	Violating conditions of limited driving privilege[39, 40]	20-179.3(j) 20-28(a)	Class 1 misdemeanor (mandatory app.)
Failure to Dim Lights			
20-181	Failure to dim headlights when meeting another vehicle or when following another at a distance of less than 200 feet	20-181	Infraction (up to $10 penalty)
Equipment Inspection Laws			
20-183.8(a)	Failing to display a current and valid inspection certificate[41]	20-183.8(a)	Infraction
20-183.8(c)	Forging inspection certificate	20-183.8(c)	Class I felony (mandatory app.)
Passing Stopped School Bus			
20-217(a) (comm.)	Failure to stop and remain stopped when approaching a stopped school bus engaged in receiving or discharging passengers and while bus has mechanical stop signal (or stop lights) displayed (exceptions listed in statute)	20-217(e)	Class 2 misdemeanor (mandatory app.)
Bus Driver Rules			
20-217(d)	Stopping school bus to receive or discharge passengers where passengers would have to cross a roadway	20-217(e)	Class 2 misdemeanor
20-218(b)	Driving a loaded school bus over 45 mph, or driving a school activity bus over 55 mph	20-218(c)	Class 3 misdemeanor
20-218.2	Driving an activity bus for nonprofit organization for a nonprofit purpose over 55 mph	20-218.2	Class 3 misdemeanor

*Pursuant to G.S. 20-24(a), the court must require the driver convicted of this offense to surrender his or her driver's license to the court.

39. Under G.S. 20-16.1(b)(4) the punishment is the same as for driving while license suspended in violation of G.S. 20-28.

40. For a first offense under this section, the license is revoked for an additional year; for a second offense, 2 additional years; a third or subsequent offense brings permanent revocation. The licensee is entitled to apply for restoration of the license early according to schedule set forth in G.S. 20-28(c).

41. Penalty of no more than $50.

Offense Statute	Description of Offense	Punishment Statute	Punishment
Insurance Violations			
20-313(a) (comm.)	Operating or allowing one's vehicle registered in this state to be operated without the "required financial responsibility"	20-313(a)	Class 1 misdemeanor (mandatory app.)
20-313.1(a)	Making a false certification concerning financial responsibility	20-313.1(a)	Class 1 misdemeanor (mandatory app.)
20-313.1(b)	Giving false information to DMV concerning another's financial responsibility, knowing or having reason to believe that such information is false	20-313.1(b)	Class 1 misdemeanor (mandatory app.)

Index to Punishment Chart for North Carolina Motor Vehicle Offenses

Major offenses are listed in alphabetical order, showing the section number for each.

Accident responsibility laws
  failure to give information, 20-166(c), (c1)
  hit-and-run, death or injury, 20-166(a)
  hit-and-run, property damage, 20-166(c)
  report of accident, 20-166.1
Activity bus speed limits, 20-218.2

Backing vehicle, 20-154(a)

Car theft and related offenses
  altered serial number, 20-108, -109
  false report of theft, 20-102.1
  removing vehicle parts, 20-107
  rented vehicle (failure to return), 20-106.1
  stolen vehicles, 20-106
Certificates of title, 20-72 through -74
Child care vehicle, 20-138.2B
Commercial licenses
  driving while impaired, 20-138.2, -138.2A
  driving without a commercial license, 20-37.12(a)
  failure to report traffic conviction, 20-37.18
  license suspended, revoked, cancelled, 20-37.19(a), (b)
  more than one license, 20-37.19(b)(2)

Dealer plates, 20-79
Death by vehicle, 20-141.4
Dim lights, 20-181
Driver's license violations
  age limits, 20-10, -10.1
  driving without license (NOL) or violating restrictions, 20-7, -29.1
  illegal activity relating to license, 20-29, -29.1, -30 through -32, and -34
  learner's permit, 20-11, -12.1
  no operator's license, 20-7(a)
  parking privileges for handicapped drivers, 20-37.6
  special I.D. card, 20-37.7
  suspended or revoked license, 20-16.1(b), -28
Driving while impaired, 20-138.1, -138.2, -138.5

Equipment violations
  brakes, 20-124
  child restraint systems, 20-137.1
  horns and warning devices, 20-125
  lights, 20-129, -129.1, -130.1, -130.3, and -134
  mirrors, 20-126
  mufflers, 20-128
  seat belts, 20-135.2A, -135.2B
  selling unapproved brake fluid or lining, 20-124(h)
  smoke screens, 20-136
  speedometer, 20-123.2
  steering mechanism, 20-123.1
  tires, 20-122.1
  windshields, 20-127

Following too closely, 20-152

Inspection laws, 20-183.8(a), -183.8(c)
Insurance violations, 20-313(a), -313.1

Limited driving privileges, 20-16.1, -179.3

No operator's license (NOL), 20-7
Nuclear fuel, 20-167.1

Passing, 20-149 through -150.1
Pedestrian crosswalks, 20-173
Perjury, 20-112
Pickup truck, transporting children, 20-135.2B
Police or fire directions, 20-114.1

Racing, 20-141.3
Right-of-way, 20-155 through -158
Rules of the road violations
- controlled-access highways, 20-140.3
- death by vehicle, 20-141.4
- dim lights, 20-181
- driving after consuming alcohol, 20-138.2A, -138.2B, and -138.3
- driving commercial vehicle while possessing alcoholic beverage, 20-138.2C
- driving while impaired (DWI), 20-12.1, -138.1, 138.2, -138.5, and -138.7
- fire, police, and rescue vehicles, 20-156, -157
- following too closely, 20-152
- motorcycles and mopeds, 20-140.4, -146.1
- one-way streets, 20-165.1
- parking, 20-161, -161.1, -162, and -163
- passing, 20-149 through -150.1
- passing stopped school bus, 20-217
- racing, 20-141.3
- railroad grade crossings, 20-142.1 through -142.5
- reckless driving, 20-140
- right-of-way, 20-155 through -157(a)
- safety zones or sidewalks, 20-160
- school zones, 20-141.1
- speeding, 20-141
- speeding to elude arrest, 20-141.5
- stop signs and red lights, 20-158
- turning, 20-153, -154
- work zone, 20-141
- wrong side of road or improper lane, 20-146 through -148
- wrong way on one-way street, 20-165.1
- yield signs, 20-158.1

Salvage titles, 20-71.4
School activity bus, 20-138.2B, -218
School bus driver consuming alcohol, 20-138.2B
School bus speed limits, 20-218
Soliciting rides, employment, or business on highways, 20-175
Speeding, 20-141
Standing, sitting, or lying in street, 20-174.1
Stopped school bus, 20-217

Transfer of title or interest, 20-72 through -74
Transporting open container of alcoholic beverage, 20-138.7

Vehicle registration
- altered or forged title, 20-71
- altered plate, 20-63
- failure to display registration card, 20-57(c)
- registration or plate violations, 20-50, -111

Waiver list, see Chapter 4 of Part One

Yield signs, 20-158.1

Appendix B
North Carolina Motor Vehicle Statutes

Appendix B
North Carolina Motor Vehicle Statutes Chapter 20

Article 1. Division of Motor Vehicles

§ 20-4.01. Definitions

Unless the context requires otherwise, the following definitions apply throughout this Chapter to the defined words and phrases and their cognates:

(1a) Alcohol.—Any substance containing any form of alcohol, including ethanol, methanol, propanol, and isopropanol.

(1b) Alcohol Concentration.—The concentration of alcohol in a person, expressed either as:

- a. Grams of alcohol per 100 milliliters of blood; or
- b. Grams of alcohol per 210 liters of breath.

The results of a defendant's alcohol concentration determined by a chemical analysis of the defendant's breath or blood shall be reported to the hundredths. Any result between hundredths shall be reported to the next lower hundredth.

(1c) Business District.—The territory prescribed as such by ordinance of the Board of Transportation.

(2) Canceled.—As applied to driver's licenses and permits, a declaration that a license or permit which was issued through error or fraud is void and terminated.

(2a) Class A Motor Vehicle.—A combination of motor vehicles that meets either of the following descriptions:

- a. Has a combined GVWR of at least 26,001 pounds and includes as part of the combination a towed unit that has a GVWR of at least 10,001 pounds.
- b. Has a combined GVWR of less than 26,001 pounds and includes as part of the combination a towed unit that has a GVWR of at least 10,001 pounds.

(2b) Class B Motor Vehicle.—Any of the following:

- a. A single motor vehicle that has a GVWR of at least 26,001 pounds.
- b. A combination of motor vehicles that includes as part of the combination a towing unit that has a GVWR of at least 26,001 pounds and a towed unit that has a GVWR of less than 10,001 pounds.

(2c) Class C Motor Vehicle.—Any of the following:

- a. A single motor vehicle not included in Class B.
- b. A combination of motor vehicles not included in Class A or Class B.

(3) Repealed by Session Laws 1979, c. 667, s. 1.

(3a) Chemical Analysis.—A test or tests of the breath, blood, or other bodily fluid or substance of a person to determine the person's alcohol concentration or presence of an impairing substance, performed in accordance with G.S. 20-139.1, including duplicate or sequential analyses.

(3b) Chemical Analyst.—A person granted a permit by the Department of Health and Human Services under G.S. 20-139.1 to perform chemical analyses.

(3c) Commercial Driver's License (CDL).—A license issued by a state to an individual who resides in the state that authorizes the individual to drive a class of commercial motor vehicle. A "nonresident commercial driver's license (NRCDL)" is issued by a state to an individual who resides in a foreign jurisdiction.

(3d) Commercial Motor Vehicle.—Any of the following motor vehicles that are designed or used to transport passengers or property:

a. A Class A motor vehicle that has a combined GVWR of at least 26,001 pounds and includes as part of the combination a towed unit that has a GVWR of at least 10,001 pounds.

b. A Class B motor vehicle.

c. A Class C motor vehicle that meets either of the following descriptions:

1. Is designed to transport 16 or more passengers, including the driver.
2. Is transporting hazardous materials and is required to be placarded in accordance with 49 C.F.R. Part 172, Subpart F.

d. Repealed by Session Laws 1999, c. 330, s. 9, effective December 1, 1999.

(4) Commissioner.—The Commissioner of Motor Vehicles.

(4a) Conviction.—A conviction for an offense committed in North Carolina or another state:

a. In-State. When referring to an offense committed in North Carolina, the term means any of the following:

1. A final conviction of a criminal offense, including a no contest plea.
2. A determination that a person is responsible for an infraction, including a no contest plea.
3. An unvacated forfeiture of cash in the full amount of a bond required by Article 26 of Chapter 15A of the General Statutes.
4. A third or subsequent prayer for judgment continued within any five-year period.

b. Out-of-State. When referring to an offense committed outside North Carolina, the term means any of the following:

1. An unvacated adjudication of guilt.
2. A determination that a person has violated or failed to comply with the law in a court of original jurisdiction or an authorized administrative tribunal.
3. An unvacated forfeiture of bail or collateral deposited to secure the person's appearance in court.
4. A violation of a condition of release without bail, regardless of whether or not the penalty is rebated, suspended, or probated.

(4b) Crash.—Any event that results in injury or property damage attributable directly to the motion of a motor vehicle or its load. The terms collision, accident, and crash and their cognates are synonymous.

(5) Dealer.—Every person engaged in the business of buying, selling, distributing, or exchanging motor vehicles, trailers or semitrailers in this State, having an established place of business in this State and being subject to the tax levied by G.S. 105-89.

The terms "motor vehicle dealer," "new motor vehicle dealer," and "used motor vehicle dealer" shall have the meaning set forth in G.S. 20-286.

(5a) Disqualification.—A withdrawal of the privilege to drive a commercial motor vehicle.

(6) Division.—The Division of Motor Vehicles acting directly or through its duly authorized officers and agents.

(7) Driver.—The operator of a vehicle, as defined in subdivision (25). The terms "driver" and "operator" and their cognates are synonymous.

(7a) Employer.—Any person who owns or leases a commercial motor vehicle or assigns a person to drive a commercial motor vehicle.

(8) Essential Parts.—All integral and body parts of a vehicle of any type required to be registered hereunder, the removal, alteration, or substitution of which would tend to conceal the identity of the vehicle or substantially alter its appearance, model, type, or mode of operation.

(9) Established Place of Business.—Except as provided in G.S. 20-286, the place actually occupied by a dealer or manufacturer at which a permanent business of bargaining, trading, and selling motor vehicles is or will be carried on and at which the books, records, and files necessary and incident to the conduct of the business of automobile dealers or manufacturers shall be kept and maintained.

(10) Explosives.—Any chemical compound or mechanical mixture that is commonly used or intended for the purpose of producing an explosion and which contains any oxidizing and com-

bustive units or other ingredients in such proportions, quantities, or packing that an ignition by fire, by friction, by concussion, by percussion, or by detonator of any part of the compound or mixture may cause such a sudden generation of highly heated gases that the resultant gaseous pressures are capable of producing destructible effects on contiguous objects or of destroying life or limb.

(11) Farm Tractor.—Every motor vehicle designed and used primarily as a farm implement for drawing plows, mowing machines, and other implements of husbandry.

(11a) For-Hire Motor Carrier.—A person who transports passengers or property by motor vehicle for compensation.

(12) Foreign Vehicle.—Every vehicle of a type required to be registered hereunder brought into this State from another state, territory, or country, other than in the ordinary course of business, by or through a manufacturer or dealer and not registered in this State.

(12a) Gross Vehicle Weight Rating (GVWR).—The value specified by the manufacturer as the maximum loaded weight of a vehicle. The GVWR of a combination vehicle is the GVWR of the power unit plus the GVWR of the towed unit or units. When a vehicle is determined by an enforcement officer to be structurally altered from the manufacturer's original design, the license weight or the total weight of the vehicle or combination of vehicles may be deemed as the GVWR for the purpose of enforcing this Chapter.

(12b) Hazardous Materials.—Materials designated as hazardous by the United States Secretary of Transportation under 49 U.S.C. § 1803.

(13) Highway.—The entire width between property or right-of-way lines of every way or place of whatever nature, when any part thereof is open to the use of the public as a matter of right for the purposes of vehicular traffic. The terms "highway" and "street" and their cognates are synonymous.

(14) House Trailer.—Any trailer or semitrailer designed and equipped to provide living or sleeping facilities and drawn by a motor vehicle.

(14a) Impairing Substance.—Alcohol, controlled substance under Chapter 90 of the General Statutes, any other drug or psychoactive substance capable of impairing a person's physical or mental faculties, or any combination of these substances.

(15) Implement of Husbandry.—Every vehicle which is designed for agricultural purposes and used exclusively in the conduct of agricultural operations.

(16) Intersection.—The area embraced within the prolongation of the lateral curblines or, if none, then the lateral edge of roadway lines of two or more highways which join one another at any angle whether or not one such highway crosses the other.

Where a highway includes two roadways 30 feet or more apart, then every crossing of each roadway of such divided highway by an intersecting highway shall be regarded as a separate intersection. In the event that such intersecting highway also includes two roadways 30 feet or more apart, then every crossing of two roadways of such highways shall be regarded as a separate intersection.

(17) License.—Any driver's license or any other license or permit to operate a motor vehicle issued under or granted by the laws of this State including:

a. Any temporary license or learner's permit;
b. The privilege of any person to drive a motor vehicle whether or not such person holds a valid license; and
c. Any nonresident's operating privilege.

(18) Local Authorities.—Every county, municipality, or other territorial district with a local board or body having authority to adopt local police regulations under the Constitution and laws of this State.

(19) Manufacturer.—Every person, resident, or nonresident of this State, who manufactures or assembles motor vehicles.

(20) Manufacturer's Certificate.—A certification on a form approved by the Division, signed by the manufacturer, indicating the name of the person or dealer to whom the therein-described vehicle is transferred, the date of transfer and that such vehicle is the first transfer of such vehicle in ordinary trade and commerce. The description of the vehicle shall include the make, model, year, type of body, identification number or numbers, and such other information as the Division may require.

(21) Metal Tire.—Every tire the surface of which in contact with the highway is wholly or partly of metal or other hard, nonresilient material.

(21a) Moped.—A type of passenger vehicle as defined in G.S. 105-164.3.

(21b) Motor Carrier.—A for-hire motor carrier or a private motor carrier.

(22) Motorcycle.—A type of passenger vehicle as defined in G.S. 20-4.01(27).

(23) Motor Vehicle.—Every vehicle which is self-propelled and every vehicle designed to run upon the highways which is pulled by a self-propelled vehicle. This shall not include mopeds as defined in G.S. 20-4.01(27)d1.

(24) Nonresident.—Any person whose legal residence is in some state, territory, or jurisdiction other than North Carolina or in a foreign country.

(24a) Offense Involving Impaired Driving.—Any of the following offenses:

a. Impaired driving under G.S. 20-138.1.
b. Death by vehicle under G.S. 20-141.4 when conviction is based upon impaired driving or a substantially equivalent offense under previous law.
c. First or second degree murder under G.S. 14-17 or involuntary manslaughter under G.S. 14-18 when conviction is based upon impaired driving or a substantially equivalent offense under previous law.
d. An offense committed in another jurisdiction which prohibits substantially similar conduct prohibited by the offenses in this subsection.
e. A repealed or superseded offense substantially equivalent to impaired driving, including offenses under former G.S. 20-138 or G.S. 20-139.
f. Impaired driving in a commercial motor vehicle under G.S. 20-138.2, except that convictions of impaired driving under G.S. 20-138.1 and G.S. 20-138.2 arising out of the same transaction shall be considered a single conviction of an offense involving impaired driving for any purpose under this Chapter.
g. Habitual impaired driving under G.S. 20-138.5.

A conviction under former G.S. 20-140(c) is not an offense involving impaired driving.

(25) Operator.—A person in actual physical control of a vehicle which is in motion or which has the engine running. The terms "operator" and "driver" and their cognates are synonymous.

(25a) Out of Service Order.—A declaration that a driver, a commercial motor vehicle, or a motor carrier operation is out-of-service.

(26) Owner.—A person holding the legal title to a vehicle, or in the event a vehicle is the subject of a chattel mortgage or an agreement for the conditional sale or lease thereof or other like agreement, with the right of purchase upon performance of the conditions stated in the agreement, and with the immediate right of possession vested in the mortgagor, conditional vendee or lessee, said mortgagor, conditional vendee or lessee shall be deemed the owner for the purpose of this Chapter. For the purposes of this Chapter, the lessee of a vehicle owned by the government of the United States shall be considered the owner of said vehicle.

(27) Passenger Vehicles.

a. Excursion passenger vehicles.—Vehicles transporting persons on sight-seeing or travel tours.
b. For hire passenger vehicles.—Vehicles transporting persons for compensation. This classification shall not include vehicles operated as ambulances; vehicles operated by the owner where the costs of operation are shared by the passengers; vehicles operated pursuant to a ridesharing arrangement as defined in G.S. 136-44.21; vehicles transporting students for the public school system under contract with the State Board of Education or vehicles leased to the United States of America or any of its agencies on a nonprofit basis; or vehicles used for human service or volunteer transportation.
c. Common carriers of passengers.—Vehicles operated under a certificate of authority issued by the Utilities Commission for operation on the highways of this State between fixed termini or over a regular route for the transportation of persons for compensation.
c1. Child care vehicles.—Vehicles under the direction and control of a child care facility, as defined in G.S. 110-86(3), and driven by an owner, employee, or agent of the child care facility for the primary purpose of transporting children to and from the child care facility, or to and from a place for participation in an event or activity in connection with the child care facility.

d. Motorcycles.—Vehicles having a saddle for the use of the rider and designed to travel on not more than three wheels in contact with the ground, including motor scooters and motor-driven bicycles, but excluding tractors and utility vehicles equipped with an additional form of device designed to transport property, three-wheeled vehicles while being used by law-enforcement agencies and mopeds as defined in subdivision d1 of this subsection.

d1. Moped.—Defined in G.S. 105-164.3.

d2. Motor home or house car.—A vehicular unit, designed to provide temporary living quarters, built into as an integral part, or permanently attached to, a self-propelled motor vehicle chassis or van. The vehicle must provide at least four of the following facilities: cooking, refrigeration or icebox, self-contained toilet, heating or air conditioning, a portable water supply system including a faucet and sink, separate 110-125 volt electrical power supply, or an LP gas supply.

d3. School activity bus.—A vehicle, generally painted a different color from a school bus, whose primary purpose is to transport school students and others to or from a place for participation in an event other than regular classroom work. The term includes a public, private, or parochial vehicle that meets this description.

d4. School bus.—A vehicle whose primary purpose is to transport school students over an established route to and from school for the regularly scheduled school day, that is equipped with alternately flashing red lights on the front and rear and a mechanical stop signal, and that bears the words "School Bus" on the front and rear in letters at least 8 inches in height. The term includes a public, private, or parochial vehicle that meets this description.

e. U-drive-it passenger vehicles.—Passenger vehicles included in the definition of U-drive-it vehicles set forth in this section.

f. Ambulances.—Vehicles equipped for transporting wounded, injured, or sick persons.

g. Private passenger vehicles.—All other passenger vehicles not included in the above definitions.

(28) Person.—Every individual, firm, partnership, association, corporation, governmental agency, or combination thereof of whatsoever form or character.

(29) Pneumatic Tire.—Every tire in which compressed air is designed to support the load.

(29a) Private Motor Carrier.—A person who transports passengers or property by motor vehicle in interstate commerce and is not a for-hire motor carrier.

(30) Private Road or Driveway.—Every road or driveway not open to the use of the public as a matter of right for the purpose of vehicular traffic.

(31) Property-Hauling Vehicles.

a. Vehicles used for the transportation of property.

b., c. Repealed by Session Laws 1995 (Reg. Sess., 1996), c. 756, s. 4.

d. Semitrailers.—Vehicles without motive power designed for carrying property or persons and for being drawn by a motor vehicle, and so constructed that part of their weight or their load rests upon or is carried by the pulling vehicle.

e. Trailers.—Vehicles without motive power designed for carrying property or persons wholly on their own structure and to be drawn by a motor vehicle, including "pole trailers" or a pair of wheels used primarily to balance a load rather than for purposes of transportation.

f. Repealed by Session Laws 1995 (Reg. Sess., 1996), c. 756, s. 4.

(31a) Provisional Licensee.—A person under the age of 18 years.

(32) Public Vehicular Area.—Any area within the State of North Carolina that is generally open to and used by the public for vehicular traffic, including by way of illustration and not limitation any drive, driveway, road, roadway, street, alley, or parking lot upon the grounds and premises of:

a. Any public or private hospital, college, university, school, orphanage, church, or any of the institutions, parks or other facilities maintained and supported by the State of North Carolina or any of its subdivisions; or

b. Any service station, drive-in theater, supermarket, store, restaurant, or office building, or any other business, residential, or municipal establishment providing parking space for customers, patrons, or the public; or

c. Any property owned by the United States and subject to the jurisdiction of the State of North Carolina. (The inclusion of property owned by the United States in this definition shall not limit assimilation of North Carolina law when applicable under the provisions of Title 18, *United States Code*, Section 13.)

The term "public vehicular area" shall also include any beach area used by the public for vehicular traffic as well as any road opened to vehicular traffic within or leading to a subdivision for use by subdivision residents, their guests, and members of the public, whether or not the subdivision roads have been offered for dedication to the public. The term "public vehicular area" shall not be construed to mean any private property not generally open to and used by the public.

(32a) Regular Driver's License.—A license to drive a commercial motor vehicle that is exempt from the commercial driver's license requirements or a noncommercial motor vehicle.

(33) a. Flood Vehicle.—A motor vehicle that has been submerged or partially submerged in water to the extent that damage to the body, engine, transmission, or differential has occurred.

b. Non-U.S.A. Vehicle.—A motor vehicle manufactured outside of the United States and not intended by the manufacturer for sale in the United States.

c. Reconstructed Vehicle.—A motor vehicle of a type required to be registered hereunder that has been materially altered from original construction due to removal, addition or substitution of new or used essential parts; and includes glider kits and custom assembled vehicles.

d. Salvage Motor Vehicle.—Any motor vehicle damaged by collision or other occurrence to the extent that the cost of repairs to the vehicle and rendering the vehicle safe for use on the public streets and highways would exceed seventy-five percent (75%) of its fair retail market value, whether or not the motor vehicle has been declared a total loss by an insurer. Repairs shall include the cost of parts and labor. Fair market retail values shall be as found in the NADA Pricing Guide Book or other publications approved by the Commissioner.

e. Salvage Rebuilt Vehicle.—A salvage vehicle that has been rebuilt for title and registration.

f. Junk Vehicle.—A motor vehicle which is incapable of operation or use upon the highways and has no resale value except as a source of parts or scrap, and shall not be titled or registered.

(33a) Relevant Time after the Driving.—Any time after the driving in which the driver still has in his body alcohol consumed before or during the driving.

(33b) Reportable Crash.—A crash involving a motor vehicle that results in one or more of the following:

a. Death or injury of a human being.

b. Total property damage of one thousand dollars ($1,000) or more, or property damage of any amount to a vehicle seized pursuant to G. S. 20-28.3.

(34) Resident.—Any person who resides within this State for other than a temporary or transitory purpose for more than six months shall be presumed to be a resident of this State; but absence from the State for more than six months shall raise no presumption that the person is not a resident of this State.

(35) Residential District.—The territory prescribed as such by ordinance of the Department of Transportation.

(36) Revocation or Suspension.—Termination of a licensee's or permittee's privilege to drive or termination of the registration of a vehicle for a period of time stated in an order of revocation or suspension. The terms "revocation" or "suspension" or a combination of both terms shall be used synonymously.

(37) Road Tractors.—Vehicles designed and used for drawing other vehicles upon the highway and not so constructed as to carry any part of the load, either independently or as a part of the weight of the vehicle so drawn.

(38) Roadway.—That portion of a highway improved, designed, or ordinarily used for vehicular travel, exclusive of the shoulder. In the event a highway includes two or more separate roadways the term "roadway" as used herein shall refer to any such roadway separately but not to all such roadways collectively.

(39) Safety Zone.—Traffic island or other space officially set aside within a highway for the exclusive use of pedestrians and which is so plainly marked or indicated by proper signs as to be plainly visible at all times while set apart as a safety zone.

(40) Security Agreement.—Written agreement which reserves or creates a security interest.

(41) Security Interest.—An interest in a vehicle reserved or created by agreement and which secures payments or performance of an obligation. The term includes but is not limited to the interest of a chattel mortgagee, the interest of a vendor under a conditional sales contract, the interest of a trustee under a chattel deed of trust, and the interest of a lessor under a lease intended as security. A security interest is "perfected" when it is valid against third parties generally.

(41a) Serious Traffic Violation.—A conviction of one of the following offenses when operating a commercial motor vehicle:

a. Excessive speeding, involving a single charge of any speed 15 miles per hour or more above the posted speed limit.
b. Careless and reckless driving.
c. A violation of any State or local law relating to motor vehicle traffic control, other than a parking violation, arising in connection with a fatal accident.
d. Improper or erratic lane changes.
e. Following the vehicle ahead too closely.

(42) Solid Tire.—Every tire of rubber or other resilient material which does not depend upon compressed air for the support of the load.

(43) Specially Constructed Vehicles.—Vehicles of a type required to be registered hereunder not originally constructed under a distinctive name, make, model, or type by a generally recognized manufacturer of vehicles and not materially altered from their original construction.

(44) Special Mobile Equipment.—Defined in G.S. 105-164.3.

(45) State.—A state, territory, or possession of the United States, District of Columbia, Commonwealth of Puerto Rico, or a province of Canada.

(46) Street.—A highway, as defined in subdivision (13). The terms "highway" and "street" and their cognates are synonymous.

(47) Suspension.—Termination of a licensee's or permittee's privilege to drive or termination of the registration of a vehicle for a period of time stated in an order of revocation or suspension. The terms "revocation" or "suspension" or a combination of both terms shall be used synonymously.

(48) Truck Tractors.—Vehicles designed and used primarily for drawing other vehicles and not so constructed as to carry any load independent of the vehicle so drawn.

(48a) U-drive-it vehicles.—The following vehicles that are rented to a person, to be operated by that person:

a. A private passenger vehicle other than the following:
   1. A private passenger vehicle of nine-passenger capacity or less that is rented for a term of one year or more.
   2. A private passenger vehicle that is rented to public school authorities for driver-training instruction.
b. A property-hauling vehicle under 7,000 pounds that does not haul products for hire and that is rented for a term of less than one year.
c. Motorcycles.

(48b) Under the Influence of an Impairing Substance.—The state of a person having his physical or mental faculties, or both, appreciably impaired by an impairing substance.

(49) Vehicle.—Every device in, upon, or by which any person or property is or may be transported or drawn upon a highway, excepting devices moved by human power or used exclusively upon fixed rails or tracks; provided, that for the purposes of this Chapter bicycles shall be deemed vehicles and every rider of a bicycle upon a highway shall be subject to the provisions of this Chapter applicable to the driver of a vehicle except those which by their nature can have no application. This term shall not include a device which is designed for and intended to be used as a means of transportation for a person with a mobility impairment, is suitable for use both inside and outside a building, and whose maximum speed does not exceed 12 miles per hour when the device is being operated by a person with a mobility impairment.

(50) Wreckers.—Vehicles with permanently attached cranes used to move other vehicles; provided, that said wreckers shall be equipped with adequate brakes for units being towed.

History: 1973, c. 1330, s. 1; 1975, cc. 94, 208; c. 716, s. 5; c. 743; c. 859, s. 1; 1977, c. 313; c. 464, s. 34; 1979, c. 39; c. 423, s. 1; c. 574, ss. 1–4; c. 667, s. 1; c. 680; 1981, c. 606, s. 3; c. 792, s. 2; 1983, c. 435, s. 8; 1983 (Reg. Sess., 1984), c. 1101, ss. 1–3; 1985, c. 509, s. 6; 1987, c. 607, s. 2; c. 658, s. 1; 1987 (Reg. Sess., 1988), c. 1069; c. 1105, s. 1; c. 1112, ss. 1–3; 1989, c. 455, ss. 1, 2; c. 727, s. 219(1); c. 771, ss. 1, 18; 1991, c. 449, s. 2; c. 726, ss. 1–4; 1991 (Reg. Sess., 1992), c. 1015, s. 1; 1993 (Reg. Sess., 1994), c. 761, s. 22; 1995,

c. 191, s. 1; 1995 (Reg. Sess., 1996), c. 756, ss. 2–4; 1997-379, s. 5.1; 1997-443, s. 11A.8; 1997-456, s. 27; 1998-149, s. 1; 1998-182, ss. 1, 1.1, 26; 1998-217, s. 62(e); 1999-330, s. 9; 1999-337, s. 28(c)-(e); 1999-406, s. 14; 1999-452, ss. 1–5.

Article 1B. Reciprocal Provisions as to Arrest of Nonresidents

§ 20-4.18. Definitions

Unless the context otherwise requires, the following words and phrases, for the purpose of this Article, shall have the following meanings:

(1) Citation.—Any citation, summons, ticket, or other document issued by a law-enforcement officer for the violation of a traffic law, ordinance, rule or regulation.

(2) Collateral or Bond.—Any cash or other security deposited to secure an appearance following a citation by a law-enforcement officer.

(3) Repealed by Session Laws 1979, c. 667, s. 2.

(4) Nonresident.—A person who holds a license issued by a reciprocating state.

(5) Personal Recognizance.—An agreement by a nonresident to comply with the terms of the citation issued to the nonresident.

(6) Reciprocating State.—Any state or other jurisdiction which extends by its laws to residents of North Carolina substantially the rights and privileges provided by this Article.

(7) State.—The State of North Carolina.

History: 1973, c. 736; 1979, c. 667, s. 2; 1981, c. 508; 1999-452, s. 6.

§ 20-4.19. Issuance of citation to nonresident; officer to report noncompliance

(a) Notwithstanding other provisions of this Chapter, a law-enforcement officer observing a violation of this Chapter or other traffic regulation by a nonresident shall issue a citation as appropriate and shall not, subject to the provisions of subsection (b) of this section, require such nonresident to post collateral or bond to secure appearance for trial, but shall accept such nonresident's personal recognizance; provided, however, that the nonresident shall have the right upon request to post collateral or bond in a manner provided by law and in such case the provisions of this Article shall not apply.

(b) A nonresident may be required to post collateral or bond to secure appearance for trial if the offense is one which would result in the suspension or revocation of a person's license under the laws of this State.

(c) Upon the failure of the nonresident to comply with the citation, the clerk of court shall report the noncompliance to the Division. The report of noncompliance shall clearly identify the nonresident; describe the violation, specifying the section of the statute, code, or ordinance violated; indicate the location and date of offense; and identify the vehicle involved.

History: 1973, c. 736; 1975, c. 716, s. 5; 1991, c. 682, s. 1; 1999-452, s. 7.

§ 20-4.20. Division to transmit report to reciprocating state; suspension of license for noncompliance with citation issued by reciprocating state

(a) Upon receipt of a report of noncompliance, the Division shall transmit a certified copy of such report to the official in charge of the issuance of licenses in the reciprocating state in which the nonresident resides or by which he is licensed.

(b) When the licensing authority of a reciprocating state reports that a person holding a North Carolina license has failed to comply with a citation issued in such state, the Commissioner shall forthwith suspend such person's license. The order of suspension shall indicate the reason for the order, and shall notify the person that his license shall remain suspended until he has furnished evidence satisfactory to the Commissioner that he has complied with the terms of the citation which was the basis for the suspension order by appearing before the tribunal to which he was cited and complying with any order entered by said tribunal.

(c) A copy of any suspension order issued hereunder may be furnished to the licensing authority of the reciprocating state.

(d) The Commissioner shall maintain a current listing of reciprocating states hereunder. Such lists shall from time to time be disseminated among the appropriate departments, divisions, bureaus, and agencies of this State; the principal law-enforcement officers of the several counties, cities, and towns of this State; and the licensing authorities in reciprocating states.

(e) The Commissioner shall have the authority to execute or make agreements, arrangements, or declarations to carry out the provisions of this Article.

History: 1973, c. 736; 1975, c. 716, s. 5; 1979, c. 104.

Article 2. Uniform Driver's License Act

§ 20-7. Issuance and renewal of driver's licenses

(a) License Required.—To drive a motor vehicle on a highway, a person must be licensed by the Division under this Article or Article 2C of this Chapter to drive the vehicle and must carry the license while driving the vehicle. The Division issues regular driver's licenses under this Article and issues commercial driver's licenses under Article 2C.

A license authorizes the holder of the license to drive any vehicle included in the class of the license and any vehicle included in a lesser class of license, except a vehicle for which an endorsement is required. To drive a vehicle for which an endorsement is required, a person must obtain both a license and an endorsement for the vehicle. A regular driver's license is considered a lesser class of license than its commercial counterpart.

The classes of regular driver's licenses and the motor vehicles that can be driven with each class of license are:

(1) Class A.—A Class A license authorizes the holder to drive any of the following:
- a. A Class A motor vehicle that is exempt under G.S. 20-37.16 from the commercial driver's license requirements.
- b. A Class A motor vehicle that has a combined GVWR of less than 26,001 pounds and includes as part of the combination a towed unit that has a GVWR of at least 10,001 pounds.

(2) Class B.—A Class B license authorizes the holder to drive any Class B motor vehicle that is exempt under G.S. 20-37.16 from the commercial driver's license requirements.

(3) Class C.—A Class C license authorizes the holder to drive any of the following:
- a. A Class C motor vehicle that is not a commercial motor vehicle.
- b. When operated by a volunteer member of a fire department, a rescue squad, or an emergency medical service (EMS) in the performance of duty, a Class A or Class B fire-fighting, rescue, or EMS motor vehicle or a combination of these vehicles.

The Commissioner may assign a unique motor vehicle to a class that is different from the class in which it would otherwise belong.

A new resident of North Carolina who has a driver's license issued by another jurisdiction must obtain a license from the Division within 60 days after becoming a resident.

(a1) Motorcycles and Mopeds.—To drive a motorcycle, a person shall have:

(1) A full provisional license with a motorcycle learner's permit;

(2) A regular driver's license with a motorcycle learner's permit; or

(3) Either:
- a. A full provisional license; or
- b. A regular driver's license, with a motorcycle endorsement.

Subsection (a2) of this section sets forth the requirements for a motorcycle learner's permit.

To obtain a motorcycle endorsement, a person shall demonstrate competence to drive a motorcycle by:

(1) Passing a road test;

(2) Passing a written or oral test concerning motorcycles; and

(3) Paying the fee for a motorcycle endorsement.

Neither a driver's license nor a motorcycle endorsement is required to drive a moped.

(a2) Motorcycle Learner's Permit.—The following persons are eligible for a motorcycle learner's permit:

(1) A person who is at least 16 years old but less than 18 years old and has a full provisional license issued by the Division.

(2) A person who is at least 18 years old and has a license issued by the Division.

To obtain a motorcycle learner's permit, an applicant shall pass a vision test, a road sign test, and a written test specified by the Division. A motorcycle learner's permit expires 18 months after it is issued. The holder of a motorcycle learner's permit may not drive a motorcycle with a passenger. The fee for a motorcycle learner's permit is the amount set in G.S. 20-7(l) for a learner's permit.

(b) Repealed by Session Laws 1993, c. 368, s. 1, c. 533, s. 12.

(b1) Application.—To obtain a driver's license from the Division, a person must complete an application form provided by the Division, present at least two forms of identification approved by the Commissioner, be a resident of this State, and demonstrate his or her physical and mental ability to drive safely a motor vehicle included in the class of license for which the person has applied. The Division may copy the identification presented or hold it for a brief period of time to verify its authenticity. To obtain an endorsement, a person must demonstrate his or her physical and mental ability to drive safely the type of motor vehicle for which the endorsement is required.

The application form must request all of the following information:

(1) The applicant's full name.
(2) The applicant's mailing address and residence address.
(3) A physical description of the applicant, including the applicant's sex, height, eye color, and hair color.
(4) The applicant's date of birth.
(5) The applicant's social security number. The Division shall not issue a license to an applicant who fails to provide the applicant's social security number. The applicant's social security number shall not be printed on the license and may be released only to the Department of Health and Human Services, Child Support Enforcement Program, upon its request and for the purpose of establishing paternity or child support, or enforcing a child support order.
(6) The applicant's signature.

The application form must also contain the disclosures concerning the request for an applicant's social security number required by section 7 of the federal Privacy Act of 1974, Pub. L. No. 93-579. In accordance with 42 U.S.C. 405 and 42 U.S.C. 666, and amendments thereto, the Division may disclose a social security number obtained under this subsection only for the purpose of administering the driver's license laws or to assist the State Child Support Enforcement Program in establishing paternity or establishing or enforcing child support and may not disclose the social security number for any other purpose. The social security number of an applicant for a license or of a licensed driver is therefore not a public record. A violation of the disclosure restrictions is punishable as provided in 42 U.S.C. 408, and amendments thereto.

(c) Tests.—To demonstrate physical and mental ability, a person must pass an examination. The examination may include road tests, vision tests, oral tests, and, in the case of literate applicants, written tests, as the Division may require. The tests must ensure that an applicant recognizes the handicapped international symbol of access, as defined in G.S. 20-37.5. The Division may not require a person who applies to renew a license that has not expired to take a written test or a road test unless one or more of the following applies:

(1) The person has been convicted of a traffic violation since the person's license was last issued.
(2) The applicant suffers from a mental or physical condition that impairs the person's ability to drive a motor vehicle.

The Division may not require a person who is at least 60 years old to parallel park a motor vehicle as part of a road test.

(c1) Insurance.—The Division may not issue a driver's license to a person until the person has furnished proof of financial responsibility. Proof of financial responsibility shall be in one of the following forms:

(1) A written certificate or electronically-transmitted facsimile thereof from any insurance carrier duly authorized to do business in this State certifying that there is in effect a nonfleet private passenger motor vehicle liability policy for the benefit of the person required to furnish proof of financial responsibility. The certificate or facsimile shall state the effective date and expiration date of the nonfleet private passenger motor vehicle liability policy and shall state the date that the certificate or facsimile is issued. The certificate or facsimile shall remain effective proof of financial responsibility for a period of 30 consecutive days following the date the certificate or facsimile is issued but shall not in and of itself constitute a binder or policy of insurance.
(2) A binder for or policy of nonfleet private passenger motor vehicle liability insurance under which the applicant is insured, provided that the binder or policy states the effective date and expiration date of the nonfleet private passenger motor vehicle liability policy.

The preceding provisions of this subsection do not apply to applicants who do not own currently registered motor vehicles and who do not operate nonfleet private passenger motor vehicles that are owned by other persons and that are not insured under commercial motor vehicle liability insurance policies. In such cases, the applicant shall sign a written certificate to that effect. Such certificate shall be furnished by the Division and may be incorporated into the license application form. Any material misrepresentation made by such person on such certificate shall be grounds for suspension of that person's license for a period of 90 days.

For the purpose of this subsection, the term "nonfleet private passenger motor vehicle" has the definition ascribed to it in Article 40 of General Statute Chapter 58.

The Commissioner may require that certificates required by this subsection be on a form approved by the Commissioner.

The requirement of furnishing proof of financial responsibility does not apply to a person who applies for a renewal of his or her driver's license.

Nothing in this subsection precludes any person from showing proof of financial responsibility in any other manner authorized by Articles 9A and 13 of this Chapter.

(d) Repealed by Session Laws 1993, c. 368, s. 1.

(e) Restrictions.—The Division may impose any restriction it finds advisable on a driver's license. It is unlawful for the holder of a restricted license to operate a motor vehicle without complying with the restriction and is the equivalent of operating a motor vehicle without a license. If any applicant shall suffer from any physical defect or disease which affects his or her operation of a motor vehicle, the Division may require to be filed with it a certificate of such applicant's condition signed by some medical authority of the applicant's community designated by the Division. This certificate shall in all cases be treated as confidential. Nothing in this subsection shall be construed to prevent the Division from refusing to issue a license, either restricted or unrestricted, to any person deemed to be incapable of safely operating a motor vehicle. This subsection does not prohibit deaf persons from operating motor vehicles who in every other way meet the requirements of this section.

(f) Expiration and Temporary License.—The first driver's license the Division issues to a person expires on the person's fourth or subsequent birthday that occurs after the license is issued and on which the individual's age is evenly divisible by five, unless this subsection sets a different expiration date. The first driver's license the Division issues to a person who is at least 17 years old but is less than 18 years old expires on the person's twentieth birthday. The first driver's license the Division issues to a person who is at least 62 years old expires on the person's birthday in the fifth year after the license is issued, whether or not the person's age on that birthday is evenly divisible by five.

A driver's license that was issued by the Division and is renewed by the Division expires five years after the expiration date of the license that is renewed. A person may apply to the Division to renew a license during the 180-day period before the license expires. The Division may not accept an application for renewal made before the 180-day period begins.

The Division may renew by mail a driver's license issued by the Division to a person who meets any of the following descriptions:

(1) Is serving on active duty in the armed forces of the United States and is stationed outside this State.

(2) Is a resident of this State and has been residing outside the State for at least 30 continuous days.

When renewing a license by mail, the Division may waive the examination that would otherwise be required for the renewal and may impose any conditions it finds advisable. A license renewed by mail is a temporary license that expires 60 days after the person to whom it is issued returns to this State.

(g) Repealed by Session Laws 1979, c. 667, s. 6.

(h) Repealed by Session Laws 1979, c. 113, s. 1.

(i) Fees.—The fee for a regular driver's license is the amount set in the following table multiplied by the number of years in the period for which the license is issued:

Class of Regular License	Fee for Each Year
Class A	$3.75
Class B	3.75
Class C	2.50

The fee for a motorcycle endorsement is one dollar and twenty-five cents ($1.25) for each year of the period for which the endorsement is issued. The appropriate fee must be paid before a person receives a regular driver's license or an endorsement.

(i1) Restoration Fee.—Any person whose driver's license has been revoked pursuant to the provisions of this Chapter, other than G.S. 20-17(2), shall pay a restoration fee of twenty-five dollars ($25.00). A person whose driver's license has been revoked under G.S. 20-17(2) shall pay a restoration fee of fifty dollars ($50.00) until the end of the fiscal year in which the cumulative total amount of fees deposited under this subsection in the General Fund exceeds ten million dollars ($10,000,000), and shall pay a restoration fee of twenty-five dollars ($25.00) thereafter. The fee shall be paid to the Division prior to the issuance to such person of a new driver's license or the restoration of the driver's license. The restoration fee shall be paid to the Division in addition to any and all fees which may be provided by law. This restoration fee shall not be required from any licensee whose license was revoked or voluntarily surrendered for medical or health reasons whether or not a medical evaluation was conducted pursuant to this Chapter. The twenty-five dollar ($25.00) fee, and the first twenty-five dollars ($25.00) of the fifty-dollar ($50.00) fee, shall be deposited in the Highway Fund. The remaining twenty-five dollars ($25.00) of the fifty-dollar ($50.00) fee shall be deposited in the General Fund of the State. The Office of State Budget and Management shall certify to the Department of Transportation and the General Assembly when the cumulative total amount of fees deposited in the General Fund under this subsection exceeds ten million dollars ($10,000,000), and shall annually report to the General Assembly the amount of fees deposited in the General Fund under this subsection.

It is the intent of the General Assembly to annually appropriate the funds deposited in the General Fund under this subsection to the Board of Governors of The University of North Carolina to be used for the Center for Alcohol Studies Endowment at The University of North Carolina at Chapel Hill, but not to exceed this cumulative total of ten million dollars ($10,000,000).

(j) Highway Fund.—The fees collected under this section and G.S. 20-14 shall be placed in the Highway Fund.

(k) Repealed by Session Laws 1991, c. 726, s. 5.

(l) Learner's Permit.—A person who is at least 18 years old may obtain a learner's permit. A learner's permit authorizes the permit holder to drive a specified type or class of motor vehicle while in possession of the permit. A learner's permit is valid for a period of 18 months after it is issued. The fee for a learner's permit is ten dollars ($10.00). A learner's permit may be renewed, or a second learner's permit may be issued, for an additional period of 18 months. The permit holder must, while operating a motor vehicle over the highways, be accompanied by a person who is licensed to operate the motor vehicle being driven and is seated beside the permit holder.

(l-1) Repealed by Session Laws 1991, c. 726, s. 5.

(m) Instruction Permit.—The Division upon receiving proper application may in its discretion issue a restricted instruction permit effective for a school year or a lesser period to any of the following applicants:

(1) An applicant who is less than 18 years old and is enrolled in a driver's education program that is approved by the State Superintendent of Public Instruction and is offered at a public high school, a nonpublic secondary school, or a licensed drivers' training school.

(2) An applicant for certification under G.S. 20-218 as a school bus driver.

A restricted instruction permit authorizes the holder of the permit to drive a specified type or class of motor vehicle when in possession of the permit, subject to any restrictions imposed by the Division. The restrictions the Division may impose on a permit include restrictions to designated areas and highways and restrictions prohibiting operation except when an approved instructor is occupying a seat beside the permittee. A restricted instruction permit is not required to have a distinguishing number or a picture of the person to whom the permit is issued.

(n) Format.—A driver's license issued by the Division must be tamperproof and must contain all of the following information:

(1) An identification of this State as the issuer of the license.

(2) The license holder's full name.

(3) The license holder's residence address.

(4) A color photograph of the license holder, taken by the Division.

(5) A physical description of the license holder, including sex, height, eye color, and hair color.

(6) The license holder's date of birth.

(7) The license holder's social security number or another identifying number assigned by the Division.

(8) Each class of motor vehicle the license holder is authorized to drive and any endorsements or restrictions that apply.

(9) The license holder's signature.

(10) The date the license was issued and the date the license expires.

The Commissioner may waive the requirement of a color photograph on a license if the license holder proves to the satisfaction of the Commissioner that taking the photograph would violate the license holder's religious convictions. In taking photographs of license holders, the Division must distinguish between license holders who are less than 21 years old and license holders who are at least 21 years old by using different color backgrounds or borders for each group. The Division shall determine the different colors to be used.

At the request of an applicant for a driver's license, a license issued to the applicant must contain the applicant's race.

(o) Repealed by Session Laws 1991, c. 726, s. 5.

(p) The Division must give the clerk of superior court in each county at least 50 copies of the driver license handbook free of charge. The clerk must give a copy to a person who requests it.

History: 1935, c. 52, s. 2; 1943, c. 649, s. 1; c. 787, s. 1; 1947, c. 1067, s. 10; 1949, c. 583, ss. 9, 10; c. 826, ss. 1, 2; 1951, c. 542, ss. 1, 2; c. 1196, ss. 1–3; 1953, cc. 839, 1284, 1311; 1955, c. 1187, ss. 2–6; 1957, c. 1225; 1963, cc. 754, 1007, 1022; 1965, c. 410, s. 5; 1967, c. 509; 1969, c. 183; c. 783, s. 1; c. 865; 1971, c. 158; 1973, cc. 73, 705; c. 1057, ss. 1, 3; 1975, c. 162, s. 1; c. 295; c. 296, ss. 1, 2; c. 684; c. 716, s. 5; c. 841; c. 875, s. 4; c. 879, s. 46; 1977, c. 6; c. 340, s. 3; c. 865, ss. 1, 3; 1979, c. 37, s. 1; c. 113; c. 178, s. 2; c. 667, ss. 3–11, 41; c. 678, ss. 1–3; c. 801, ss. 5, 6; 1981, c. 42; c. 690, ss. 8–10; c. 792, s. 3; 1981 (Reg. Sess., 1982), c. 1257, s. 1; 1983, c. 443, s. 1; 1985, c. 141, s. 4; c. 682, ss. 1, 2; 1987, c. 869, ss. 10, 11; 1989, c. 436, ss. 1, 2; c. 771, s. 5; c. 786, s. 4; 1991, c. 478, s. 1; c. 689, s. 325; c. 726, s. 5; 1991 (Reg. Sess., 1992), c. 1007, s. 27; c. 1030, s. 10; 1993, c. 368, s. 1; c. 533, ss. 2, 3, 12; 1993 (Reg. Sess., 1994), c. 595, ss. 1, 2; c. 750, s. 1; c. 761, s. 1.1; 1995 (Reg. Sess., 1996), c. 675, s. 1; 1997-16, ss. 5, 8, 9; 1997-122, ss. 2, 3; 1997-377, s. 1; 1997-433, s. 4; 1997-443, ss. 11A.122, 32.20; 1997-456, s. 32, 33; 1998-17, s. 1; 1998-149, s. 2.

§ 20-8. Persons exempt from license

The following are exempt from license hereunder:

(1) Any person while operating a motor vehicle the property of and in the service of the armed forces of the United States. This shall not be construed to exempt any operators of the United States Civilian Conservation Corps motor vehicles;

(2) Any person while driving or operating any road machine, farm tractor, or implement of husbandry temporarily operated or moved on a highway;

(3) A nonresident who is at least 16 years of age who has in his immediate possession a valid driver's license issued to him in his home state or country if the nonresident is operating a motor vehicle in this State in accordance with the license restrictions and vehicle classifications that would be applicable to him under the laws and regulations of his home state or country if he were driving in his home state or country. This exemption specifically applies to nonresident military spouses, regardless of their employment status, who are temporarily residing in North Carolina due to the active duty military orders of a spouse.

(4) to (6) Repealed by Session Laws 1979, c. 667, s. 13.

(7) Any person who is at least 16 years of age and while operating a moped.

History: 1935, c. 52, s. 3; 1963, c. 1175; 1973, c. 1017; 1975, c. 859, s. 2; 1979, c. 574, s. 7; c. 667, s. 13; 1983, c. 436.

§ 20-10.1. Mopeds

It shall be unlawful for any person who is under the age of 16 years to operate a moped as defined in G.S. 20-4.01(27)d1 upon any highway or public vehicular area of this State.

History: 1979, c. 574, s. 8.

§ 20-11. Issuance of limited learner's permit and provisional driver's license to person who is less than 18 years old

(a) Process.—Safe driving requires instruction in driving and experience. To ensure that a person who is less than 18 years old has both instruction and experience before obtaining a driver's license, driving privileges are granted first on a limited basis and are then expanded in accordance with the following process:

(1) Level 1.—Driving with a limited learner's permit.

(2) Level 2.—Driving with a limited provisional license.

(3) Level 3.—Driving with a full provisional license.

A permit or license issued under this section must have a color background or border that indicates the level of driving privileges granted by the permit or license.

(b) Level 1.—A person who is at least 15 years old but less than 18 years old may obtain a limited learner's permit if the person meets all of the following requirements:

(1) Passes a course of driver education prescribed in G.S. 20-88.1 or a course of driver instruction at a licensed commercial driver training school.

(2) Passes a written test administered by the Division.

(3) Has a driving eligibility certificate or a high school diploma or its equivalent.

(c) Level 1 Restrictions.—A limited learner's permit authorizes the permit holder to drive a specified type or class of motor vehicle only under the following conditions:

(1) The permit holder must be in possession of the permit.

(2) A supervising driver must be seated beside the permit holder in the front seat of the vehicle when it is in motion. No person other than the supervising driver can be in the front seat.

(3) For the first six months after issuance, the permit holder may drive only between the hours of 5:00 a.m. and 9:00 p.m.

(4) After the first six months after issuance, the permit holder may drive at any time.

(5) Every person occupying the vehicle being driven by the permit holder must have a safety belt properly fastened about his or her body, or be restrained by a child passenger restraint system as provided in G.S. 20-137.1(a), when the vehicle is in motion.

(d) Level 2.—A person who is at least 16 years old but less than 18 years old may obtain a limited provisional license if the person meets all of the following requirements:

(1) Has held a limited learner's permit issued by the Division for at least 12 months.

(2) Has not been convicted of a motor vehicle moving violation or seat belt infraction during the preceding six months.

(3) Passes a road test administered by the Division.

(4) Has a driving eligibility certificate or a high school diploma or its equivalent.

(e) Level 2 Restrictions.—A limited provisional license authorizes the license holder to drive a specified type or class of motor vehicle only under the following conditions:

(1) The license holder must be in possession of the license.

(2) The license holder may drive without supervision in any of the following circumstances:

a. From 5:00 a.m. to 9:00 p.m.

b. When driving to or from work.

c. When driving to or from an activity of a volunteer fire department, volunteer rescue squad, or volunteer emergency medical service, if the driver is a member of the organization.

(3) The license holder may drive with supervision at any time. When the license holder is driving with supervision, the supervising driver must be seated beside the license holder in the front seat of the vehicle when it is in motion. The supervising driver need not be the only other occupant of the front seat, but must be the person seated next to the license holder.

(4) Every person occupying the vehicle being driven by the license holder must have a safety belt properly fastened about his or her body, or be restrained by a child passenger restraint system as provided in G.S. 20-137.1(a), when the vehicle is in motion.

(f) Level 3.—A person who is at least 16 years old but less than 18 years old may obtain a full provisional license if the person meets all of the following requirements:

(1) Has held a limited provisional license issued by the Division for at least six months.

(2) Has not been convicted of a motor vehicle moving violation or seat belt infraction during the preceding six months.

(3) Has a driving eligibility certificate or a high school diploma or its equivalent.

A person who meets these requirements may obtain a full provisional license by mail.

(g) Level 3 Restrictions.—The restrictions on Level 1 and Level 2 drivers concerning time of driving, supervision, and passenger limitations do not apply to a full provisional license.

(h) Exception for Persons 16 to 18 Who Have an Unrestricted Out-of-State License.—A person who is at least 16 years old but less than 18 years old, who was a resident of another state and has an unrestricted driver's license issued by that state, and who becomes a resident of this State may obtain one of the following upon the submission of a driving eligibility certificate or a high school diploma or its equivalent:

(1) A temporary permit, if the person has not completed a drivers' education program that meets the requirements of the Superintendent of Public Instruction but is currently enrolled in a drivers' education program that meets these requirements. A temporary permit is valid for the period specified in the permit and authorizes the holder of the permit to drive a specified type or class of motor vehicle when in possession of the permit, subject to any restrictions imposed

by the Division concerning time of driving, supervision, and passenger limitations. The period must end within 10 days after the expected completion date of the drivers' education program in which the applicant is enrolled.

(2) A full provisional license, if the person has completed a drivers' education program that meets the requirements of the Superintendent of Public Instruction, has held the license issued by the other state for at least 12 months, and has not been convicted during the preceding six months of a motor vehicle moving violation, a seat belt infraction, or an offense committed in another jurisdiction that would be a motor vehicle moving violation or seat belt infraction if committed in this State.

(3) A limited provisional license, if the person has completed a drivers' education program that meets the requirements of the Superintendent of Public Instruction but either did not hold the license issued by the other state for at least 12 months or was convicted during the preceding six months of a motor vehicle moving violation, a seat belt infraction, or an offense committed in another jurisdiction that would be a motor vehicle moving violation or seat belt infraction if committed in this State.

(h1) Exception for Persons 16 to 18 Who Have an Out-of-State Restricted License.—A person who is at least 16 years old but less than 18 years old, who was a resident of another state and has a restricted driver's license issued by that state, and who becomes a resident of this State may obtain one of the following:

(1) A limited provisional license, if the person has completed a drivers' education program that meets the requirements of the Superintendent of Public Instruction, held the restricted license issued by the other state for at least 12 months, and whose parent or guardian certifies that the person has not been convicted during the preceding six months of a motor vehicle moving violation, a seat belt infraction, or an offense committed in another jurisdiction that would be a motor vehicle moving violation or seat belt infraction if committed in this State.

(2) A limited learner's permit, if the person has completed a drivers' education program that meets the requirements of the Superintendent of Public Instruction but either did not hold the restricted license issued by the other state for at least 12 months or was convicted during the preceding six months of a motor vehicle moving violation, a seat belt infraction, or an offense committed in another jurisdiction that would be a motor vehicle moving violation or seat belt infraction if committed in this State. A person who qualifies for a limited learner's permit under this subdivision and whose parent or guardian certifies that the person has not been convicted of a moving violation in the preceding six months shall be deemed to have held a limited learners permit in this State for each month the person held a restricted license in another state.

(h2) Exception for Persons Age 15 Who Have an Out-of-State Unrestricted or Restricted License.—A person who is age 15, who was a resident of another state, has an unrestricted or restricted driver's license issued by that state, and who becomes a resident of this State may obtain a limited learner's permit if the person has completed a drivers' education program that meets the requirements of the Superintendent of Public Instruction. A person who qualifies for a limited learner's permit under this subsection and whose parent or guardian certifies that the person has not been convicted of a moving violation in the preceding six months shall be deemed to have held a limited learner's permit in this State for each month the person held an unrestricted or restricted license in another state.

(h3) Exception for Persons Less Than Age 18 Who Have a Federally Issued Unrestricted or Restricted License.—A person who is less than age 18, who has an unrestricted or restricted driver's license issued by the federal government, and who becomes a resident of this State may obtain a limited provisional license or a provisional license if the person has completed a drivers' education program substantially equivalent to the drivers' education program that meets the requirements of the Superintendent of Public Instruction. A person who qualifies for a limited provisional license or a provisional license under this subsection and whose parent or guardian certifies that the person has not been convicted of a moving violation in the preceding six months shall be deemed to have held a limited provisional license or a provisional license in this State for each month the person held an unrestricted or restricted license issued by the federal government.

(i) Application.—An application for a permit or license authorized by this section must be signed by both the applicant and another person. That person must be:

(1) The applicant's parent or guardian;

(2) A person approved by the applicant's parent or guardian; or

(3) A person approved by the Division.

(j) Duration and Fee.—A limited learner's permit expires on the eighteenth birthday of the permit holder. A limited provisional license expires on the eighteenth birthday of the license holder. A full provisional license expires on the date set under G.S. 20-7(f). The fee for a limited learner's permit or a limited provisional license is ten dollars ($10.00). The fee for a full provisional license is the amount set under G.S. 20-7(i).

(k) Supervising Driver.—A supervising driver shall be a parent or guardian of the permit holder or license holder or a responsible person approved by the parent or guardian or the Division. A supervising driver shall be a licensed driver who has been licensed for at least five years. At least one supervising driver shall sign the application for a permit or license.

(l) Violations.—It is unlawful for the holder of a limited learner's permit, a temporary permit, or a limited provisional license to drive a motor vehicle in violation of the restrictions that apply to the permit or license. Failure to comply with a restriction concerning the time of driving or the presence of a supervising driver in the vehicle constitutes operating a motor vehicle without a license. Failure to comply with any other restriction, including seating and passenger limitations, is an infraction punishable by a monetary penalty as provided in G.S. 20-176.

(m) Insurance Status.—The holder of a limited learner's permit is not considered a licensed driver for the purpose of determining the inexperienced operator premium surcharge under automobile insurance policies.

(n) (Effective until July 1, 2000) Driving Eligibility Certificate.—A person who desires to obtain a permit or license issued under this section and who does not have a high school diploma or its equivalent must have a driving eligibility certificate. A driving eligibility certificate must meet the following conditions:

- (1) The person who is required to sign the certificate under subdivision (4) of this subsection must show that he or she has determined that one of the following requirements is met:
  - a. The person is currently enrolled in school and is making progress toward obtaining a high school diploma or its equivalent.
  - b. A substantial hardship would be placed on the person or the person's family if the person does not receive a certificate.
  - c. The person cannot make progress toward obtaining a high school diploma or its equivalent.
- (2) It must be on a form approved by the Division.
- (3) It must be dated within 30 days of the date the person applies for a permit or license issuable under this section.
- (4) It must be signed by the applicable person named below:
  - a. The principal, or the principal's designee, of the public school in which the person is enrolled.
  - b. The administrator, or the administrator's designee, of the nonpublic school in which the person is enrolled.
  - c. The person who provides the academic instruction in the home school in which the person is enrolled.
  - c1. The person who provides the academic instruction in the home in accordance with an educational program found by a court, prior to July 1, 1998, to comply with the compulsory attendance law.
  - d. The designee of the board of directors of the charter school in which the person is enrolled.
  - e. The president, or the president's designee, of the community college in which the person is enrolled.

Notwithstanding any other law, the decision concerning whether a driving eligibility certificate was properly issued or improperly denied shall be appealed only as provided under the rules adopted in accordance with G.S. 115C-12(27), G.S. 115D-5(a3), or G.S. 115C-566, whichever is applicable, and may not be appealed under this Chapter.

(n) (Effective July 1, 2000) Driving Eligibility Certificate.—A person who desires to obtain a permit or license issued under this section must have a high school diploma or its equivalent or must have a driving eligibility certificate. A driving eligibility certificate must meet the following conditions:

- (1) The person who is required to sign the certificate under subdivision (4) of this subsection must show that he or she has determined that one of the following requirements is met:
  - a. The person is currently enrolled in school and is making progress toward obtaining a high school diploma or its equivalent.
  - b. A substantial hardship would be placed on the person or the person's family if the person does not receive a certificate.
  - c. The person cannot make progress toward obtaining a high school diploma or its equivalent.
- (1a) The person who is required to sign the certificate under subdivision (4) of this subsection also must show that one of the following requirements is met:

a. The person who seeks a permit or license issued under this section is not subject to subsection (n1) of this section.
b. The person who seeks a permit or license issued under this section is subject to subsection (n1) of this section and is eligible for the certificate under that subsection.

(2) It must be on a form approved by the Division.

(3) It must be dated within 30 days of the date the person applies for a permit or license issuable under this section.

(4) It must be signed by the applicable person named below:
a. The principal, or the principal's designee, of the public school in which the person is enrolled.
b. The administrator, or the administrator's designee, of the nonpublic school in which the person is enrolled.
c. The person who provides the academic instruction in the home school in which the person is enrolled.
c1. The person who provides the academic instruction in the home in accordance with an educational program found by a court, prior to July 1, 1998, to comply with the compulsory attendance law.
d. The designee of the board of directors of the charter school in which the person is enrolled.
e. The president, or the president's designee, of the community college in which the person is enrolled.

Notwithstanding any other law, the decision concerning whether a driving eligibility certificate was properly issued or improperly denied shall be appealed only as provided under the rules adopted in accordance with G.S. 115C-12(28), 115D-5(a3), or 115C-566, whichever is applicable, and may not be appealed under this Chapter.

(n1) (Effective July 1, 2000) Lose Control; Lose License.

(1) The following definitions apply in this subsection:
a. Applicable State entity.—The State Board of Education for public schools and charter schools, the State Board of Community Colleges for community colleges, or the Secretary of Administration for nonpublic schools and home schools.
b. Certificate.—A driving eligibility certificate that meets the conditions of subsection (n) of this section.
c. Disciplinary action.—An expulsion, a suspension for more than 10 consecutive days, or an assignment to an alternative educational setting for more than 10 consecutive days.
d. Enumerated student conduct.—One of the following behaviors that results in disciplinary action:
1. The possession or sale of an alcoholic beverage or an illegal controlled substance on school property.
2. The bringing, possession, or use on school property of a weapon or firearm that resulted in disciplinary action under G.S. 115C-391(d1) or that could have resulted in that disciplinary action if the conduct had occurred in a public school.
3. The physical assault on a teacher or other school personnel on school property.
e. School.—A public school, charter school, community college, nonpublic school, or home school.
f. School administrator.—The person who is required to sign certificates under subdivision (4) of subsection (n) of this section.
g. School property.—The physical premises of the school, school buses or other vehicles under the school's control or contract and that are used to transport students, and school-sponsored curricular or extracurricular activities that occur on or off the physical premises of the school.
h. Student.—A person who desires to obtain a permit or license issued under this section.

(2) Any student who was subject to disciplinary action for enumerated student conduct that occurred either after the first day of July before the school year in which the student enrolled in the eighth grade or after the student's fourteenth birthday, whichever event occurred first, is subject to this subsection.

(3) A student who is subject to this subsection is eligible for a certificate when the school administrator determines that the student has exhausted all administrative appeals connected to the disciplinary action and that one of the following conditions is met:

a. The enumerated student conduct occurred before the student reached the age of 15, and the student is now at least 16 years old.
b. The enumerated student conduct occurred after the student reached the age of 15, and it is at least one year after the date the student exhausted all administrative appeals connected to the disciplinary action.
c. The student needs the certificate in order to drive to and from school, a drug or alcohol treatment counseling program, as appropriate, or a mental health treatment program, and no other transportation is available.

(4) A student whose permit or license is denied or revoked due to ineligibility for a certificate under this subsection may otherwise be eligible for a certificate if, after six months from the date of the ineligibility, the school administrator determines that one of the following conditions is met:
a. The student has returned to school or has been placed in an alternative educational setting, and has displayed exemplary student behavior, as defined by the applicable State entity.
b. The disciplinary action was for the possession or sale of an alcoholic beverage or an illegal controlled substance on school property, and the student subsequently attended and successfully completed, as defined by the applicable State entity, a drug or alcohol treatment counseling program, as appropriate.

History: 1935, c. 52, s. 6; 1953, c. 355; 1955, c. 1187, s. 8; 1963, c. 968, ss. 2, 2A; 1965, c. 410, s. 3; c. 1171; 1967, c. 694; 1969, c. 37; 1973, c. 191, ss. 1, 2; c. 664, ss. 1, 2; 1975, c. 79; c. 716, s. 5; 1979, c. 101; c. 667, ss. 15, 16, 41; 1981 (Reg. Sess., 1982), c. 1257, s. 2; 1989 (Reg. Sess., 1990), c. 1021, s. 11; 1991, c. 689, s. 326; 1993, c. 539, s. 319; 1994, Ex. Sess., c. 24, s. 14(c); 1997-16, s. 1; 1997-443, s. 32.20; 1997-507, s. 1; 1998-149, ss. 2.1, 2.2, 2.3, 2.4, 2.5; 1998-212, s. 9.21(c); 1999-243, ss. 1, 2; 1999-276, s. 1; 1999-387, s. 4; 1999-452, s. 9.

§ 20-12.1. Impaired supervision or instruction

(a) It is unlawful for a person to serve as a supervising driver under G.S. 20-7(l) or G.S. 20-11 or as an approved instructor under G.S. 20-7(m) in any of the following circumstances:

(1) While under the influence of an impairing substance.
(2) After having consumed sufficient alcohol to have, at any relevant time after the driving, an alcohol concentration of 0.08 or more.

(b) An offense under this section is an implied-consent offense under G.S. 20-16.2.

History: 1977, c. 116, ss. 1, 2; 1981, c. 412, s. 4; c. 747, s. 66; 1983, c. 435, s. 9; 1993, c. 285, s. 2; 1997-16, s. 7; 1997-443, s. 32.20.

§ 20-13. Suspension of license of provisional licensee

(a) The Division may suspend, with or without a preliminary hearing, the operator's license of a provisional licensee upon receipt of notice of the licensee's conviction of a motor vehicle moving violation, in accordance with subsection (b), if the offense was committed while the person was still a provisional licensee. As used in this section, the phrase "motor vehicle moving violation" does not include the offenses listed in the third paragraph of G.S. 20-16(c) for which no points are assessed, nor does it include equipment violations specified in Part 9 of Article 3 of this Chapter. However, if the Division revokes without a preliminary hearing and the person whose license is being revoked requests a hearing before the effective date of the revocation, the licensee retains his license unless it is revoked under some other provision of the law, until the hearing is held, the person withdraws his request, or he fails to appear at a scheduled hearing.

(b) The Division may suspend the license of a provisional licensee as follows:

(1) For the first motor vehicle moving violation, the Division may not suspend the license of the provisional licensee.
(2) For conviction of a second motor vehicle moving violation committed within 12 months of the date the first offense was committed, the Division may suspend the licensee's license for up to 30 days.
(3) For conviction of a third motor vehicle moving violation committed within 12 months of the date the first offense was committed, the Division may suspend the licensee's license for up to 90 days.
(4) For conviction of a fourth motor vehicle moving violation committed within 12 months of the date the first offense was committed, the Division may suspend the licensee's license for up to six months.

The Division may, in lieu of suspension and with the written consent of the licensee, place the licensee on probation for a period of not more than 12 months on such terms and conditions as the Division sees fit to impose.

If the Division suspends the provisional licensee's license for at least 90 days without a preliminary hearing, the parent, guardian or other person standing in loco parentis of the provisional licensee may request a hearing to determine if the provisional licensee's license should be restored on a probationary status. The Division may wait until one-half the period of suspension has expired to hold the hearing. The Division may place the licensee on probation for up to 12 months on such terms and conditions as the Division sees fit to impose, if the licensee consents in writing to the terms and conditions of probation.

(c) In the event of conviction of two or more motor vehicle moving offenses committed on a single occasion, a licensee shall be charged, for purposes of this section, with only one moving offense, except as otherwise provided.

(d) The suspension provided for in this section is in addition to any other remedies which the Division may have against a licensee under other provisions of law; however, when the license of any person is suspended under this section and at the same time is also suspended under other provisions of law, the suspensions run concurrently.

(e) Repealed by Session Laws 1987, c. 869, s. 14, effective January 1, 1988.

History: 1963, c. 968, s. 1; 1965, c. 897; 1967, c. 295, s. 1; 1971, c. 120, ss. 1, 2; 1973, c. 439; 1975, c. 716, s. 5; 1979, c. 555, s. 1; 1983, c. 538, ss. 1, 2; 1983 (Reg. Sess., 1984), c. 1101, s. 3; 1987, c. 744, ss. 3, 4; c. 869, s. 14.

§ 20-13.2. Grounds for revoking provisional license

(a) The Division must revoke the license of a person convicted of violating the provisions of G.S. 20-138.3 upon receipt of a record of the licensee's conviction.

(b) If a person is convicted of an offense involving impaired driving and the offense occurs while he is less than 21 years old, his license must be revoked under this section in addition to any other revocation required or authorized by law.

(c) If a person willfully refuses to submit to a chemical analysis pursuant to G.S. 20-16.2 while he is less than 21 years old, his license must be revoked under this section, in addition to any other revocation required or authorized by law. A revocation order entered under authority of this subsection becomes effective at the same time as a revocation order issued under G.S. 20-16.2 for the same willful refusal.

(c1) (Effective until July 1, 2000) The Division must revoke the permit or license of a person under the age of 18 if the proper school authority notifies the Division that the person no longer meets the requirements for a driving eligibility certificate under G.S. 20-11(n). Notwithstanding subsection (d) of this section, the length of revocation must last until the person's eighteenth birthday or until the Division restores the permit or license under this subsection. The Division must restore a person's permit or license before the person's eighteenth birthday, if the person submits to the Division one of the following:

(1) A high school diploma or its equivalent.

(2) A driving eligibility certificate as required under G.S. 20-11(n).

Notwithstanding any other law, the decision concerning whether a driving eligibility certificate was properly issued or improperly denied shall be appealed only as provided under the rules adopted in accordance with G.S. 115C-12(27), G.S. 115D-5(a3), or G.S. 115C-566, whichever is applicable, and may not be appealed under this Chapter.

(c1) (Effective July 1, 2000) Upon receipt of notification from the proper school authority that a person no longer meets the requirements for a driving eligibility certificate under G.S. 20-11(n), the Division must expeditiously notify the person that his or her permit or license is revoked effective on the tenth calendar day after the mailing of the revocation notice. The Division must revoke the permit or license of that person on the tenth calendar day after the mailing of the revocation notice. Notwithstanding subsection (d) of this section, the length of revocation must last for the following periods:

(1) If the revocation is because of ineligibility for a driving eligibility certificate under G.S. 20-11(n)(1), then the revocation shall last until the person's eighteenth birthday.

(2) If the revocation is because of ineligibility for a driving eligibility certificate under G.S. 20-11(n1), then the revocation shall be for a period of one year.

For a person whose permit or license was revoked due to ineligibility for a driving eligibility certificate under G.S. 20-11(n)(1), the Division must restore a person's permit or license before the person's eighteenth birthday, if the person submits to the Division one of the following:

(1) A high school diploma or its equivalent.

(2) A driving eligibility certificate as required under G.S. 20-11(n).

For a person whose permit or license was revoked due to ineligibility for a driving eligibility certificate under G.S. 20-11(n1), the Division shall restore a person's permit or license before the end of the revocation period, if the person submits to the Division a driving eligibility certificate as required under G.S. 20-11(n).

Notwithstanding any other law, the decision concerning whether a driving eligibility certificate was properly issued or improperly denied shall be appealed only as provided under the rules adopted in accordance with G.S. 115C-12(28), 115D-5(a3), or 115C-566, whichever is applicable, and may not be appealed under this Chapter.

(c2) The Division must revoke the permit or license of a person under the age of 18 upon receiving a record of the person's conviction for malicious use of an explosive or incendiary device to damage property (G.S. 14-49(b) and (b1)); conspiracy to injure or damage by use of an explosive or incendiary device (G.S. 14-50); making a false report concerning a destructive device in a public building (G.S. 14-69.1(c)); perpetrating a hoax concerning a destructive device in a public building (G.S. 14-69.2(c)); possessing or carrying a dynamite cartridge, bomb, grenade, mine, or powerful explosive on educational property (G.S. 14-269.2(b1)); or causing, encouraging, or aiding a minor to possess or carry a dynamite cartridge, bomb, grenade, mine, or powerful explosive on educational property (G.S. 14-269.2(c1)).

(d) The length of revocation under this section shall be one year. Revocations under this section run concurrently with any other revocations.

(e) Before the Division restores a driver's license that has been suspended or revoked under any provision of this Article, other than G.S. 20-24.1, the person seeking to have his driver's license restored shall submit to the Division proof that he has notified his insurance agent or company of his seeking the restoration and that he is financially responsible. Proof of financial responsibility shall be in one of the following forms:

(1) A written certificate or electronically-transmitted facsimile thereof from any insurance carrier duly authorized to do business in this State certifying that there is in effect a nonfleet private passenger motor vehicle liability policy for the benefit of the person required to furnish proof of financial responsibility. The certificate or facsimile shall state the effective date and expiration date of the nonfleet private passenger motor vehicle liability policy and shall state the date that the certificate or facsimile is issued. The certificate or facsimile shall remain effective proof of financial responsibility for a period of 30 consecutive days following the date the certificate or facsimile is issued but shall not in and of itself constitute a binder or policy of insurance or

(2) A binder for or policy of nonfleet private passenger motor vehicle liability insurance under which the applicant is insured, provided that the binder or policy states the effective date and expiration date of the nonfleet private passenger motor vehicle liability policy.

The preceding provisions of this subsection do not apply to applicants who do not own currently registered motor vehicles and who do not operate nonfleet private passenger motor vehicles that are owned by other persons and that are not insured under commercial motor vehicle liability insurance policies. In such cases, the applicant shall sign a written certificate to that effect. Such certificate shall be furnished by the Division and may be incorporated into the restoration application form. Any material misrepresentation made by such person on such certificate shall be grounds for suspension of that person's license for a period of 90 days.

For the purposes of this subsection, the term "nonfleet private passenger motor vehicle" has the definition ascribed to it in Article 40 of General Statute Chapter 58.

The Commissioner may require that certificates required by this subsection be on a form approved by the Commissioner. The financial responsibility required by this subsection shall be kept in effect for not less than three years after the date that the license is restored. Failure to maintain financial responsibility as required by this subsection shall be grounds for suspending the restored driver's license for a period of thirty (30) days. Nothing in this subsection precludes any person from showing proof of financial responsibility in any other manner authorized by Articles 9A and 13 of this Chapter.

History: 1983, c. 435, s. 33; 1987, c. 869, s. 12; 1989, c. 436, s. 3; 1993, c. 285, s. 8; 1995, c. 506, ss. 3, 4, 5; 1997-507, s. 2; 1999-243, s. 3; 1999-257, s. 4.

§ 20-16. Authority of Division to suspend license

(a) The Division shall have authority to suspend the license of any operator with or without a preliminary hearing upon a showing by its records or other satisfactory evidence that the licensee:

(1) through (4) Repealed by Session Laws 1979, c. 36;

(5) Has, under the provisions of subsection (c) of this section, within a three-year period, accumulated 12 or more points, or eight or more points in the three-year period immediately following the reinstatement of a license which has been suspended or revoked because of a conviction for one or more traffic offenses;

(6) Has made or permitted an unlawful or fraudulent use of such license or a learner's permit, or has displayed or represented as his own, a license or learner's permit not issued to him;

(7) Has committed an offense in another state, which if committed in this State would be grounds for suspension or revocation;

(8) Has been convicted of illegal transportation of alcoholic beverages;

(8a) Has been convicted of impaired instruction under G.S. 20-12.1;

(8b) Has violated on a military installation a regulation of that installation prohibiting conduct substantially equivalent to conduct that constitutes impaired driving under G.S. 20-138.1 and, as a result of that violation, has had his privilege to drive on that installation revoked or suspended after an administrative hearing authorized by the commanding officer of the installation and that commanding officer has general court martial jurisdiction;

(9) Has, within a period of 12 months, been convicted of two or more charges of speeding in excess of 55 and not more than 80 miles per hour, or of one or more charges of reckless driving and one or more charges of speeding in excess of 55 and not more than 80 miles per hour;

(10) Has been convicted of operating a motor vehicle at a speed in excess of 75 miles per hour on a public road or highway where the maximum speed is less than 70 miles per hour;

(10a) Has been convicted of operating a motor vehicle at a speed in excess of 80 miles per hour on a public highway where the maximum speed is 70 miles per hour; or

(11) Has been sentenced by a court of record and all or a part of the sentence has been suspended and a condition of suspension of the sentence is that the operator not operate a motor vehicle for a period of time.

However, if the Division revokes without a preliminary hearing and the person whose license is being revoked requests a hearing before the effective date of the revocation, the licensee retains his license unless it is revoked under some other provision of the law, until the hearing is held, the person withdraws his request, or he fails to appear at a scheduled hearing.

(b) Pending an appeal from a conviction of any violation of the motor vehicle laws of this State, no driver's license shall be suspended by the Division of Motor Vehicles because of such conviction or because of evidence of the commission of the offense for which the conviction has been had.

(c) The Division shall maintain a record of convictions of every person licensed or required to be licensed under the provisions of this Article as an operator and shall enter therein records of all convictions of such persons for any violation of the motor vehicle laws of this State and shall assign to the record of such person, as of the date of commission of the offense, a number of points for every such conviction in accordance with the following schedule of convictions and points, except that points shall not be assessed for convictions resulting in suspensions or revocations under other provisions of laws: Further, any points heretofore charged for violation of the motor vehicle inspection laws shall not be considered by the Division of Motor Vehicles as a basis for suspension or revocation of driver's license:

Schedule of Point Values

Passing stopped school bus	5
Reckless driving	4
Hit and run, property damage only	4
Following too close	4
Driving on wrong side of road	4
Illegal passing	4
Running through stop sign	3
Speeding in excess of 55 miles per hour	3
Failing to yield right-of-way	3
Running through red light	3
No driver's license or license expired more than one year	3
Failure to stop for siren	3
Driving through safety zone	3
No liability insurance	3
Failure to report accident where such report is required	3
Speeding in a school zone in excess of the posted school zone speed limit	3

All other moving violations 2
Littering pursuant to G.S. 14-399 when the littering involves
the use of a motor vehicle 1

Schedule of Point Values for Violations While Operating a Commercial Motor Vehicle

Passing stopped school bus 8
Rail-highway crossing violation 6
Reckless driving 5
Hit and run, property damage only 5
Following too close 5
Driving on wrong side of road 5
Illegal passing 5
Running through stop sign 4
Speeding in excess of 55 miles per hour 4
Failing to yield right-of-way 4
Running through red light 4
No driver's license or license expired more than one year 4
Failure to stop for siren 4
Driving through safety zone 4
No liability insurance 4
Failure to report accident where such report is required 4
Speeding in a school zone in excess of the posted school zone speed limit 4
Possessing alcoholic beverages in the passenger area of a
commercial motor vehicle 4
All other moving violations 3
Littering pursuant to G.S. 14-399 when the littering involves
the use of a motor vehicle 1

The above provisions of this subsection shall only apply to violations and convictions which take place within the State of North Carolina. The Schedule of Point Values for Violations While Operating a Commercial Motor Vehicle shall not apply to any commercial motor vehicle known as an "aerial lift truck" having a hydraulic arm and bucket station, and to any commercial motor vehicle known as a "line truck" having a hydraulic lift for cable, if the vehicle is owned, operated by or under contract to a public utility, electric or telephone membership corporation or municipality and used in connection with installation, restoration or maintenance of utility services.

No points shall be assessed for conviction of the following offenses:

Overloads
Over length
Over width
Over height
Illegal parking
Carrying concealed weapon
Improper plates
Improper registration
Improper muffler
Improper display of license plates or dealers' tags
Unlawful display of emblems and insignia
Failure to display current inspection certificate.

In case of the conviction of a licensee of two or more traffic offenses committed on a single occasion, such licensee shall be assessed points for one offense only and if the offenses involved have a different point value, such licensee shall be assessed for the offense having the greater point value.

Upon the restoration of the license or driving privilege of such person whose license or driving privilege has been suspended or revoked because of conviction for a traffic offense, any points that might previously have been accumulated in the driver's record shall be cancelled.

Whenever any licensee accumulates as many as seven points or accumulates as many as four points during a three-year period immediately following reinstatement of his license after a period of suspension or revocation, the Division may request the licensee to attend a conference regarding such licensee's driving record.

The Division may also afford any licensee who has accumulated as many as seven points or any licensee who has accumulated as many as four points within a three-year period immediately following reinstatement of his license after a period of suspension or revocation an opportunity to attend a driver improvement clinic operated by the Division and, upon the successful completion of the course taken at the clinic, three points shall be deducted from the licensee's conviction record; provided, that only one deduction of points shall be made on behalf of any licensee within any five-year period.

When a license is suspended under the point system provided for herein, the first such suspension shall be for not more than 60 days; the second such suspension shall not exceed six months and any subsequent suspension shall not exceed one year.

Whenever the driver's license of any person is subject to suspension under this subsection and at the same time also subject to suspension or revocation under other provisions of laws, such suspensions or revocations shall run concurrently.

In the discretion of the Division, a period of probation not to exceed one year may be substituted for suspension or for any unexpired period of suspension under subsections (a)(1) through (a)(10a) of this section. Any violation of probation during the probation period shall result in a suspension for the unexpired remainder of the suspension period. Any accumulation of three or more points under this subsection during a period of probation shall constitute a violation of the condition of probation.

(d) Upon suspending the license of any person as authorized in this section, the Division shall immediately notify the licensee in writing and upon his request shall afford him an opportunity for a hearing, not to exceed 60 days after receipt of the request, unless a preliminary hearing was held before his license was suspended. Upon such hearing the duly authorized agents of the Division may administer oaths and may issue subpoenas for the attendance of witnesses and the production of relevant books and papers and may require a reexamination of the licensee. Upon such hearing the Division shall either rescind its order of suspension, or good cause appearing therefor, may extend the suspension of such license. Provided further upon such hearing, preliminary or otherwise, involving subsections (a)(1) through (a)(10a) of this section, the Division may for good cause appearing in its discretion substitute a period of probation not to exceed one year for the suspension or for any unexpired period of suspension. Probation shall mean any written agreement between the suspended driver and a duly authorized representative of the Division and such period of probation shall not exceed one year, and any violation of the probation agreement during the probation period shall result in a suspension for the unexpired remainder of the suspension period. The authorized agents of the Division shall have the same powers in connection with a preliminary hearing prior to suspension as this subsection provided in connection with hearings held after suspension. These agents shall also have the authority to take possession of a surrendered license on behalf of the Division if the suspension is upheld and the licensee requests that the suspension begin immediately.

(e) The Division may conduct driver improvement clinics for the benefit of those who have been convicted of one or more violations of this Chapter. Each driver attending a driver improvement clinic shall pay a fee of twenty-five dollars ($25.00).

(e1) Notwithstanding any other provision of this Chapter, if the Division suspends the license of an operator pursuant to subdivisions (a)(9), (a)(10), or (a)(10a) of this section, upon the first suspension only, a district court judge may allow the licensee a limited driving privilege or license for a period not to exceed 12 months, provided he has not been convicted of any other motor vehicle moving violation within the previous 12 months. The limited driving privilege shall be issued in the same manner and under the terms and conditions prescribed in G.S. 20-16.1(b)(1), (2), (3), (4), and (5).

History: 1935, c. 52, s. 11; 1947, c. 893, ss. 1, 2; c. 1067, s. 13; 1949, c. 373, ss. 1, 2; c. 1032, s. 2; 1953, c. 450; 1955, c. 1152, s. 15; c. 1187, ss. 9–12; 1957, c. 499, s. 1; 1959, c. 1242, ss. 1–2; 1961, c. 460, ss. 1, 2(a); 1963, c. 1115; 1965, c. 130; 1967, c. 16; 1971, c. 234, ss. 1, 2; c. 793, ss. 1, 2; c. 1198, ss. 1, 2; 1973, c. 17, ss. 1, 2; 1975, c. 716, s. 5; 1977, c. 902, s. 1; 1979, c. 36; c. 667, ss. 18, 41; 1981, c. 412, s. 4; c. 747, ss. 33, 66; 1981 (Reg. Sess., 1982), c. 1256; 1983, c. 435, s. 10; c. 538, ss. 3–5; c. 798; 1983 (Reg. Sess., 1984), c. 1101, s. 4; 1987, c. 744, ss. 1, 2; 1987 (Reg. Sess., 1988), c. 1037, s. 75; 1989, c. 784, s. 9; 1991, c. 682, s. 3; 1999-330, s. 7; 1999-452, s. 10.

§ 20-16.1. Mandatory suspension of driver's license upon conviction of excessive speeding; limited driving permits for first offenders

(a) Notwithstanding any other provisions of this Article, the Division shall suspend for a period of 30 days the license of any driver without preliminary hearing on receiving a record of the driver's conviction of either (i) exceeding by more than 15 miles per hour the speed limit, either within or outside the corporate limits of a municipality, if the person was also driving at a speed in excess of 55 miles per hour at the time of the offense, or (ii) driving at a speed in excess of 80 miles per hour at the time of the offense.

(b) (1) Upon a first conviction only of violating subsection (a), the trial judge may when feasible allow a limited driving privilege or license to the person convicted for proper purposes reasonably connected with the health, education and welfare of the person convicted and his family. For purposes of determining whether conviction is a first conviction, no prior offense occurring more than seven years before the date of the current offense shall be considered. The judge may impose upon such limited driving privilege any restrictions as in his discretion are deemed advisable including, but not limited to, conditions of days, hours, types of vehicles, routes, geographical boundaries and specific purposes for which limited driving privilege is allowed. Any such limited driving privilege allowed and restrictions imposed thereon shall be specifically recorded in a written judgment which shall be as near as practical to that hereinafter set forth and shall be signed by the trial judge and shall be affixed with the seal of the court and shall be made a part of the records of the said court. A copy of said judgment shall be transmitted to the Division of Motor Vehicles along with any driver's license in the possession of the person convicted and a notice of the conviction. Such permit issued hereunder shall be valid for 30 days from the date of issuance by trial court. Such permit shall constitute a valid license to operate motor vehicles of the class or type that would be allowed by the person's license if it were not currently revoked upon the streets and highways of this or any other state in accordance with the restrictions noted thereon and shall be subject to all provisions of law relating to driver's license, not by their nature, rendered inapplicable.

(2) The judgment issued by the trial judge as herein permitted shall as near as practical be in form and content as follows:

This cause coming on to be heard and being heard before the Honorable ...., Judge Presiding, and it appearing to the court that the defendant, ..., has been convicted of the offense of excessive speeding in violation of G.S. 20-16.1(a), and it further appearing to the court that the defendant should be issued a restrictive driving license and is entitled to the issuance of a restrictive driving privilege under and by the authority of G.S. 20-16.1(b);

Now, therefore, it is ordered, adjudged and decreed that the defendant be allowed to operate a motor vehicle under the following conditions and under no other circumstances.

Name: ....
Race: .... Sex: ....
Height: .... Weight: ....
Color of Hair: .... Color of Eyes: ....
Birth Date: ....
Driver's License Number: ....
Signature of Licensee: ....
Conditions of Restriction: ....
Type of Vehicle: ....
Geographic Restrictions: ....
Hours of Restriction: ....
Other Restrictions: ....

This limited license shall be effective from .... to .... subject to further orders as the court in its discretion may deem necessary and proper.

This the .... day of ....,

....
(Judge Presiding)

(3) Upon conviction of such offense outside the jurisdiction of this State the person so convicted may apply to the resident judge of the superior court of the district or set of districts as defined in G.S. 7A-41.1(a) in which he resides for limited driving privileges hereinbefore defined. Upon such application the judge shall have the authority to issue such limited driving privileges in the same manner as if he were the trial judge.

(4) Any violation of the restrictive driving privileges as set forth in the judgment of the trial judge allowing such privileges shall constitute the offense of driving while license has been suspended as set forth in G.S. 20-28. Whenever a person is charged with operating a motor vehicle in violation of the restrictions, the limited driving privilege shall be suspended pending the final disposition of the charge.

(5) This section is supplemental and in addition to existing law and shall not be construed so as to repeal any existing provision contained in the General Statutes of North Carolina.

(c) Upon conviction of a similar second or subsequent offense which offense occurs within one year of the first or prior offense, the license of such operator shall be suspended for 60 days, provided such first or prior offense occurs subsequent to July 1, 1953.

(d) Notwithstanding any other provisions of this Article, the Division shall suspend for a period of 60 days the license of any driver without preliminary hearing on receiving a record of such driver's conviction of having violated the laws against speeding described in subsection (a) and of having violated the laws against reckless driving on the same occasion as the speeding offense occurred.

(e) The provisions of this section shall not prevent the suspension or revocation of a license for a longer period of time where the same may be authorized by other provisions of law.

(f) Repealed by Session Laws 1987, c. 869, s. 14.

(g) Any judge granting limited driving privileges under this section shall, prior to granting such privileges, be furnished proof and be satisfied that the person being granted such privileges is financially responsible. Proof of financial responsibility shall be in one of the following forms:

(1) A written certificate or electronically-transmitted facsimile thereof from any insurance carrier duly authorized to do business in this State certifying that there is in effect a nonfleet private passenger motor vehicle liability policy for the benefit of the person required to furnish proof of financial responsibility. The certificate or facsimile shall state the effective date and expiration date of the nonfleet private passenger motor vehicle liability policy and shall state the date that the certificate or facsimile is issued. The certificate or facsimile shall remain effective proof of financial responsibility for a period of 30 consecutive days following the date the certificate or facsimile is issued but shall not in and of itself constitute a binder or policy of insurance or

(2) A binder for or policy of nonfleet private passenger motor vehicle liability insurance under which the applicant is insured, provided that the binder or policy states the effective date and expiration date of the nonfleet private passenger motor vehicle liability policy.

The preceding provisions of this subsection do not apply to applicants who do not own currently registered motor vehicles and who do not operate nonfleet private passenger motor vehicles that are owned by other persons and that are not insured under commercial motor vehicle liability insurance policies. In such cases, the applicant shall sign a written certificate to that effect. Such certificate shall be furnished by the Division. Any material misrepresentation made by such person on such certificate shall be grounds for suspension of that person's license for a period of 90 days.

For the purpose of this subsection "nonfleet private passenger motor vehicle" has the definition ascribed to it in Article 40 of General Statute Chapter 58.

The Commissioner may require that certificates required by this subsection be on a form approved by the Commissioner. Such granting of limited driving privileges shall be conditioned upon the maintenance of such financial responsibility during the period of the limited driving privilege. Nothing in this subsection precludes any person from showing proof of financial responsibility in any other manner authorized by Articles 9A and 13 of this Chapter.

History: 1953, c. 1223; 1955, c. 1187, s. 15; 1959, c. 1264, s. 4; 1965, c. 133; 1975, c. 716, s. 5; c. 763; 1979, c. 667, ss. 19, 41; 1983, c. 77; 1987, c. 869, ss. 13, 14; 1989, c. 436, s. 4; 770, s. 57; 1995 (Reg. Sess., 1996), c. 652, s. 2; 1999-456, s. 59.

FIRST OF TWO VERSIONS OF THIS SECTION
(THIS SECTION HAS MORE THAN ONE DOCUMENT WITH VARYING EFFECTIVE DATES)

§ 20-16.2. (Effective until July 1, 2000) Implied consent to chemical analysis; mandatory revocation of license in event of refusal; right of driver to request analysis

(a) Basis for Charging Officer to Require Chemical Analysis; Notification of Rights.—Any person who drives a vehicle on a highway or public vehicular area thereby gives consent to a chemical analysis if charged with an implied-consent offense. The charging officer shall designate the type of chemical analysis to be administered, and it may be administered when the officer has reasonable grounds to believe that the person charged has committed the implied-consent offense.

Except as provided in this subsection or subsection (b), before any type of chemical analysis is administered the person charged shall be taken before a chemical analyst authorized to administer a test of a person's breath, who shall inform the person orally and also give the person a notice in writing that:

(1) The person has a right to refuse to be tested.
(2) Refusal to take any required test or tests will result in an immediate revocation of the person's driving privilege for at least 30 days and an additional 12-month revocation by the Division of Motor Vehicles.
(3) The test results, or the fact of the person's refusal, will be admissible in evidence at trial on the offense charged.
(4) The person's driving privilege will be revoked immediately for at least 30 days if:
    a. The test reveals an alcohol concentration of 0.08 or more;
    b. The person was driving a commercial motor vehicle and the test reveals an alcohol concentration of 0.04 or more; or
    c. The person is under 21 years of age and the test reveals any alcohol concentration.
(5) The person may choose a qualified person to administer a chemical test or tests in addition to any test administered at the direction of the charging officer.
(6) The person has the right to call an attorney and select a witness to view for him or her the testing procedures, but the testing may not be delayed for these purposes longer than 30 minutes from the time when the person is notified of his or her rights.

If the charging officer or an arresting officer is authorized to administer a chemical analysis of a person's breath, the charging officer or the arresting officer may give the person charged the oral and written notice of rights required by this subsection. This authority applies regardless of the type of chemical analysis designated.

(a1) Meaning of Terms.—Under this section, an "implied-consent offense" is an offense involving impaired driving or an alcohol-related offense made subject to the procedures of this section. A person is "charged" with an offense if the person is arrested for it or if criminal process for the offense has been issued. A "charging officer" is a law-enforcement officer who arrests the person charged, lodges the charge, or assists the officer who arrested the person or lodged the charge by assuming custody of the person to make the request required by subsection (c) and, if necessary, to present the person to a judicial official for an initial appearance.

(b) Unconscious Person May Be Tested.—If a charging officer has reasonable grounds to believe that a person has committed an implied-consent offense, and the person is unconscious or otherwise in a condition that makes the person incapable of refusal, the charging officer may direct the taking of a blood sample by a person qualified under G.S. 20-139.1 or may direct the administration of any other chemical analysis that may be effectively performed. In this instance the notification of rights set out in subsection (a) and the request required by subsection (c) are not necessary.

(c) Request to Submit to Chemical Analysis; Procedure upon Refusal.—The charging officer, in the presence of the chemical analyst who has notified the person of his or her rights under subsection (a), must request the person charged to submit to the type of chemical analysis designated. If the person charged willfully refuses to submit to that chemical analysis, none may be given under the provisions of this section, but the refusal does not preclude testing under other applicable procedures of law. If the person refuses to submit to the chemical analysis, the charging officer and the chemical analyst must without unnecessary delay go before an official authorized to administer oaths and execute an affidavit stating that the person charged, after being advised of his or her rights under subsection (a), willfully refused to submit to a chemical analysis at the request of the charging officer. The charging officer must immediately mail the affidavit to the Division. If the person's refusal to submit to a chemical analysis occurs in a case involving death or critical injury to another person, the charging officer must include that fact in the affidavit mailed to the Division. If the charging officer is also the chemical analyst who has notified the person of his or her rights under subsection (a), the charging officer may perform alone the duties of this subsection.

(d) Consequences of Refusal; Right to Hearing before Division; Issues.—Upon receipt of a properly executed affidavit required by subsection (c), the Division must expeditiously notify the person charged that the person's license to drive is revoked for 12 months, effective on the tenth calendar day after the mailing of the revocation order unless, before the effective date of the order, the person requests in writing a hearing before the Division. Except for the time referred to in G.S. 20-16.5, if the person shows to the satisfaction of the Division that his or her license was surrendered to the court, and remained in the court's possession, then the Division shall credit the amount of time for which the license was in the possession of the court against the 12-month revocation period required by this subsection. If the person properly requests a hearing, the person retains his or her license, unless it is revoked under some other provision of law, until the hearing is held, the person withdraws the request, or the person fails to appear at a scheduled hearing. The hearing officer may subpoena any witnesses or documents that the hearing officer deems necessary. The person may request the hearing officer to subpoena the charging officer, the chemical analyst, or both to appear at the hearing if the person makes the request in writing at least three days before the hearing. The person may subpoena any other witness whom the person deems necessary, and the provisions of G.S. 1A-1, Rule 45, apply to the issuance and service of all subpoenas issued under the authority of this section. The hearing officer is authorized to administer oaths to witnesses appearing at the hearing. The hearing must be conducted in the county where the charge was brought, and must be limited to consideration of whether:

(1) The person was charged with an implied-consent offense;
(2) The charging officer had reasonable grounds to believe that the person had committed an implied-consent offense;
(3) The implied-consent offense charged involved death or critical injury to another person, if this allegation is in the affidavit;
(4) The person was notified of his or her rights as required by subsection (a); and
(5) The person willfully refused to submit to a chemical analysis upon the request of the charging officer.

If the Division finds that the conditions specified in this subsection are met, it must order the revocation sustained. If the Division finds that any of the conditions (1), (2), (4), or (5) is not met, it must rescind the revocation. If it finds that condition (3) is alleged in the affidavit but is not met, it must order the revocation sustained if that is the only condition that is not met; in this instance subsection (d1) does not apply to that revocation. If the revocation is sustained, the person must surrender his or her license immediately upon notification by the Division.

(d1) Consequences of Refusal in Case Involving Death or Critical Injury.—If the refusal occurred in a case involving death or critical injury to another person, no limited driving privilege may be issued. The 12-month revocation begins only after all other periods of revocation have terminated unless the person's license is revoked under G.S. 20-28, 20-28.1, 20-19(d), or 20-19(e). If the revocation is based on those sections, the revocation under this subsection begins at the time and in the manner specified in subsection (d) for revocations under this section. However, the person's eligibility for a hearing to determine if the revocation under those sections should be rescinded is postponed for one year from the date on which the person would otherwise have been eligible for such a hearing. If the person's driver's license is again revoked while the 12-month revocation under this subsection is in effect, that revocation, whether imposed by a court or by the Division, may only take effect after the period of revocation under this subsection has terminated.

(e) Right to Hearing in Superior Court.—If the revocation is sustained after the hearing, the person whose license has been revoked has the right to file a petition in the superior court for a hearing de novo upon the issues listed in subsection (d), in the same manner and under the same conditions as provided in G.S. 20-25 except that the de novo hearing is conducted in the superior court district or set of districts as defined in G.S. 7A-41.1 where the charge was made.

(e1) Limited Driving Privilege after Six Months in Certain Instances.—A person whose driver's license has been revoked under this section may apply for and a judge authorized to do so by this subsection may issue a limited driving privilege if:

(1) At the time of the refusal the person held either a valid driver's license or a license that had been expired for less than one year;
(2) At the time of the refusal, the person had not within the preceding seven years been convicted of an offense involving impaired driving;

(3) At the time of the refusal, the person had not in the preceding seven years willfully refused to submit to a chemical analysis under this section;

(4) The implied-consent offense charged did not involve death or critical injury to another person;

(5) The underlying charge for which the defendant was requested to submit to a chemical analysis has been finally disposed of:

a. Other than by conviction; or

b. By a conviction of impaired driving under G.S. 20-138.1, at a punishment level authorizing issuance of a limited driving privilege under G.S. 20-179.3(b), and the defendant has complied with at least one of the mandatory conditions of probation listed for the punishment level under which the defendant was sentenced;

(6) Subsequent to the refusal the person has had no unresolved pending charges for or additional convictions of an offense involving impaired driving;

(7) The person's license has been revoked for at least six months for the refusal; and

(8) The person has obtained a substance abuse assessment from a mental health facility and successfully completed any recommended training or treatment program.

Except as modified in this subsection, the provisions of G.S. 20-179.3 relating to the procedure for application and conduct of the hearing and the restrictions required or authorized to be included in the limited driving privilege apply to applications under this subsection. If the case was finally disposed of in the district court, the hearing shall be conducted in the district court district as defined in G.S. 7A-133 in which the refusal occurred by a district court judge. If the case was finally disposed of in the superior court, the hearing shall be conducted in the superior court district or set of districts as defined in G.S. 7A-41.1 in which the refusal occurred by a superior court judge. A limited driving privilege issued under this section authorizes a person to drive if the person's license is revoked solely under this section or solely under this section and G.S. 20-17(2). If the person's license is revoked for any other reason, the limited driving privilege is invalid.

(f) Notice to Other States as to Nonresidents.—When it has been finally determined under the procedures of this section that a nonresident's privilege to drive a motor vehicle in this State has been revoked, the Division must give information in writing of the action taken to the motor vehicle administrator of the state of the person's residence and of any state in which the person has a license.

(g) Repealed by Session Laws 1973, c. 914.

(h) Repealed by Session Laws 1979, c. 423, s. 2.

(i) Right to Chemical Analysis before Arrest or Charge.—A person stopped or questioned by a law-enforcement officer who is investigating whether the person may have committed an implied-consent offense may request the administration of a chemical analysis before any arrest or other charge is made for the offense. Upon this request, the officer shall afford the person the opportunity to have a chemical analysis of his or her breath, if available, in accordance with the procedures required by G.S. 20-139.1(b). The request constitutes the person's consent to be transported by the law-enforcement officer to the place where the chemical analysis is to be administered. Before the chemical analysis is made, the person shall confirm the request in writing and shall be notified:

(1) That the test results will be admissible in evidence and may be used against the person in any implied-consent offense that may arise;

(2) That the person's license will be revoked for at least 30 days if:

a. The test reveals an alcohol concentration of 0.08 or more; or

b. The person was driving a commercial motor vehicle and the test results reveal an alcohol concentration of 0.04 or more; or

c. The person is under 21 years of age and the test reveals any alcohol concentration.

(3) That if the person fails to comply fully with the test procedures, the officer may charge the person with any offense for which the officer has probable cause, and if the person is charged with an implied-consent offense, the person's refusal to submit to the testing required as a result of that charge would result in revocation of the person's driver's license. The results of the chemical analysis are admissible in evidence in any proceeding in which they are relevant.

History: 1963, c. 966, s. 1; 1965, c. 1165; 1969, c. 1074, s. 1; 1971, c. 619, ss. 3–6; 1973, c. 206, ss. 1, 2; cc. 824, 914; 1975, c. 716, s. 5; 1977, c. 812; 1979, c. 423, s. 2; 1979, 2d Sess., c. 1160; 1981, c. 412, s. 4; c. 747, s. 66; 1983, c. 87; c. 435, s. 11; 1983 (Reg. Sess., 1984), c. 1101, ss. 5–8; 1987, c. 797, s. 3; 1987 (Reg. Sess., 1988), c. 1037, ss. 76, 77; c. 1112; 1989, c. 771, ss. 13, 14, 18; 1991, c. 689, s. 233.1(c); 1993, c. 285, ss. 3, 4; 1995, c. 163, s. 1; 1997-379, ss. 3.1–3.3; 1998-182, s. 28; 1999-406, s. 10.

SECOND OF TWO VERSIONS OF THIS SECTION

§ 20-16.2. (Effective July 1, 2000) Implied consent to chemical analysis; mandatory revocation of license in event of refusal; right of driver to request analysis

(a) Basis for Charging Officer to Require Chemical Analysis; Notification of Rights.—Any person who drives a vehicle on a highway or public vehicular area thereby gives consent to a chemical analysis if charged with an implied-consent offense. The charging officer shall designate the type of chemical analysis to be administered, and it may be administered when the officer has reasonable grounds to believe that the person charged has committed the implied-consent offense.

Except as provided in this subsection or subsection (b), before any type of chemical analysis is administered the person charged shall be taken before a chemical analyst authorized to administer a test of a person's breath, who shall inform the person orally and also give the person a notice in writing that:

(1) The person has a right to refuse to be tested.

(2) Refusal to take any required test or tests will result in an immediate revocation of the person's driving privilege for at least 30 days and an additional 12-month revocation by the Division of Motor Vehicles.

(3) The test results, or the fact of the person's refusal, will be admissible in evidence at trial on the offense charged.

(4) The person's driving privilege will be revoked immediately for at least 30 days if:

a. The test reveals an alcohol concentration of 0.08 or more;

b. The person was driving a commercial motor vehicle and the test reveals an alcohol concentration of 0.04 or more; or

c. The person is under 21 years of age and the test reveals any alcohol concentration.

(5) The person may choose a qualified person to administer a chemical test or tests in addition to any test administered at the direction of the charging officer.

(6) The person has the right to call an attorney and select a witness to view for him or her the testing procedures, but the testing may not be delayed for these purposes longer than 30 minutes from the time when the person is notified of his or her rights.

If the charging officer or an arresting officer is authorized to administer a chemical analysis of a person's breath, the charging officer or the arresting officer may give the person charged the oral and written notice of rights required by this subsection. This authority applies regardless of the type of chemical analysis designated.

(a1) Meaning of Terms.—Under this section, an "implied-consent offense" is an offense involving impaired driving or an alcohol-related offense made subject to the procedures of this section. A person is "charged" with an offense if the person is arrested for it or if criminal process for the offense has been issued. A "charging officer" is a law-enforcement officer who arrests the person charged, lodges the charge, or assists the officer who arrested the person or lodged the charge by assuming custody of the person to make the request required by subsection (c) and, if necessary, to present the person to a judicial official for an initial appearance.

(b) Unconscious Person May Be Tested.—If a charging officer has reasonable grounds to believe that a person has committed an implied-consent offense, and the person is unconscious or otherwise in a condition that makes the person incapable of refusal, the charging officer may direct the taking of a blood sample by a person qualified under G.S. 20-139.1 or may direct the administration of any other chemical analysis that may be effectively performed. In this instance the notification of rights set out in subsectio) and the request required by subsection (c) are not necessary.

(c) Request to Submit to Chemical Analysis.—The charging officer, in the presence of the chemical analyst who has notified the person of his or her rights under subsection (a), must request the person charged to submit to the type of chemical analysis designated. If the person charged willfully refuses to submit to that chemical analysis, none may be given under the provisions of this section, but the refusal does not preclude testing under other applicable procedures of law.

(c1) Procedure for Reporting Results and Refusal to Division.—Whenever a person refuses to submit to a chemical analysis or a person's driver's license has an alcohol concentration restriction and the results of the chemical analysis establish a violation of the restriction, the charging officer and the chemical analyst must without unnecessary delay go before an official authorized to administer oaths and execute an affidavit(s) stating that:

(1) The person was charged with an implied-consent offense or had an alcohol concentration restriction on the driver's license;
(2) The charging officer had reasonable grounds to believe that the person had committed an implied-consent offense or violated the alcohol concentration restriction on the driver's license;
(3) Whether the implied-consent offense charged involved death or critical injury to another person, if the person willfully refused to submit to chemical analysis;
(4) The person was notified of the rights in subsection (a); and
(5) The results of any tests given or that the person willfully refused to submit to a chemical analysis upon the request of the charging officer.

The charging officer must immediately mail the affidavit(s) to the Division. If the charging officer is also the chemical analyst who has notified the person of the rights under subsection (a), the charging officer may perform alone the duties of this subsection.

(d) Consequences of Refusal; Right to Hearing before Division; Issues.—Upon receipt of a properly executed affidavit required by subsection (c1), the Division must expeditiously notify the person charged that the person's license to drive is revoked for 12 months, effective on the tenth calendar day after the mailing of the revocation order unless, before the effective date of the order, the person requests in writing a hearing before the Division. Except for the time referred to in G.S. 20-16.5, if the person shows to the satisfaction of the Division that his or her license was surrendered to the court, and remained in the court's possession, then the Division shall credit the amount of time for which the license was in the possession of the court against the 12-month revocation period required by this subsection. If the person properly requests a hearing, the person retains his or her license, unless it is revoked under some other provision of law, until the hearing is held, the person withdraws the request, or the person fails to appear at a scheduled hearing. The hearing officer may subpoena any witnesses or documents that the hearing officer deems necessary. The person may request the hearing officer to subpoena the charging officer, the chemical analyst, or both to appear at the hearing if the person makes the request in writing at least three days before the hearing. The person may subpoena any other witness whom the person deems necessary, and the provisions of G.S. 1A-1, Rule 45, apply to the issuance and service of all subpoenas issued under authority of this section. The hearing officer is authorized to administer oaths to witnesses appearing at the hearing. The hearing must be conducted in the county where the charge was brought, and must be limited to consideration of whether:

(1) The person was charged with an implied-consent offense or the driver had an alcohol concentration restriction on the driver's license pursuant to G.S. 20-19;
(2) The charging officer had reasonable grounds to believe that the person had committed an implied-consent offense or violated the alcohol concentration restriction on the driver's license;
(3) The implied-consent offense charged involved death or critical injury to another person, if this allegation is in the affidavit;
(4) The person was notified of the person's rights as required by subsection (a); and
(5) The person willfully refused to submit to a chemical analysis upon the request of the charging officer.

If the Division finds that the conditions specified in this subsection are met, it must order the revocation sustained. If the Division finds that any of the conditions (1), (2), (4), or (5) is not met, it must rescind the revocation. If it finds that condition (3) is alleged in the affidavit but is not met, it must order the revocation sustained if that is the only condition that is not met; in this instance subsection (d1) does not apply to that revocation. If the revocation is sustained, the person must surrender his or her license immediately upon notification by the Division.

(d1) Consequences of Refusal in Case Involving Death or Critical Injury.—If the refusal occurred in a case involving death or critical injury to another person, no limited driving privilege may be issued. The 12-month revocation begins only after all other periods of revocation have terminated unless the person's license is revoked under G.S. 20-28, 20-28.1, 20-19(d), or 20-19(e). If the revocation is based on those sections, the revocation under this subsection begins at the time and in the manner specified in subsection (d) for revocations under this section. However, the person's eligibility for a hearing to determine if the revocation under those sections should be rescinded is postponed for one year from the date on which the person would otherwise have been eligible for such a hearing. If the person's driver's license is again revoked while the 12-month revocation under this subsection is in effect, that revocation, whether imposed by a court or by the Division, may only take effect after the period of revocation under this subsection has terminated.

(e) Right to Hearing in Superior Court.—If the revocation for a willful refusal is sustained after the hearing, the person whose license has been revoked has the right to file a petition in the superior court for a hearing de novo upon the issues listed in subsection (d), in the same manner and under the same conditions as provided in G.S. 20-25 except that the de novo hearing is conducted in the superior court district or set of districts as defined in G.S. 7A-41.1 where the charge was made.

(e1) Limited Driving Privilege after Six Months in Certain Instances.—A person whose driver's license has been revoked under this section may apply for and a judge authorized to do so by this subsection may issue a limited driving privilege if:

(1) At the time of the refusal the person held either a valid driver's license or a license that had been expired for less than one year;

(2) At the time of the refusal, the person had nithin the preceding seven years been convicted of an offense involving impaired driving;

(3) At the time of the refusal, the person had not in the preceding seven years willfully refused to submit to a chemical analysis under this section;

(4) The implied-consent offense charged did not involve death or critical injury to another person;

(5) The underlying charge for which the defendant was requested to submit to a chemical analysis has been finally disposed of:

a. Other than by conviction; or

b. By a conviction of impaired driving under G.S. 20-138.1, at a punishment level authorizing issuance of a limited driving privilege under G.S. 20-179.3(b), and the defendant has complied with at least one of the mandatory conditions of probation listed for the punishment level under which the defendant was sentenced;

(6) Subsequent to the refusal the person has had no unresolved pending charges for or additional convictions of an offense involving impaired driving;

(7) The person's license has been revoked for at least six months for the refusal; and

(8) The person has obtained a substance abuse assessment from a mental health facility and successfully completed any recommended training or treatment program.

Except as modified in this subsection, the provisions of G.S. 20-179.3 relating to the procedure for application and conduct of the hearing and the restrictions required or authorized to be included in the limited driving privilege apply to applications under this subsection. If the case was finally disposed of in the district court, the hearing shall be conducted in the district court district as defined in G.S. 7A-133 in which the refusal occurred by a district court judge. If the case was finally disposed of in the superior court, the hearing shall be conducted in the superior court district or set of districts as defined in G.S. 7A-41.1 in which the refusal occurred by a superior court judge. A limited driving privilege issued under this section authorizes a person to drive if the person's license is revoked solely under this section or solely under this section and G.S. 20-17(2). If the person's license is revoked for any other reason, the limited driving privilege is invalid.

(f) Notice to Other States as to Nonresidents.—When it has been finally determined under the procedures of this section that a nonresident's privilege to drive a motor vehicle in this State has been revoked, the Division must give information in writing of the action taken to the motor vehicle administrator of the state of the person's residence and of any state in which the person has a license.

(g) Repealed by Session Laws 1973, c. 914.

(h) Repealed by Session Laws 1979, c. 423, s. 2.

(i) Right to Chemical Analysis before Arrest or Charge.—A person stopped or questioned by a law-enforcement officer who is investigating whether the person may have committed an implied-consent offense may request the administration of a chemical analysis before any arrest or other charge is made for the offense. Upon this request, the officer shall afford the person the opportunity to have a chemical analysis of his or her breath, if available, in accordance with the procedures required by G.S. 20-139.1(b). The request constitutes the person's consent to be transported by the law-enforcement officer to the place where the chemical analysis is to be administered. Before the chemical analysis is made, the person shall confirm the request in writing and shall be notified:

(1) That the test results will be admissible in evidence and may be used against the person in any implied-consent offense that may arise;

(2) That the person's license will be revoked for at least 30 days if:

a. The test reveals an alcohol concentration of 0.08 or more; or

b. The person was driving a commercial motor vehicle and the test results reveal an alcohol concentration of 0.04 or more; or

c. The person is under 21 years of age and the test reveals any alcohol concentration.

(3) That if the person fails to comply fully with the test procedures, the officer may charge the person with any offense for which the officer has probable cause, and if the person is charged

with an implied-consent offense, the person's refusal to submit to the testing required as a result of that charge would result in revocation of the person's driver's license. The results of the chemical analysis are admissible in evidence in any proceeding in which they are relevant.

History: 1963, c. 966, s. 1; 1965, c. 1165; 1969, c. 1074, s. 1; 1971, c. 619, ss. 3–6; 1973, c. 206, ss. 1, 2; cc. 824, 914; 1975, c. 716, s. 5; 1977, c. 812; 1979, c. 423, s. 2; 1979, 2d Sess., c. 1160; 1981, c. 412, s. 4; c. 747, s. 66; 1983, c. 87; c. 435, s. 11; 1983 (Reg. Sess., 1984), c. 1101, ss. 5–8; 1987, c. 797, s. 3; 1987 (Reg. Sess., 1988), c. 1037, ss. 76, 77; 1989, c. 771, ss. 13, 14; 1991, c. 689, s. 233.1(c); 1993, c. 285, ss. 3, 4; 1995, c. 163, s. 1; 1997-379, ss. 3.1–3.3; 1998-182, s. 28; 1999-406, ss. 1, 10.

§ 20-16.3. Alcohol screening tests required of certain drivers; approval of test devices and manner of use by Commission for Health Services; use of test results or refusal

(a) When Alcohol Screening Test May Be Required; Not an Arrest.—A law-enforcement officer may require the driver of a vehicle to submit to an alcohol screening test within a relevant time after the driving if the officer has:

(1) Reasonable grounds to believe that the driver has consumed alcohol and has:

a. Committed a moving traffic violation; or

b. Been involved in an accident or collision; or

(2) An articulable and reasonable suspicion that the driver has committed an implied-consent offense under G.S. 20-16.2, and the driver has been lawfully stopped for a driver's license check or otherwise lawfully stopped or lawfully encountered by the officer in the course of the performance of the officer's duties.

Requiring a driver to submit to an alcohol screening test in accordance with this section does not in itself constitute an arrest.

(b) Approval of Screening Devices and Manner of Use.—The Commission for Health Services is directed to examine and approve devices suitable for use by law-enforcement officers in making on-the-scene tests of drivers for alcohol concentration. For each alcohol screening device or class of devices approved, the Commission must adopt regulations governing the manner of use of the device. For any alcohol screening device that tests the breath of a driver, the Commission is directed to specify in its regulations the shortest feasible minimum waiting period that does not produce an unacceptably high number of false positive test results.

(c) Tests Must Be Made with Approved Devices and in Approved Manner.—No screening test for alcohol concentration is a valid one under this section unless the device used is one approved by the Commission for Health Services and the screening test is conducted in accordance with the applicable regulations of the Commission as to the manner of its use.

(d) Use of Screening Test Results or Refusal by Officer.—The results of an alcohol screening test or a driver's refusal to submit may be used by a law-enforcement officer, a court, or an administrative agency in determining if there are reasonable grounds for believing that the driver has committed an implied-consent offense under G.S. 20-16.2. Negative or low results on the alcohol screening test may be used in factually appropriate cases by the officer, a court, or an administrative agency in determining whether a person's alleged impairment is caused by an impairing substance other than alcohol. Except as provided in this subsection, the results of an alcohol screening test may not be admitted in evidence in any court or administrative proceeding.

History: 1973, c. 312, s. 1; c. 476, s. 128; 1981, c. 412, s. 4; c. 747, s. 66; 1983, c. 435, s. 12.

§ 20-16.3A. Impaired driving checks

A law-enforcement agency may make impaired driving checks of drivers of vehicles on highways and public vehicular areas if the agency:

(1) Develops a systematic plan in advance that takes into account the likelihood of detecting impaired drivers, traffic conditions, number of vehicles to be stopped, and the convenience of the motoring public.

(2) Designates in advance the pattern both for stopping vehicles and for requesting drivers that are stopped to submit to alcohol screening tests. The plan may include contingency provisions for altering either pattern if actual traffic conditions are different from those anticipated, but no individual officer may be given discretion as to which vehicle is stopped or, of the vehicles stopped, which driver is requested to submit to an alcohol screening test.

(3) Marks the area in which checks are conducted to advise the public that an authorized impaired driving check is being made.

This section does not prevent an officer from using the authority of G.S. 20-16.3 to request a screening test if, in the course of dealing with a driver under the authority of this section, he develops grounds for requesting such a test under G.S. 20-16.3. Alcohol screening tests and the results from them are subject to the provisions of subsections (b), (c), and (d) of G.S. 20-16.3. This section does not limit the authority of a law-enforcement officer or agency to conduct a license check independently or in conjunction with the impaired driving check, to administer psychophysical tests to screen for impairment, or to utilize roadblocks or other types of vehicle checks or checkpoints that are consistent with the laws of this State and the Constitution of North Carolina and of the United States.

History: 1983, c. 435, s. 22.

§ 20-16.5. Immediate civil license revocation for certain persons charged with implied-consent offenses

(a) Definitions.—As used in this section the following words and phrases have the following meanings:

(1) Charging Officer.—As described in G.S. 20-16.2(a1).

(2) Clerk.—As defined in G.S. 15A-101(2).

(3) Judicial Official.—As defined in G.S. 15A-101(5).

(4) Revocation Report.—A sworn statement by a charging officer and a chemical analyst containing facts indicating that the conditions of subsection (b) have been met, and whether the person has a pending offense for which their license had been or is revoked under this section. When one chemical analyst analyzes a person's blood and another chemical analyst informs a person of his rights and responsibilities under G.S. 20-16.2, the report must include the statements of both analysts.

(5) Surrender of a Driver's License.—The act of turning over to a court or a law-enforcement officer the person's most recent, valid driver's license or learner's permit issued by the Division or by a similar agency in another jurisdiction, or a limited driving privilege issued by a North Carolina court. A person who is validly licensed but who is unable to locate his license card may file an affidavit with the clerk setting out facts that indicate that he is unable to locate his license card and that he is validly licensed; the filing of the affidavit constitutes a surrender of the person's license.

(b) Revocations for Persons Who Refuse Chemical Analyses or Who Are Charged With Certain Implied-Consent Offenses.—A person's driver's license is subject to revocation under this section if:

(1) A charging officer has reasonable grounds to believe that the person has committed an offense subject to the implied-consent provisions of G.S. 20-16.2;

(2) The person is charged with that offense as provided in G.S. 20-16.2(a);

(3) The charging officer and the chemical analyst comply with the procedures of G.S. 20-16.2 and G.S. 20-139.1 in requiring the person's submission to or procuring a chemical analysis; and

(4) The person:

a. Willfully refuses to submit to the chemical analysis;

b. Has an alcohol concentration of 0.08 or more within a relevant time after the driving;

c. Has an alcohol concentration of 0.04 or more at any relevant time after the driving of a commercial vehicle; or

d. Has any alcohol concentration at any relevant time after the driving and the person is under 21 years of age.

(b1) Precharge Test Results as Basis for Revocation.—Notwithstanding the provisions of subsection (b), a person's driver's license is subject to revocation under this section if:

(1) The person requests a precharge chemical analysis pursuant to G.S. 20-16.2(i); and

(2) The person has:

a. An alcohol concentration of 0.08 or more at any relevant time after driving;

b. An alcohol concentration of 0.04 or more at any relevant time after driving a commercial motor vehicle; or

c. Any alcohol concentration at any relevant time after driving and the person is under 21 years of age; and

(3) The person is charged with an implied-consent offense.

(c) Duty of Charging Officers and Chemical Analysts to Report to Judicial Officials.—If a person's driver's license is subject to revocation under this section, the charging officer and the chemical analyst must execute a revocation report. If the person has refused to submit to a chemical analysis, a copy of the affidavit to be submitted to the Division under G.S. 20-16.2(c) may be substituted for the revocation report if it contains the information required by this section. It is the specific duty of the charging officer to make sure that the report is expeditiously filed with a judicial official as required by this section.

(d) Which Judicial Official Must Receive Report.—The judicial official with whom the revocation report must be filed is:

(1) The judicial official conducting the initial appearance on the underlying criminal charge if:
  a. No revocation report has previously been filed; and
  b. At the time of the initial appearance the results of the chemical analysis, if administered, or the reports indicating a refusal, are available.

(2) A judicial official conducting any other proceeding relating to the underlying criminal charge at which the person is present, if no report has previously been filed.

(3) The clerk of superior court in the county in which the underlying criminal charge has been brought if subdivisions (1) and (2) are not applicable at the time the charging officer must file the report.

(e) Procedure if Report Filed with Judicial Official When Person Is Present.—If a properly executed revocation report concerning a person is filed with a judicial official when the person is present before that official, the judicial official shall, after completing any other proceedings involving the person, determine whether there is probable cause to believe that each of the conditions of subsection (b) has been met. If he determines that there is such probable cause, he shall enter an order revoking the person's driver's license for the period required in this subsection. The judicial official shall order the person to surrender his license and if necessary may order a law-enforcement officer to seize the license. The judicial official shall give the person a copy of the revocation order. In addition to setting it out in the order the judicial official shall personally inform the person of his right to a hearing as specified in subsection (g), and that his license remains revoked pending the hearing. The revocation under this subsection begins at the time the revocation order is issued and continues until the person's license has been surrendered for the period specified in this subsection, and the person has paid the applicable costs. The period of revocation is 30 days, if there are no pending offenses for which the person's license had been or is revoked under this section. If at the time of the current offense, the person has one or more pending offenses for which his license had been or is revoked under this section, the revocation shall remain in effect until a final judgment, including all appeals, has been entered for the current offense and for all pending offenses. In no event, may the period of revocation under this subsection be less than 30 days. If within five working days of the effective date of the order, the person does not surrender his license or demonstrate that he is not currently licensed, the clerk shall immediately issue a pick-up order. The pick-up order shall be issued to a member of a local law-enforcement agency if the charging officer was employed by the agency at the time of the charge and the person resides in or is present in the agency's territorial jurisdiction. In all other cases, the pick-up order shall be issued to an officer or inspector of the Division. A pick-up order issued pursuant to this section is to be served in accordance with G.S. 20-29 as if the order had been issued by the Division.

(f) Procedure if Report Filed with Clerk of Court When Person Not Present.—When a clerk receives a properly executed report under subdivision (d) (3) and the person named in the revocation report is not present before the clerk, the clerk shall determine whether there is probable cause to believe that each of the conditions of subsection (b) has been met. If he determines that there is such probable cause, he shall mail to the person a revocation order by first-class mail. The order shall direct that the person on or before the effective date of the order either surrender his license to the clerk or appear before the clerk and demonstrate that he is not currently licensed, and the order shall inform the person of the time and effective date of the revocation and of its duration, of his right to a hearing as specified in subsection (g), and that the revocation remains in effect pending the hearing. Revocation orders mailed under this subsection become effective on the fourth day after the order is deposited in the United States mail. If within five working days of the effective date of the order, the person does not surrender his license to the clerk or appear before the clerk to demonstrate that he is not currently licensed, the clerk shall immediately issue a pick-up order. The pick-up order shall be issued and served in the same manner as specified in subsection (e) for pick-up orders issued pursuant to that subsection. A revocation under this subsection begins at the date specified in the order and continues until the person's license has been revoked for the period specified in this subsection and the person has paid the applicable costs. If the person has no pending offenses for which his license had been or is revoked under this section, the period of revocation under this subsection is:

(1) Thirty days from the time the person surrenders his license to the court, if the surrender occurs within five working days of the effective date of the order; or
(2) Thirty days after the person appears before the clerk and demonstrates that he is not currently licensed to drive, if the appearance occurs within five working days of the effective date of the revocation order; or
(3) Forty-five days from the time:
   a. The person's driver's license is picked up by a law-enforcement officer following service of a pick-up order; or
   b. The person demonstrates to a law-enforcement officer who has a pick-up order for his license that he is not currently licensed; or
   c. The person's driver's license is surrendered to the court if the surrender occurs more than five working days after the effective date of the revocation order; or
   d. The person appears before the clerk to demonstrate that he is not currently licensed, if he appears more than five working days after the effective date of the revocation order.

If at the time of the current offense, the person has one or more pending offenses for which his license had been or is revoked under this section, the revocation shall remain in effect until a final judgment, including all appeals, has been entered for the current offense and for all pending offenses. In no event may the period of revocation for the current offense be less than the applicable period of revocation in subdivision (1), (2), or (3) of this subsection. When a pick-up order is issued, it shall inform the person of his right to a hearing as specified in subsection (g), and that the revocation remains in effect pending the hearing. An officer serving a pick-up order under this subsection shall return the order to the court indicating the date it was served or that he was unable to serve the order. If the license was surrendered, the officer serving the order shall deposit it with the clerk within three days of the surrender.

(g) Hearing before Magistrate or Judge if Person Contests Validity of Revocation.—A person whose license is revoked under this section may request in writing a hearing to contest the validity of the revocation. The request may be made at the time of the person's initial appearance, or within 10 days of the effective date of the revocation to the clerk or a magistrate designated by the clerk, and may specifically request that the hearing be conducted by a district court judge. The Administrative Office of the Courts must develop a hearing request form for any person requesting a hearing. Unless a district court judge is requested, the hearing must be conducted within the county by a magistrate assigned by the chief district judge to conduct such hearings. If the person requests that a district court judge hold the hearing, the hearing must be conducted within the district court district as defined in G.S. 7A-133 by a district court judge assigned to conduct such hearings. The revocation remains in effect pending the hearing, but the hearing must be held within three working days following the request if the hearing is before a magistrate or within five working days if the hearing is before a district court judge. The request for the hearing must specify the grounds upon which the validity of the revocation is challenged and the hearing must be limited to the grounds specified in the request. A witness may submit his evidence by affidavit unless he is subpoenaed to appear. Any person who appears and testifies is subject to questioning by the judicial official conducting the hearing, and the judicial official may adjourn the hearing to seek additional evidence if he is not satisfied with the accuracy or completeness of evidence. The person contesting the validity of the revocation may, but is not required to, testify in his own behalf. Unless contested by the person requesting the hearing, the judicial official may accept as true any matter stated in the revocation report. If any relevant condition under subsection (b) is contested, the judicial official must find by the greater weight of the evidence that the condition was met in order to sustain the revocation. At the conclusion of the hearing the judicial official must enter an order sustaining or rescinding the revocation. The judicial official's findings are without prejudice to the person contesting the revocation and to any other potential party as to any other proceedings, civil or criminal, that may involve facts bearing upon the conditions in subsection (b) considered by the judicial official. The decision of the judicial official is final and may not be appealed in the General Court of Justice. If the hearing is not held and completed within three working days of the written request for a hearing before a magistrate or within five working days of the written request for a hearing before a district court judge, the judicial official must enter an order rescinding the revocation, unless the person contesting the revocation contributed to the delay in completing the hearing. If the person requesting the hearing fails to appear at the hearing or any rescheduling thereof after having been properly notified, he forfeits his right to a hearing.

(h) Return of License.—After the applicable period of revocation under this section, or if the magistrate or judge orders the revocation rescinded, the person whose license was revoked may apply to the clerk for return of his surrendered license. Unless the clerk finds that the person is not eligible to use the surrendered license, he must return it if:

(1) The applicable period of revocation has passed and the person has tendered payment for the costs under subsection (j); or

(2) The magistrate or judge has ordered the revocation rescinded.

If the license has expired, he may return it to the person with a caution that it is no longer valid. Otherwise, if the person is not eligible to use the license and the license was issued by the Division or in another state, the clerk must mail it to the Division. If the person has surrendered his copy of a limited driving privilege and he is no longer eligible to use it, the clerk must make a record that he has withheld the limited driving privilege and forward that record to the clerk in the county in which the limited driving privilege was issued for filing in the case file. If the person's license is revoked under this section and under another section of this Chapter, the clerk must surrender the license to the Division if the revocation under this section can terminate before the other revocation; in such cases, the costs required by subsection (j) must still be paid before the revocation under this section is terminated.

(i) Effect of Revocations.—A revocation under this section revokes a person's privilege to drive in North Carolina whatever the source of his authorization to drive. Revocations under this section are independent of and run concurrently with any other revocations. No court imposing a period of revocation following conviction of an offense involving impaired driving may give credit for any period of revocation imposed under this section. A person whose license is revoked pursuant to this section is not eligible to receive a limited driving privilege except as specifically authorized by G.S. 20-16.5(p).

(j) Costs.—Unless the magistrate or judge orders the revocation rescinded, a person whose license is revoked under this section must pay a fee of fifty dollars ($50.00) as costs for the action before the person's license may be returned under subsection (h). The costs collected under this section shall be credited to the General Fund. Fifty percent (50%) of the costs collected shall be used to fund a statewide chemical alcohol testing program administered by the Injury Control Section of the Department of Health and Human Services.

(k) Report to Division.—Except as provided below, the clerk shall mail a report to the Division:

(1) If the license is revoked indefinitely, within 10 working days of the revocation of the license; and

(2) In all cases, within 10 working days of the return of a license under this section or of the termination of a revocation of the driving privilege of a person not currently licensed.

The report shall identify the person whose license has been revoked, specify the date on which his license was revoked, and indicate whether the license has been returned. The report must also provide, if applicable, whether the license is revoked indefinitely. No report need be made to the Division, however, if there was a surrender of the driver's license issued by the Division, a 30-day minimum revocation was imposed, and the license was properly returned to the person under subsection (h) within five working days after the 30-day period had elapsed.

(l) Restoration Fee for Unlicensed Persons.—If a person whose license is revoked under this section has no valid license, he must pay the restoration fee required by G.S. 20-7 before he may apply for a license from the Division.

(m) Modification of Revocation Order.—Any judicial official presiding over a proceeding under this section may issue a modified order if he determines that an inappropriate order has been issued.

(n) Exception for Revoked Licenses.—Notwithstanding any other provision of this section, if the judicial official required to issue a revocation order under this section determines that the person whose license is subject to revocation under subsection (b):

(1) Has a currently revoked driver's license;

(2) Has no limited driving privilege; and

(3) Will not become eligible for restoration of his license or for a limited driving privilege during the period of revocation required by this section, the judicial official need not issue a revocation order under this section. In this event the judicial official must file in the records of the civil proceeding a copy of any documentary evidence and set out in writing all other evidence on which he relies in making his determination.

(o) Designation of Proceedings.—Proceedings under this section are civil actions, and must be identified by the caption "In the Matter of _________" and filed as directed by the Administrative Office of the Courts.

(p) Limited Driving Privilege.—A person whose driver's license has been revoked for a specified period of 30 or 45 days under this section may apply for a limited driving privilege if:

(1) At the time of the alleged offense the person held either a valid driver's license or a license that had been expired for less than one year;

(2) Does not have an unresolved pending charge involving impaired driving except the charge for which the license is currently revoked under this section or additional convictions of an offense involving impaired driving since being charged for the violation for which the license is currently revoked under this section;

(3) The person's license has been revoked for at least 10 days if the revocation is for 30 days or 30 days if the revocation is for 45 days; and

(4) The person has obtained a substance abuse assessment from a mental health facility and registers for and agrees to participate in any recommended training or treatment program.

A person whose license has been indefinitely revoked under this section may, after completion of 30 days under subsection (e) or the applicable period of time under subdivision (1), (2), or (3) of subsection (f), apply for a limited driving privilege. In the case of an indefinite revocation, a judge of the division in which the current offense is pending may issue the limited driving privilege only if the privilege is necessary to overcome undue hardship and the person meets the eligibility requirements of G.S. 20-179.3, except that the requirements in G.S. 20-179.3(b)(1)c. and G.S. 20-179.3(e) shall not apply. Except as modified in this subsection, the provisions of G.S. 20-179.3 relating to the procedure for application and conduct of the hearing and the restrictions required or authorized to be included in the limited driving privilege apply to applications under this subsection. Any district court judge authorized to hold court in the judicial district is authorized to issue such a limited driving privilege. A limited driving privilege issued under this section authorizes a person to drive if the person's license is revoked solely under this section. If the person's license is revoked for any other reason, the limited driving privilege is invalid.

History: 1983, c. 435, s. 14; 1983 (Reg. Sess., 1984), c. 1101, ss. 11–17; 1985, c. 690, ss. 1, 2; 1987 (Reg. Sess., 1988), c. 1037, s. 80, c. 1112; 1989, c. 771, ss. 15, 16, 18; 1991, c. 689, s. 233.1(a); 1993, c. 285, ss. 5, 6; 1997-379, ss. 3.4–3.8; 1997-443, s. 11A.9; 1997-486, ss. 2–6; 1998-182, ss. 29, 30; 1999-406, s. 13.

§ 20-17. Mandatory revocation of license by Division

(a) The Division shall forthwith revoke the license of any driver upon receiving a record of the driver's conviction for any of the following offenses:

(1) Manslaughter (or negligent homicide) resulting from the operation of a motor vehicle.

(2) Either of the following impaired driving offenses:

a. Impaired driving under G.S. 20-138.1.

b. Impaired driving under G.S. 20-138.2.

(3) Any felony in the commission of which a motor vehicle is used.

(4) Failure to stop and render aid in violation of G.S. 20-166(a) or (b).

(5) Perjury or the making of a false affidavit or statement under oath to the Division under this Article or under any other law relating to the ownership of motor vehicles.

(6) Conviction upon two charges of reckless driving committed within a period of 12 months.

(7) Conviction upon one charge of reckless driving while engaged in the illegal transportation of intoxicants for the purpose of sale.

(8) Conviction of using a false or fictitious name or giving a false or fictitious address in any application for a driver's license, or learner's permit, or any renewal or duplicate thereof, or knowingly making a false statement or knowingly concealing a material fact or otherwise committing a fraud in any such application or procuring or knowingly permitting or allowing another to commit any of the foregoing acts.

(9) Death by vehicle as defined in G.S. 20-141.4.

(10) Repealed by Session Laws 1997-443, s. 19.26(b).

(11) Conviction of assault with a motor vehicle.

(12) A second or subsequent conviction of transporting an open container of alcoholic beverage under G.S. 20-138.7.

(13) A second or subsequent conviction, as defined in G.S. 20-138.2A(d), of driving a commercial motor vehicle after consuming alcohol under G.S. 20-138.2A.

(14) A conviction of driving a school bus, school activity bus, or child care vehicle after consuming alcohol under G.S. 20-138.2B.

(15) A conviction of malicious use of an explosive or incendiary device to damage property (G.S. 14-49(b) and (b1)); conspiracy to injure or damage by use of an explosive or incendiary device (G.S. 14-50); making a false report concerning a destructive device in a public building

(G.S. 14-69.1(c)); perpetrating a hoax concerning a destructive device in a public building (G.S. 14-69.2(c)); possessing or carrying a dynamite cartridge, bomb, grenade, mine, or powerful explosive on educational property (G.S. 14-269.2(b1)); or causing, encouraging, or aiding a minor to possess or carry a dynamite cartridge, bomb, grenade, mine, or powerful explosive on educational property (G.S. 14-269.2(c1)).

(b) On the basis of information provided by the child support enforcement agency or the clerk of court, the Division shall:

(1) Ensure that no license or right to operate a motor vehicle under this Chapter is renewed or issued to an obligor who is delinquent in making child support payments when a court of record has issued a revocation order pursuant to G.S. 110-142.2 or G.S. 50-13.12. The obligor shall not be entitled to any other hearing before the Division as a result of the revocation of his license pursuant to G.S. 110-142.2 or G.S. 50-13.12; or

(2) Revoke the driver's license of any person who has willfully failed to complete court-ordered community service and a court has issued a revocation order. This revocation shall continue until the Division receives certification from the clerk of court that the person has completed the court-ordered community service. No person whose driver's license is revoked pursuant to this subdivision shall be entitled to any other hearing before the Division as a result of this revocation.

History: 1935, c. 52, s. 12; 1947, c. 1067, s. 14; 1967, c. 1098, s. 2; 1971, c. 619, s. 7; 1973, c. 18, s. 1; c. 1081, s. 3; c. 1330, s. 2; 1975, c. 716, s. 5; c. 831; 1979, c. 667, ss. 20, 41; 1981, c. 412, s. 4; c. 747, s. 66; 1983, c. 435, s. 15; 1989, c. 771, s. 11; 1991, c. 726, s. 7; 1993 (Reg. Sess., 1994), c. 761, s. 1; 1995, c. 506, s. 7; c. 538, s. 2(b); 1997-234, s. 3; 1997-443, s. 19.26(b); 1998-182, s. 18; 1999-257, s. 4.1.

§ 20-17.2. Court-ordered revocations for offenses involving impaired driving; procedure for notice

When a person convicted of an offense involving impaired driving is ordered by a court not to operate a motor vehicle for a specified period of time as a condition of probation, the Division, upon receiving a copy of the judgment, must revoke the person's driver's license for the period and dates specified in the order of the court. The entry of the probationary judgment by the court is notice to the person that his license is revoked, and the Division need not notify the person of his revocation. In judgment forms for use in impaired driving cases under G.S. 20-138.1 the Administrative Office of the Courts must provide for inclusion of a notice provision, when applicable, of the terms of this section.

History: 1983, c. 435, s. 16.

§ 20-17.3. Revocation for underage purchasers of alcohol

The Division shall revoke for one year the driver's license of any person who has been convicted of violating any of the following:

(1) G.S. 18B-302(c)(1), (e), or (f); or

(2) G.S. 18B-302(b), if the violation occurred while the person was purchasing or attempting to purchase an alcoholic beverage.

If the person's license is currently suspended or revoked, then the revocation under this section shall begin at the termination of that revocation.

History: 1983, c. 435, s. 36.

§ 20-17.4. Disqualification to drive a commercial motor vehicle

(a) One Year.—Any of the following disqualifies a person from driving a commercial motor vehicle for one year:

(1) A first conviction of G.S. 20-138.1, driving while impaired, that occurred while the person was driving a motor vehicle not a commercial motor vehicle.

(2) A first conviction of G.S. 20-138.2, driving a commercial motor vehicle while impaired.

(3) A first conviction of G.S. 20-166, hit and run, involving a commercial motor vehicle driven by the person.

(4) A first conviction of a felony in the commission of which a commercial motor vehicle was used.

(5) Refusal to submit to a chemical test when charged with an implied-consent offense, as defined in G.S. 20-16.2, that occurred while the person was driving a commercial motor vehicle.

(6) A second or subsequent conviction, as defined in G.S. 20-138.2A(d), of driving a commercial motor vehicle after consuming alcohol under G.S. 20-138.2A.

(a1) Ten-Day Disqualification.—A person who is convicted for a first offense of driving a commercial motor vehicle after consuming alcohol under G.S. 20-138.2A is disqualified from driving a commercial motor vehicle for 10 days.

(b) Modified Life.—A person who has been disqualified from driving a commercial motor vehicle for a conviction or refusal described in subsection (a) who, as the result of a separate incident, is subsequently convicted of an offense or commits an act requiring disqualification under subsection (a) is disqualified for life. The Division may adopt guidelines, including conditions, under which a disqualification for life under this subsection may be reduced to 10 years.

(b1) Life Without Reduction.—A person is disqualified from driving a commercial motor vehicle for life, without the possibility of reinstatement after 10 years, if that person is convicted of a third or subsequent violation of G.S. 20-138.2, a fourth or subsequent violation of G.S. 20-138.2A, or if the person refuses to submit to a chemical test a third time when charged with an implied-consent offense, as defined in G.S. 20-16.2, that occurred while the person was driving a commercial motor vehicle.

(c) Life.—A person is disqualified from driving a commercial motor vehicle for life if that person uses a commercial motor vehicle in the commission of any felony involving the manufacture, distribution, or dispensing of a controlled substance, or possession with intent to manufacture, distribute, or dispense a controlled substance.

(d) Less Than a Year.—A person is disqualified from driving a commercial motor vehicle for 60 days if that person is convicted of two serious traffic violations, or 120 days if convicted of three or more serious traffic violations, committed in a commercial motor vehicle arising from separate incidents occurring within a three-year period.

(e) Three Years.—A person is disqualified from driving a commercial motor vehicle for three years if that person is convicted of an offense or commits an act requiring disqualification under subsection (a) and the offense or act occurred while the person was transporting a hazardous material that required the motor vehicle driven to be placarded.

(f) Revocation Period.—A person is disqualified from driving a commercial motor vehicle for the period during which the person's regular or commercial driver's license is revoked.

(g) Violation of Out-of-Service Order.—Any person convicted for violating an out-of-service order, except as described in subsection (h) of this section, shall be disqualified as follows:

(1) A person is disqualified from driving a commercial vehicle for a period of 90 days if convicted of a first violation of an out-of-service order.

(2) A person is disqualified for a period of one year if convicted of a second violation of an out-of-service order during any 10-year period, arising from separate incidents.

(3) A person is disqualified for a period of three years if convicted of a third or subsequent violation of an out-of-service order during any 10-year period, arising from separate incidents.

(h) Violation of Out-of-Service Order; Special Rule for Hazardous Materials and Passenger Offenses.—Any person convicted for violating an out-of-service order while transporting hazardous materials or while operating a commercial vehicle designed or used to transport more than 15 passengers, including the driver, shall be disqualified as follows:

(1) A person is disqualified for a period of 180 days if convicted of a first violation of an out-of-service order.

(2) A person is disqualified for a period of three years if convicted of a second or subsequent violation of an out-of-service order during any 10-year period, arising from separate incidents.

(i) Disqualification for Out-of-State Violations.—The Division shall withdraw the privilege to operate a commercial vehicle of any resident of this State upon receiving notice of the person's conviction in another state for an offense that, if committed in this State, would be grounds for disqualification. The period of disqualification shall be the same as if the offense occurred in this State.

(j) Disqualification of Persons Without Commercial Driver's Licenses.—Any person convicted of an offense that requires disqualification under this section, but who does not hold a commercial driver's license, shall be disqualified from operating a commercial vehicle in the same manner as if the person held a valid commercial driver's license.

History: 1989, c. 771, s. 3; 1991, c. 726, s. 8; 1993, c. 533, s. 5; 1998-149, s. 3; 1998-182, s. 19.

§ 20-17.5. Effect of disqualification

(a) When No Accompanying Revocation.—A person who is disqualified as the result of a conviction that requires disqualification but not revocation may keep any regular Class C driver's license the person had at the time of the offense resulting in disqualification. If the person had a Class A or Class B regular driver's license or a commercial driver's license when the offense occurred, all of the following apply:

(1) The person must give the license to the court that convicts the person or, if the person is not present when convicted, to the Division.

(2) The person may apply for a regular Class C driver's license.

(b) When Revocation and Disqualification.—When a person is disqualified as the result of a conviction that requires both disqualification and revocation, all of the following apply:

(1) The person must give any driver's license the person has to the court that convicts the person or, if the person is not present when convicted, to the Division.

(2) The person may obtain limited driving privileges to drive a noncommercial motor vehicle during the revocation period to the extent the law would allow limited driving privileges if the person had been driving a noncommercial motor vehicle when the offense occurred. The same procedure, eligibility requirements, and mandatory conditions apply to limited driving privileges authorized by this subdivision that would apply if the person had been driving a noncommercial motor vehicle when the offense occurred.

(3) If the disqualification period is longer than the revocation period, the person may apply for a regular Class C driver's license at the end of the revocation period.

(c) Refusal to Take Chemical Test.—When a person is disqualified for refusing to take a chemical test, all of the following apply:

(1) The person must give any license the person has to a court, a law enforcement officer, or the Division, in accordance with G.S. 20-16.2 and G.S. 20-16.5.

(2) The person may obtain limited driving privileges to drive a noncommercial motor vehicle during the period the person's license is revoked for the refusal that disqualified the person to the extent the law would allow limited driving privileges if the person had been driving a noncommercial motor vehicle at the time of the refusal. The same procedure, eligibility requirements, and mandatory conditions apply to limited driving privileges authorized by this subdivision that would apply if the person had been driving a noncommercial motor vehicle at the time of the refusal.

(3) If the disqualification period is longer than the revocation period, the person may apply for a regular Class C driver's license at the end of the revocation period.

(d) Obtaining Class C Regular License.—A person who is authorized by this section to apply for a regular Class C driver's license and who meets all of the following criteria may obtain a regular Class C driver's license without taking a test:

(1) The person must have had a Class A or Class B regular driver's license or a commercial driver's license when the person was disqualified.

(2) The person's license must have been issued by the Division.

(3) The person's license must not have expired by the date the person applies for a regular Class C driver's license.

Upon application and payment of the fee set in G.S. 20-14 for a duplicate license, the Division shall issue a person who meets these criteria a regular Class C driver's license. The license shall include the same endorsements and restrictions as the former Class A regular, Class B regular, or commercial driver's license, to the extent they apply to a regular Class C driver's license. A regular Class C driver's license issued to a person who meets these criteria expires the same day as the license it replaces.

G.S. 20-7 governs the issuance of a regular Class C driver's license to a person who is authorized by this section to apply for a regular Class C driver's license but who does not meet the listed criteria. In accordance with that statute, the Division may require the person to take a test and the person must pay the license fee.

(e) Restoration Fee.—A person who is disqualified must pay the restoration fee set in G.S. 20-7(i1) the first time any of the following events occurs as a result of the same disqualification:

(1) The Division reinstates a Class A regular driver's license, a Class B regular driver's license, or a commercial driver's license the person had at the time of the disqualification by issuing the person a duplicate license.

(2) The Division issues a Class A regular driver's license, a Class B regular driver's license, or a commercial driver's license to the person.

(3) If the person's license was revoked because of the conviction or act requiring disqualification, the Division issues a regular Class C driver's license to the person.

The restoration fee does not apply the second time any of these events occurs as a result of the same disqualification.

History: 1991, c. 726, s. 9.

§ 20-17.6. Restoration of a license after a conviction of driving while impaired or driving while less than 21 years old after consuming alcohol or drugs

(a) Scope.—This section applies to a person whose license was revoked as a result of a conviction of any of the following offenses:

(1) G.S. 20-138.1, driving while impaired (DWI).

(2) G.S. 20-138.2, commercial DWI.

(3) G.S. 20-138.3, driving while less than 21 years old after consuming alcohol or drugs.

(4) G.S. 20-138.2A, driving a commercial motor vehicle with an alcohol concentration of greater than 0.00 and less than 0.04, if the person's driver's license was revoked under G.S. 20-17(a)(13).

(5) G.S. 20-138.2B, driving a school bus, a school activity bus, or a child care vehicle with an alcohol concentration of greater than 0.00, if the person's driver's license was revoked under G.S. 20-17(a)(14).

(b) Requirement for Restoring License.—The Division must receive a certificate of completion for a person who is subject to this section before the Division can restore that person's license. The revocation period for a person who is subject to this section is extended until the Division receives the certificate of completion.

(c) Certificate of Completion.—To obtain a certificate of completion, a person must have a substance abuse assessment and, depending on the results of the assessment, must complete either an alcohol and drug education traffic (ADET) school or a substance abuse treatment program. The substance abuse assessment must be conducted by one of the entities authorized by the Department of Health and Human Services to conduct assessments. G.S. 122C-142.1 describes the procedure for obtaining a certificate of completion.

(d) Notice of Requirement.—When a court reports to the Division a conviction of a person who is subject to this section, the Division must send the person written notice of the requirements of this section and of the consequences of failing to comply with these requirements. The notification must include a statement that the person may contact the local area mental health, developmental disabilities, and substance abuse program for a list of agencies and entities in the person's area that are authorized to make a substance abuse assessment and provide the education or treatment needed to obtain a certificate of completion.

(e) Effect on Limited Driving Privileges.—A person who is subject to this section is not eligible for limited driving privileges if the revocation period for the offense that caused the person to become subject to this section has ended and the person's license remains revoked only because the Division has not obtained a certificate of completion for that person. The issuance of limited driving privileges during the revocation period for the offense that caused the person to become subject to this section is governed by the statutes that apply to that offense.

History: 1995, c. 496, ss. 1, 11, 12; 1997-443, s. 11A.118(a); 1998-182, s. 20.

§ 20-17.7. Commercial motor vehicle out-of-service fines authorized

The Commissioner may adopt rules implementing fines for violation of out-of-service criteria as defined in 49 C.F.R. § 390.5. These fines may not exceed the schedule of fines adopted by the Commercial Motor Vehicle Safety Alliance that is in effect on the date of the violations.

History: 1999-330, s. 1.

§ 20-17.8. (Effective July 1, 2000) Restoration of a license after certain driving while impaired convictions; ignition interlock

(a) Scope.—This section applies to a person whose license was revoked as a result of a conviction of driving while impaired, G.S. 20-138.1, and:

(1) The person had an alcohol concentration of 0.16 or more; or

(2) The person has been convicted of another offense involving impaired driving, which offense occurred within seven years immediately preceding the date of the offense for which the person's license has been revoked.

(b) Ignition Interlock Required.—When the Division restores the license of a person who is subject to this section, in addition to any other restriction or condition, it shall require the person to agree to and shall indicate on the person's driver's license the following restrictions for the period designated in subsection (c):

(1) A restriction that the person may operate only a vehicle that is equipped with a functioning ignition interlock system of a type approved by the Commissioner. The Commissioner shall not unreasonably withhold approval of an ignition interlock system and shall consult with the Division of Purchase and Contract in the Department of Administration to ensure that potential vendors are not discriminated against.

(2) A requirement that the person personally activate the ignition interlock system before driving the motor vehicle.

(3) A requirement that the person not drive with an alcohol concentration of 0.04 or greater.

(c) Length of Requirement.—The requirements of subsection (b) shall remain in effect for:

(1) One year from the date of restoration if the original revocation period was one year;

(2) Three years from the date of restoration if the original revocation period was four years; or

(3) Seven years from the date of restoration if the original revocation was a permanent revocation.

(d) Effect of Limited Driving Privileges.—If the person was eligible for and received a limited driving privilege under G.S. 20-179.3, with the ignition interlock requirement contained in G.S. 20-179.3(g5), the period of time for which that limited driving privilege was held shall be applied towards the requirements of subsection (c).

(e) Notice of Requirement.—When a court reports to the Division a conviction of a person who is subject to this section, the Division must send the person written notice of the requirements of this section and of the consequences of failing to comply with these requirements. The notification must include a statement that the person may contact the Division for information on obtaining and having installed an ignition interlock system of a type approved by the Commissioner.

(f) Effect of Violation of Restriction.—A person subject to this section who violates any of the restrictions of this section commits the offense of driving while license revoked under G.S. 20-28(a) and is subject to punishment and license revocation as provided in that section. If a law enforcement officer has reasonable grounds to believe that a person subject to this section has consumed alcohol while driving or has driven while he has remaining in his body any alcohol previously consumed, the suspected offense of driving while license is revoked is an alcohol-related offense subject to the implied-consent provisions of G.S. 20-16.2. If a person subject to this section is charged with driving while license revoked by violating a condition of subsection (b) of this section, and a judicial official determines that there is probable cause for the charge, the person's license is suspended pending the resolution of the case, and the judicial official must require the person to surrender the license. The judicial official must also notify the person that he is not entitled to drive until his case is resolved. An alcohol concentration report from the ignition interlock system shall not be admissible as evidence of driving while license revoked, nor shall it be admissible in an administrative revocation proceeding as provided in subsection (g) of this section; provided that the person did not operate a vehicle until the ignition interlock system indicated an alcohol concentration of less than 0.04.

(g) Effect of Violation of Restriction When Driving While License Revoked Not Charged.—A person subject to this section who violates any of the restrictions of this section, but is not charged or convicted of driving while license revoked pursuant to G.S. 20-28(a), shall have the person's license revoked by the Division for a period of one year.

(h) Beginning of Revocation Period.—If the original period of revocation was imposed pursuant to G.S. 20-19(d) or (e), any remaining period of the original revocation, prior to its reduction, shall be reinstated and the revocation required by subsection (f) or (g) of this section begins after all other periods of revocation have terminated.

(i) Notification of Revocation.—If the person's license has not already been surrendered to the court, the Division must expeditiously notify the person that the person's license to drive is revoked pursuant to subsection (f) or (g) of this section effective on the tenth calendar day after the mailing of the revocation order.

(j) Right to Hearing Before Division; Issues.—If the person's license is revoked pursuant to subsection (g) of this section, before the effective date of the order issued under subsection (i) of this section, the person may request in writing a hearing before the Division. Except for the time referred to in G.S. 20-16.5, if the person shows to the satisfaction of the Division that the person's license was surrendered to the court and remained in the court's possession, then the Division shall credit the amount of time for which the license was in the possession of the court against the revocation period required by subsection (g) of this section. If the person properly requests a hearing, the person retains the person's license, unless it is revoked under some other provision of law, until the hearing is held, the person withdraws the request, or the person fails to appear at a scheduled hearing. The hearing officer may subpoena any witnesses or documents that the hearing officer deems necessary. The person may request the hearing officer to subpoena the charging officer, the chemical analyst, or both to appear at the hearing if the person makes the request in writing at least three days before the hearing. The person may subpoena any other witness whom the person deems necessary, and the provisions of G.S. 1A-1, Rule 45, apply to the issuance and service of all subpoenas issued under the authority of this section. The hearing officer is authorized to administer oaths to witnesses appearing at the hearing. The hearing must be conducted in the county where the charge was brought, and must be limited to consideration of whether:

(1) The driver's license of the person had an ignition interlock requirement; and

(2) The person:

a. Was driving a vehicle that was not equipped with a functioning ignition interlock system; or

b. Did not personally activate the ignition interlock system before driving the vehicle; or

c. Drove the vehicle with an alcohol concentration of 0.04 or greater.

If the Division finds that the conditions specified in this subsection are met, it must order the revocation sustained. If the Division finds that the condition of subdivision (1) is not met, or that none of the conditions of subdivision (2) are met, it must rescind the revocation. If the revocation is sustained, the person must surrender the person's license immediately upon notification by the Division. If the revocation is sustained, the person may appeal the decision of the Division pursuant to G.S. 20-25.

(k) Restoration After Violation.—When the Division restores the license of a person whose license was revoked pursuant to subsection (f) or (g) of this section and the revocation occurred prior to completion of time period required by subsection (c) of this section, in addition to any other restriction or condition, it shall require the person to comply with the conditions of subsection (b) of this section until the person has complied with those conditions for the cumulative period of time as set forth in subsection (c) of this section. The period of time for which the person successfully complied with subsection (b) of this section prior to revocation pursuant to subsection (f) or (g) of this section shall be applied towards the requirements of subsection (c) of this section.

History: 1999-406, s. 3.

FIRST OF TWO VERSIONS OF THIS SECTION
(THIS SECTION HAS MORE THAN ONE DOCUMENT WITH VARYING EFFECTIVE DATES)

§ 20-19. (Effective until July 1, 2000) Period of suspension or revocation

(a) When a license is suspended under subdivision (8) or (9) of G.S. 20-16(a), the period of suspension shall be in the discretion of the Division and for such time as it deems best for public safety but shall not exceed six months.

(b) When a license is suspended under subdivision (10) of G.S. 20-16(a), the period of suspension shall be in the discretion of the Division and for such time as it deems best for public safety but shall not exceed a period of 12 months.

(c) When a license is suspended under any other provision of this Article which does not specifically provide a period of suspension, the period of suspension shall be not more than one year.

(c1) When a license is revoked under subdivision (2) of G.S. 20-17, and the period of revocation is not determined by subsection (d) or (e) of this section, the period of revocation is one year.

(c2) When a license is suspended under G.S. 20-17(a)(14), the period of revocation for a first conviction shall be for 10 days. For a second or subsequent conviction as defined in G.S. 20-138.2B(d), the period of revocation shall be one year.

(d) When a person's license is revoked under G.S. 20-17(a)(2) and the person has another offense involving impaired driving for which he has been convicted, which offense occurred within three years immediately preceding the date of the offense for which his license is being revoked, the period of revocation is four years, and this period may be reduced only as provided in this section. The Division may conditionally restore the person's license after it has been revoked for at least two years under this subsection if he provides the Division with satisfactory proof that:

(1) He has not in the period of revocation been convicted in North Carolina or any other state or federal jurisdiction of a motor vehicle offense, an alcoholic beverage control law offense, a drug law offense, or any other criminal offense involving the possession or consumption of alcohol or drugs; and

(2) He is not currently an excessive user of alcohol or drugs.

If the Division restores the person's license, it may place reasonable conditions or restrictions on the person for the duration of the original revocation period.

(e) When a person's license is revoked under G.S. 20-17(a)(2) and the person has two or more previous offenses involving impaired driving for which he has been convicted, and the most recent offense occurred within the five years immediately preceding the date of the offense for which his license is being revoked, the revocation is permanent. The Division may, however, conditionally restore the person's license after it has been revoked for at least three years under this subsection if he provides the Division with satisfactory proof that:

(1) In the three years immediately preceding the person's application for a restored license, he has not been convicted in North Carolina or in any other state or federal court of a motor vehicle offense, an alcohol beverage control law offense, a drug law offense, or any criminal offense involving the consumption of alcohol or drugs; and

(2) He is not currently an excessive user of alcohol or drugs.

If the Division restores the person's license, it may place reasonable conditions or restrictions on the person for any period up to three years from the date of restoration.

(f) When a license is revoked under any other provision of this Article which does not specifically provide a period of revocation, the period of revocation shall be one year.

(g) When a license is suspended under subdivision (11) of G.S. 20-16(a), the period of suspension shall be for a period of time not in excess of the period of nonoperation imposed by the court as a condition of the suspended sentence; further, in such case, it shall not be necessary to comply with the Motor Vehicle Safety and Financial Responsibility Act in order to have such license returned at the expiration of the suspension period.

(g1) When a license is revoked under subdivision (12) of G.S. 20-17, the period of revocation is six months for conviction of a second offense and one year for conviction of a third or subsequent offense.

(h) Repealed by Session Laws 1983, c. 435, s. 17.

(i) When a person's license is revoked under subdivision (1) or (9) of G.S. 20-17 and the offense is one involving impaired driving, the revocation is permanent. The Division may, however, conditionally restore the person's license after it has been revoked for at least three years in accordance with the procedure in subsection (e) of this section.

(j) The Division is authorized to issue amended revocation orders issued under subsections (d) and (e), if necessary because convictions do not respectively occur in the same order as offenses for which the license may be revoked under those subsections.

(k) Before the Division restores a driver's license that has been suspended or revoked under any provision of this Article, other than G.S. 20-24.1, the person seeking to have his driver's license restored shall submit to the Division proof that he has notified his insurance agent or company of his seeking the restoration and that he is financially responsible. Proof of financial responsibility shall be in one of the following forms:

(1) A written certificate or electronically-transmitted facsimile thereof from any insurance carrier duly authorized to do business in this State certifying that there is in effect a nonfleet private passenger motor vehicle liability policy for the benefit of the person required to furnish proof of financial responsibility. The certificate or facsimile shall state the effective date and expiration date of the nonfleet private passenger motor vehicle liability policy and shall state the date that the certificate or facsimile is issued. The certificate or facsimile shall remain effective proof of financial responsibility for a period of 30 consecutive days following the date the certificate or facsimile is issued but shall not in and of itself constitute a binder or policy of insurance or

(2) A binder for or policy of nonfleet private passenger motor vehicle liability insurance under which the applicant is insured, provided that the binder or policy states the effective date and expiration date of the nonfleet private passenger motor vehicle liability policy.

The preceding provisions of this subsection do not apply to applicants who do not own currently registered motor vehicles and who do not operate nonfleet private passenger motor vehicles that are owned by other persons and that are not insured under commercial motor vehicle liability insurance policies. In such cases, the applicant shall sign a written certificate to that effect. Such certificate shall be furnished by the

Division and may be incorporated into the restoration application form. Any material misrepresentation made by such person on such certificate shall be grounds for suspension of that person's license for a period of 90 days.

For the purposes of this subsection, the term "nonfleet private passenger motor vehicle" has the definition ascribed to it in Article 40 of General Statute Chapter 58.

The Commissioner may require that certificates required by this subsection be on a form approved by the Commissioner. The financial responsibility required by this subsection shall be kept in effect for not less than three years after the date that the license is restored. Failure to maintain financial responsibility as required by this subsection shall be grounds for suspending the restored driver's license for a period of thirty (30) days. Nothing in this subsection precludes any person from showing proof of financial responsibility in any other manner authorized by Articles 9A and 13 of this Chapter.

History: 1935, c. 52, s. 13; 1947, c. 1067, s. 15; 1951, c. 1202, ss. 2–4; 1953, c. 1138; 1955, c. 1187, ss. 13, 17, 18; 1957, c. 499, s. 2; c. 515, s. 1; 1959, c. 1264, s. 11A; 1969, c. 242; 1971, c. 619, ss. 8–10; 1973, c. 1445, ss. 1–4; 1975, c. 716, s. 5; 1979, c. 903, ss. 4–6; 1981, c. 412, s. 4; c. 747, ss. 34, 66; 1983, c. 435, s. 17; 1983 (Reg. Sess., 1984), c. 1101, s. 18; 1987, c. 869, s. 12; 1987 (Reg. Sess., 1988), c. 1112; 1989, c. 436, s. 5; c. 771, s. 18; 1995, c. 506, s. 8; 1998-182, s. 21; 1999-452, ss. 11, 12.

SECOND OF TWO VERSIONS OF THIS SECTION

§ 20-19. (Effective July 1, 2000) Period of suspension or revocation; conditions of restoration

(a) When a license is suspended under subdivision (8) or (9) of G.S. 20-16(a), the period of suspension shall be in the discretion of the Division and for such time as it deems best for public safety but shall not exceed six months.

(b) When a license is suspended under subdivision (10) of G.S. 20-16(a), the period of suspension shall be in the discretion of the Division and for such time as it deems best for public safety but shall not exceed a period of 12 months.

(c) When a license is suspended under any other provision of this Article which does not specifically provide a period of suspension, the period of suspension shall be not more than one year.

(c1) When a license is revoked under subdivision (2) of G.S. 20-17, and the period of revocation is not determined by subsection (d) or (e) of this section, the period of revocation is one year.

(c2) When a license is suspended under G.S. 20-17(a)(14), the period of revocation for a first conviction shall be for 10 days. For a second or subsequent conviction as defined in G.S. 20-138.2B(d), the period of revocation shall be one year.

(c3) Restriction; Revocations.—When the Division restores a person's driver's license which was revoked pursuant to G.S. 20-13.2 (a), G.S. 20-23 when the offense involved impaired driving, G.S. 20-23.2, subdivision (2) of G.S. 20-17(a), subdivision (1) or (9) of G.S. 20-17(a) when the offense involved impaired driving, or this subsection, in addition to any other restriction or condition, it shall place the applicable restriction on the person's driver's license as follows:

(1) For the first restoration of a driver's license for a person convicted of driving while impaired, G.S. 20-138.1, or a driver's license revoked pursuant to G.S. 20-23 or G.S. 20-23.2 when the offense for which the person's license was revoked prohibits substantially similar conduct which if committed in this State would result in a conviction of driving while impaired under G.S. 20-138.1, that the person not operate a vehicle with an alcohol concentration of 0.04 or more at any relevant time after the driving;

(2) For the second or subsequent restoration of a driver's license for a person convicted of driving while impaired, G.S. 20-138.1, or a driver's license revoked pursuant to G.S. 20-23 or G.S. 20-23.2 when the offense for which the person's license was revoked prohibits substantially similar conduct which if committed in this State would result in a conviction of driving while impaired under G.S. 20-138.1, that the person not operate a vehicle with an alcohol concentration greater than 0.00 at any relevant time after the driving;

(3) For any restoration of a driver's license for a person convicted of driving while impaired in a commercial motor vehicle, G.S. 20-138.2, driving while less than 21 years old after consuming alcohol or drugs, G.S. 20-138.3, felony death by vehicle, G.S. 20-141.4(a1), manslaughter or negligent homicide resulting from the operation of a motor vehicle when the offense

involved impaired driving, or a revocation under this subsection, that the person not operate a vehicle with an alcohol concentration of 0.00 or more at any relevant time after the driving;

(4) For any restoration of a driver's license revoked pursuant to G.S. 20-23 or G.S. 20-23.2 when the offense for which the person's license was revoked prohibits substantially similar conduct which if committed in this State would result in a conviction of driving while impaired in a commercial motor vehicle, G.S. 20-138.2, driving while lesan 21 years old after consuming alcohol or drugs, G.S. 20-138.3, felony death by vehicle, G.S. 20-141.4(a1), or manslaughter or negligent homicide resulting from the operation of a motor vehicle when the offense involved impaired driving, that the person not operate a vehicle with an alcohol concentration of 0.00 or more at any relevant time after the driving.

In addition, the person seeking restoration of a license must agree to submit to a chemical analysis in accordance with G.S. 20-16.2 at the request of a law enforcement officer who has reasonable grounds to believe the person is operating a motor vehicle on a highway in violation of the restriction specified in this subsection. The person must also agree that, when requested by a law enforcement officer, the person will agree to be transported by the law enforcement officer to the place where chemical analysis is to be administered.

The restrictions placed on a license under this subsection shall be in effect (i) seven years from the date of restoration if the person's license was permanently revoked, (ii) until the person's twenty-first birthday if the revocation was for a conviction under G.S. 20-138.3, and (iii) three years in all other cases.

On the basis of information reported pursuant to G.S. 20-16.2, the Division shall revoke the driver's license of any person who violates a condition of reinstatement imposed under this subsection. An alcohol concentration report from an ignition interlock system shall not be used as the basis for revocation under this subsection. A violation of a restriction imposed under this subsection or the willful refusal to submit to a chemical analysis shall result in a one-year revocation. If the period of revocation was imposed pursuant to subsection (d) or (e), any remaining period of the original revocation, prior to its reduction, shall be reinstated and the one-year revocation begins after all other periods of revocation have terminated.

(c4) Applicable Procedures.—When a person has violated a condition of restoration by refusing a chemical analysis, the notice and hearing procedures of G.S. 20-16.2 apply. When a person has submitted to a chemical analysis and the results show a violation of the alcohol concentration restriction, the notification and hearing procedures of this section apply.

(c5) Right to Hearing Before Division; Issues.—Upon receipt of a properly executed affidavit required by G.S. 20-16.2(c1), the Division must expeditiously notify the person charged that the person's license to drive is revoked for the period of time specified in this section, effective on the tenth calendar day after the mailing of the revocation order unless, before the effective date of the order, the person requests in writing a hearing before the Division. Except for the time referred to in G.S. 20-16.5, if the person shows to the satisfaction of the Division that the person's license was surrendered to the court and remained in the court's possession, then the Division shall credit the amount of time for which the license was in the possession of the court against the revocation period required by this section. If the person properly requests a hearing, the person retains the person's license, unless it is revoked under some other provision of law, until the hearing is held, the person withdraws the request, or the person fails to appear at a scheduled hearing. The hearing officer may subpoena any witnesses or documents that the hearing officer deems necessary. The person may request the hearing officer to subpoena the chargifficer, the chemical analyst, or both to appear at the hearing if the person makes the request in writing at least three days before the hearing. The person may subpoena any other witness whom the person deems necessary, and the provisions of G.S. 1A-1, Rule 45, apply to the issuance and service of all subpoenas issued under the authority of this section. The hearing officer is authorized to administer oaths to witnesses appearing at the hearing. The hearing must be conducted in the county where the charge was brought, and must be limited to consideration of whether:

(1) The charging officer had reasonable grounds to believe that the person had violated the alcohol concentration restriction;

(2) The person was notified of the person's rights as required by G.S. 20-16.2(a);

(3) The driver's license of the person had an alcohol concentration restriction; and

(4) The person submitted to a chemical analysis upon the request of the charging officer, and the analysis revealed an alcohol concentration in excess of the restriction on the person's driver's license.

If the Division finds that the conditions specified in this subsection are met, it must order the revocation sustained. If the Division finds that any of the conditions (1), (2), (3), or (4) is not met, it must rescind the revocation. If the revocation is sustained, the person must surrender the person's license immediately upon notification by the Division.

(c6) Appeal to Court.—There is no right to appeal the decision of the Division. However, if the person properly requested a hearing before the Division under subsection (c5) and the Division held such a hearing, the person may within 30 days of the date the Division's decision is mailed to the person, petition the superior court of the county in which the hearing took place for discretionary review on the record of the revocation. The superior court may stay the imposition of the revocation only if the court finds that the person is likely to succeed on the merits of the case and will suffer irreparable harm if such a stay is not granted. The stay shall not exceed 30 days. The reviewing court shall review the record only and shall be limited to determining if the Division hearing officer followed proper procedures and if the hearing officer made sufficient findings of fact to support the revocation. There shall be no further appeal.

(d) When a person's license is revoked under G.S. 20-17(a)(2) and the person has another offense involving impaired driving for which he has been convicted, which offense occurred within three years immediately preceding the date of the offense for which his license is being revoked, the period of revocation is four years, and this period may be reduced only as provided in this section. The Division may conditionally restore the person's license after it has been revoked for at least two years under this subsection if he provides the Division with satisfactory proof that:

(1) He has not in the period of revocation been convicted in North Carolina or any other state or federal jurisdiction of a motor vehicle offense, an alcoholic beverage control law offense, a drug law offense, or any other criminal offense involving the possession or consumption of alcohol or drugs; and

(2) He is not currently an excessive user of alcohol or drugs.

If the Division restores the person's license, it may place reasonable conditions or restrictions on the person for the duration of the original revocation period.

(e) When a person's license is revounder G.S. 20-17(a)(2) and the person has two or more previous offenses involving impaired driving for which he has been convicted, and the most recent offense occurred within the five years immediately preceding the date of the offense for which his license is being revoked, the revocation is permanent. The Division may, however, conditionally restore the person's license after it has been revoked for at least three years under this subsection if he provides the Division with satisfactory proof that:

(1) In the three years immediately preceding the person's application for a restored license, he has not been convicted in North Carolina or in any other state or federal court of a motor vehicle offense, an alcohol beverage control law offense, a drug law offense, or any criminal offense involving the consumption of alcohol or drugs; and

(2) He is not currently an excessive user of alcohol or drugs.

If the Division restores the person's license, it may place reasonable conditions or restrictions on the person for any period up to three years from the date of restoration.

(f) When a license is revoked under any other provision of this Article which does not specifically provide a period of revocation, the period of revocation shall be one year.

(g) When a license is suspended under subdivision (11) of G.S. 20-16(a), the period of suspension shall be for a period of time not in excess of the period of nonoperation imposed by the court as a condition of the suspended sentence; further, in such case, it shall not be necessary to comply with the Motor Vehicle Safety and Financial Responsibility Act in order to have such license returned at the expiration of the suspension period.

(g1) When a license is revoked under subdivision (12) of G.S. 20-17, the period of revocation is six months for conviction of a second offense and one year for conviction of a third or subsequent offense.

(h) Repealed by Session Laws 1983, c. 435, s. 17.

(i) When a person's license is revoked under subdivision (1) or (9) of G.S. 20-17 and the offense is one involving impaired driving, the revocation is permanent. The Division may, however, conditionally restore the person's license after it has been revoked for at least three years in accordance with the procedure in subsection (e) of this section.

(j) The Division is authorized to issue amended revocation orders issued under subsections (d) and (e), if necessary because convictions do not respectively occur in the same order as offenses for which the license may be revoked under those subsections.

(k) Before the Division restores a driver's license that has been suspended or revoked under any provision of this Article, other than G.S. 20-24.1, the person seeking to have his driver's license restored shall submit to the Division proof that he has notified his insurance agent or company of his seeking the restoration and that he is financially responsible. Proof of financial responsibility shall be in one of the following forms:

(1) A written certificate or electronically-transmitted facsimile thereof from any insurance carrier duly authorized to do business in this State certifying that there is in effect a nonfleet private passenger motor vehicle liability policy for the benefit of the person required to furnish proof of financial responsibility. The certificate or facsimile shall state the effective date and expiration date of the nonfleet private passenger motor vehicle liability policy and shall state the date that the certificate or facsimile is issued. The ificate or facsimile shall remain effective proof of financial responsibility for a period of 30 consecutive days following the date the certificate or facsimile is issued but shall not in and of itself constitute a binder or policy of insurance or

(2) A binder for or policy of nonfleet private passenger motor vehicle liability insurance under which the applicant is insured, provided that the binder or policy states the effective date and expiration date of the nonfleet private passenger motor vehicle liability policy.

The preceding provisions of this subsection do not apply to applicants who do not own currently registered motor vehicles and who do not operate nonfleet private passenger motor vehicles that are owned by other persons and that are not insured under commercial motor vehicle liability insurance policies. In such cases, the applicant shall sign a written certificate to that effect. Such certificate shall be furnished by the Division and may be incorporated into the restoration application form. Any material misrepresentation made by such person on such certificate shall be grounds for suspension of that person's license for a period of 90 days.

For the purposes of this subsection, the term "nonfleet private passenger motor vehicle" has the definition ascribed to it in Article 40 of General Statute Chapter 58.

The Commissioner may require that certificates required by this subsection be on a form approved by the Commissioner. The financial responsibility required by this subsection shall be kept in effect for not less than three years after the date that the license is restored. Failure to maintain financial responsibility as required by this subsection shall be grounds for suspending the restored driver's license for a period of thirty (30) days. Nothing in this subsection precludes any person from showing proof of financial responsibility in any other manner authorized by Articles 9A and 13 of this Chapter.

History: 1935, c. 52, s. 13; 1947, c. 1067, s. 15; 1951, c. 1202, ss. 2–4; 1953, c. 1138; 1955, c. 1187, ss. 13, 17, 18; 1957, c. 499, s. 2; c. 515, s. 1; 1959, c. 1264, s. 11A; 1969, c. 242; 1971, c. 619, ss. 8–10; 1973, c. 1445, ss. 1–4; 1975, c. 716, s. 5; 1979, c. 903, ss. 4–6; 1981, c. 412, s. 4; c. 747, ss. 34, 66; 1983, c. 435, s. 17; 1983 (Reg. Sess., 1984), c. 1101, s. 18; 1987, c. 869, s. 12; 1989, c. 436, s. 5; 1995, c. 506, s. 8; 1998-182, s. 21; 1999-406, s. 2; 1999-452, ss. 11, 12.

§ 20-22. Suspending privileges of nonresidents and reporting convictions

(a) The privilege of driving a motor vehicle on the highways of this State given to a nonresident hereunder shall be subject to suspension or revocation by the Division in like manner and for like cause as a driver's license issued hereunder may be suspended or revoked.

(b) The Division is further authorized, upon receiving a record of the conviction in this State of a nonresident driver of a motor vehicle of any offense under the motor vehicle laws of this State, to forward a certified copy of such record to the motor vehicle administrator in the state wherein the person so convicted is a resident.

History: 1935, c. 52, s. 16; 1975, c. 716, s. 5; 1979, c. 667, s. 41.

§ 20-23. Revoking resident's license upon conviction in another state

The Division may revoke the license of any resident of this State upon receiving notice of the person's conviction in another state of an offense set forth in G.S. 20-26(a).

History: 1935, c. 52, s. 17; 1971, c. 486, s. 2; 1975, c. 716, s. 5; 1979, c. 667, s. 22; 1993, c. 533, s. 6.

§ 20-23.1. Suspending or revoking operating privilege of person not holding license

In any case where the Division would be authorized to suspend or revoke the license of a person but such person does not hold a license, the Division is authorized to suspend or revoke the operating privilege of such a person in like manner as it could suspend or revoke his license if such person held a driver's license, and the provisions of this Chapter governing suspensions, revocations, issuance of a license, and driving after license suspended or revoked, shall apply in the discretion of the Division in the same manner as if the license has been suspended or revoked.

History: 1955, c. 1187, s. 19; 1969, c. 186, s. 2; 1975, c. 716, s. 5; 1979, c. 667, s. 41.

§ 20-23.2. Suspension of license for conviction of offense involving impaired driving in federal court

Upon receipt of notice of conviction in any court of the federal government of an offense involving impaired driving, the Division is authorized to revoke the driving privilege of the person convicted in the same manner as if the conviction had occurred in a court of this State.

History: 1969, c. 988; 1971, c. 619, s. 11; 1975, c. 716, s. 5; 1979, c. 903, s. 12; 1981, c. 412, s. 4; c. 747, s. 66; 1983, c. 435, s. 18.

§ 20-24. When court or child support enforcement agency to forward license to Division and report convictions, child support delinquencies, and prayers for judgment continued

(a) License.—A court that convicts a person of an offense that requires revocation of the person's driver's license or revokes a person's driver's license pursuant to G.S. 50-13.12 shall require the person to give the court any regular or commercial driver's license issued to that person. A court that convicts a person of an offense that requires disqualification of the person but would not require revocation of a regular driver's license issued to that person shall require the person to give the court any Class A or Class B regular driver's license and any commercial driver's license issued to that person.

The clerk of court in a non-IV-D case, and the child support enforcement agency in a IV-D case, shall accept a driver's license required to be given to the court under this subsection. A clerk of court or the child support enforcement agency who receives a driver's license shall give the person whose license is received a copy of a dated receipt for the license. The receipt must be on a form approved by the Commissioner. A revocation or disqualification for which a license is received under this subsection is effective as of the date on the receipt for the license.

The clerk of court or the child support enforcement agency shall notify the Division of a license received under this subsection either by forwarding to the Division the license, a record of the conviction for which the license was received, a copy of the court order revoking the license for failure to pay child support for which the license was received, and the original dated receipt for the license or by electronically sending to the Division the information on the license, the record of conviction or court order revoking the license for failure to pay child support, and the receipt given for the license. The clerk of court or the child support enforcement agency must forward the required items unless the Commissioner has given the clerk of court or the child support enforcement agency approval to notify the Division electronically. If the clerk of court or the child support enforcement agency notifies the Division electronically, the clerk of court or the child support enforcement agency must destroy a license received after sending to the Division the required information. The clerk of court or the child support enforcement agency shall notify the Division within 30 days after entry of the conviction or court order revoking the license for failure to pay child support for which the license was received.

(b) Convictions, Court Orders of Driver's License Revocations, and PJCs.—The clerk of court shall send the Division a record of any of the following:

- (1) A conviction of a violation of a law regulating the operation of a vehicle.
- (2) A conviction for which the convicted person is placed on probation and a condition of probation is that the person not drive a motor vehicle for a period of time, stating the period of time for which the condition applies.
- (3) A conviction of a felony in the commission of which a motor vehicle is used, when the judgment includes a finding that a motor vehicle was used in the commission of the felony.
- (4) A conviction that requires revocation of the driver's license of the person convicted and is not otherwise reported under subdivision (1).
- (4a) A court order revoking driver's license pursuant to G.S. 50-13.12.
- (5) An order entering prayer for judgment continued in a case involving an alleged violation of a law regulating the operation of a vehicle.

The child support enforcement agency shall send the Division a record of any court order revoking driver's license pursuant to G.S. 110-142.2(a)(1).

With the approval of the Commissioner, the clerk of court or the child support enforcement agency may forward a record of conviction, court order revoking driver's license, or prayer for judgment continued to the Division by electronic data processing means.

(b1) In any case in which the Division, for any reason, does not receive a record of a conviction or a prayer for judgment continued until more than one year after the date it is entered, the Division may, in its discretion, substitute a period of probation for all or any part of a revocation or disqualification required because of the conviction or prayer for judgment continued.

(c) Repealed by Session Laws 1991, c. 726, s. 10.

(d) Scope.—This Article governs driver's license revocation and disqualification. A driver's license may not be revoked and a person may not be disqualified except in accordance with this Article.

(e) Special Information.—A judgment for a conviction for an offense for which special information is required under this subsection shall, when appropriate, include a finding of the special information. The convictions for which special information is required and the specific information required is as follows:

(1) Homicide.—If a conviction of homicide involves impaired driving, the judgment must indicate that fact.

(2) G.S. 20-138.1, Driving While Impaired.—If a conviction under G.S. 20-138.1 involves a commercial motor vehicle, the judgment must indicate that fact. If a conviction under G.S. 20-138.1 involves a commercial motor vehicle that was transporting a hazardous substance required to be placarded, the judgment must indicate that fact.

(3) G.S. 20-138.2, Driving Commercial Motor Vehicle While Impaired.—If the commercial motor vehicle involved in an offense under G.S. 20-138.2 was transporting a hazardous material required to be placarded, a judgment for that offense must indicate that fact.

(4) G.S. 20-166, Hit and Run.—If a conviction under G.S. 20-166 involves a commercial motor vehicle, the judgment must indicate that fact. If a conviction under G.S. 20-166 involves a commercial motor vehicle that was transporting a hazardous substance required to be placarded, the judgment must indicate that fact.

(5) Felony Using Commercial Motor Vehicle.—If a conviction of a felony in which a commercial motor vehicle was used involves the manufacture, distribution, or dispensing of a controlled substance, or possession with intent to manufacture, distribute, or dispense a controlled substance, the judgment must indicate that fact. If a commercial motor vehicle used in a felony was transporting a hazardous substance required to be placarded, the judgment for that felony must indicate that fact.

History: 1935, c. 52, s. 18; 1949, c. 373, ss. 3, 4; 1955, c. 1187, s. 14; 1959, c. 47; 1965, c. 38; 1973, c. 19; 1975, cc. 46, 445; c. 716, s. 5; c. 871, s. 1; 1979, c. 667, s. 41; 1981, c. 416; c. 839; 1983, c. 294, s. 5; c. 435, s. 19; 1985, c. 764, s. 18; 1985 (Reg. Sess., 1986), c. 852, s. 17; 1987, c. 581, s. 1; c. 658, s. 2; 1989, c. 771, s. 10; 1991, c. 726, s. 10; 1993, c. 533, s. 7; 1995, c. 538, s. 2(c).

§ 20-24.1. Revocation for failure to appear or pay fine, penalty or costs for motor vehicle offenses

(a) The Division must revoke the driver's license of a person upon receipt of notice from a court that the person was charged with a motor vehicle offense and he:

(1) failed to appear, after being notified to do so, when the case was called for a trial or hearing; or

(2) failed to pay a fine, penalty, or court costs ordered by the court.

Revocation orders entered under the authority of this section are effective on the sixtieth day after the order is mailed or personally delivered to the person.

(b) A license revoked under this section remains revoked until the person whose license has been revoked:

(1) disposes of the charge in the trial division in which he failed to appear when the case was last called for trial or hearing; or

(2) demonstrates to the court that he is not the person charged with the offense; or

(3) pays the penalty, fine, or costs ordered by the court; or

(4) demonstrates to the court that his failure to pay the penalty, fine, or costs was not willful and that he is making a good faith effort to pay or that the penalty, fine, or costs should be remitted.

Upon receipt of notice from the court that the person has satisfied the conditions of this subsection applicable to his case, the Division must restore the person's license as provided in subsection (c). In addition, if the person whose license is revoked is not a resident of this State, the Division may notify the driver licensing agency in the person's state of residence that the person's license to drive in this State has been revoked.

(b1) A defendant must be afforded an opportunity for a trial or a hearing within a reasonable time of the defendant's appearance. Upon motion of a defendant, the court must order that a hearing or a trial be heard within a reasonable time.

(c) If the person satisfies the conditions of subsection (b) that are applicable to his case before the effective date of the revocation order, the revocation order and any entries on his driving record relating to it shall be deleted and the person does not have to pay the restoration fee set by G.S. 20-7(i1). For all other revocation orders issued pursuant to this section, G.S. 50-13.12 or G.S. 110-142.2, the person must pay the restoration fee and satisfy any other applicable requirements of this Article before the person may be relicensed.

(d) To facilitate the prompt return of licenses and to prevent unjustified charges of driving while license revoked, the clerk of court, upon request, must give the person a copy of the notice it sends to the Division to indicate that the person has complied with the conditions of subsection (b) applicable to his case. If the person complies with the condition before the effective date of the revocation, the notice must indicate that the person is eligible to drive if he is otherwise validly licensed.

(e) As used in this section and in G.S. 20-24.2, the word offense includes crimes and infractions created by this Chapter.

History: 1985, c. 764, s. 19; 1985 (Reg. Sess., 1986), c. 852, ss. 4–6, 9, 17; 1987, c. 581, s. 4; 1991, c. 682, s. 4; 1993, c. 313, s. 1; 1995, c. 538, s. 2(d).

§ 20-25. Right of appeal to court

Any person denied a license or whose license has been canceled, suspended or revoked by the Division, except where such cancellation is mandatory under the provisions of this Article, shall have a right to file a petition within 30 days thereafter for a hearing in the matter in the superior court of the county wherein such person shall reside, or to the resident judge of the district or judge holding the court of that district, or special or emergency judge holding a court in such district in which the violation was committed, and such court or judge is hereby vested with jurisdiction and it shall be its or his duty to set the matter for hearing upon 30 days' written notice to the Division, and thereupon to take testimony and examine into the facts of the case, and to determine whether the petitioner is entitled to a license or is subject to suspension, cancellation or revocation of license under the provisions of this Article. Provided, a judge of the district court shall have limited jurisdiction under this section to sign and enter a temporary restraining order only.

History: 1935, c. 52, s. 19; 1975, c. 716, s. 5; 1987, c. 659, s. 1.

§ 20-26. Records; copies furnished; charge

(a) The Division shall keep a record of all applications for a driver's license, all tests given an applicant for a driver's license, all applications for a driver's license that are denied, all driver's licenses issued, renewed, cancelled, or revoked, all disqualifications, all convictions affecting a driver's license, and all prayers for judgment continued that may lead to a license revocation. When the Division cancels or revokes a commercial driver's license or disqualifies a person, the Division shall update its records to reflect that action within 10 days after the cancellation, revocation, or disqualification becomes effective. When a person who is not a resident of this State is convicted of an offense or commits an act requiring revocation of the person's commercial driver's license or disqualification of the person, the Division shall notify the licensing authority of the person's state of residence.

The Division shall keep records of convictions occurring outside North Carolina for the offenses of exceeding a stated speed limit of 55 miles per hour or more by more than 15 miles per hour, driving while license suspended or revoked, careless and reckless driving, engaging in prearranged speed competition, engaging willfully in speed competition, hit-and-run driving resulting in damage to property, unlawfully passing a stopped school bus, illegal transportation of alcoholic beverages, and the offenses included in G.S. 20-17. The Division shall also keep records of convictions occurring outside North Carolina for any serious traffic violation that involves a commercial motor vehicle and is not otherwise required to be kept under this subsection.

(b) The Division shall furnish certified copies of license records required to be kept by subsection (a) of this section to State, county, municipal and court officials of this State for official use only, without charge. A certified copy of a driver's records kept pursuant to subsection (a) may be sent by the Police Information Network. In addition to the uses authorized by G.S. 8-35.1, a copy certified under the authority of this section is admissible as prima facie evidence of the status of the person's license. The Attorney General and the Commissioner of Motor Vehicles are authorized to promulgate such rules and regulations as may be necessary to implement the provision of this subsection.

(b1) The registered or declared weight set forth on the vehicle registration card or a certified copy of the Division record sent by the Division of Criminal Information or otherwise is admissible in any judicial or administrative proceeding and shall be prima facie evidence of the registered or declared weight.

(c) The Division shall furnish copies of license records required to be kept by subsection (a) of this section in accordance with G.S. 20-43.1 to other persons for uses other than official upon prepayment of the following fees:

(1)	Limited extract copy of license record, for period up to three years	$5.00
(2)	Complete extract copy of license record	5.00
(3)	Certified true copy of complete license record	7.00.

All fees received by the Division under this subsection shall be credited to the Highway Fund.

(d) The charge for records provided pursuant to this section shall not be subject to the provisions of Chapter 132 of the General Statutes.

(e) In the event of a mistake on the part of any person in ordering license records under subsection (c) of this section, the Commissioner may refund or credit to that person up to sixty-five percent (65%) of the amount paid for the license records.

(f) On and after July 1, 1988, the Division shall expeditiously furnish to insurance agents, insurance companies, and to insurance support organizations as defined in G.S. 58-39-15(12), for the purpose of rating nonfleet private passenger motor vehicle insurance policies, through electronic data processing means or otherwise, copies of or information pertaining to license records that are required to be kept pursuant to subsection (a) of this section.

History: 1935, c. 52, s. 20; 1961, c. 307; 1969, c. 783, s. 3; 1971, c. 486, s. 1; 1975, c. 716, s. 5; 1979, c. 667, s. 23; c. 903, ss. 9, 10; 1981, c. 145, s. 1; c. 412, s. 4; c. 690, s. 13; c. 747, s. 66; 1983, c. 435, s. 20; c. 761, s. 149; 1987, c. 869, s. 16; 1987 (Reg. Sess., 1988), c. 1112, ss. 14, 17; 1989, c. 771, ss. 9, 17, 18; 1991, c. 689, s. 330; c. 726, s. 11; 1997-443, s. 32.25(b).

§ 20-27. Availability of records

(a) All records of the Division pertaining to application and to driver's' licenses, except the confidential medical report referred to in G.S. 20-7, of the current or previous five years shall be open to public inspection in accordance with G.S. 20-43.1, at any reasonable time during office hours and copies shall be provided pursuant to the provisions of G.S. 20-26.

(b) All records of the Division pertaining to chemical tests as provided in G.S. 20-16.2 shall be available to the courts as provided in G.S. 20-26(b).

History: 1935, c. 52, s. 21; 1975, c. 716, s. 5; 1979, c. 667, s. 24; c. 903, s. 11; 1981, c. 145, s. 2; 1997-443, s. 32.25(c).

§ 20-28. Unlawful to drive while license revoked or while disqualified

(a) Driving While License Revoked.—Except as provided in subsection (a1) of this section, any person whose driver's license has been revoked who drives any motor vehicle upon the highways of the State while the license is revoked is guilty of a Class 1 misdemeanor. Upon conviction, the person's license shall be revoked for an additional period of one year for the first offense, two years for the second offense, and permanently for a third or subsequent offense.

The restoree of a revoked driver's license who operates a motor vehicle upon the highways of the State without maintaining financial responsibility as provided by law shall be punished as for driving without a license.

(a1) Driving Without Reclaiming License.—A person convicted under subsection (a) shall be punished as if the person had been convicted of driving without a license under G.S. 20-35 if the person demonstrates to the court that either subdivisions (1) and (2), or subdivision (3) of this subsection is true:

(1) At the time of the offense, the person's license was revoked solely under G.S. 20-16.5; and

(2) a. The offense occurred more than 30 days after the effective date of a revocation order issued under G.S. 20-16.5(f) and the period of revocation was 30 days as provided under subdivision (3) of that subsection; or

b. The offense occurred more than 10 days after the effective date of the revocation order issued under any other provision of G.S. 20-16.5; or

(3) At the time of the offense the person had met the requirements of G.S. 50-13.12, or G.S. 110-142.2 and was eligible for reinstatement of the person's driver's license privilege as provided therein.

In addition, a person punished under this subsection shall be treated for driver's license and insurance rating purposes as if the person had been convicted of driving without a license under G.S. 20-35, and the conviction report sent to the Division must indicate that the person is to be so treated.

(b) Repealed by Session Laws 1993 (Reg. Sess., 1994), c. 761, s. 3.

(c) When Person May Apply for License.—A person whose license has been revoked under this section for one year may apply for a license after 90 days. A person whose license has been revoked under this section for two years may apply for a license after 12 months. A person whose license has been revoked under this section permanently may apply for a license after three years. Upon the filing of an application the Division may, with or without a hearing, issue a new license upon satisfactory proof that the former licensee has not been convicted of a moving violation under this Chapter or the laws of another state, a violation of any provision of the alcoholic beverage laws of this State or another state, or a violation of any provisions of the drug laws of this State or another state when any of these violations occurred during the revocation period. The Division may impose any restrictions or conditions on the new license that the Division considers appropriate for the balance of the revocation period. When the revocation period is permanent, the restrictions and conditions imposed by the Division may not exceed three years.

(d) Driving While Disqualified.—A person who was convicted of a violation that disqualified the person and required the person's driver's license to be revoked who drives a motor vehicle during the revocation period is punishable as provided in the other subsections of this section. A person who has been disqualified who drives a commercial motor vehicle during the disqualification period is guilty of a Class 1 misdemeanor and is disqualified for an additional period as follows:

(1) For a first offense of driving while disqualified, a person is disqualified for a period equal to the period for which the person was disqualified when the offense occurred.

(2) For a second offense of driving while disqualified, a person is disqualified for a period equal to two times the period for which the person was disqualified when the offense occurred.

(3) For a third offense of driving while disqualified, a person is disqualified for life.

The Division may reduce a disqualification for life under this subsection to 10 years in accordance with the guidelines adopted under G.S. 20-17.4(b). A person who drives a commercial motor vehicle while the person is disqualified and the person's driver's license is revoked is punishable for both driving while the person's license was revoked and driving while disqualified.

History: 1935, c. 52, s. 22; 1945, c. 635; 1947, c. 1067, s. 16; 1955, c. 1020, s. 1; c. 1152, s. 18; c. 1187, s. 20; 1957, c. 1046; 1959, c. 515; 1967, c. 447; 1973, c. 47, s. 2; cc. 71, 1132; 1975, c. 716, s. 5; 1979, c 377, ss. 1, 2; c. 667, s. 41; 1981, c. 412, s. 4; c. 747, s. 66; 1983, c. 51; 1983 (Reg. Sess., 1984), c. 1101, s. 18A; 1989, c. 771, s. 4; 1991, c. 509, s. 2; c. 726, s. 12; 1993, c. 539, ss. 320–322; 1994, Ex. Sess., c. 24, s. 14(c); 1993 (Reg. Sess., 1994), c. 761, ss. 2, 3; 1995, c. 538, s. 2(e), (f).

§ 20-28.1. Conviction of moving offense committed while driving during period of suspension or revocation of license

(a) Upon receipt of notice of conviction of any person of a motor vehicle moving offense, except a conviction punishable under G.S. 20-28(a1), such offense having been committed while such person's driving privilege was in a state of suspension or revocation, the Division shall revoke such person's driving privilege for an additional period of time as set forth in subsection (b) hereof.

(b) When a driving privilege is subject to revocation under this section, the additional period of revocation shall be as follows:

(1) A first such revocation shall be for one year;

(2) A second such revocation shall be for two years; and

(3) A third or subsequent such revocation shall be permanent.

(c) A person whose license has been revoked under this section for one year may apply for a license after 90 days. A person whose license has been revoked under this section for two years may apply for a license after 12 months. A person whose license has been revoked under this section permanently may apply for a license after three years. Upon the filing of an application, the Division may, with or without a hearing, issue a new license upon satisfactory proof that the former licensee has not been convicted of a moving violation under this Chapter or the laws of another state, or a violation of any provision of the alcoholic beverage laws of this State or another state, or a violation of any provision of the drug laws of this State or another state when any of these violations occurred during the revocation period. The Division may impose any restrictions or conditions on the new license that the Division considers appropriate for the balance of the revocation period. When the revocation period is permanent, the restrictions and conditions imposed by the Division may not exceed three years.

(d) Repealed by Session Laws 1979, c. 378, s. 2.

History: 1965, c. 286; 1969, c. 348; 1971, c. 163; 1973, c. 47, s. 2; 1975, c. 716, s. 5; 1979, c. 378, ss. 1, 2; 1981, c. 412, s. 4; c. 747, s. 66; 1991, c. 509, s. 1; c. 682, s. 6; c. 726, s. 22.1.

§ 20-28.2. Forfeiture of motor vehicle for impaired driving after impaired driving license revocation

(a) Meaning of "Impaired Driving License Revocation".—The revocation of a person's driver's license is an impaired driving license revocation if the revocation is pursuant to:

(1) G.S. 20-13.2, 20-16(a)(8b), 20-16.2, 20-16.5, 20-17(a)(2), 20-17(a)(12), 20-17.2, or 20-138.5; or

(2) G.S. 20-16(a)(7), 20-17(a)(1), 20-17(a)(3), 20-17(a)(9), or 20-17(a)(11), if the offense involves impaired driving; or

(3) The laws of another state and the offense for which the person's license is revoked prohibits substantially similar conduct which if committed in this State would result in a revocation listed in subdivisions (1) or (2).

(a1) Definitions.—As used in this section and in G.S. 20-28.3, 20-28.4, 20-28.5, 20-28.7, 20-28.8, and 20-28.9, the following terms mean:

(1) Acknowledgment.—A written document acknowledging that:

a. The motor vehicle was operated by a person charged with an offense involving impaired driving while that person's driver's license was revoked as a result of a prior impaired driver's license revocation;

b. If the motor vehicle is again operated by this particular person, at any time while that person's driver's license is revoked, and the person is charged with an offense involving impaired driving, the motor vehicle is subject to impoundment and forfeiture; and

c. A lack of knowledge or consent to the operation will not be a defense in the future, unless the motor vehicle owner has taken all reasonable precautions to prevent the use of the motor vehicle by this particular person and immediately reports, upon discovery, any unauthorized use to the appropriate law enforcement agency.

(1a) Fair Market Value.—The value of the seized motor vehicle, as determined in accordance with the schedule of values adopted by the Commissioner pursuant to G.S. 105-187.3.

(2) Innocent Owner.—A motor vehicle owner:

a. Who did not know and had no reason to know that the defendant's driver's license was revoked; or

b. Who knew that the defendant's driver's license was revoked, but the defendant drove the vehicle without the person's expressed or implied permission, and the owner files a police report for unauthorized use of the motor vehicle and agrees to prosecute the unauthorized operator of the motor vehicle;

c. Whose vehicle was reported stolen;

d. Repealed by Session Laws 1999-406, s. 17, effective December 1, 1999.

e. Who is in the business of renting vehicles, and the vehicle was driven by a person who is not listed as an authorized driver on the rental contract; or

f. Who is in the business of leasing motor vehicles, who holds legal title to the motor vehicle as a lessor at the time of seizure and who has no actual knowledge of the revocation of the lessee's driver's license at the time the lease is entered.

(2a) Insurance Company.—Any insurance company that has coverage on or is otherwise liable for repairs or damages to the motor vehicle at the time of the seizure.

(2b) Insurance Proceeds.—Proceeds paid under an insurance policy for damage to a seized motor vehicle less any payments actually paid to valid lienholders and for towing and storage costs incurred for the motor vehicle after the time the motor vehicle became subject to seizure.

(3) Lienholder.—A person who holds a perfected security interest in a motor vehicle at the time of seizure.

(3a) Motor Vehicle Owner.—A person in whose name a registration card or certificate of title for a motor vehicle is issued at the time of seizure.

(4) Order of Forfeiture.—An order by the court which terminates the rights and ownership interest of a motor vehicle owner in a motor vehicle and any insurance proceeds or proceeds of sale in accordance with G.S. 20-28.2.

(5) Repealed by Session Laws 1998-182, s. 2, effective December 1, 1998.

(6) Registered Owner.—A person in whose name a registration card for a motor vehicle is issued at the time of seizure.

(7) Repealed by Session Laws 1998-182, s. 2, effective December 1, 1998.

(b) When Motor Vehicle Becomes Property Subject to Order of Forfeiture.—If at a sentencing hearing for the underlying offense involving impaired driving, at a separate hearing after conviction of the defendant, or at a forfeiture hearing held at least 60 days after the defendant failed to appear at the scheduled trial for the underlying offense and the defendant's order of arrest for failing to appear has not been set aside, the judge determines by the greater weight of the evidence that the defendant is guilty of an offense involving impaired driving and that the defendant's license was revoked pursuant to an impaired driving license revocation as defined in subsection (a) of this section, the motor vehicle that was driven by the defendant at the time the defendant committed the offense becomes property subject to an order of forfeiture.

(c) Duty of Prosecutor to Notify Possible Innocent Parties.—In any case in which a prosecutor determines that a motor vehicle driven by a defendant may be subject to forfeiture under this section and the motor vehicle has not been permanently released to a nondefendant vehicle owner pursuant to G.S. 20-28.3(e1), a defendant owner pursuant to G.S. 20-28.3(e2), or a lienholder, pursuant to G.S. 20-28.3(e3), the prosecutor shall notify the defendant, each motor vehicle owner, and each lienholder that the motor vehicle may be subject to forfeiture and that the defendant, motor vehicle owner, or the lienholder may intervene to protect that person's interest. The notice may be served by any means reasonably likely to provide actual notice, and shall be served at least 10 days before the hearing at which an order of forfeiture may be entered.

(c1) Motor Vehicles Involved in Accidents.—If a motor vehicle subject to forfeiture was damaged while the defendant operator was committing the underlying offense involving impaired driving, or was damaged incident to the seizure of the motor vehicle, the Division shall determine the name of any insurance companies that are the insurers of record with the Division for the motor vehicle at the time of the seizure or that may otherwise be liable for repair to the motor vehicle. In any case where a seized motor vehicle was involved in an accident, the Division shall notify the insurance companies that the claim for insurance proceeds for damage to the seized motor vehicle shall be paid to the clerk of superior court of the county where the motor vehicle driver was charged to be held and disbursed pursuant to further orders of the court. Any insurance company that receives written or other actual notice of seizure pursuant to this section shall not be relieved of any legal obligation under any contract of insurance unless the claim for property damage to the seized motor vehicle minus the policy owner's deductible is paid directly to the clerk of court. The insurance company paying insurance proceeds to the clerk of court pursuant to this section shall be immune from suit by the motor vehicle owner for any damages alleged to have occurred as a result of the motor vehicle seizure. The proceeds shall be held by the clerk. The clerk shall disburse the insurance proceeds pursuant to further orders of the court.

(d) Forfeiture Hearing.—Unless a motor vehicle that has been seized pursuant to G.S. 20-28.3 has been permanently released to an innocent owner pursuant to G.S. 20-28.3(e1), a defendant owner pursuant to G.S. 20-28.3(e2), or to a lienholder pursuant to G.S. 20-28.3(e3), the court shall conduct a hearing on the forfeiture of the motor vehicle. The hearing may be held at the sentencing hearing on the underlying offense involving impaired driving, at a separate hearing after conviction of the defendant, or at a separate forfeiture hearing held not less than 60 days after the defendant failed to appear at the scheduled trial for the underlying offense and the defendant's order of arrest for failing to appear has not been set aside. If at the forfeiture hearing, the judge determines that the motor vehicle is subject to forfeiture pursuant to this section and proper notice of the hearing has been given, the judge shall order the motor vehicle forfeited. If at the sentencing hearing or at a forfeiture hearing, the judge determines that the motor vehicle is subject to forfeiture pursuant to this section and proper notice of the hearing has been given, the judge shall order the motor vehicle forfeited unless another motor vehicle owner establishes, by the greater weight of the evidence, that such motor vehicle owner is an innocent owner as defined in this section, in which case the trial judge shall order the motor vehicle released to the innocent owner pursuant to the provisions of subsection (e) of this section. In any case where the motor vehicle is ordered forfeited, the judge shall:

(1) a. Authorize the sale of the motor vehicle at public sale or allow the county board of education to retain the motor vehicle for its own use pursuant to G.S. 20-28.5; or

b. Order the motor vehicle released to a lienholder pursuant to the provisions of subsection (f) of this section; and

(2) a. Order any proceeds of sale or insurance proceeds held by the clerk of court to be disbursed to the county board of education; and

b. Order any outstanding insurance claims be assigned to the county board of education in the event the motor vehicle has been damaged in an accident incident to the seizure of the motor vehicle.

If the judge determines that the motor vehicle is subject to forfeiture pursuant to this section, but that notice as required by subsection (c) has not been given, the judge shall continue the forfeiture proceeding until adequate notice has been given. In no circumstance shall the sentencing of the defendant be delayed as a result of the failure of the prosecutor to give adequate notice.

(e) Release of Vehicle to Innocent Motor Vehicle Owner.—At a forfeiture hearing, if a nondefendant motor vehicle owner establishes by the greater weight of the evidence that: (i) the motor vehicle was being driven by a person who was not the only motor vehicle owner or had no ownership interest in the motor vehicle at the time of the underlying offense and (ii) the petitioner is an "innocent owner", as defined by this section, a judge shall order the motor vehicle released to that owner, conditioned upon payment of all towing and storage charges incurred as a result of the seizure and impoundment of the motor vehicle.

Release to an innocent owner shall only be ordered upon satisfactory proof of:

(1) The identity of the person as a motor vehicle owner;

(2) The existence of financial responsibility to the extent required by Article 13 of this Chapter or by the laws of the state in which the vehicle is registered; and

(3) Repealed by Session Laws 1998-182, s. 2, effective December 1, 1998.

(4) The execution of an acknowledgment as defined in subdivision (a1)(1) of this section.

If the nondefendant owner is a lessor, the release shall also be conditioned upon the lessor agreeing not to sell, give, or otherwise transfer possession of the forfeited motor vehicle to the defendant or any person acting on the defendant's behalf. A lessor who refuses to sell, give, or transfer possession of a seized motor vehicle to the defendant or any person acting on the behalf of the defendant shall not be liable for damages arising out of the refusal.

No motor vehicle subject to forfeiture under this section shall be released to a nondefendant motor vehicle owner if the records of the Division indicate the motor vehicle owner had previously signed an acknowledgment, as required by this section, and the same person was operating the motor vehicle while that person's license was revoked unless the innocent owner shows by the greater weight of the evidence that the motor vehicle owner has taken all reasonable precautions to prevent the use of the motor vehicle by this particular person and immediately reports, upon discovery, any unauthorized use to the appropriate law enforcement agency. A determination by the court at the forfeiture hearing held pursuant to subsection (d) of this section that the petitioner is not an innocent owner is a final judgment and is immediately appealable to the Court of Appeals.

(f) Release to Lienholder.—At a forfeiture hearing, the trial judge shall order a forfeited motor vehicle released to the lienholder upon payment of all towing and storage charges incurred as a result of the seizure of the motor vehicle if the judge determines, by the greater weight of the evidence, that:

(1) The lienholder's interest has been perfected and appears on the title to the forfeited vehicle;

(2) The lienholder agrees not to sell, give, or otherwise transfer possession of the forfeited motor vehicle to the defendant or to the motor vehicle owner who owned the motor vehicle immediately prior to forfeiture, or any person acting on the defendant's or motor vehicle owner's behalf;

(3) The forfeited motor vehicle had not previously been released to the lienholder;

(4) The owner is in default under the terms of the security instrument evidencing the interest of the lienholder and as a consequence of the default the lienholder is entitled to possession of the motor vehicle; and

(5) The lienholder agrees to sell the motor vehicle in accordance with the terms of its agreement and pursuant to the provisions of Part 5 of Article 9 of Chapter 25 of the General Statutes. Upon the sale of the motor vehicle, the lienholder will pay to the clerk of court of the county in which the vehicle was forfeited all proceeds from the sale, less the amount of the lien in favor of the lienholder, and any towing and storage costs paid by the lienholder.

A lienholder who refuses to sell, give, or transfer possession of a forfeited motor vehicle to the defendant, the vehicle owner who owned the motor vehicle immediately prior to forfeiture, or any person acting on the behalf of the defendant or motor vehicle owner shall not be liable for damages arising out of such refusal. The defendant, the motor vehicle owner who owned the motor vehicle immediately prior to forfeiture, and any person acting on the defendant's or motor vehicle owner's behalf are prohibited from purchasing the motor vehicle at any sale conducted by the lienholder.

(g) Repealed by Session Laws 1998-182, s. 2, effective December 1, 1998.

History: 1983, c. 435, s. 21; 1983 (Reg. Sess., 1984), c. 1101, s. 19; 1989 (Reg. Sess., 1990), c. 1024, s. 6; 1997-379, s. 1.1; 1997-456, s. 30; 1998-182, s. 2; 1999-406, ss. 11, 12, 17.

§ 20-28.3. Seizure, impoundment, forfeiture of motor vehicles for offenses involving impaired driving while license revoked

(a) Motor Vehicles Subject to Seizure.—A motor vehicle that is driven by a person who is charged with an offense involving impaired driving is subject to seizure if at the time of the violation the driver's license of the person driving the motor vehicle was revoked as a result of a prior impaired driving license revocation as defined in G.S. 20-28.2(a).

(b) Duty of Officer.—If the charging officer has probable cause to believe that a motor vehicle driven by the defendant may be subject to forfeiture under this section, the officer shall seize the motor vehicle and have it impounded. If the officer determines prior to seizure that the motor vehicle had been reported stolen, the officer shall not seize the motor vehicle pursuant to this section. If the officer determines prior to seizure that the motor vehicle was a rental vehicle driven by a person not listed as an authorized driver on the rental contract, the officer shall not seize the motor vehicle pursuant to this section, but shall make a reasonable effort to notify the owner of the rental vehicle that the vehicle was stopped and that the driver of the vehicle was not listed as an authorized driver on the rental contract. Probable cause may be based on the officer's personal knowledge, reliable information conveyed by another officer, records of the Division, or other reliable source. The seizing officer shall notify the executive agency designated under subsection (b1) of this section as soon as practical but no later than 72 hours after seizure of the motor vehicle of the seizure in accordance with procedures established by the executive agency designated under subsection (b1) of this section.

(b1) Notification of Impoundment.—Within 48 hours of receipt of the notice of seizure, an executive agency designated by the Governor shall issue written notification of impoundment to the Division, to any lienholder of record and to any motor vehicle owner who was not operating the motor vehicle at the time of the offense. This notice shall be sent by first-class mail to the most recent address contained in the Division's records. If the motor vehicle is registered in another state, notice shall be sent to the address shown on the records of the state where the motor vehicle is registered. This written notification shall provide notice that the motor vehicle has been seized, state the reason for the seizure and the procedure for requesting release of the motor vehicle. Additionally, if the motor vehicle was damaged while the defendant operator was committing an offense involving impaired driving or incident to the seizure, the agency shall issue written notification of the seizure to the owner's insurance company of record and to any other insurance companies that may be insuring other motor vehicles involved in the accident. The Division shall prohibit title to a seized motor vehicle from being transferred by a motor vehicle owner unless authorized by court order.

(c) Review by Magistrate.—Upon determining that there is probable cause for seizing a motor vehicle, the seizing officer shall present to a magistrate within the county where the driver was charged an affidavit of impoundment setting forth the basis upon which the motor vehicle has been or will be seized for forfeiture. The magistrate shall review the affidavit of impoundment and if the magistrate determines the requirements of this section have been met, shall order the motor vehicle held. The magistrate may request additional information and may hear from the defendant if the defendant is present. If the magistrate determines the requirements of this section have not been met, the magistrate shall order the motor vehicle released to a motor vehicle owner upon payment of towing and storage fees. If the motor vehicle has not yet been seized, and the magistrate determines that seizure is appropriate, the magistrate shall issue an order of seizure of the motor vehicle. The magistrate shall provide a copy of the order of seizure to the clerk of court. The clerk shall provide copies of the order of seizure to the district attorney and the attorney for the county board of education.

(c1) Effecting an Order of Seizure.—An order of seizure shall be valid anywhere in the State. Any officer with territorial jurisdiction and who has subject matter jurisdiction for violations of this Chapter may use such force as may be reasonable to seize the motor vehicle and to enter upon the property of the defendant to accomplish the seizure. An officer who has probable cause to believe the motor vehicle is concealed or stored on private property of a person other than the defendant may obtain a search warrant to enter upon that property for the purpose of seizing the motor vehicle.

(d) Custody of Motor Vehicle.—Unless the motor vehicle is towed pursuant to a statewide or regional contract, or a contract with the county board of education, the seized motor vehicle shall be towed by a commercial towing company designated by the law enforcement agency that seized the motor vehicle. Seized motor vehicles not towed pursuant to a statewide or regional contract or a contract with a county board of education shall be retrieved from the commercial towing company within a reasonable time, not to exceed 10 days, by the county board of education or their agent who must pay towing and storage fees to the commercial towing company when the motor vehicle is retrieved. If either a statewide or regional contractor, or the county board of education, chooses to contract for local towing services, all towing companies on the towing list for each law enforcement agency with jurisdiction within the county shall be given written notice and an opportunity to submit proposals prior to a contract for local towing services being awarded. The seized motor vehicle is under the constructive possession of the county board of education for the county in which the operator of the vehicle is charged at the time the vehicle is delivered to a location designated by the county board of education or delivered to its agent pending release or sale, or in the event a statewide or regional contract is in place, under the constructive possession of the Department of Public Instruction, on behalf of the State at the time the vehicle is delivered to a location designated by the Department of Public Instruction or delivered to its agent pending release or sale. Absent a statewide or regional contract that provides otherwise, each county board of education may elect to have seized motor vehicles stored on property owned or leased by the county board of education and charge a reasonable fee for storage, not to exceed ten dollars ($10.00) per day. In the alternative, the county board of education may contract with a commercial towing and storage facility or other private entity for the towing, storage, and disposal of seized motor vehicles, and a storage fee of not more than ten dollars ($10.00) per day may be charged. Except for gross negligence or intentional misconduct, the county board of education, or any of its employees, shall not be liable to the owner or lienholder for damage to or loss of the motor vehicle or its contents, or to the owner of personal property in a seized vehicle, during the time the motor vehicle is being towed or stored pursuant to this subsection.

(e) Release of Motor Vehicle Pending Trial.—A motor vehicle owner, other than the driver at the time of the underlying offense resulting in the seizure, may apply to the clerk of superior court in the county where the charges are pending for pretrial release of the motor vehicle.

The clerk shall release the motor vehicle to a nondefendant motor vehicle owner conditioned upon payment of all towing and storage charges incurred as a result of seizure and impoundment of the motor vehicle under the following conditions:

(1) The motor vehicle has been seized for not less than 24 hours;

(2) Repealed by Session Laws 1998-182, s. 3, effective December 1, 1998.

(3) A bond in an amount equal to the fair market value of the motor vehicle as defined by G.S. 20-28.2 has been executed and is secured by a cash deposit in the full amount of the bond, by a recordable deed of trust to real property in the full amount of the bond, by a bail bond under G.S. 58-71-1(2), or by at least one solvent surety, payable to the county school fund and conditioned on return of the motor vehicle, in substantially the same condition as it was at the time of seizure and without any new or additional liens or encumbrances, on the day of any hearing scheduled and noticed by the district attorney under G.S. 20-28.2(c), unless the motor vehicle has been permanently released;

(4) Execution of an acknowledgment as described in G.S. 20-28.2(a1);

(5) A check of the records of the Division indicates that the requesting motor vehicle owner has not previously executed an acknowledgment naming the operator of the seized motor vehicle; and

(6) A bond posted to secure the release of this motor vehicle under this subsection has not been previously ordered forfeited under G.S. 20-28.5.

In the event a nondefendant motor vehicle owner who obtains temporary possession of a seized motor vehicle pursuant to this subsection does not return the motor vehicle on the day of the forfeiture hearing as noticed by the district attorney under G.S. 20-28.3(c) or otherwise violates a condition of pretrial release of the seized motor vehicle as set forth in this subsection, the bond posted shall be ordered forfeited and an order of seizure shall be issued by the court. Additionally, a nondefendant motor vehicle owner or lienholder who willfully violates any condition of pretrial release may be held in civil or criminal contempt.

(e1) Pretrial Release of Motor Vehicle to Innocent Owner.—A nondefendant motor vehicle owner may file a petition with the clerk of court seeking a pretrial determination that the petitioner is an innocent owner. The clerk shall schedule a hearing before a judge to be held within 10 business days or as soon as thereafter may be feasible. Notice of the hearing shall be given to the petitioner, the district attorney, and the attorney for the county board of education. The clerk shall forward a copy of the petition to the district attorney for the district attorney's review. If, based on available information, the district attorney determines that the petitioner is an innocent owner and that the motor vehicle is not subject to forfeiture, the district attorney may note the State's consent to the release of the motor vehicle on the petition and return the petition to the clerk of court who shall enter an order releasing the motor vehicle to the petitioner subject to the conditions of release as set forth in G.S. 20-28.2(e) and no hearing shall be held. The clerk shall send a copy of the order of release to the county board of education attorney. At any pretrial hearing conducted pursuant to this subsection, the court is not required to determine the issue of forfeiture, only the issue of whether the petitioner is an innocent owner. Accordingly, the State shall not be required to prove the underlying offense of impaired driving or the existence of a prior driver's license revocation. If the court determines that the petitioner is an innocent owner, the court shall release the motor vehicle to the petitioner subject to the same conditions as if the petitioner were an innocent owner under G.S. 20-28.2(e). An order issued under this subsection finding that the petitioner failed to establish that the petitioner is an innocent owner may be reconsidered by the court as part of the forfeiture hearing conducted pursuant to G.S. 20-28.2(d).

(e2) Pretrial Release of Motor Vehicle to Defendant Owner.—A defendant motor vehicle owner may file a petition with the clerk of court seeking a pretrial determination that the defendant's license was not revoked pursuant to an impaired driving license revocation as defined in G.S. 20-28.2(a). The clerk shall schedule a hearing before a judge of the division in which the underlying criminal charge is pending for a hearing to be held within 10 business days or as soon thereafter as may be feasible. Notice of the hearing shall be given to the defendant, the district attorney, and the attorney for the county board of education. The clerk shall forward a copy of the petition to the district attorney for the district attorney's review. If, based on available information, the district attorney determines that the defendant's motor vehicle is not subject to forfeiture, the district attorney may note the State's consent to the release of the motor vehicle on the petition and return the petition to the clerk of court who shall enter an order releasing the motor vehicle to the defendant upon payment of all towing and storage charges incurred as a result of the seizure and impoundment of the motor vehicle, subject to the satisfactory proof of the identity of the defendant as a motor vehicle owner and the existence of financial responsibility to the extent required by Article 13 of this Chapter, and no hearing shall be held. The clerk shall send a copy of the order of release to the attorney for the county board of education. At any pretrial hearing conducted pursuant to this subsection, the court is not required to determine the issue of the underlying offense of impaired driving only the existence of a prior driver's license revocation as an impaired driving license revocation. Accordingly, the State shall not be required to prove the underlying offense of impaired driving. An order issued under this subsection finding that the defendant failed to establish that the defendant's license was not revoked pursuant to an impaired driving license revocation as defined in G.S. 20-28.2(a) may be reconsidered by the court as part of the forfeiture hearing conducted pursuant to G.S. 20-28.2(d).

(e3) Pretrial Release of Motor Vehicle to Lienholder.

(1) A lienholder may file a petition with the clerk of court requesting the court to order pretrial release of a seized motor vehicle. The lienholder shall serve a copy of the petition on all interested parties which shall include the registered owner, the titled owner, the district attorney, and the county board of education attorney. Upon 10 days' prior notice of the date, time, and location of the hearing sent by the lienholder to all interested parties, a judge, after a hearing, shall order a seized motor vehicle released to the lienholder conditioned upon payment of all towing and storage costs incurred as a result of the seizure and impoundment of the motor vehicle if the judge determines, by the greater weight of the evidence, that:
   a. Default on the obligation secured by the motor vehicle has occurred;
   b. As a consequence of default, the lienholder is entitled to possession of the motor vehicle;
   c. The lienholder agrees to sell the motor vehicle in accordance with the terms of its agreement and pursuant to the provisions of Part 5 of Article 9 of Chapter 25 of the General Statutes. Upon sale of the motor vehicle, the lienholder will pay to the clerk of court of the county in which the driver was charged all proceeds from the sale, less the amount of the lien in favor of the lienholder, and any towing and storage costs paid by the lienholder;
   d. The lienholder agrees not to sell, give, or otherwise transfer possession of the seized motor vehicle while the motor vehicle is subject to forfeiture, or the forfeited motor vehicle after the forfeiture hearing, to the defendant or the motor vehicle owner; and
   e. The seized motor vehicle while the motor vehicle is subject to forfeiture, or the forfeited motor vehicle after the forfeiture hearing, had not previously been released to the lienholder as a result of a prior seizure involving the same defendant or motor vehicle owner.

(2) The clerk of superior court may order a seized vehicle released to the lienholder conditioned upon payment of all towing and storage costs incurred as a result of the seizure and impoundment of the motor vehicle at any time when all interested parties have, in writing, waived any rights that they may have to notice and a hearing, and the lienholder has agreed to the provision of subdivision (4 above. A lienholder who refuses to sell, give, or transfer possession of a seized motor vehicle while the motor vehicle is subject to forfeiture, or a forfeited motor vehicle after the forfeiture hearing, to:

a. The defendant;
b. The motor vehicle owner who owned the motor vehicle immediately prior to seizure pending the forfeiture hearing, or to forfeiture after the forfeiture hearing; or
c. Any person acting on the behalf of the defendant or the motor vehicle owner, shall not be liable for damages arising out of such refusal. However, any subsequent violation of the conditions of release by the lienholder shall be punishable by civil or criminal contempt.

(f), (g) Repealed by Session Laws 1998-182, s. 3, effective December 1, 1998.

(h) Insurance Proceeds.—In the event a motor vehicle is damaged incident to the conduct of the defendant which gave rise to the defendant's arrest and seizure of the motor vehicle pursuant to this section, the county board of education, or its authorized designee, is authorized to negotiate the county board of education's interest with the insurance company and to compromise and accept settlement of any claim for damages. Property insurance proceeds accruing to the defendant, or other owner of the seized motor vehicle, shall be paid by the responsible insurance company directly to the clerk of superior court in the county where the motor vehicle driver was charged. If the motor vehicle is declared a total loss by the insurance company liable for the damages to the motor vehicle, the clerk of superior court, upon application of the county board of education, shall enter an order that the motor vehicle be released to the insurance company upon payment into the court of all insurance proceeds for damage to the motor vehicle after payment of towing and storage costs and all valid liens. The clerk of superior court shall provide the Division with a certified copy of the order entered pursuant to this subsection, and the Division shall transfer title to the insurance company or to such other person or entity as may be designated by the insurance company. Insurance proceeds paid to the clerk of court pursuant to this subsection shall be subject to forfeiture pursuant to G.S. 20-28.5 and shall be disbursed pursuant to further orders of the court. An affected motor vehicle owner or lienholder who objects to any agreed upon settlement under this subsection may file an independent claim with the insurance company for any additional monies believed owed. Notwithstanding any other provisions in this Chapter, nothing in this section or G.S. 20-28.2 shall require an insurance company to make payments in excess of those required pursuant to its policy of insurance on the seized motor vehicle.

(i) Expedited Sale of Seized Motor Vehicles in Certain Cases.—In order to avoid additional liability for towing and storage costs pending resolution of the criminal proceedings of the defendant, the county board of education may, after expiration of 90 days from the date of seizure, sell any motor vehicle having a fair market value of one thousand five hundred dollars ($1,500) or less. The county board of education may also sell a motor vehicle, regardless of the fair market value, any time the outstanding towing and storage costs exceed eighty-five percent (85%) of the fair market value of the vehicle, or with the consent of all the motor vehicle owners. Any sale conducted pursuant to this subsection shall be conducted in accordance with the provisions of G.S. 20-28.5(a), and the proceeds of the sale, after the payment of outstanding towing and storage costs or reimbursement of towing and storage costs paid by a person other than the defendant, shall be deposited with the clerk of superior court. If an order of forfeiture is entered by the court, the court shall order the proceeds held by the clerk to be disbursed as provided in G.S. 20-28.5(b). If the court determines that the motor vehicle is not subject to forfeiture, the court shall order the proceeds held by the clerk to be disbursed first to pay the sale, towing, and storage costs, second to pay outstanding liens on the motor vehicle, and the balance to be paid to the motor vehicle owners.

(j) Retrieval of Certain Personal Property.—At reasonable times, the entity charged with storing the motor vehicle may permit owners of personal property not affixed to the motor vehicle to retrieve those items from the motor vehicle, provided satisfactory proof of ownership of the motor vehicle or the items of personal property is presented to the storing entity.

(k) County Board of Education Right to Appear and Participate in Proceedings.—The attorney for the county board of education shall be given notice of all proceedings regarding offenses involving impaired driving related to a motor vehicle subject to forfeiture. The attorney for the county board of education shall also have the right to appear and to be heard on all issues relating to the seizure, possession, release, forfeiture, sale, and other matters related to the seized vehicle under this section. With the prior consent of the county board of education, the district attorney may delegate to the attorney for the county board of education any or all of the duties of the district attorney under this section. Clerks of superior court, law enforcement agencies, and all other agencies with information relevant to the seizure, impoundment, release, or forfeiture of motor vehicles are authorized and directed to provide county boards of education with access to that information and to do so by electronic means when existing technology makes this type of transmission possible.

(l) Payment of Fees Upon Conviction.—If the driver of a motor vehicle seized pursuant to this section is convicted of an offense involving impaired driving, the defendant shall be ordered to pay as restitution to the county board of education, the motor vehicle owner, or the lienholder the cost paid or owing for the towing, storage, and sale of the motor vehicle to the extent the costs were not covered by the proceeds from the forfeiture and sale of the motor vehicle. In addition, a civil judgment for the costs under this section in favor of the party to whom the restitution is owed shall be docketed by the clerk of superior court. If the defendant is sentenced to an active term of imprisonment, the civil judgment shall become effective and be docketed when the defendant's conviction becomes final. If the defendant is placed on probation, the civil judgment in the amount found by a judge during the probation revocation or termination hearing to be due shall become effective and be docketed by the clerk when the defendant's probation is revoked or terminated.

(m) Trial Priority.—District court trials of impaired driving offenses involving forfeitures of motor vehicles pursuant to G.S. 20-28.2 shall be scheduled on the arresting officer's next court date or within 30 days of the offense, whichever comes first.

Once scheduled, the case shall not be continued unless all of the following conditions are met:

(1) A written motion for continuance is filed with notice given to the opposing party prior to the motion being heard.

(2) The judge makes a finding of a "compelling reason" for the continuance.

(3) The motion and finding are attached to the court case record.

Upon a determination of guilt, the issue of vehicle forfeiture shall be heard by the judge immediately, or as soon thereafter as feasible, and the judge shall issue the appropriate orders pursuant to G.S. 20-28.2(d).

Should a defendant appeal the conviction to superior court, any party who has not previously been heard on a petition for pretrial release under subsections (e1) or (e3) of this section or any party whose motor vehicle has not been the subject of a forfeiture hearing held pursuant to G.S. 20-28.2(d) may be heard on a petition for pretrial release pursuant to subsections (e1) or (e3) of this section. The provisions of subsection (e) of this section shall also apply to seized motor vehicles pending trial in superior court. Where a motor vehicle was released pursuant to subsection (e) of this section pending trial in district court, the release of the motor vehicle continues, and the terms and conditions of the original bond remain the same as those required for the initial release of the motor vehicle under subsection (e) of this section, pending the resolution of the underlying offense involving impaired driving in superior court.

History: 1997-379, s. 1.2; 1997-456, s. 31; 1998-182, s. 3; 1998-217, s. 62(a)-(c).

§ 20-28.4. Release of impounded motor vehicles by judge

Release Upon Conclusion of Trial.—If the driver of a motor vehicle seized pursuant to G.S. 20-28.3:

(1) Is subsequently not convicted of an offense involving impaired driving due to dismissal or a finding of not guilty; or

(2) The judge at a forfeiture hearing conducted pursuant to G.S. 20-28.2(d) fails to find that the driver's license was revoked as a result of a prior impaired driving license revocation as defined in G.S. 20-28.2; and

(3) The vehicle has not previously been released to a lienholder pursuant to G.S. 20-28.3(e3),

the seized motor vehicle or insurance proceeds held by the clerk of court pursuant to G.S. 20-28.2(c1) or G.S. 20-28.3(h) shall be released to the motor vehicle owner conditioned upon payment of towing and storage costs. Notwithstanding G.S. 44A-2(d), if the owner of the seized motor vehicle does not obtain release of the vehicle within 30 days from the date of the court's order, the possessor of the seized motor vehicle has a mechanics' lien on the seized motor vehicle for the full amount of the towing and storage charges incurred since the motor vehicle was seized and may dispose of the seized motor vehicle pursuant to Article 1 of Chapter 44A of the General Statutes.

History: 1997-379, s. 1.3; 1998-182, s. 4.

§ 20-28.5. Forfeiture of impounded motor vehicle or funds

(a) Sale.—A motor vehicle ordered forfeited and sold or a seized motor vehicle authorized to be sold pursuant to G.S. 20-28.3(i), shall be sold at a public sale conducted in accordance with the provisions of Article 12 of Chapter 160A of the General Statutes, applicable to sales authorized pursuant to G.S. 160A-266(a)(2), (3), or (4), subject to the notice requirements of this subsection, and shall be conducted by the county board of education or a person acting on its behalf. Notice of sale, including the date, time, location, and manner of sale, shall be given by first-class mail to all motor vehicle owners of the vehicle to be sold at the address shown by the records of the Division. Written notice of sale shall also be given to all lienholders on file with the Division. Notice of sale shall be given to the Division in accordance with the procedures established by the Division. Notices required to be given under this subsection shall be mailed at least 10 days prior to the date of sale. A lienholder shall be permitted to purchase the motor vehicle at any such sale by bidding in the amount of its lien, if that should be the highest bid, without being required to tender any additional funds, other than the towing and storage fees. The county board of education, or its agent, shall not sell, give, or otherwise transfer possession of the forfeited motor vehicle to the defendant, the motor vehicle owner who owned the motor vehicle immediately prior to forfeiture, or any person acting on the defendant's or motor vehicle owner's behalf.

(b) Proceeds of Sale.—Proceeds of any sale conducted under this section, G.S. 20-28.2(f)(5), or G.S. 20-28.3(e3)(3), shall first be applied to the cost of sale and then to satisfy towing and storage costs. The balance of the proceeds of sale, if any, shall be used to satisfy any other existing liens of record that were properly recorded prior to the date of initial seizure of the vehicle. Any remaining balance shall be paid to the county school fund in the county in which the motor vehicle was ordered forfeited. If there is more than one school board in the county, then the net proceeds of sale, after reimbursement to the county board of education of reasonable administrative costs incurred in connection with the forfeiture and sale of the motor vehicle, shall be distributed in the same manner as fines and other forfeitures. The sale of a motor vehicle pursuant to this section shall be deemed to extinguish all existing liens on the motor vehicle and the motor vehicle shall be transferred free and clear of any liens.

(c) Retention of Motor Vehicle.—A board of education may, at its option, retain any forfeited motor vehicle for its use upon payment of towing and storage costs. If the motor vehicle is retained, any valid lien of record at the time of the initial seizure of the motor vehicle shall be satisfied by the county board of education relieving the motor vehicle owner of all liability for the obligation secured by the motor vehicle. If there is more than one school board in the county, and the motor vehicle is retained by a board of education, then the fair market value of the motor vehicle, less the costs for towing, storage, reasonable administrative costs, and liens paid, shall be used to determine and pay the share due each of the school boards in the same manner as fines and other forfeitures.

(d) Repealed by Session Laws 1998-182, s. 5, effective December 1, 1998.

(e) Order of Forfeiture; Appeals.—An order of forfeiture is stayed pending appeal of a conviction for an offense that is the basis for the order. When the conviction of an offense that is the basis for an order of forfeiture is appealed from district court, the issue of forfeiture shall be heard in superior court de novo. Appeal from a final order of forfeiture shall be to the Court of Appeals.

History: 1997-379, s. 1.4; 1998-182, s. 5; 1998-217, s. 62(d); 1999-456, s. 11.

§ 20-28.7. Responsibility of Division of Motor Vehicles

The Division shall establish procedures by rule to provide for the orderly seizure, forfeiture, sale, and transfer of motor vehicles pursuant to the provisions of G.S. 20-28.2, 20-28.3, 20-28.4, and 20-28.5.

History: 1997-379, s. 1.6; 1998-182, s. 7.

§ 20-28.8. Reports to the Division

In any case in which a vehicle has been seized pursuant to G.S. 20-28.3, in addition to any other information that must be reported pursuant to this Chapter, the clerk of superior court shall report to the Division by electronic means the execution of an acknowledgment as defined in G.S. 20-28.2(a1)(1), the entry of an order of forfeiture as defined in G.S. 20-28.2(a1)(4), and the entry of an order of release as defined in G.S. 20-28.3 and G.S. 20-28.4. Each report shall include any of the following information that has not previously been reported to the Division in the case: the name, address, and driver's license number of the defendant; the name, address, and driver's license number of the nondefendant motor vehicle owner, if known; and the make, model, year, vehicle identification number, state of registration, and vehicle registration plate number of the seized vehicle, if known.

History: 1998-182, s. 8.

§ 20-28.9. Authority for the Department of Public Instruction to administer a statewide or regional towing, storage, and sales program for driving while impaired vehicles forfeited

(a) The Department of Public Instruction is authorized to enter into a contract for a statewide service or contracts for regional services to tow, store, process, maintain, and sell motor vehicles seized pursuant to G.S. 20-28.3. All motor vehicles seized under G.S. 20-28.3 shall be subject to contracts entered into pursuant to this section. Contracts shall be let by the Department of Public Instruction in accordance with the provisions of Article 3 of Chapter 143 of the General Statutes. All contracts shall ensure the safety of the motor vehicles while held and any funds arising from the sale of any seized motor vehicle. The contract shall require the contractor to maintain and make available to the agency a computerized up-to-date inventory of all motor vehicles held under the contract, together with an accounting of all accrued charges, the status of the vehicle, and the county school fund to which the proceeds of sale are to be paid. The contract shall provide that the contractor shall pay the towing and storage charges owed on a seized vehicle to a commercial towing company at the time the seized vehicle is obtained from the commercial towing company, with the contractor being reimbursed this expense when the vehicle is released or sold. The Department shall not enter into any contract under this section under which the State will be obligated to pay a deficiency arising from the sale of any forfeited motor vehicle.

(b) The Department, through its contractor or contractors designated in accordance with subsection (a) of this section, may charge a reasonable fee for storage not to exceed ten dollars ($10.00) per day for the storage of seized vehicles pursuant to G.S. 20-28.3.

(c) In order to help defray the administrative costs associated with the administration of this section, the Department shall collect a ten dollar ($10.00) administrative fee from a person to whom a seized vehicle is released at the time the motor vehicle is released and shall collect a ten dollar ($10.00) administrative fee out of the proceeds of the sale of any forfeited motor vehicle. The funds collected under this subsection shall be paid to the General Fund.

History: 1998-182, s. 8.

§ 20-30. Violations of license or learner's permit provisions

It shall be unlawful for any person to commit any of the following acts:

(1) To display or cause to be displayed or to have in possession a driver's license or learner's permit, knowing the same to be fictitious or to have been canceled, revoked, suspended or altered.

(2) To counterfeit, sell, lend to, or knowingly permit the use of, by one not entitled thereto, a driver's license or learner's permit.

(3) To display or to represent as one's own a license or learner's permit not issued to the person so displaying same.

(4) To fail or refuse to surrender to the Division upon demand any driver's license or learner's permit that has been suspended, canceled or revoked as provided by law.

(5) To use a false or fictitious name or give a false or fictitious address in any application for a driver's license or learner's permit, or any renewal or duplicate thereof, or knowingly to make a false statement or knowingly conceal a material fact or otherwise commit a fraud in any such application, or for any person to procure, or knowingly permit or allow another to commit any of the foregoing acts. Any license or learner's permit procured as aforesaid shall be void from the issuance thereof, and any moneys paid therefor shall be forfeited to the State.

(6) To photostat or otherwise reproduce a driver's license or learner's permit or to possess a driver's license or learner's permit which has been photostated or otherwise reproduced, unless such photostat or other reproduction was authorized by the Commissioner.

(7) To sell or offer for sale any reproduction or facsimile or simulation of a driver's license or learner's permit. The provisions of this subdivision shall not apply to agents or employees of the Division while acting in the course and scope of their employment. Any person, firm or corporation violating the provisions of this subsection shall be guilty of a Class I felony.

(8) To possess more than one commercial driver's license or to possess a commercial driver's license and a regular driver's license. Any commercial driver's license other than the one most recently issued is subject to immediate seizure by any law enforcement officer or judicial official. Any regular driver's license possessed at the same time as a commercial driver's license is subject to immediate seizure by any law enforcement officer or judicial official.

(9) To present, display, or use a driver's license or learner's permit that contains a false or fictitious name in the commission or attempted commission of a felony. Any person violating the provisions of this subdivision shall be guilty of a Class I felony.

History: 1935, c. 52, s. 24; 1951, c. 542, s. 4; 1967, c. 1098, s. 1; 1973, c. 18, s. 2; 1975, c. 716, s. 5; 1979, c. 415; c. 667, ss. 27, 41; 1979, 2d Sess., c. 1316, s. 22; 1989, c. 771, s. 8; 1991, c. 726, s. 13; 1991 (Reg. Sess., 1992), c. 1007, s. 29; 1993, c. 539, s. 1247; 1994, Ex. Sess., c. 24, s. 14(c); 1999-299, s. 1.

§ 20-32. Unlawful to permit unlicensed minor to drive motor vehicle

It shall be unlawful for any person to cause or knowingly permit any minor under the age of 18 years to drive a motor vehicle upon a highway as an operator, unless such minor shall have first obtained a license to so drive a motor vehicle under the provisions of this Article.

History: 1935, c. 52, s. 26; 1973, c. 684.

§ 20-34. Unlawful to permit violations of this Article

No person shall authorize or knowingly permit a motor vehicle owned by him or under his control to be driven by any person who has no legal right to do so or in violation of any of the provisions of this Article.

History: 1935, c. 52, s. 28.

§ 20-35. Penalties for violating Article; defense to driving without a license

(a) Penalty.—A violation of this Article is a Class 2 misdemeanor unless a statute in the Article sets a different punishment for the violation. If a statute in this Article sets a different punishment for a violation of the Article, the different punishment applies.

(b) Repealed by Session Laws 1993 (Reg. Sess., 1994), c. 761, s. 4.

(c) Defenses.—A person may not be convicted of failing to carry a regular driver's license if, when tried for that offense, the person produces in court a regular driver's license issued to the person that was valid when the person was charged with the offense. A person may not be convicted of driving a motor vehicle without a regular driver's license if, when tried for that offense, the person shows all the following:

(1) That, at the time of the offense, the person had an expired license.

(2) The person renewed the expired license within 30 days after it expired and now has a driver's license.

(3) The person could not have been charged with driving without a license if the person had the renewed license when charged with the offense.

History: 1935, c. 52, s. 29; 1991, c. 726, s. 14; 1993, c. 539, s. 324; 1994, Ex. Sess., c. 24, s. 14(c); 1993 (Reg. Sess., 1994), c. 761, s. 4.

Article 2C. Commercial Driver's License

§ 20-37.12. Commercial driver's license required

(a) On or after April 1, 1992, no person shall operate a commercial motor vehicle on the highways of this State unless he has first been issued and is in immediate possession of a commercial driver's license with applicable endorsements valid for the vehicle he is driving; provided, a person may operate a commercial motor vehicle after being issued and while in possession of a commercial driver learner's permit and while accompanied by the holder of a commercial driver's license valid for the vehicle being driven.

(b) The out-of-service criteria as referred to in 49 C.F.R. Subchapter B apply to a person who drives a commercial motor vehicle. No person shall drive a commercial motor vehicle on the highways of this State in violation of an out-of-service order.

(c) Repealed by Session Laws 1991, c. 726, s. 15.

(d) Any person who is not a resident of this State, who has been issued a commercial driver's license by his state of residence, who has that license in his immediate possession, whose privilege to drive any motor vehicle is not suspended, revoked, or cancelled, and who has not been disqualified from driving a commercial motor vehicle shall be permitted without further examination or licensure by the Division to drive a commercial motor vehicle in this State.

(e) G.S. 20-7 sets the time period in which a new resident of North Carolina must obtain a license from the Division. The Commissioner may establish by rule the conditions under which the test requirements for a commercial driver's license may be waived for a new resident who is licensed in another state.

History: 1989, c. 771, s. 2; 1991, c. 726, s. 15; 1997-122, s. 5; 1998-149, s. 4.

§ 20-37.16. Content of license; classifications and endorsements; fees

(a) A commercial driver's license must be marked "Commercial Driver's License" or "CDL" and must contain the information required by G.S. 20-7 for a regular driver's license.

(b) The classes of commercial driver's licenses are:

(1) Class A CDL—A Class A commercial driver's license authorizes the holder to drive any Class A motor vehicle.

(2) Class B CDL—A Class B commercial driver's license authorizes the holder to drive any Class B motor vehicle.

(3) Class C CDL—A Class C commercial driver's license authorizes the holder to drive any Class C motor vehicle.

(c) Endorsements.—The endorsements required to drive certain motor vehicles are as follows:

Endorsement	Vehicles That Can Be Driven
H	Vehicles, regardless of size or class, except tank vehicles, when transporting hazardous materials that require the vehicle to be placarded
M	Motorcycles
N	Tank vehicles not carrying hazardous materials
P	Vehicles carrying passengers
T	Double trailers
X	Tank vehicles carrying hazardous materials.

To obtain an H or an X endorsement, an applicant must take a test. This requirement applies when a person first obtains an H or an X endorsement and each time a person renews an H or an X endorsement. An applicant who has an H or an X endorsement issued by another state who applies for an H or an X endorsement must take a test unless the person has passed a test that covers the information set out in 49 C.F.R. § 383.121 within the preceding two years.

(d) The fee for a Class A, B, or C commercial driver's license is ten dollars ($10.00) for each year of the period for which the license is issued. The fee for each endorsement is one dollar and twenty-five cents ($1.25) for each year of the period for which the endorsement is issued. The fees required under this section do not apply to a person whose license is restricted to driving a school bus or school activity bus or to employees of the Driver License Section of the Division who are designated by the Commissioner.

(e) The requirements for a commercial driver's license do not apply to vehicles used for personal use such as recreational vehicles. A commercial driver's license is also waived for the following classes of vehicles as permitted by regulation of the United States Department of Transportation:

(1) Vehicles owned or operated by the Department of Defense, including the National Guard, while they are driven by active duty military personnel, or members of the National Guard when on active duty, in the pursuit of military purposes.

(2) Any vehicle when used as firefighting or emergency equipment for the purpose of preserving life or property or to execute emergency governmental functions.

(3) A farm vehicle that meets all of the following criteria:

a. Is controlled and operated by the farmer or the farmer's employee and used exclusively for farm use.

b. Is used to transport either agricultural products, farm machinery, or farm supplies, both to or from a farm.

c. Is not used in the operations of a for-hire motor carrier.

d. Is used within 150 miles of the farmer's farm.

A farm vehicle includes a forestry vehicle that meets the listed criteria when applied to the forestry operation.

History: 1989, c. 771, s. 2; 1991, c. 726, s. 18; 1993, c. 368, s. 4; 1993 (Reg. Sess., 1994), c. 750, ss. 4, 6; 1995 (Reg. Sess., 1996), c. 695, s. 1; c. 756, s. 5; 1998-149, s. 5.

§ 20-37.21. Penalties

(a) Any person who drives a commercial motor vehicle in violation of G.S. 20-37.12 shall be guilty of a Class 3 misdemeanor and, upon conviction, shall be fined not less than two hundred fifty dollars ($250.00) for a first offense and not less than five hundred dollars ($500.00) for a second or subsequent offense.

(b) Any person who violates G.S. 20-37.18 shall have committed an infraction and, upon being found responsible, shall pay a penalty of not less than one hundred dollars ($100.00) nor more than five hundred dollars ($500.00).

(c) Any employer who violates G.S. 20-37.19 shall have committed an infraction and, upon being found responsible, shall pay a penalty of not less than five hundred dollars ($500.00) nor more than one thousand dollars ($1,000).

History: 1989, c. 771, s. 2; 1993, c. 539, s. 327; 1994, Ex. Sess., c. 24, s. 14(c).

Article 3. Motor Vehicle Act of 1937

Part 2. Authority and Duties of Commissioner and Division [N.C. Gen. Stat. § 20-48 (1999)]

§ 20-48. Giving of notice

(a) Whenever the Division is authorized or required to give any notice under this Chapter or other law regulating the operation of vehicles, unless a different method of giving such notice is otherwise expressly prescribed, such notice shall be given either by personal delivery thereof to the person to be so notified or by deposit in the United States mail of such notice in an envelope with postage prepaid, addressed to such person at his address as shown by the records of the Division. The giving of notice by mail is complete upon the expiration of four days after such deposit of such notice. Proof of the giving of notice in either such manner may be made by the certificate of any officer or employee of the Division or affidavit of any person over 18 years of age, naming the person to whom such notice was given and specifying the time, place, and manner of the giving thereof.

(b) Notwithstanding any other provision of this Chapter at any time notice is now required by registered mail with return receipt requested, certified mail with return receipt requested may be used in lieu thereof and shall constitute valid notice to the same extent and degree as notice by registered mail with return receipt requested.

(c) The Commissioner shall appoint such agents of the Division as may be needed to serve revocation notices required by this Chapter. The fee for service of a notice shall be fifty dollars ($50.00).

History: 1937, c. 407, s. 13; 1955, c. 1187, s. 21; 1971, c. 1231, s. 1; 1975, c. 326, s. 3; c. 716, s. 5; 1983, c. 761, s. 148; 1985, c. 479, s. 171.

Part 3. Registration and Certificate of Title of Motor Vehicles

§ 20-50. Owner to secure registration and certificate of title; temporary registration markers

(a) A vehicle intended to be operated upon any highway of this State must be registered with the Division in accordance with G.S. 20-52, and the owner of the vehicle must comply with G.S. 20-52 before operating the vehicle. A vehicle that is leased to an individual who is a resident of this State is a vehicle intended to be operated upon a highway of this State.

The Commissioner of Motor Vehicles or the Commissioner's duly authorized agent is empowered to grant a special one-way trip permit to move a vehicle without license upon good cause being shown. When the owner of a vehicle leases the vehicle to a carrier of passengers or property and the vehicle is actually used by the carrier in the operation of its business, the license plates may be obtained by the lessee, upon written consent of the owner, after the certificate of title has been obtained by the owner. When the owner of a vehicle leases the vehicle to a farmer and the vehicle is actually used by the farmer in the operation of a farm, the license plates may be obtained by the farmer at the applicable farmer rate, upon written consent of the owner, after the certificate of title has been obtained by the owner. The lessee shall make application on an appropriate form furnished by the Division and file such evidence of the lease as the Division may require.

(b) The Division may issue a temporary license plate for a vehicle. A temporary license plate is valid for the period set by the Division. The period may not be less than 10 days nor more than 60 days.

A person may obtain a temporary license plate for a vehicle by filing an application with the Division and paying the required fee. An application must be filed on a form provided by the Division.

The fee for a temporary license plate that is valid for 10 days is three dollars ($3.00). The fee for a temporary license plate that is valid for more than 10 days is the amount that would be required with an application for a license plate for the vehicle. If a person obtains for a vehicle a temporary license plate that is valid for more than 10 days and files an application for a license plate for that vehicle before the temporary license plate expires, the person is not required to pay the fee that would otherwise be required for the license plate.

A temporary license plate is subject to the following limitations and conditions:

(1) It may be issued only upon proper proof that the applicant has met the applicable financial responsibility requirements.

(2) It expires on midnight of the day set for expiration.

(3) It may be used only on the vehicle for which issued and may not be transferred, loaned, or assigned to another.

(4) If it is lost or stolen, the person who applied for it must notify the Division.

(5) It may not be issued by a dealer.

(6) The provisions of G.S. 20-63, 20-71, 20-110 and 20-111 that apply to license plates apply to temporary license plates insofar as possible.

History: 1937, c. 407, s. 15; 1943, c. 648; 1945, c. 956, s. 3; 1947, c. 219, s. 2; 1953, c. 831, s. 3; 1957, c. 246, s. 2; 1961, c. 360, s. 1; 1963, c. 552, s. 1; 1973, c. 919; 1975, c. 462; c. 716, s. 5; c. 767, s. 1; 1995, c. 394, s. 1; 1999-438, s. 26.

§ 20-51. Exempt from registration

The following shall be exempt from the requirement of registration and certificate of title:

(1) Any such vehicle driven or moved upon a highway in conformance with the provisions of this Article relating to manufacturers, dealers, or nonresidents.

(2) Any such vehicle which is driven or moved upon a highway only for the purpose of crossing such highway from one property to another.

(3) Any implement of husbandry, farm tractor, road construction or maintenance machinery or other vehicle which is not self-propelled that was designed for use in work off the highway and which is operated on the highway for the purpose of going to and from such nonhighway projects.

(4) Any vehicle owned and operated by the government of the United States.

(5) Farm tractors equipped with rubber tires and trailers or semitrailers when attached thereto and when used by a farmer, his tenant, agent, or employee in transporting his own farm implements, farm supplies, or farm products from place to place on the same farm, from one farm to another, from farm to market, or from market to farm. This exemption shall extend also to any tractor, implement of husbandry, and trailer or semitrailer while on any trip within a radius of 10 miles from the point of loading, provided that the vehicle does not exceed a speed of 35 miles per hour. This section shall not be construed as granting any exemption to farm tractors, implements of husbandry, and trailers or semitrailers which are operated on a for-hire basis, whether money or some other thing of value is paid or given for the use of such tractors, implements of husbandry, and trailers or semitrailers.

(6) Any trailer or semitrailer attached to and drawn by a properly licensed motor vehicle when used by a farmer, his tenant, agent, or employee in transporting unginned cotton, peanuts, soybeans, corn, hay, tobacco, silage, cucumbers, potatoes, fertilizers or chemicals purchased or owned by the farmer or tenant for personal use in implementing husbandry, irrigation pipes, loaders, or equipment owned by the farmer or tenant from place to place on the same farm, from one farm to another, from farm to gin, from farm to dryer, or from farm to market, and when not operated on a for-hire basis. The term "transporting" as used herein shall include the actual hauling of said products and all unloaded travel in connection therewith.

(7) Those small farm trailers known generally as tobacco-handling trailers, tobacco trucks or tobacco trailers when used by a farmer, his tenant, agent or employee, when transporting or otherwise handling tobacco in connection with the pulling, tying or curing thereof.

(8) Any vehicle which is driven or moved upon a highway only for the purpose of crossing or traveling upon such highway from one side to the other provided the owner or lessee of the vehicle owns the fee or a leasehold in all the land along both sides of the highway at the place or crossing.

(9) Mopeds as defined in G.S. 20-4.01(27)d1.

(10) Devices which are designed for towing private passenger motor vehicles or vehicles not exceeding 5,000 pounds gross weight. These devices are known generally as "tow dollies." A tow dolly is a two-wheeled device without motive power designed for towing disabled motor vehicles and is drawn by a motor vehicle in the same manner as a trailer.

(11) Devices generally called converter gear or dollies consisting of a tongue attached to either a single or tandem axle upon which is mounted a fifth wheel and which is used to convert a semi-trailer to a full trailer for the purpose of being drawn behind a truck tractor and semitrailer.

(12) Motorized wheelchairs or similar vehicles not exceeding 1,000 pounds gross weight when used for pedestrian purposes by a handicapped person with a mobility impairment as defined in G.S. 20-37.5.

(13) Any vehicle registered in another state and operated temporarily within this State by a public utility, a governmental or cooperative provider of utility services, or a contractor for one of these entities for the purpose of restoring utility services in an emergency outage.

History: 1937, c. 407, s. 16; 1943, c. 500; 1949, c. 429; 1951, c. 705, s. 2; 1953, c. 826, ss. 2, 3; c. 1316, s. 1; 1961, cc. 334, 817; 1963, c. 145; 1965, c. 1146; 1971, c. 107; 1973, cc. 478, 757, 964; 1979, c. 574, s. 6; 1981 (Reg. Sess., 1982), c. 1286; 1983, cc. 288, 732; 1987, c. 608; 1989, c. 157, s. 2; 1991, c. 411, s. 4; 1995, c. 50, s. 4; 1999-281, s. 2.

§ 20-54.1. Forfeiture of right of registration

(a) Upon receipt of notice of conviction of a violation of an offense involving impaired driving while the person's license is revoked as a result of a prior impaired driving license revocation as defined in G.S. 20-28.2, the Division shall revoke the registration of all motor vehicles registered in the convicted person's name and shall not register a motor vehicle in the convicted person's name until the convicted person's license is restored. Upon receipt of notice of revocation of registration from the Division, the convicted person shall surrender the registration on all motor vehicles registered in the convicted person's name to the Division within 10 days of the date of the notice.

(b) Upon receipt of a notice of conviction under subsection (a) of this section, the Division shall revoke the registration of the motor vehicle seized, and the owner shall not be allowed to register the motor vehicle seized until the convicted operator's driver's license has been restored. The Division shall not revoke the registration of the owner of the seized motor vehicle if the owner is determined to be an innocent owner. The Division shall revoke the owner's registration only after the owner is given an opportunity for a hearing to demonstrate that the owner is an innocent owner as defined in G.S. 20-28.2. Upon receipt of notice of revocation of registration from the Division, the owner shall surrender the registration on the motor vehicle seized to the Division within 10 days of the date of the notice.

History: 1998-182, s. 10.

§ 20-63. Registration plates furnished by Division; requirements; replacement of regular plates with First in Flight plates; surrender and reissuance; displaying; preservation and cleaning; alteration or concealment of numbers; commission contracts for issuance

(a) The Division upon registering a vehicle shall issue to the owner one registration plate for a motorcycle, trailer or semitrailer and for every other motor vehicle. Registration plates issued by the Division under this Article shall be and remain the property of the State, and it shall be lawful for the Commissioner or his duly authorized agents to summarily take possession of any plate or plates which he has reason to believe is being illegally used, and to keep in his possession such plate or plates pending investigation and legal disposition of the same. Whenever the Commissioner finds that any registration plate issued for any vehicle pursuant to the provisions of this Article has become illegible or is in such a condition that the numbers thereon may not be readily distinguished, he may require that such registration plate, and its companion when there are two registration plates, be surrendered to the Division. When said registration plate or plates are so surrendered to the Division, a new registration plate or plates shall be issued in lieu thereof without charge. The owner of any vehicle who receives notice to surrender illegible plate or plates on which the numbers are not readily distinguishable and who willfully refuses to surrender said plates to the Division shall be guilty of a Class 2 misdemeanor.

(b) Every license plate shall have displayed upon it the registration number assigned to the vehicle for which it is issued, the name of the State of North Carolina, which may be abbreviated, and the year number for which it is issued or the date of expiration. A plate issued for a commercial vehicle, as defined in G.S. 20-4.2(1), must bear the word "commercial," unless the plate is a special registration plate authorized in G.S. 20-79.4 or the commercial vehicle is a trailer or is licensed for 6,000 pounds or less.

A registration plate issued by the Division for a private passenger vehicle or for a private hauler vehicle licensed for 6,000 pounds or less, other than a Friends of the Great Smoky Mountains National Park special registration plate, shall be a "First in Flight" plate. A "First in Flight" plate shall have the words "First in Flight" printed at the top of the plate above all other letters and numerals. The background of the plate shall depict the Wright Brothers biplane flying over Kitty Hawk Beach, with the plane flying slightly upward and to the right.

(c) Such registration plate and the required numerals thereon, except the year number for which issued, shall be of sufficient size to be plainly readable from a distance of 100 feet during daylight.

(d) Registration plates issued for a motor vehicle other than a motorcycle, trailer, or semitrailer shall be attached thereto, one in the front and the other in the rear: Provided, that when only one registration plate is issued for a motor vehicle other than a truck-tractor, said registration plate shall be attached to the rear of the motor vehicle. The registration plate issued for a truck-tractor shall be attached to the front thereof. Provided further, that when only one registration plate is issued for a motor vehicle and this motor vehicle is transporting a substance that may adhere to the plate so as to cover or discolor the plate or if the motor vehicle has a mechanical loading device that may damage the plate, the registration plate may be attached to the front of the motor vehicle.

Any motor vehicle of the age of 35 years or more from the date of manufacture may bear the license plates of the year of manufacture instead of the current registration plates, if the current registration plates are maintained within the vehicle and produced upon the request of any person.

The Division shall provide registered owners of motorcycles and motorcycle trailers with suitably reduced size registration plates.

(e) Preservation and Cleaning of Registration Plates.—It shall be the duty of each and every registered owner of a motor vehicle to keep the registration plates assigned to such motor vehicle reasonably clean and free from dust and dirt, and such registered owner, or any person in his employ, or who operates such motor vehicle by his authority, shall, upon the request of any proper officer, immediately clean such registration plates so that the numbers thereon may be readily distinguished, and any person who shall neglect or refuse to so clean a registration plate, after having been requested to do so, shall be guilty of a Class 3 misdemeanor.

(f) Operating with False Numbers.—Any person who shall willfully operate a motor vehicle with a registration plate which has been repainted or altered or forged shall be guilty of a Class 2 misdemeanor.

(g) Alteration, Disguise, or Concealment of Numbers.—Any operator of a motor vehicle who shall willfully mutilate, bend, twist, cover or cause to be covered or partially covered by any bumper, light, spare tire, tire rack, strap, or other device, or who shall paint, enamel, emboss, stamp, print, perforate, or alter or add to or cut off any part or portion of a registration plate or the figures or letters thereon, or who shall place or deposit or cause to be placed or deposited any oil, grease, or other substance upon such registration plates for the purpose of making dust adhere thereto, or who shall deface, disfigure, change, or attempt to change any letter or figure thereon, or who shall display a number plate in other than a horizontal upright position, shall be guilty of a Class 2 misdemeanor. Any operator of a motor vehicle who shall otherwise intentionally cover any number or registration renewal sticker on a registration plate with any material that makes the number or registration renewal sticker illegible commits an infraction and shall be fined under G.S. 14-3.1.

(h) Commission Contracts for Issuance of Plates and Certificates.—All registration plates, registration certificates and certificates of title issued by the Division, outside of those issued from the Raleigh offices of the said Division and those issued and handled through the United States mail, shall be issued insofar as practicable and possible through commission contracts entered into by the Division for the issuance of such plates and certificates in localities throughout North Carolina with persons, firms, corporations or governmental subdivisions of the State of North Carolina and the Division shall make a reasonable effort in every locality, except as hereinbefore noted, to enter into a commission contract for the issuance of such plates and certificates and a record of these efforts shall be maintained in the Division. In the event the Division is unsuccessful in making commission contracts as hereinbefore set out it shall then issue said plates and certificates through the regular employees of the Division. Whenever registration plates, registration certificates and certificates of title are issued by the Division through commission contract arrangements, the Division shall provide proper supervision of such distribution. Commission contracts entered under this subsection shall provide for the payment of compensation for all transactions as set forth below. Nothing contained in this subsection will allow or permit the operation of fewer outlets in any county in this State than are now being operated.

A transaction is any of the following activities:

(1) Issuance of a registration plate, a registration card, a registration renewal sticker, or a certificate of title.

(2) Issuance of a handicapped placard or handicapped identification card.

(3) Acceptance of an application for a personalized registration plate.
(4) Acceptance of a surrendered registration plate, registration card, or registration renewal sticker, or acceptance of an affidavit stating why a person cannot surrender a registration plate, registration card, or registration renewal sticker.
(5) Cancellation of a title because the vehicle has been junked.
(6) Acceptance of an application for, or issuance of, a refund for a fee or a tax, other than the highway use tax.
(7) Receipt of the civil penalty imposed by G.S. 20-309 for a lapse in financial responsibility or receipt of the restoration fee imposed by that statute.
(8) Acceptance of a notice of failure to maintain financial responsibility for a motor vehicle.
(8a) Collection of civil penalties imposed for violations of G.S. 20-183.8A.
(8b) Sale of one or more inspection stickers in a single transaction to a licensed inspection station.
(9) Collection of the highway use tax.

Performance at the same time of any combination of the items that are listed within each subdivision or are listed within subdivisions (1) through (8b) of this section is a single transaction for which a dollar and thirty-five cent ($1.35) compensation shall be paid. Performance of the item listed in subdivision (9) of this subsection in combination with any other items listed in this subsection is a separate transaction for which a one dollar and twenty cent ($1.20) compensation shall be paid.

(i) Electronic Applications and Collections.—The Division is authorized to accept electronic applications for the issuance of registration plates, registration certificates, and certificates of title, and to electronically collect fees and penalties.

History: 1937, c. 407, s. 27; 1943, c. 726; 1951, c. 102, ss. 1–3; 1955, c. 119, s. 1; 1961, c. 360, s. 4; c. 861, s. 2; 1963, c. 552, s. 6; c. 1071; 1965, c. 1088; 1969, c. 1140; 1971, c. 945; 1973, c. 629; 1975, c. 716, s. 5; 1979, c. 470, s. 1; c. 604, s. 1; c. 917, s. 4; 1981, c. 750; c. 859, s. 76; 1983, c. 253, ss. 1–3; 1985, c. 257; 1991 (Reg. Sess., 1992), c. 1007, s. 32; 1993, c. 539, ss. 333–336; 1994, Ex. Sess., c. 24, s. 14(c); 1997-36, s. 1; 1997-443, s. 32.7(a); 1997-461, s. 1; 1998-160, s. 3; 1998-212, ss. 15.4(a), 27.6(a); 1999-452, ss. 13, 14.

Part 8. Anti-Theft and Enforcement Provisions

§ 20-111. Violation of registration provisions

It shall be unlawful for any person to commit any of the following acts:

(1) To drive a vehicle on a highway, or knowingly permit a vehicle owned by that person to be driven on a highway, when the vehicle is not registered with the Division in accordance with this Article or does not display a current registration plate.
(2) To display or cause or permit to be displayed or to have in possession any registration card, certificate of title or registration number plate knowing the same to be fictitious or to have been canceled, revoked, suspended or altered, or to willfully display an expired license or registration plate on a vehicle knowing the same to be expired.
(3) The giving, lending, or borrowing of a license plate for the purpose of using same on some motor vehicle other than that for which issued shall make the giver, lender, or borrower guilty of a Class 3 misdemeanor. Where license plate is found being improperly used, such plate or plates shall be revoked or canceled, and new license plates must be purchased before further operation of the motor vehicle.
(4) To fail or refuse to surrender to the Division, upon demand, any title certificate, registration card or registration number plate which has been suspended, canceled or revoked as in this Article provided. Service of the demand shall be in accordance with G.S. 20-48.
(5) To use a false or fictitious name or address in any application for the registration of any vehicle or for a certificate of title or for any renewal or duplicate thereof, or knowingly to make a false statement or knowingly to conceal a material fact or otherwise commit a fraud in any such application. A violation of this subdivision shall constitute a Class 1 misdemeanor.
(6) To give, lend, sell or obtain a certificate of title for the purpose of such certificate being used for any purpose other than the registration, sale, or other use in connection with the vehicle for which the certificate was issued. Any person violating the provisions of this subdivision shall be guilty of a Class 2 misdemeanor.

History: 1937, c. 407, s. 75; 1943, c. 592, s. 2; 1945, c. 576, s. 6; c. 635; 1949, c. 360; 1955, c. 294,

s. 2; 1961, c. 360, s. 20; 1975, c. 716, s. 5; 1981, c. 938, s. 3; 1993, c. 440, s. 9; c. 539, ss. 351–353; 1994, Ex. Sess., c. 24, s. 14(c).

Part 9. The Size, Weight, Construction, and Equipment of Vehicles

§ 20-129. Required lighting equipment of vehicles

(a) When Vehicles Must Be Equipped.—Every vehicle upon a highway within this State shall be equipped with lighted headlamps and rear lamps as required for different classes of vehicles, and subject to exemption with reference to lights on parked vehicles as declared in G.S. 20-134:

(1) During the period from sunset to sunrise,

(2) When there is not sufficient light to render clearly discernible any person on the highway at a distance of 400 feet ahead, or

(3) Repealed by Session Laws 1989 (Reg. Sess., 1990), c. 822, s. 1.

(4) At any other time when windshield wipers are in use as a result of smoke, fog, rain, sleet, or snow, or when inclement weather or environmental factors severely reduce the ability to clearly discern persons and vehicles on the street and highway at a distance of 500 feet ahead, provided, however, the provisions of this subdivision shall not apply to instances when windshield wipers are used intermittently in misting rain, sleet, or snow. Any person violating this subdivision during the period from October 1, 1990, through December 31, 1991, shall be given a warning of the violation only. Thereafter, any person violating this subdivision shall have committed an infraction and shall pay a fine of five dollars ($5.00) and shall not be assessed court costs. No driver's license points, insurance points or premium surcharge shall be assessed on account of violation of this subdivision and no negligence or liability shall be assessed on or imputed to any party on account of a violation of this subdivision. The Commissioner of Motor Vehicles and the Superintendent of Public Instruction shall incorporate into driver education programs and driver licensing programs instruction designed to encourage compliance with this subdivision as an important means of reducing accidents by making vehicles more discernible during periods of limited visibility.

(b) Headlamps on Motor Vehicles.—Every self-propelled motor vehicle other than motorcycles, road machinery, and farm tractors shall be equipped with at least two headlamps, all in good operating condition with at least one on each side of the front of the motor vehicle. Headlamps shall comply with the requirements and limitations set forth in G.S. 20-131 or 20-132.

(c) Headlamps on Motorcycles.—Every motorcycle shall be equipped with at least one and not more than two headlamps which shall comply with the requirements and limitations set forth in G.S. 20-131 or 20-132. The headlamps on a motorcycle shall be lighted at all times while the motorcycle is in operation on highways or public vehicular areas.

(d) Rear Lamps.—Every motor vehicle, and every trailer or semitrailer attached to a motor vehicle and every vehicle which is being drawn at the end of a combination of vehicles, shall have all originally equipped rear lamps or the equivalent in good working order, which lamps shall exhibit a red light plainly visible under normal atmospheric conditions from a distance of 500 feet to the rear of such vehicle. One rear lamp or a separate lamp shall be so constructed and placed that the number plate carried on the rear of such vehicle shall under like conditions be illuminated by a white light as to be read from a distance of 50 feet to the rear of such vehicle. Every trailer or semitrailer shall carry at the rear, in addition to the originally equipped lamps, a red reflector of the type which has been approved by the Commissioner and which is so located as to height and is so maintained as to be visible for at least 500 feet when opposed by a motor vehicle displaying lawful undimmed lights at night on an unlighted highway.

Notwithstanding the provisions of the first paragraph of this subsection, it shall not be necessary for a trailer weighing less than 4,000 pounds, or a trailer described in G.S. 20-51(6) weighing less than 6,500 pounds, to carry or be equipped with a rear lamp, provided such vehicle is equipped with and carries at the rear two red reflectors of a diameter of not less than three inches, such reflectors to be approved by the Commissioner, and which are so designed and located as to height and are maintained so that each reflector is visible for at least 500 feet when approached by a motor vehicle displaying lawful undimmed headlights at night on an unlighted highway.

The rear lamps of a motorcycle shall be lighted at all times while the motorcycle is in operation on highways or public vehicular areas.

(e) Lamps on Bicycles.—Every bicycle shall be equipped with a lighted lamp on the front thereof, visible under normal atmospheric conditions from a distance of at least 300 feet in front of such bicycle, and shall also be equipped with a reflex mirror or lamp on the rear, exhibiting a red light visible under like conditions from a distance of at least 200 feet to the rear of such bicycle, when used at night.

(f) Lights on Other Vehicles.—All vehicles not heretofore in this section required to be equipped with specified lighted lamps shall carry on the left side one or more lighted lamps or lanterns projecting a white light, visible under normal atmospheric conditions from a distance of not less than 500 feet to the front of such vehicle and visible under like conditions from a distance of not less than 500 feet to the rear of such vehicle, or in lieu of said lights shall be equipped with reflectors of a type which is approved by the Commissioner. Farm tractors operated on a highway at night must be equipped with at least one white lamp visible at a distance of 500 feet from the front of the tractor and with at least one red lamp visible at a distance of 500 feet to the rear of the tractor. Two red reflectors each having a diameter of at least four inches may be used on the rear of the tractor in lieu of the red lamp.

(g) No person shall sell or operate on the highways of the State any motor vehicle, motorcycle or motor-driven cycle, manufactured after December 31, 1955, unless it shall be equipped with a stop lamp on the rear of the vehicle. The stop lamp shall display a red or amber light visible from a distance of not less than 100 feet to the rear in normal sunlight, and shall be actuated upon application of the service (foot) brake. The stop lamp may be incorporated into a unit with one or more other rear lamps.

History: 1937, c. 407, s. 92; 1939, c. 275; 1947, c. 526; 1955, c. 1157, ss. 3–5, 8; 1957, c. 1038, s. 1; 1967, cc. 1076, 1213; 1969, c. 389; 1973, c. 531, ss. 1, 2; 1979, c. 175; 1981, c. 549, s. 1; 1985, c. 66; 1987, c. 611; 1989 (Reg. Sess., 1990), c. 822, s. 1; 1991, c. 18, s. 1; 1999-281, s. 1.

§ 20-130.1. Use of red or blue lights on vehicles prohibited; exceptions

(a) It is unlawful for any person to install or activate or operate a red light in or on any vehicle in this State. As used in this subsection, unless the context requires otherwise, "red light" means an operable red light not sealed in the manufacturer's original package which: (i) is designed for use by an emergency vehicle or is similar in appearance to a red light designed for use by an emergency vehicle; and (ii) can be operated by use of the vehicle's battery, vehicle's electrical system, or a dry cell battery.

(b) The provisions of subsection (a) of this section do not apply to the following:

(1) A police car;

(2) A highway patrol car;

(3) A vehicle owned by the Wildlife Resources Commission and operated exclusively for law-enforcement purposes;

(4) An ambulance;

(5) A vehicle used by an organ procurement organization or agency for the recovery and transportation of blood, human tissues, or organs for transplantation;

(6) A fire-fighting vehicle;

(7) A school bus;

(8) A vehicle operated by any member of a municipal or rural fire department in the performance of his duties, regardless of whether members of that fire department are paid or voluntary;

(9) A vehicle of a voluntary lifesaving organization (including the private vehicles of the members of such an organization) that has been officially approved by the local police authorities and which is manned or operated by members of that organization while answering an official call;

(10) A vehicle operated by medical doctors or anesthetists in emergencies;

(11) A motor vehicle used in law enforcement by the sheriff, or any salaried rural policeman in any county, regardless of whether or not the county owns the vehicle;

(11a) A vehicle operated by the State Fire Marshal or his representatives in the performance of their duties, whether or not the State owns the vehicle;

(12) A vehicle operated by any county fire marshal, assistant fire marshal, or emergency management coordinator in the performance of his duties, regardless of whether or not the county owns the vehicle;

(13) A light required by the Federal Highway Administration;

(14) A vehicle operated by a transplant coordinator who is an employee of an organ procurement organization or agency when the transplant coordinator is responding to a call to recover or transport human tissues or organs for transplantation;

(15) A vehicle operated by an emergency medical service as an emergency support vehicle; and
(16) A State emergency management vehicle.

(c) It is unlawful for any person to possess a blue light or to install, activate, or operate a blue light in or on any vehicle in this State, except for a publicly owned vehicle used for law enforcement purposes or any other vehicle when used by law enforcement officers in the performance of their official duties. As used in this subsection, unless the context requires otherwise, "blue light" means an operable blue light which:

(1) Is not (i) being installed on, held in inventory for the purpose of being installed on, or held in inventory for the purpose of sale for installation on a vehicle on which it may be lawfully operated or (ii) installed on a vehicle which is used solely for the purpose of demonstrating the blue light for sale to law enforcement personnel;
(1a) Is designed for use by an emergency vehicle, or is similar in appearance to a blue light designed for use by an emergency vehicle; and
(2) Can be operated by use of the vehicle's battery, the vehicle's electrical system, or a dry cell battery.

(d) Repealed by Session Laws 1999-249, s. 1, effective December 1, 1999.

(e) Violation of subsection (a) or (c) of this section is a Class 1 misdemeanor.

History: 1943, c. 726; 1947, c. 1032; 1953, c. 354; 1955, c. 528; 1957, c. 65, s. 11; 1959, c. 166, s. 2; c. 1170, s. 2; 1967, c. 651, s. 1; 1971, c. 1214; 1977, c. 52, s. 2; c. 438, s. 2; 1979, c. 653, s. 1; c. 887; 1983, c. 32, s. 1; c. 768, s. 6; 1985 (Reg. Sess., 1986), c. 1027, s. 50; 1989, c. 537, s. 2; 1989 (Reg. Sess., 1990), c. 1020, s. 2; 1991, c. 263, s. 1; 1993, c. 539, s. 361; 1994, Ex. Sess., c. 24, s. 14(c); 1993 (Reg. Sess., 1994), c. 719, s. 1; 1995, c. 168, s. 1; 1995 (Reg. Sess., 1996), c. 756, s. 16; 1999-249, s. 1.

§ 20-135.2A. Seat belt use mandatory

(a) Each front seat occupant who is 16 years of age or older and each driver of a passenger motor vehicle manufactured with seat belts shall have a seat belt properly fastened about his or her body at all times when the vehicle is in forward motion on a street or highway in this State.

(b) "Passenger Motor Vehicle," as used in this section, means a motor vehicle with motive power designed for carrying 10 passengers or fewer, but does not include a motorcycle, a motorized pedacycle or a trailer.

(c) This section shall not apply to any of the following:

(1) A driver or occupant with a medical or physical condition that prevents appropriate restraint by a safety belt or with a professionally certified mental phobia against the wearing of vehicle restraints;
(2) A motor vehicle operated by a rural letter carrier of the United States Postal Service while performing duties as a rural letter carrier and a motor vehicle operated by a newspaper delivery person while actually engaged in delivery of newspapers along the person's specified route;
(3) A driver or passenger frequently stopping and leaving the vehicle or delivering property from the vehicle if the speed of the vehicle between stops does not exceed 20 miles per hour;
(4) Any vehicle registered and licensed as a property-carrying vehicle in accordance with G.S. 20-88, while being used for agricultural or commercial purposes; or
(5) A motor vehicle not required to be equipped with seat safety belts under federal law.

(d) Evidence of failure to wear a seat belt shall not be admissible in any criminal or civil trial, action, or proceeding except in an action based on a violation of this section or as justification for the stop of a vehicle or detention of a vehicle operator and passengers.

(e) Any driver or passenger who fails to wear a seat belt as required by this section shall have committed an infraction and shall pay a penalty of twenty-five dollars ($25.00). Conviction of an infraction under this section has no consequence other than payment of a penalty. A person found responsible for a violation of this section may not be assessed court costs.

(f) No driver's license points or insurance surcharge shall be assessed on account of violation of this section.

(g) The Commissioner of the Division of Motor Vehicles and the Department of Public Instruction shall incorporate in driver education programs and driver licensing programs instructions designed to encourage compliance with this section as an important means of reducing the severity of injury to the users of restraint devices and on the requirements and penalties specified in this law.

(h) Repealed by Session Laws 1999-183, s. 3, effective October 1, 1999.

History: 1985, c. 222, s. 1; 1987, c. 623; 1991, c. 448, s. 1; 1994, Ex. Sess., c. 5, s. 1; 1997-16, s. 2; 1997-443, s. 32.20; 1999-183, ss. 1–3.

§ 20-137.1. Child restraint systems required

(a) Every driver who is transporting one or more passengers of less than 16 years of age shall have all such passengers properly secured in a child passenger restraint system or seat belt which meets federal standards applicable at the time of its manufacture.

(a1) A child less than five years of age and less than 40 pounds in weight shall be properly secured in a weight-appropriate child passenger restraint system. In vehicles equipped with an active passenger-side front air bag, if the vehicle has a rear seat, a child less than five years of age and less than 40 pounds in weight shall be properly secured in a rear seat, unless the child restraint system is designed for use with air bags.

(b) The provisions of this section shall not apply: (i) to ambulances or other emergency vehicles; (ii) when the child's personal needs are being attended to; (iii) if all seating positions equipped with child passenger restraint systems or seat belts are occupied; or (iv) to vehicles which are not required by federal law or regulation to be equipped with seat belts.

(c) Any driver found responsible for a violation of this section may be punished by a penalty not to exceed twenty-five dollars ($25.00), even when more than one child less than 16 years of age was not properly secured in a restraint system. Conviction of an infraction under this section has no consequence other than payment of a penalty. No driver charged under this section for failure to have a child under five years of age properly secured in a restraint system shall be convicted if he produces at the time of his trial proof satisfactory to the court that he has subsequently acquired an approved child passenger restraint system.

(d) No driver license points or insurance points shall be assessed for a violation of this section; nor shall a violation constitute negligence per se or contributory negligence per se nor shall it be evidence of negligence or contributory negligence.

History: 1981, c. 804, ss. 1, 4, 5; 1985, c. 218; 1993 (Reg. Sess., 1994), c. 748, s. 1; 1999-183, ss. 6, 7.

Part 10. Operation of Vehicles and Rules of the Road

§ 20-138.1. Impaired driving

(a) Offense.—A person commits the offense of impaired driving if he drives any vehicle upon any highway, any street, or any public vehicular area within this State:

(1) While under the influence of an impairing substance; or

(2) After having consumed sufficient alcohol that he has, at any relevant time after the driving, an alcohol concentration of 0.08 or more.

(b) Defense Precluded.—The fact that a person charged with violating this section is or has been legally entitled to use alcohol or a drug is not a defense to a charge under this section.

(c) Pleading.—In any prosecution for impaired driving, the pleading is sufficient if it states the time and place of the alleged offense in the usual form and charges that the defendant drove a vehicle on a highway or public vehicular area while subject to an impairing substance.

(d) Sentencing Hearing and Punishment.—Impaired driving as defined in this section is a misdemeanor. Upon conviction of a defendant of impaired driving, the presiding judge must hold a sentencing hearing and impose punishment in accordance with G.S. 20-179.

(e) Exception.—Notwithstanding the definition of "vehicle" pursuant to G.S. 20-4.01(49), for purposes of this section the word "vehicle" does not include a horse, bicycle, or lawnmower.

History: 1983, c. 435, s. 24; 1989, c. 711, s. 2; 1993, c. 285, s. 1.

§ 20-138.2. Impaired driving in commercial vehicle

(a) Offense.—A person commits the offense of impaired driving in a commercial motor vehicle if he drives a commercial motor vehicle upon any highway, any street, or any public vehicular area within the State:

(1) While under the influence of an impairing substance; or

(2) After having consumed sufficient alcohol that he has, at any relevant time after the driving, an alcohol concentration of 0.04 or more.

(b) Defense Precluded.—The fact that a person charged with violating this section is or has been legally entitled to use alcohol or a drug is not a defense to a charge under this section.

(c) Pleading.—To charge a violation of this section, the pleading is sufficient if it states the time and place of the alleged offense in the usual form and charges the defendant drove a commercial motor vehicle on a highway, street, or public vehicular area while subject to an impairing substance.

(d) Implied Consent Offense.—An offense under this section is an implied consent offense subject to the provisions of G.S. 20-16.2.

(e) Punishment.—The offense in this section is a misdemeanor and any defendant convicted under this section shall be sentenced under G.S. 20-179. This offense is not a lesser included offense of impaired driving under G.S. 20-138.1, and if a person is convicted under this section and of an offense involving impaired driving under G.S. 20-138.1 arising out of the same transaction, the aggregate punishment imposed by the Court may not exceed the maximum punishment applicable to the offense involving impaired driving under G.S. 20-138.1.

(f) Repealed by Session Laws 1991, c. 726, s. 19.

(g) Chemical Analysis Provisions.—The provisions of G.S. 20-139.1 shall apply to the offense of impaired driving in a commercial motor vehicle.

History: 1989, c. 771, s. 12; 1991, c. 726, s. 19; 1993, c. 539, s. 363; 1994, Ex. Sess., c. 24, s. 14(c); 1998-182, s. 24.

§ 20-138.2A. Operating a commercial vehicle after consuming alcohol

(a) Offense.—A person commits the offense of operating a commercial motor vehicle after consuming alcohol if the person drives a commercial motor vehicle, as defined in G.S. 20-4.01(3d)a. and b., upon any highway, any street, or any public vehicular area within the State while consuming alcohol or while alcohol remains in the person's body.

(b) Implied-Consent Offense.—An offense under this section is an implied-consent offense subject to the provisions of G.S. 20-16.2. The provisions of G.S. 20-139.1 shall apply to an offense committed under this section.

(b1) Odor Insufficient.—The odor of an alcoholic beverage on the breath of the driver is insufficient evidence by itself to prove beyond a reasonable doubt that alcohol was remaining in the driver's body in violation of this section unless the driver was offered an alcohol screening test or chemical analysis and refused to provide all required samples of breath or blood for analysis.

(b2) Alcohol Screening Test.—Notwithstanding any other provision of law, an alcohol screening test may be administered to a driver suspected of violation of subsection (a) of this section, and the results of an alcohol screening test or the driver's refusal to submit may be used by a law enforcement officer, a court, or an administrative agency in determining if alcohol was present in the driver's body. No alcohol screening tests are valid under this section unless the device used is one approved by the Commission on Health Services, and the screening test is conducted in accordance with the applicable regulations of the Commission as to its manner and use.

(c) Punishment.—Except as otherwise provided in this subsection, a violation of the offense described in subsection (a) of this section is a Class 3 misdemeanor and, notwithstanding G.S. 15A-1340.23, is punishable by a penalty of one hundred dollars ($100.00). A second or subsequent violation of this section is a misdemeanor punishable under G.S. 20-179. This offense is a lesser included offense of impaired driving of a commercial vehicle under G.S. 20-138.2.

(d) Second or Subsequent Conviction Defined.—A conviction for violating this offense is a second or subsequent conviction if at the time of the current offense the person has a previous conviction under this section, and the previous conviction occurred in the seven years immediately preceding the date of the current offense. This definition of second or subsequent conviction also applies to G.S. 20-17(a)(13) and G.S. 20-17.4(a)(6).

History: 1998-182, s. 23; 1999-406, s. 15.

§ 20-138.2B. Operating a school bus, school activity bus, or child care vehicle after consuming alcohol

(a) Offense.—A person commits the offense of operating a school bus, school activity bus, or child care vehicle after consuming alcohol if the person drives a school bus, school activity bus, or child care vehicle upon any highway, any street, or any public vehicular area within the State while consuming alcohol or while alcohol remains in the person's body.

(b) Implied-Consent Offense.—An offense under this section is an implied-consent offense subject to the provisions of G.S. 20-16.2. The provisions of G.S. 20-139.1 shall apply to an offense committed under this section.

(b1) Odor Insufficient.—The odor of an alcoholic beverage on the breath of the driver is insufficient evidence by itself to prove beyond a reasonable doubt that alcohol was remaining in the driver's body in violation of this section unless the driver was offered an alcohol screening test or chemical analysis and refused to provide all required samples of breath or blood for analysis.

(b2) Alcohol Screening Test.—Notwithstanding any other provision of law, an alcohol screening test may be administered to a driver suspected of violation of subsection (a) of this section, and the results of an alcohol screening test or the driver's refusal to submit may be used by a law enforcement officer, a court, or an administrative agency in determining if alcohol was present in the driver's body. No alcohol screening tests are valid under this section unless the device used is one approved by the Commission on Health Services, and the screening test is conducted in accordance with the applicable regulations of the Commission as to its manner and use.

(c) Punishment.—Except as otherwise provided in this subsection, a violation of the offense described in subsection (a) of this section is a Class 3 misdemeanor and, notwithstanding G.S. 15A-1340.23, is punishable by a penalty of one hundred dollars ($100.00). A second or subsequent violation of this section is a misdemeanor punishable under G.S. 20-179. This offense is a lesser included offense of impaired driving of a commercial vehicle under G.S. 20-138.1.

(d) Second or Subsequent Conviction Defined.—A conviction for violating this offense is a second or subsequent conviction if at the time of the current offense the person has a previous conviction under this section, and the previous conviction occurred in the seven years immediately preceding the date of the current offense. This definition of second or subsequent conviction also applies to G.S. 20-19(c2).

History: 1998-182, s. 27; 1999-406, s. 16.

§ 20-138.2C. Possession of alcoholic beverages while operating a commercial motor vehicle

A person commits the offense of operating a commercial motor vehicle while possessing alcoholic beverages if the person drives a commercial motor vehicle, as defined in G.S. 20-4.01(3d), upon any highway, any street, or any public vehicular area within the State while having an open or closed alcoholic beverage in the passenger area of the commercial motor vehicle. This section shall not apply to the driver of a commercial motor vehicle that is also an excursion passenger vehicle, a for-hire passenger vehicle, a common carrier of passengers, or a motor home, if the alcoholic beverage is in possession of a passenger or is in the passenger area of the vehicle.

History: 1999-330, s. 2.

§ 20-138.3. Driving by person less than 21 years old after consuming alcohol or drugs

(a) Offense.—It is unlawful for a person less than 21 years old to drive a motor vehicle on a highway or public vehicular area while consuming alcohol or at any time while he has remaining in his body any alcohol or controlled substance previously consumed, but a person less than 21 years old does not violate this section if he drives with a controlled substance in his body which was lawfully obtained and taken in therapeutically appropriate amounts.

(b) Subject to Implied-Consent Law.—An offense under this section is an alcohol-related offense subject to the implied-consent provisions of G.S. 20-16.2.

(b1) Odor Insufficient.—The odor of an alcoholic beverage on the breath of the driver is insufficient evidence by itself to prove beyond a reasonable doubt that alcohol was remaining in the driver's body in violation of this section unless the driver was offered an alcohol screening test or chemical analysis and refused to provide all required samples of breath or blood for analysis.

(b2) Alcohol Screening Test.—Notwithstanding any other provision of law, an alcohol screening test may be administered to a driver suspected of violation of subsection (a) of this section, and the results of an alcohol screening test or the driver's refusal to submit may be used by a law enforcement officer, a court, or an administrative agency in determining if alcohol was present in the driver's body. No alcohol screening tests are valid under this section unless the device used is one approved by the Commission on Health Services, and the screening test is conducted in accordance with the applicable regulations of the Commission as to its manner and use.

(c) Punishment; Effect When Impaired Driving Offense Also Charged.—The offense in this section is a Class 2 misdemeanor. It is not, in any circumstances, a lesser included offense of impaired driving under G.S. 20-138.1, but if a person is convicted under this section and of an offense involving impaired driving arising out of the same transaction, the aggregate punishment imposed by the court may not exceed the maximum applicable to the offense involving impaired driving, and any minimum punishment applicable shall be imposed.

(d) Limited Driving Privilege.—A person who is convicted of violating subsection (a) of this section and whose driver's license is revoked solely based on that conviction may apply for a limited driving privilege as provided in G.S. 20-179.3. This subsection shall apply only if the person meets both of the following requirements:

(1) Is 18, 19, or 20 years old on the date of the offense.
(2) Has not previously been convicted of a violation of this section.

The judge may issue the limited driving privilege only if the person meets the eligibility requirements of G.S. 20-179.3, other than the requirement in G.S. 20-179.3(b) (1)c. G.S. 20-179.3(e) shall not apply. All other terms, conditions, and restrictions provided for in G.S. 20-179.3 shall apply. G.S. 20-179.3, rather than this subsection, governs the issuance of a limited driving privilege to a person who is convicted of violating subsection (a) of this section and of driving while impaired as a result of the same transaction.

History: 1983, c. 435, s. 34; 1985 (Reg. Sess., 1986), c. 852, s. 11; 1993, c. 539, s. 364; 1994, Ex. Sess., c. 24, s. 14(c); 1995, c. 506, s. 6; 1997-379, ss. 4, 5.2.

§ 20-138.4. Requirement that prosecutor explain reduction or dismissal of charge involving impaired driving

Any prosecutor must enter detailed facts in the record of any case involving impaired driving explaining the reasons for his action if he:

(1) Enters a voluntary dismissal; or
(2) Accepts a plea of guilty or no contest to a lesser included offense; or
(3) Substitutes another charge, by statement of charges or otherwise, if the substitute charge carries a lesser mandatory minimum punishment or is not an offense involving impaired driving; or
(4) Otherwise takes a discretionary action that effectively dismisses or reduces the original charge in the case involving impaired driving.

General explanations such as "interests of justice" or "insufficient evidence" are not sufficiently detailed to meet the requirements of this section.

History: 1983, c. 435, s. 25; 1987 (Reg. Sess., 1988), c. 1112; 1989, c. 771, s. 18.

§ 20-138.5. Habitual impaired driving

(a) A person commits the offense of habitual impaired driving if he drives while impaired as defined in G.S. 20-138.1 and has been convicted of three or more offenses involving impaired driving as defined in G.S. 20-4.01(24a) within seven years of the date of this offense.

(b) A person convicted of violating this section shall be punished as a Class F felon and shall be sentenced to a minimum active term of not less than 12 months of imprisonment, which shall not be suspended. Sentences imposed under this subsection shall run consecutively with and shall commence at the expiration of any sentence being served.

(c) An offense under this section is an implied consent offense subject to the provisions of G.S. 20-16.2.

(d) A person convicted under this section shall have his license permanently revoked.

(e) If a person is convicted under this section, the motor vehicle that was driven by the defendant at the time the defendant committed the offense of impaired driving becomes property subject to forfeiture in accordance with the procedure set out in G.S. 20-28.2. In applying the procedure set out in that statute, an owner or a holder of a security interest is considered an innocent party with respect to a motor vehicle subject to forfeiture under this subsection if any of the following applies:

(1) The owner or holder of the security interest did not know and had no reason to know that the defendant had been convicted within the previous seven years of three or more offenses involving impaired driving.
(2) The defendant drove the motor vehicle without the consent of the owner or the holder of the security interest.

History: 1989 (Reg. Sess., 1990), c. 1039, s. 7; 1993, c. 539, s. 1258; 1994, Ex. Sess., c. 14, s. 32; c. 24, s. 14(c); 1993 (Reg. Sess., 1994), c. 761, s. 34.1; c. 767, s. 32; 1997-379, s. 6.

§ 20-138.7. Transporting an open container of alcoholic beverage after consuming alcohol

(a) Offense.—No person shall drive a motor vehicle on a highway or public vehicular area:

(1) While there is an alcoholic beverage other than in the unopened manufacturer's original container in the passenger area; and

(2) While the driver is consuming alcohol or while alcohol remains in the driver's body.

(b) Subject to Implied-Consent Law.—An offense under this section is an alcohol-related offense subject to the implied-consent provisions of G.S. 20-16.2.

(c) Odor Insufficient.—The odor of an alcoholic beverage on the breath of the driver is insufficient evidence to prove beyond a reasonable doubt that alcohol was remaining in the driver's body in violation of this section, unless the driver was offered an alcohol screening test or chemical analysis and refused to provide all required samples of breath or blood for analysis.

(d) Alcohol Screening Test.—Notwithstanding any other provision of law, an alcohol screening test may be administered to a driver suspected of violating subsection (a) of this section, and the results of an alcohol screening test or the driver's refusal to submit may be used by a law enforcement officer, a court, or an administrative agency in determining if alcohol was present in the driver's body. No alcohol screening tests are valid under this section unless the device used is one approved by the Commission for Health Services, and the screening test is conducted in accordance with the applicable regulations of the Commission as to the manner of its use.

(e) Punishment; Effect When Impaired Driving Offense Also Charged.—Violation of this section shall be punished as a Class 3 misdemeanor for the first offense and shall be punished as a Class 2 misdemeanor for a second or subsequent offense. A fine imposed for a second or subsequent offense may not exceed one thousand dollars ($1,000). Violation of this section is not a lesser included offense of impaired driving under G.S. 20-138.1, but if a person is convicted under this section and of an offense involving impaired driving arising out of the same transaction, the punishment imposed by the court shall not exceed the maximum applicable to the offense involving impaired driving, and any minimum applicable punishment shall be imposed. A violation of this section shall be considered a moving violation for purposes of G.S. 20-16(c).

(f) Definitions.—If the seal on a container of alcoholic beverages has been broken, it is opened within the meaning of this section. For purposes of this section, "passenger area of a motor vehicle" means the area designed to seat the driver and passengers and any area within the reach of a seated driver or passenger, including the glove compartment. The area of the trunk or the area behind the last upright back seat of a station wagon, hatchback, or similar vehicle shall not be considered part of the passenger area. The term "alcoholic beverage" is as defined in G.S. 18B-101(4).

(g) Pleading.—In any prosecution for a violation of this section, the pleading is sufficient if it states the time and place of the alleged offense in the usual form and charges that the defendant drove a motor vehicle on a highway or public vehicular area with an open container of alcoholic beverage after drinking.

(h) Limited Driving Privilege.—A person who is convicted of violating subsection (a) of this section and whose driver's license is revoked solely based on that conviction may apply for a limited driving privilege as provided for in G.S. 20-179.3. The judge may issue the limited driving privilege only if the driver meets the eligibility requirements of G.S. 20-179.3, other than the requirement in G.S. 20-179.3(b)(1)c. G.S. 20-179.3(e) shall not apply. All other terms, conditions, and restrictions provided for in G.S. 20-179.3 shall apply. G.S. 20-179.3, rather than this subsection, governs the issuance of a limited driving privilege to a person who is convicted of violating subsection (a) of this section and of driving while impaired as a result of the same transaction.

History: 1995, c. 506, s. 9.

§ 20-139.1. Procedures governing chemical analyses; admissibility; evidentiary provisions; controlled-drinking programs

(a) Chemical Analysis Admissible.—In any implied-consent offense under G.S. 20-16.2, a person's alcohol concentration or the presence of any other impairing substance in the person's body as shown by a chemical analysis is admissible in evidence. This section does not limit the introduction of other competent evidence as to a person's alcohol concentration or results of other tests showing the presence of an impairing substance, including other chemical tests.

(b) Approval of Valid Test Methods; Licensing Chemical Analysts.—A chemical analysis, to be valid, shall be performed in accordance with the provisions of this section. The chemical analysis shall be performed according to methods approved by the Commission for Health Services by an individual possessing a current permit issued by the Department of Health and Human Services for that type of chemical analysis. The Commission for Health Services may adopt rules approving satisfactory methods or techniques for performing chemical analyses, and the Department of Health and Human Services may ascertain the qualifications and competence of individuals to conduct particular chemical analyses. The Department may issue permits to conduct chemical analyses to individuals it finds qualified subject to periodic renewal, termination, and revocation of the permit in the Department's discretion.

(b1) When Officer May Perform Chemical Analysis.—Except as provided in this subsection, a chemical analysis is not valid in any case in which it is performed by an arresting officer or by a charging officer under the terms of G.S. 20-16.2. A chemical analysis of the breath may be performed by an arresting officer or by a charging officer when both of the following apply:

(1) The officer possesses a current permit issued by the Department of Health and Human Services for the type of chemical analysis.

(2) The officer performs the chemical analysis by using an automated instrument that prints the results of the analysis.

(b2) Breath Analysis Results Inadmissible if Preventive Maintenance Not Performed.—Notwithstanding the provisions of subsection (b), the results of a chemical analysis of a person's breath performed in accordance with this section are not admissible in evidence if:

(1) The defendant objects to the introduction into evidence of the results of the chemical analysis of the defendant's breath; and

(2) The defendant demonstrates that, with respect to the instrument used to analyze the defendant's breath, preventive maintenance procedures required by the regulations of the Commission for Health Services had not been performed within the time limits prescribed by those regulations.

(b3) Sequential Breath Tests Required.—By January 1, 1985, the regulations of the Commission for Health Services governing the administration of chemical analyses of the breath shall require the testing of at least duplicate sequential breath samples. Those regulations must provide:

(1) A specification as to the minimum observation period before collection of the first breath sample and the time requirements as to collection of second and subsequent samples.

(2) That the test results may only be used to prove a person's particular alcohol concentration if:
   a. The pair of readings employed are from consecutively administered tests; and
   b. The readings do not differ from each other by an alcohol concentration greater than 0.02.

(3) That when a pair of analyses meets the requirements of subdivision (2), only the lower of the two readings may be used by the State as proof of a person's alcohol concentration in any court or administrative proceeding.

A person's willful refusal to give the sequential breath samples necessary to constitute a valid chemical analysis is a willful refusal under G.S. 20-16.2(c).

A person's willful refusal to give the second or subsequent breath sample shall make the result of the first breath sample, or the result of the sample providing the lowest alcohol concentration if more than one breath sample is provided, admissible in any judicial or administrative hearing for any relevant purpose, including the establishment that a person had a particular alcohol concentration for conviction of an offense involving impaired driving.

(b4) Introducing Routine Records Kept as Part of Breath-Testing Program.—In civil and criminal proceedings, any party may introduce, without further authentication, simulator logs and logs for other devices used to verify a breath-testing instrument, certificates and other records concerning the check of ampoules and of simulator stock solution and the stock solution used in any other equilibration device, preventive maintenance records, and other records that are routinely kept concerning the maintenance and operation of breath-testing instruments. In a criminal case, however, this subsection does not authorize the State to introduce records to prove the results of a chemical analysis of the defendant or of any validation test of the instrument that is conducted during that chemical analysis.

(b5) Subsequent Tests Allowed.—A person may be requested, pursuant to G.S. 20-16.2, to submit to a chemical analysis of the person's blood or other bodily fluid or substance in addition to or in lieu of a chemical analysis of the breath, in the discretion of the charging officer. If a subsequent chemical analysis is requested pursuant to this subsection, the person shall again be advised of the implied consent rights in accordance with G.S. 20-16.2(a). A person's willful refusal to submit to a chemical analysis of the blood or other bodily fluid or substance is a willful refusal under G.S. 20-16.2.

(c) Withdrawal of Blood for Chemical Analysis.—When a blood test is specified as the type of chemical analysis by the charging officer, only a physician, registered nurse, or other qualified person may withdraw the blood sample. If the person withdrawing the blood requests written confirmation of the charging officer's request for the withdrawal of blood, the officer shall furnish it before blood is withdrawn. When blood is withdrawn pursuant to a charging officer's request, neither the person withdrawing the blood nor any hospital, laboratory, or other institution, person, firm, or corporation employing that person, or contracting for the service of withdrawing blood, may be held criminally or civilly liable by reason of withdrawing that blood, except that there is no immunity from liability for negligent acts or omissions.

(d) Right to Additional Test.—A person who submits to a chemical analysis may have a qualified person of his own choosing administer an additional chemical test or tests, or have a qualified person withdraw a blood sample for later chemical testing by a qualified person of his own choosing. Any law-enforcement officer having in his charge any person who has submitted to a chemical analysis shall assist the person in contacting someone to administer the additional testing or to withdraw blood, and shall allow access to the person for that purpose. The failure or inability of the person who submitted to a chemical analysis to obtain any additional test or to withdraw blood does not preclude the admission of evidence relating to the chemical analysis.

(e) Recording Results of Chemical Analysis of Breath.—The chemical analyst who administers a test of a person's breath shall record the following information after making any chemical analysis:

(1) The alcohol concentration or concentrations revealed by the chemical analysis.

(2) The time of the collection of the breath sample or samples used in the chemical analysis.

A copy of the record of this information shall be furnished to the person submitting to the chemical analysis, or to his attorney, before any trial or proceeding in which the results of the chemical analysis may be used.

(e1) Use of Chemical Analyst's Affidavit in District Court.—An affidavit by a chemical analyst sworn to and properly executed before an official authorized to administer oaths is admissible in evidence without further authentication in any hearing or trial in the District Court Division of the General Court of Justice with respect to the following matters:

(1) The alcohol concentration or concentrations or the presence or absence of an impairing substance of a person given a chemical analysis and who is involved in the hearing or trial.

(2) The time of the collection of the blood, breath, or other bodily fluid or substance sample or samples for the chemical analysis.

(3) The type of chemical analysis administered and the procedures followed.

(4) The type and status of any permit issued by the Department of Health and Human Services that the analyst held on the date the analyst performed the chemical analysis in question.

(5) If the chemical analysis is performed on a breath-testing instrument for which regulations adopted pursuant to subsection (b) require preventive maintenance, the date the most recent preventive maintenance procedures were performed on the breath-testing instrument used, as shown on the maintenance records for that instrument.

The Department of Health and Human Services shall develop a form for use by chemical analysts in making this affidavit. If any person who submitted to a chemical analysis desires that a chemical analyst personally testify in the hearing or trial in the District Court Division, the person may subpoena the chemical analyst and examine him as if he were an adverse witness.

(f) Evidence of Refusal Admissible.—If any person charged with an implied-consent offense refuses to submit to a chemical analysis, evidence of that refusal is admissible in any criminal action against him for an implied-consent offense under G.S. 20-16.2.

(g) Controlled-Drinking Programs.—The Department of Health and Human Services may adopt rules concerning the ingestion of controlled amounts of alcohol by individuals submitting to chemical testing as a part of scientific, experimental, educational, or demonstration programs. These regulations shall prescribe procedures consistent with controlling federal law governing the acquisition, transportation, possession, storage, administration, and disposition of alcohol intended for use in the programs. Any person in charge of a controlled-drinking program who acquires alcohol under these regulations must keep records accounting for the disposition of all alcohol acquired, and the records must at all reasonable times be available for inspection upon the request of any federal, State, or local law-enforcement officer with jurisdiction over the laws relating to control of alcohol. A controlled-drinking program exclusively using lawfully purchased alcoholic beverages in places in which they may be lawfully possessed, however, need not comply with the record-keeping requirements of the regulations authorized by this subsection. All acts pursuant to the regulations reasonably done in furtherance of bona fide objectives of a controlled-drinking program authorized by the regulations are lawful notwithstanding the provisions of any other general or local statute, regulation, or ordinance controlling alcohol.

History: 1963, c. 966, s. 2; 1967, c. 123; 1969, c. 1074, s. 2; 1971, c. 619, ss. 12, 13; 1973, c. 476, s. 128;

c. 1081, s. 2; c. 1331, s. 3; 1975, c. 405; 1979, 2d Sess., c. 1089; 1981, c. 412, s. 4; c. 747, s. 66; 1983, c. 435, s. 26; 1983 (Reg. Sess., 1984), c. 1101, s. 20; 1989, c. 727, s. 219(2); 1991, c. 689, s. 233.1(b); 1993, c. 285, s. 7; 1997-379, ss. 5.3–5.5; 1997-443, s. 11A.10; 1997-443, s. 11A.123; 1997-456, s. 34(b).

§ 20-140. Reckless driving

(a) Any person who drives any vehicle upon a highway or any public vehicular area carelessly and heedlessly in willful or wanton disregard of the rights or safety of others shall be guilty of reckless driving.

(b) Any person who drives any vehicle upon a highway or any public vehicular area without due caution and circumspection and at a speed or in a manner so as to endanger or be likely to endanger any person or property shall be guilty of reckless driving.

(c) Repealed by Session Laws 1983, c. 435, s. 23.

(d) Reckless driving as defined in subsections (a) and (b) is a Class 2 misdemeanor.

(e) Repealed by Session Laws 1983, c. 435, s. 23.

History: 1937, c. 407, s. 102; 1957, c. 1368, s. 1; 1959, c. 1264, s. 8; 1973, c. 1330, s. 3; 1979, c. 903, ss. 7, 8; 1981, c. 412, s. 4; c. 466, s. 7; c. 747, s. 66; 1983, c. 435, s. 23; 1985, c. 764, s. 28; 1985 (Reg. Sess., 1986), c. 852, s. 17; 1993, c. 539, s. 365; 1994, Ex. Sess., c. 24, s. 14(c).

§ 20-140.3. Unlawful use of National System of Interstate and Defense Highways and other controlled-access highways

On those sections of highways which are or become a part of the National System of Interstate and Defense Highways and other controlled-access highways, it shall be unlawful for any person:

(1) To drive a vehicle over, upon, or across any curb, central dividing section or other separation or dividing line on said highways.

(2) To make a left turn or a semicircular or U-turn except through an opening provided for that purpose in the dividing curb, separation section, or line on said highways.

(3) To drive any vehicle except in the proper lane provided for that purpose and in the proper direction and to the right of the central dividing curb, separation section, or line on said highways.

(4) To drive a vehicle onto or from any controlled-access highway except at such entrances and exits as are established by public authority.

(5) To stop, park, or leave standing any vehicle, whether attended or unattended, on any part or portion of the right-of-way of said highways, except in the case of an emergency or as directed by a peace officer, or at designated parking areas.

(6) To fail to yield the right-of-way when entering the highway to any vehicle already travelling on the highway.

(7) Notwithstanding any other subdivision of this section, a law enforcement officer may cross the median of a divided highway when the officer has reasonable grounds to believe that a felony is being or has been committed, has personal knowledge that a vehicle is being operated at a speed or in a manner which is likely to endanger persons or property, or the officer has reasonable grounds to believe that the officer's presence is immediately required at a location which would necessitate crossing a median of a divided highway for this purpose. Fire department vehicles and public or private ambulances and rescue squad emergency service vehicles traveling in response to a fire alarm or other emergency call may cross the median of a divided highway when assistance is immediately required at a location which would necessitate the vehicle crossing a median of a divided highway for this purpose.

History: 1973, c. 1330, s. 5; 1977, c. 731, s. 1; 1999-330, s. 5.

§ 20-140.4. Special provisions for motorcycles and mopeds

(a) No person shall operate a motorcycle or moped upon a highway or public vehicular area:

(1) When the number of persons upon such motorcycle or moped, including the operator, shall exceed the number of persons which it was designed to carry.

(2) Unless the operator and all passengers thereon wear safety helmets of a type approved by the Commissioner of Motor Vehicles.

(b) Violation of any provision of this section shall not be considered negligence per se or contributory negligence per se in any civil action.

(c) Any person convicted of violating this section shall have committed an infraction and shall be fined according to G.S. 20-135.2A(e) and (f).

History: 1973, c. 1330, s. 6; 1989, c. 711, s. 1.

§ 20-141. Speed restrictions

(a) No person shall drive a vehicle on a highway or in a public vehicular area at a speed greater than is reasonable and prudent under the conditions then existing.

(b) Except as otherwise provided in this Chapter, it shall be unlawful to operate a vehicle in excess of the following speeds:

(1) Thirty-five miles per hour inside municipal corporate limits for all vehicles.

(2) Fifty-five miles per hour outside municipal corporate limits for all vehicles except for school buses and school activity buses.

(c) Except while towing another vehicle, or when an advisory safe-speed sign indicates a slower speed, or as otherwise provided by law, it shall be unlawful to operate a passenger vehicle upon the interstate and primary highway system at less than the following speeds:

(1) Forty miles per hour in a speed zone of 55 miles per hour.

(2) Forty-five miles per hour in a speed zone of 60 miles per hour or greater.

These minimum speeds shall be effective only when appropriate signs are posted indicating the minimum speed.

(d) (1) Whenever the Department of Transportation determines on the basis of an engineering and traffic investigation that any speed allowed by subsection (b) is greater than is reasonable and safe under the conditions found to exist upon any part of a highway outside the corporate limits of a municipality or upon any part of a highway designated as part of the Interstate Highway System or any part of a controlled-access highway (either inside or outside the corporate limits of a municipality), the Department of Transportation shall determine and declare a reasonable and safe speed limit.

(2) Whenever the Department of Transportation determines on the basis of an engineering and traffic investigation that a higher maximum speed than those set forth in subsection (b) is reasonable and safe under the conditions found to exist upon any part of a highway designated as part of the Interstate Highway System or any part of a controlled-access highway (either inside or outside the corporate limits of a municipality) the Department of Transportation shall determine and declare a reasonable and safe speed limit. A speed limit set pursuant to this subsection may not exceed 70 miles per hour.

Speed limits set pursuant to this subsection are not effective until appropriate signs giving notice thereof are erected upon the parts of the highway affected.

(e) Local authorities, in their respective jurisdictions, may authorize by ordinance higher speeds or lower speeds than those set out in subsection (b) upon all streets which are not part of the State highway system; but no speed so fixed shall authorize a speed in excess of 55 miles per hour. Speed limits set pursuant to this subsection shall be effective when appropriate signs giving notice thereof are erected upon the part of the streets affected.

(e1) Local authorities within their respective jurisdictions may authorize, by ordinance, lower speed limits than those set in subsection (b) of this section on school property. If the lower speed limit is being set on the grounds of a public school, the local school administrative unit must request or consent to the lower speed limit. If the lower speed limit is being set on the grounds of a private school, the governing body of the school must request or consent to the lower speed limit. Speed limits established pursuant to this subsection shall become effective when appropriate signs giving notice of the speed limit are erected upon affected property. A person who drives a motor vehicle on school property at a speed greater than the speed limit set and posted under this subsection is responsible for an infraction and is required to pay a penalty of not less than twenty-five dollars ($25.00).

(f) Whenever local authorities within their respective jurisdictions determine upon the basis of an engineering and traffic investigation that a higher maximum speed than those set forth in subsection (b) is reasonable and safe, or that any speed herein before set forth is greater than is reasonable and safe, under the conditions found to exist upon any part of a street within the corporate limits of a municipality and which street is a part of the State highway system (except those highways designated as part of the interstate highway system or other controlled-access highway) said local authorities shall determine and declare a safe and reasonable speed limit. A speed limit set pursuant to this subsection may not exceed 55 miles per hour. Limits set pursuant to this subsection shall become effective when the Department of Transportation has passed a concurring ordinance and signs are erected giving notice of the authorized speed limit.

The Department of Transportation is authorized to raise or lower the statutory speed limit on all highways on the State highway system within municipalities which do not have a governing body to enact municipal ordinances as provided by law. The Department of Transportation shall determine a reasonable and safe speed limit in the same manner as is provided in G.S. 20-141(d)(1) and G.S. 20-141(d)(2) for changing the speed limits outside of municipalities, without action of the municipality.

(g) Whenever the Department of Transportation or local authorities within their respective jurisdictions determine on the basis of an engineering and traffic investigation that slow speeds on any part of a highway considerably impede the normal and reasonable movement of traffic, the Department of Transportation or such local authority may determine and declare a minimum speed below which no person shall operate a motor vehicle except when necessary for safe operation in compliance with law. Such minimum speed limit shall be effective when appropriate signs giving notice thereof are erected on said part of the highway. Provided, such minimum speed limit shall be effective as to those highways and streets within the corporate limits of a municipality which are on the State highway system only when ordinances adopting the minimum speed limit are passed and concurred in by both the Department of Transportation and the local authorities. The provisions of this subsection shall not apply to farm tractors and other motor vehicles operating at reasonable speeds for the type and nature of such vehicles.

(h) No person shall operate a motor vehicle on the highway at such a slow speed as to impede the normal and reasonable movement of traffic except when reduced speed is necessary for safe operation or in compliance with law; provided, this provision shall not apply to farm tractors and other motor vehicles operating at reasonable speeds for the type and nature of such vehicles.

(i) The Department of Transportation shall have authority to designate and appropriately mark certain highways of the State as truck routes.

(j) Repealed by Session Laws 1997, c. 443, s. 19.26(b).

(j1) A person who drives a vehicle on a highway at a speed that is either more than 15 miles per hour more than the speed limit established by law for the highway where the offense occurred or over 80 miles per hour is guilty of a Class 2 misdemeanor.

(j2) A person who drives a motor vehicle in a highway work zone at a speed greater than the speed limit set and posted under this section shall be required to pay a penalty of two hundred fifty dollars ($250.00). This penalty shall be imposed in addition to those penalties established in this Chapter. A "highway work zone" is the area between the first sign that informs motorists of the existence of a work zone on a highway and the last sign that informs motorists of the end of the work zone. This subsection applies only if a sign posted at the beginning of the highway work zone states the penalty for speeding in the work zone. The Secretary shall ensure that work zones shall only be posted with penalty signs if the Secretary determines, after engineering review, that the posting is necessary to ensure the safety of the traveling public due to a hazardous condition.

A law enforcement officer issuing a citation for a violation of this section while in a highway work zone shall indicate the vehicle speed and speed limit posted in the work zone. Upon an individual's conviction of a violation of this section while in a highway work zone, the clerk of court shall report that the vehicle was in a work zone at the time of the violation, the vehicle speed, and the speed limit of the work zone to the Division of Motor Vehicles.

(k) Repealed by Session Laws 1995 (Reg. Sess., 1996), c. 652, s. 1.

(l) Notwithstanding any other provision contained in G.S. 20-141 or any other statute or law of this State, including municipal charters, any speed limit on any portion of the public highways within the jurisdiction of this State shall be uniformly applicable to all types of motor vehicles using such portion of the highway, if on November 1, 1973, such portion of the highway had a speed limit which was uniformly applicable to all types of motor vehicles using it. Provided, however, that a lower speed limit may be established for any vehicle operating under a special permit because of any weight or dimension of such vehicle, including any load thereon. The requirement for a uniform speed limit hereunder shall not apply to any portion of the highway during such time as the condition of the highway, weather, an accident, or other condition creates a temporary hazard to the safety of traffic on such portion of the highway.

(m) The fact that the speed of a vehicle is lower than the foregoing limits shall not relieve the operator of a vehicle from the duty to decrease speed as may be necessary to avoid colliding with any person, vehicle or other conveyance on or entering the highway, and to avoid injury to any person or property.

(n) Notwithstanding any other provision contained in G.S. 20-141 or any other statute or law of this State, the failure of a motorist to stop his vehicle within the radius of its headlights or the range of his vision shall not be held negligence per se or contributory negligence per se.

History: 1937, c. 297, s. 2; c. 407, s. 103; 1939, c. 275; 1941, c. 347; 1947, c. 1067, s. 17; 1949, c. 947, s. 1; 1953, c. 1145; 1955, c. 398; c. 555, ss. 1, 2; c. 1042; 1957, c. 65, s. 11; c. 214; 1959, c. 640; c. 1264,

s. 10; 1961, cc. 99, 1147; 1963, cc. 134, 456, 949; 1967, c. 106; 1971, c. 79, ss. 1-3; 1973, c. 507, s. 5; c. 1330, s. 7; 1975, c. 225; 1977, c. 367; c. 464, s. 34; c. 470; 1983, c. 131; 1985, c. 764, ss. 29, 30; 1985 (Reg. Sess., 1986), c. 852, s. 17; 1987, c. 164; 1991 (Reg. Sess., 1992), c. 818, s. 1; c. 1034, s. 1; 1993, c. 539, ss. 366, 367; 1994, Ex. Sess., c. 24, s. 14(c); 1995 (Reg. Sess., 1996), c. 652, s. 1; 1997-341, s. 1; 1997-443, s. 19.26(b); 1997-488, s. 1; 1999-330, s. 3.

§ 20-141.1. Speed limits in school zones

The Board of Transportation or local authorities within their respective jurisdictions may, by ordinance, set speed limits lower than those designated in G.S. 20-141 for areas adjacent to or near a public, private or parochial school. Limits set pursuant to this section shall become effective when signs are erected giving notice of the school zone, the authorized speed limit, and the days and hours when the lower limit is effective, or by erecting signs giving notice of the school zone, the authorized speed limit and which indicate the days and hours the lower limit is effective by an electronic flasher operated with a time clock. Limits set pursuant to this section may be enforced only on days when school is in session, and no speed limit below 20 miles per hour may be set under the authority of this section. A person who drives a motor vehicle in a school zone at a speed greater than the speed limit set and posted under this section is responsible for an infraction and is required to pay a penalty of not less than twenty-five dollars ($25.00).

History: 1977, c. 902, s. 2; 1979, c. 613; 1997-341, s. 1.1.

§ 20-141.3. Unlawful racing on streets and highways

(a) It shall be unlawful for any person to operate a motor vehicle on a street or highway willfully in prearranged speed competition with another motor vehicle. Any person violating the provisions of this subsection shall be guilty of a Class 1 misdemeanor.

(b) It shall be unlawful for any person to operate a motor vehicle on a street or highway willfully in speed competition with another motor vehicle. Any person willfully violating the provisions of this subsection shall be guilty of a Class 2 misdemeanor.

(c) It shall be unlawful for any person to authorize or knowingly permit a motor vehicle owned by him or under his control to be operated on a public street, highway, or thoroughfare in prearranged speed competition with another motor vehicle, or to place or receive any bet, wager, or other thing of value from the outcome of any prearranged speed competition on any public street, highway, or thoroughfare. Any person violating the provisions of this subsection shall be guilty of a Class 1 misdemeanor.

(d) The Commissioner of Motor Vehicles shall revoke the driver's license or privilege to drive of every person convicted of violating the provisions of subsection (a) or subsection (c) of this section, said revocation to be for three years; provided any person whose license has been revoked under this section may apply for a new license after 18 months from revocation. Upon filing of such application the Division may issue a new license upon satisfactory proof that the former licensee has been of good behavior for the past 18 months and that his conduct and attitude are such as to entitle him to favorable consideration and upon such terms and conditions which the Division may see fit to impose for the balance of the three-year revocation period, which period shall be computed from the date of the original revocation.

(e) The Commissioner may suspend the driver's license or privilege to drive of every person convicted of violating the provisions of subsection (b) of this section. Such suspension shall be for a period of time within the discretion of the Commissioner, but not to exceed one year.

(f) All suspensions and revocations made pursuant to the provisions of this section shall be in the same form and manner and shall be subject to all procedures as now provided for suspensions and revocations made under the provisions of Article 2 of Chapter 20 of the General Statutes.

(g) When any officer of the law discovers that any person has operated or is operating a motor vehicle willfully in prearranged speed competition with another motor vehicle on a street or highway, he shall seize the motor vehicle and deliver the same to the sheriff of the county in which such offense is committed, or the same shall be placed under said sheriff's constructive possession if delivery of actual possession is impractical, and the vehicle shall be held by the sheriff pending the trial of the person or persons arrested for operating such motor vehicle in violation of subsection (a) of this section. The sheriff shall restore the seized motor vehicle to the owner upon execution by the owner of a good and valid bond, with sufficient sureties, in an amount double the value of the property, which bond shall be approved by said sheriff and shall be conditioned on the return of the motor vehicle to the custody of the sheriff on the day of trial of the person or persons accused. Upon the acquittal of the person charged with operating said motor vehicle willfully in prearranged speed competition with another motor vehicle, the sheriff shall return the motor vehicle to the owner thereof.

Notwithstanding the provisions for sale set out above, on petition by a lienholder, the court, in its discretion and upon such terms and conditions as it may prescribe, may allow reclamation of the vehicle by the lienholder. The lienholder shall file with the court an accounting of the proceeds of any subsequent sale of the vehicle and pay into the court any proceeds received in excess of the amount of the lien.

Upon conviction of the operator of said motor vehicle of a violation of subsection (a) of this section, the court shall order a sale at public auction of said motor vehicle and the officer making the sale, after deducting the expenses of keeping the motor vehicle, the fee for the seizure, and the costs of the sale, shall pay all liens, according to their priorities, which are established, by intervention or otherwise, at said hearing or in other proceeding brought for said purpose, as being bona fide, and shall pay the balance of the proceeds to the proper officer of the county who receives fines and forfeitures to be used for the school fund of the county. All liens against a motor vehicle sold under the provisions of this section shall be transferred from the motor vehicle to the proceeds of its sale. If, at the time of hearing, or other proceeding in which the matter is considered, the owner of the vehicle can establish to the satisfaction of the court that said motor vehicle was used in prearranged speed competition with another motor vehicle on a street or highway without the knowledge or consent of the owner, and that the owner had no reasonable grounds to believe that the motor vehicle would be used for such purpose, the court shall not order a sale of the vehicle but shall restore it to the owner, and the said owner shall, at his request, be entitled to a trial by jury upon such issues.

If the owner of said motor vehicle cannot be found, the taking of the same, with a description thereof, shall be advertised in some newspaper published in the city or county where taken, or, if there be no newspaper published in such city or county, in a newspaper having circulation in the county, once a week for two weeks and by handbills posted in three public places near the place of seizure, and if said owner shall not appear within 10 days after the last publication of the advertisement, the property shall be sold, or otherwise disposed of in the manner set forth in this section.

When any vehicle confiscated under the provisions of this section is found to be specially equipped or modified from its original manufactured condition so as to increase its speed, the court shall, prior to sale, order that the special equipment or modification be removed and destroyed and the vehicle restored to its original manufactured condition. However, if the court should find that such equipment and modifications are so extensive that it would be impractical to restore said vehicle to its original manufactured condition, then the court may order that the vehicle be turned over to such governmental agency or public official within the territorial jurisdiction of the court as the court shall see fit, to be used in the performance of official duties only, and not for resale, transfer, or disposition other than as junk: Provided, that nothing herein contained shall affect the rights of lienholders and other claimants to said vehicles as set out in this section.

History: 1955, c. 1156; 1957, c. 1358; 1961, c. 354; 1963, c. 318; 1967, c. 446; 1969, c. 186, s. 3; 1973, c. 1330, s. 8; 1975, c. 716, s. 5; 1979, c. 667, s. 31; 1993, c. 539, ss. 368–370; 1994, Ex. Sess., c. 24, s. 14(c); 1995, c. 163, ss. 8, 9.

§ 20-141.4. Felony and misdemeanor death by vehicle

(a) Repealed by Session Laws 1983, c. 435, s. 27.

(a1) Felony Death by Vehicle.—A person commits the offense of felony death by vehicle if he unintentionally causes the death of another person while engaged in the offense of impaired driving under G.S. 20-138.1 or G.S. 20-138.2 and commission of that offense is the proximate cause of the death.

(a2) Misdemeanor Death by Vehicle.—A person commits the offense of misdemeanor death by vehicle if he unintentionally causes the death of another person while engaged in the violation of any State law or local ordinance applying to the operation or use of a vehicle or to the regulation of traffic, other than impaired driving under G.S. 20-138.1, and commission of that violation is the proximate cause of the death.

(b) Punishments.—Felony death by vehicle is a Class G felony. Misdemeanor death by vehicle is a Class 1 misdemeanor.

(c) No Double Prosecutions.—No person who has been placed in jeopardy upon a charge of death by vehicle may be prosecuted for the offense of manslaughter arising out of the same death; and no person who has been placed in jeopardy upon a charge of manslaughter may be prosecuted for death by vehicle arising out of the same death.

History: 1973, c. 1330, s. 9; 1983, c. 435, s. 27; 1993, c. 285, s. 10; c. 539, ss. 371, 1259; 1994, Ex. Sess., c. 24, s. 14(c).

§ 20-141.5. Speeding to elude arrest

(a) It shall be unlawful for any person to operate a motor vehicle on a street, highway, or public vehicular area while fleeing or attempting to elude a law enforcement officer who is in the lawful performance of his duties. Except as provided in subsection (b) of this section, violation of this section shall be a Class 1 misdemeanor.

(b) If two or more of the following aggravating factors are present at the time the violation occurs, violation of this section shall be a Class H felony.

(1) Speeding in excess of 15 miles per hour over the legal speed limit.
(2) Gross impairment of the person's faculties while driving due to:
  a. Consumption of an impairing substance; or
  b. A blood alcohol concentration of 0.14 or more within a relevant time after the driving.
(3) Reckless driving as proscribed by G.S. 20-140.
(4) Negligent driving leading to an accident causing:
  a. Property damage in excess of one thousand dollars ($1,000); or
  b. Personal injury.
(5) Driving when the person's driver's license is revoked.
(6) Driving in excess of the posted speed limit, during the days and hours when the posted limit is in effect, on school property or in an area designated as a school zone pursuant to G.S. 20-141.1, or in a highway work zone as defined in G.S. 20-141(j2).
(7) Passing a stopped school bus as proscribed by G.S. 20-217.
(8) Driving with a child under 12 years of age in the vehicle.

(c) Whenever evidence is presented in any court or administrative hearing of the fact that a vehicle was operated in violation of this section, it shall be prima facie evidence that the vehicle was operated by the person in whose name the vehicle was registered at the time of the violation, according to the Division's records. If the vehicle is rented, then proof of that rental shall be prima facie evidence that the vehicle was operated by the renter of the vehicle at the time of the violation.

(d) The Division shall suspend, for up to one year, the driver's license of any person convicted of a misdemeanor under this section. The Division shall revoke, for two years, the driver's license of any person convicted of a felony under this section if the person was convicted on the basis of the presence of two of the aggravating factors listed in subsection (b) of this section. The Division shall revoke, for three years, the driver's license of any person convicted of a felony under this section if the person was convicted on the basis of the presence of three or more aggravating factors listed in subsection (b) of this section. In the case of a first felony conviction under this section where only two aggravating factors were present, the licensee may apply to the sentencing court for a limited driving privilege after a period of 12 months of revocation, provided the operator's license has not also been revoked or suspended under any other provision of law. A limited driving privilege issued under this subsection shall be valid for the period of revocation remaining in the same manner and under the terms and conditions prescribed in G.S. 20-16.1(b). If the person's license is revoked under any other statute, the limited driving privilege issued pursuant to this subsection is invalid.

(e) When the probable cause of the law enforcement officer is based on the prima facie evidence rule set forth in subsection (c) above, the officer shall make a reasonable effort to contact the registered owner of the vehicle prior to initiating criminal process.

(f) Each law enforcement agency shall adopt a policy applicable to the pursuit of fleeing or eluding motorists. Each policy adopted pursuant to this subsection shall specifically include factors to be considered by an officer in determining when it is advisable to break off a chase to stop and apprehend a suspect. The Attorney General shall develop a model policy or policies to be considered for use by law enforcement agencies.

History: 1997-443, s. 19.26(a).

§ 20-142.1. Obedience to railroad signal

(a) Whenever any person driving a vehicle approaches a railroad grade crossing under any of the circumstances stated in this section, the driver of the vehicle shall stop within 50 feet, but not less than 15 feet from the nearest rail of the railroad and shall not proceed until he can do so safely. These requirements apply when:

(1) A clearly visible electrical or mechanical signal device gives warning of the immediate approach of a railroad train;
(2) A crossing gate is lowered or when a human flagman gives or continues to give a signal of the approach or passage of a railroad train;

(3) A railroad train approaching within approximately 1500 feet of the highway crossing emits a signal audible from that distance, and the railroad train is an immediate hazard because of its speed or nearness to the crossing; or

(4) An approaching railroad train is plainly visible and is in hazardous proximity to the crossing.

(b) No person shall drive any vehicle through, around, or under any crossing gate or barrier at a railroad crossing while the gate or barrier is closed or is being opened or closed, nor shall any pedestrian pass through, around, over, or under any crossing gate or barrier at a railroad crossing while the gate or barrier is closed or is being opened or closed.

(c) When stopping as required at a railroad crossing, the driver shall keep as far to the right of the highway as possible and shall not form two lanes of traffic unless the roadway is marked for four or more lanes of traffic.

(d) Any person who violates any provisions of this section shall be guilty of an infraction and punished in accordance with G.S. 20-176. Violation of this section shall not constitute negligence per se.

History: 1991, c. 368, s. 1.

§ 20-142.2. Vehicles stop at certain grade crossing

The Department of Transportation may designate particularly dangerous highway crossings of railroads and erect stop signs at those crossings. When a stop sign is erected at a highway crossing of a railroad, the driver of any vehicle shall stop within 50 feet but not less than 15 feet from the nearest rail of such grade crossing and shall proceed only upon exercising due care. Any person who violates this section shall be guilty of an infraction and punished in accordance with G.S. 20-176. Violation of this section shall not constitute negligence per se.

History: 1991, c. 368, s. 1.

§ 20-142.3. Certain vehicles must stop at railroad grade crossing; placarding certain vehicles

(a) Before crossing at grade any track or tracks of a railroad, the driver of any school bus, any activity bus, any motor vehicle carrying passengers for compensation, any property-hauling motor vehicle over 10,000 pounds which is carrying hazardous materials, and any motor vehicle with a capacity of 16 or more persons shall stop the vehicle within 50 feet but not less than 15 feet from the nearest rail of the railroad. While stopped, the driver shall listen and look in both directions along the track for any approaching train and shall not proceed until he can do so safely. Upon proceeding, the driver of the vehicle shall cross the track in a gear that allows the driver to cross the track without changing gears and the driver shall not change gears while crossing the track or tracks.

(b) Except for school buses and activity buses, the provisions of this section shall not require the driver of a vehicle to stop:

(1) At railroad tracks used exclusively for industrial switching purposes within a business district.

(2) At a railroad grade crossing which a police officer or crossing flagman directs traffic to proceed.

(3) At a railroad grade crossing protected by a gate or flashing signal designed to stop traffic upon the approach of a train, when the gate or flashing signal does not indicate the approach of a train.

(4) At an abandoned railroad grade crossing which is marked with a sign indicating that the rail line is abandoned.

(5) At an industrial or spur line railroad grade crossing marked with a sign reading "Exempt" erected by or with the consent of the appropriate State or local authority.

(c) It shall be unlawful to transport by motor vehicle upon the highways of this State any hazardous material without conspicuously marking or placarding the motor vehicle on each side and on the rear with the word "DANGEROUS" or the common or generic name of the article transported or its principal hazard. Additionally, the rear of any such vehicle shall be conspicuously marked with the words "THIS VEHICLE STOPS AT RAILROAD CROSSINGS" or "WE STOP AT RR CROSSINGS" A person violating the provisions of this subsection shall be guilty of an infraction and punished in accordance with G.S. 20-176. Violation of this section shall not constitute negligence per se.

(d) "Hazardous materials," for purposes of this section only, means any hazardous material required to be placarded under 49 C.F.R. § 171-180.

(e) The provisions of this section shall not apply to vehicles subject to Federal Motor Carrier Safety rules adopted by the Division of Motor Vehicles.

History: 1991, c. 368, s. 1; 1999-274, ss. 1, 2.

§ 20-142.4. Moving heavy equipment at railroad grade crossing

(a) No person shall operate or move any crawler-type tractor, crane, or roller or any equipment or structure having a normal operating speed of five or less miles per hour upon or across any tracks at a railroad crossing without first complying with this section.

(b) Notice of any intended crossing described in subsection (a) of this section shall be given to a superintendent of the railroad and a reasonable time be given to the railroad to provide protection at the crossing.

(c) Before making any crossing described in subsection (a) of this section, the person operating or moving the vehicle or equipment shall:

(1) Stop the vehicle or equipment not less than 15 feet nor more than 50 feet from the nearest rail of the railroad;

(2) While stopped, shall listen and look both directions along the track for any approaching train and for signals indicating the approach of a train; and

(3) Shall not proceed until the crossing can be made safely.

(d) No crossing described in subsection (a) of this section shall be made when warning is given by automatic signal or crossing gates or a flagman or otherwise of the immediate approach of a railroad train or car.

(e) Subsection (c) of this section shall not apply at any railroad crossing where State or local authorities have determined that trains are not operating during certain periods or seasons of the year and have erected an official sign carrying the legend "Exempt".

(f) Any person who violates any provision of this section shall be guilty of an infraction and punished in accordance with G.S. 20-176. Violation of this section shall not constitute negligence per se.

History: 1991, c. 368, s. 1.

§ 20-142.5. Stop when traffic obstructed

No driver shall enter an intersection or a marked crosswalk or drive onto any railroad grade crossing unless there is sufficient space on the other side of the intersection, crosswalk, or railroad grade crossing to accommodate the vehicle he is operating without obstructing the passage of other vehicles, pedestrians, or railroad trains, notwithstanding the indication of any traffic control signal to proceed. Any person who violates any provision of this section shall be guilty of an infraction and punished in accordance with G.S. 20-176. Violation of this section shall not constitute negligence per se.

History: 1991, c. 368, s. 1.

§ 20-145. When speed limit not applicable

The speed limitations set forth in this Article shall not apply to vehicles when operated with due regard for safety under the direction of the police in the chase or apprehension of violators of the law or of persons charged with or suspected of any such violation, nor to fire department or fire patrol vehicles when traveling in response to a fire alarm, nor to public or private ambulances and rescue squad emergency service vehicles when traveling in emergencies, nor to vehicles operated by county fire marshals and civil preparedness coordinators when traveling in the performances of their duties. This exemption shall not, however, protect the driver of any such vehicle from the consequence of a reckless disregard of the safety of others.

History: 1937, c. 407, s. 107; 1947, c. 987; 1971, c. 5; 1977, c. 52, s. 3; 1985, c. 454, s. 5.

§ 20-146. Drive on right side of highway; exceptions

(a) Upon all [highways] of sufficient width a vehicle shall be driven upon the right half of the highway except as follows:

(1) When overtaking and passing another vehicle proceeding in the same direction under the rules governing such movement;

(2) When an obstruction exists making it necessary to drive to the left of the center of the highway; provided, any person so doing shall yield the right-of-way to all vehicles traveling in the proper direction upon the unobstructed portion of the highway within such distance as to constitute an immediate hazard;

(3) Upon a highway divided into three marked lanes for traffic under the rules applicable thereon; or

(4) Upon a highway designated and signposted for one-way traffic.

(b) Upon all highways any vehicle proceeding at less than the legal maximum speed limit shall be driven in the right-hand lane then available for thru traffic, or as close as practicable to the right-hand curb or edge of the highway, except when overtaking and passing another vehicle proceeding in the same direction or when preparing for a left turn.

(c) Upon any highway having four or more lanes for moving traffic and providing for two-way movement of traffic, no vehicle shall be driven to the left of the centerline of the highway, except when authorized by official traffic-control devices designating certain lanes to the left side of the center of the highway for use by traffic not otherwise permitted to use such lanes or except as permitted under subsection (a)(2) hereof.

(d) Whenever any street has been divided into two or more clearly marked lanes for traffic, the following rules in addition to all others consistent herewith shall apply.

(1) A vehicle shall be driven as nearly as practicable entirely within a single lane and shall not be moved from such lane until the driver has first ascertained that such movement can be made with safety.

(2) Upon a street which is divided into three or more lanes and provides for the two-way movement of traffic, a vehicle shall not be driven in the center lane except when overtaking and passing another vehicle traveling in the same direction when such center lane is clear of traffic within a safe distance, or in the preparation for making a left turn or where such center lane is at the time allocated exclusively to traffic moving in the same direction that the vehicle is proceeding and such allocation is designated by official traffic-control device.

(3) Official traffic-control devices may be erected directing specified traffic to use a designated lane or designating those lanes to be used by traffic moving in a particular direction regardless of the center of the street and drivers of vehicles shall obey the direction of every such device.

(4) Official traffic-control devices may be installed prohibiting the changing of lanes on sections of streets, and drivers of vehicles shall obey the directions of every such device.

(e) Notwithstanding any other provisions of this section, when appropriate signs have been posted, it shall be unlawful for any person to operate a motor vehicle over and upon the inside lane, next to the median of any dual-lane highway at a speed less than the posted speed limit when the operation of said motor vehicle over and upon said inside lane shall impede the steady flow of traffic except when preparing for a left turn. "Appropriate signs" as used herein shall be construed as including "Slower Traffic Keep Right" or designations of similar import.

History: 1937, c. 407, s. 108; 1965, c. 678, s. 2; 1973, c. 1330, s. 3; 1975, c. 593; 1985, c. 764, s. 25; 1985 (Reg. Sess., 1986), c. 852, s. 17.

§ 20-146.1. Operation of motorcycles

(a) All motorcycles are entitled to full use of a lane and no motor vehicle shall be driven in such a manner as to deprive any motorcycle of the full use of a lane. This subsection shall not apply to motorcycles operated two abreast in a single lane.

(b) Motorcycles shall not be operated more than two abreast in a single lane.

History: 1965, c. 909; 1973, c. 1330, s. 14; 1975, c. 786.

§ 20-147. Keep to the right in crossing intersections or railroads

In crossing an intersection of highways or the intersection of a highway by a railroad right-of-way, the driver of a vehicle shall at all times cause such vehicle to travel on the right half of the highway unless such right side is obstructed or impassable.

History: 1937, c. 407, s. 109.

§ 20-148. Meeting of vehicles

Drivers of vehicles proceeding in opposite directions shall pass each other to the right, each giving to the other at least one half of the main-traveled portion of the roadway as nearly as possible.

History: 1937, c. 407, s. 110.

§ 20-149. Overtaking a vehicle

(a) The driver of any such vehicle overtaking another vehicle proceeding in the same direction shall pass at least two feet to the left thereof, and shall not again drive to the right side of the highway until safely clear of such overtaken vehicle. This subsection shall not apply when the overtaking and passing is done pursuant to the provisions of G.S. 20-150.1.

(b) Except when overtaking and passing on the right is permitted, the driver of an overtaken vehicle shall give way to the right in favor of the overtaking vehicle while being lawfully overtaken on audible signal and shall not increase the speed of his vehicle until completely passed by the overtaking vehicle.

Failure to comply with this subsection:

(1) Is a Class 1 misdemeanor when the failure is the proximate cause of a collision resulting in serious bodily injury.

(2) Is a Class 2 misdemeanor when the failure is the proximate cause of a collision resulting in bodily injury or property damage.

(3) Is, in all other cases, an infraction.

History: 1937, c. 407, s. 111; 1955, c. 913, s. 3; 1959, c. 247; 1973, c. 1330, s. 15; 1995, c. 283, s. 1.

§ 20-150. Limitations on privilege of overtaking and passing

(a) The driver of a vehicle shall not drive to the left side of the center of a highway, in overtaking and passing another vehicle proceeding in the same direction, unless such left side is clearly visible and is free of oncoming traffic for a sufficient distance ahead to permit such overtaking and passing to be made in safety.

(b) The driver of a vehicle shall not overtake and pass another vehicle proceeding in the same direction upon the crest of a grade or upon a curve in the highway where the driver's view along the highway is obstructed within a distance of 500 feet.

(c) The driver of a vehicle shall not overtake and pass any other vehicle proceeding in the same direction at any railway grade crossing nor at any intersection of highway unless permitted so to do by a traffic or police officer. For the purposes of this section the words "intersection of highway" shall be defined and limited to intersections designated and marked by the Department of Transportation by appropriate signs, and street intersections in cities and towns.

(d) The driver of a vehicle shall not drive to the left side of the centerline of a highway upon the crest of a grade or upon a curve in the highway where such centerline has been placed upon such highway by the Department of Transportation, and is visible.

(e) The driver of a vehicle shall not overtake and pass another on any portion of the highway which is marked by signs, markers or markings placed by the Department of Transportation stating or clearly indicating that passing should not be attempted.

(f) The foregoing limitations shall not apply upon a one-way street nor to the driver of a vehicle turning left in or from an alley, private road, or driveway.

History: 1937, c. 407, s. 112; 1955, c. 862; c. 913, s. 2; 1957, c. 65, s. 11; 1969, c. 13; 1973, c. 507, s. 5; c. 1330, s. 16; 1977, c. 464, s. 34; 1979, c. 472.

§ 20-150.1. When passing on the right is permitted

The driver of a vehicle may overtake and pass upon the right of another vehicle only under the following conditions:

(1) When the vehicle overtaken is in a lane designated for left turns;

(2) Upon a street or highway with unobstructed pavement of sufficient width which have been marked for two or more lanes of moving vehicles in each direction and are not occupied by parked vehicles;

(3) Upon a one-way street, or upon a highway on which traffic is restricted to one direction of movement when such street or highway is free from obstructions and is of sufficient width and is marked for two or more lanes of moving vehicles which are not occupied by parked vehicles;

(4) When driving in a lane designating a right turn on a red traffic signal light.

History: 1953, c. 679.

§ 20-152. Following too closely

(a) The driver of a motor vehicle shall not follow another vehicle more closely than is reasonable and prudent, having due regard for the speed of such vehicles and the traffic upon and the condition of the highway.

(b) The driver of any motor vehicle traveling upon a highway outside of a business or residential district and following another motor vehicle shall, whenever conditions permit, leave sufficient space so that an overtaking vehicle may enter and occupy such space without danger, except that this shall not prevent a motor vehicle from overtaking and passing another motor vehicle. This provision shall not apply to funeral processions.

History: 1937, c. 407, s. 114; 1949, c. 1207, s. 4; 1973, c. 1330, s. 17.

§ 20-153. Turning at intersections

(a) Right Turns.—Both the approach for a right turn and a right turn shall be made as close as practicable to the right-hand curb or edge of the roadway.

(b) Left Turns.—The driver of a vehicle intending to turn left at any intersection shall approach the intersection in the extreme left-hand lane lawfully available to traffic moving in the direction of travel of that vehicle, and, after entering the intersection, the left turn shall be made so as to leave the intersection in a lane lawfully available to traffic moving in the direction upon the roadway being entered.

(c) Local authorities and the Department of Transportation, in their respective jurisdictions, may modify the foregoing method of turning at intersections by clearly indicating by buttons, markers, or other direction signs within an intersection the course to be followed by vehicles turning thereat, and it shall be unlawful for any driver to fail to turn in a manner as so directed.

History: 1937, c. 407, s. 115; 1955, c. 913, s. 5; 1973, c. 1330, s. 18; 1977, c. 464, s. 34; 1997-405, s. 1.

§ 20-154. Signals on starting, stopping or turning

(a) The driver of any vehicle upon a highway or public vehicular area before starting, stopping or turning from a direct line shall first see that such movement can be made in safety, and if any pedestrian may be affected by such movement shall give a clearly audible signal by sounding the horn, and whenever the operation of any other vehicle may be affected by such movement, shall give a signal as required in this section, plainly visible to the driver of such other vehicle, of the intention to make such movement. The driver of a vehicle shall not back the same unless such movement can be made with safety and without interfering with other traffic.

(b) The signal herein required shall be given by means of the hand and arm in the manner herein specified, or by any mechanical or electrical signal device approved by the Division, except that when a vehicle is so constructed or loaded as to prevent the hand and arm signal from being visible, both to the front and rear, the signal shall be given by a device of a type which has been approved by the Division.

Whenever the signal is given the driver shall indicate his intention to start, stop, or turn by extending the hand and arm from and beyond the left side of the vehicle as hereinafter set forth.

Left turn—hand and arm horizontal, forefinger pointing.

Right turn—hand and arm pointed upward.

Stop—hand and arm pointed downward.

All hand and arm signals shall be given from the left side of the vehicle and all signals shall be maintained or given continuously for the last 100 feet traveled prior to stopping or making a turn. Provided, that in all areas where the speed limit is 45 miles per hour or higher and the operator intends to turn from a direct line of travel, a signal of intention to turn from a direct line of travel shall be given continuously during the last 200 feet traveled before turning.

Any motor vehicle in use on a highway shall be equipped with, and required signal shall be given by, a signal lamp or lamps or mechanical signal device when the distance from the center of the top of the steering post to the left outside limit of the body, cab or load of such motor vehicle exceeds 24 inches, or when the distance from the center of the top of the steering post to the rear limit of the body or load thereof exceeds 14 feet. The latter measurement shall apply to any single vehicle, also to any combination of vehicles except combinations operated by farmers in hauling farm products.

(c) No person shall operate over the highways of this State a right-hand-drive motor vehicle or a motor vehicle equipped with the steering mechanism on the right-hand side thereof unless said motor vehicle is equipped with mechanical or electrical signal devices by which the signals for left turns and right turns may be given. Such mechanical or electrical devices shall be approved by the Division.

(d) A violation of this section shall not constitute negligence per se.

History: 1937, c. 407, s. 116; 1949, c. 1016, s. 1; 1951, cc. 293, 360; 1955, c. 1157, s. 9; 1957, c. 488, s. 2; 1965, c. 768; 1973, c. 1330, s. 19; 1975, c. 716, s. 5; 1981, c. 599, s. 4; 1985, c. 96.

§ 20-155. Right-of-way

(a) When two vehicles approach or enter an intersection from different highways at approximately the same time, the driver of the vehicle on the left shall yield the right-of-way to the vehicle on the right.

(b) The driver of a vehicle intending to turn to the left within an intersection or into an alley, private road, or driveway shall yield the right-of-way to any vehicle approaching from the opposite direction which is within the intersection or so close as to constitute an immediate hazard.

(c) The driver of any vehicle upon a highway within a business or residence district shall yield the right-of-way to a pedestrian crossing such highway within any clearly marked crosswalk, or any regular pedestrian crossing included in the prolongation of the lateral boundary lines of the adjacent sidewalk at the end of a block, except at intersections where the movement of traffic is being regulated by traffic officers or traffic direction devices.

(d) The driver of any vehicle approaching but not having entered a traffic circle shall yield the right-of-way to a vehicle already within such traffic circle.

History: 1937, c. 407, s. 117; 1949, c. 1016, s. 2; 1955, c. 913, ss. 6, 7; 1967, c. 1053; 1973, c. 1330, s. 20.

§ 20-156. Exceptions to the right-of-way rule

(a) The driver of a vehicle about to enter or cross a highway from an alley, building entrance, private road, or driveway shall yield the right-of-way to all vehicles approaching on the highway to be entered.

(b) The driver of a vehicle upon the highway shall yield the right-of-way to police and fire department vehicles and public and private ambulances, vehicles used by an organ procurement organization or agency for the recovery or transportation of human tissues and organs for transplantation or a vehicle operated by a transplant coordinator who is an employee of an organ procurement organization or agency when the transplant coordinator is responding to a call to recover or transport human tissues or organs for transplantation, and to rescue squad emergency service vehicles and vehicles operated by county fire marshals and civil preparedness coordinators when the operators of said vehicles are giving a warning signal by appropriate light and by bell, siren or exhaust whistle audible under normal conditions from a distance not less than 1,000 feet. When appropriate warning signals are being given, as provided in this subsection, an emergency vehicle may proceed through an intersection or other place when the emergency vehicle is facing a stop sign, a yield sign, or a traffic light which is emitting a flashing strobe signal or a beam of steady or flashing red light. This provision shall not operate to relieve the driver of a police or fire department vehicle or public or private ambulance or vehicles used by an organ procurement organization or agency for the recovery or transportation of human tissues and organs for transplantation or a vehicle operated by a transplant coordinator who is an employee of an organ procurement organization or agency when the transplant coordinator is responding to a call to recover or transport human tissues or organs for transplantation, or rescue squad emergency service vehicle or county fire marshals or civil preparedness coordinators from the duty to drive with due regard for the safety of all persons using the highway, nor shall it protect the driver of any such vehicle or county fire marshal or civil preparedness coordinator from the consequence of any arbitrary exercise of such right-of-way.

History: 1937, c. 407, s. 118; 1971, cc. 78, 106; 1973, c. 1330, s. 21; 1977, c. 52, s. 4; c. 438, s. 3; 1985, c. 427; 1989, c. 537, s. 3.

§ 20-157. Approach of police, fire department or rescue squad vehicles or ambulances; driving over fire hose or blocking fire-fighting equipment; parking, etc., near police, fire department, or rescue squad vehicle or ambulance

(a) Upon the approach of any police or fire department vehicle or public or private ambulance or rescue squad emergency service vehicle giving warning signal by appropriate light and by audible bell, siren or exhaust whistle, audible under normal conditions from a distance not less than 1000 feet, the driver of every other vehicle shall immediately drive the same to a position as near as possible and parallel to the right-hand edge or curb, clear of any intersection of streets or highways, and shall stop and remain in such position unless otherwise directed by a police or traffic officer until police or fire department vehicle or public or private ambulance or rescue squad emergency service vehicle shall have passed. Provided, however, this subsection shall not apply to vehicles traveling in the opposite direction of the vehicles herein enumerated when traveling on a four-lane limited access highway with a median divider dividing the highway for vehicles traveling in opposite directions, and provided further that the violation of this subsection shall not be negligence per se. Violation of this subsection is a Class 2 misdemeanor.

(b) It shall be unlawful for the driver of any vehicle other than one on official business to follow any fire apparatus traveling in response to a fire alarm closer than one block or to drive into or park such vehicle within one block where fire apparatus has stopped in answer to a fire alarm.

(c) Outside of the corporate limits of any city or town it shall be unlawful for the driver of any vehicle other than one on official business to follow any fire apparatus traveling in response to a fire alarm closer than 400 feet or to drive into or park such vehicle within a space of 400 feet from where fire apparatus has stopped in answer to a fire alarm.

(d) It shall be unlawful to drive a motor vehicle over a fire hose or any other equipment that is being used at a fire at any time, or to block a fire-fighting apparatus or any other equipment from its source of supply regardless of its distance from the fire.

(e) It shall be unlawful for the driver of a vehicle, other than one on official business, to park and leave standing such vehicle within 100 feet of police or fire department vehicles, public or private ambulances, or rescue squad emergency vehicles which are engaged in the investigation of an accident or engaged in rendering assistance to victims of such accident.

History: 1937, c. 407, s. 119; 1955, cc. 173, 744; 1971, c. 366, ss. 1, 2; 1985, c. 764, s. 31; 1985 (Reg. Sess., 1986), c. 852, s. 17; 1993, c. 539, s. 372; 1994, Ex. Sess., c. 24, s. 14(c).

§ 20-158. Vehicle control signs and signals

(a) The Department of Transportation, with reference to State highways, and local authorities, with reference to highways under their jurisdiction, are hereby authorized to control vehicles:

(1) At intersections, by erecting or installing stop signs requiring vehicles to come to a complete stop at the entrance to that portion of the intersection designated as the main traveled or through highway. Stop signs may also be erected at three or more entrances to an intersection.

(2) At appropriate places other than intersections, by erecting or installing stop signs requiring vehicles to come to a complete stop.

(3) At intersections and other appropriate places, by erecting or installing steady-beam stoplights and other traffic control devices, signs, or signals. All steady-beam stoplights emitting alternate red and green lights shall be arranged so that the red light shall appear at the top of the signaling unit and the green light shall appear at the bottom of the signaling unit.

(4) At intersections and other appropriate places, by erecting or installing flashing red or yellow lights.

(b) Control of Vehicles at Intersections.

(1) When a stop sign has been erected or installed at an intersection, it shall be unlawful for the driver of any vehicle to fail to stop in obedience thereto and yield the right-of-way to vehicles operating on the designated main-traveled or through highway. When stop signs have been erected at three or more entrances to an intersection, the driver, after stopping in obedience thereto, may proceed with caution.

(2) Vehicles facing a red light controlling traffic passing straight through an intersection from a steady or strobe beam stoplight shall not enter the intersection while the steady or strobe beam stoplight is emitting a red light controlling traffic passing straight through an intersection; provided that, except where prohibited by an appropriate sign, vehicular traffic facing a red light controlling traffic passing straight through an intersection, after coming to a complete stop at the intersection, may enter the intersection to make a right turn but such vehicle shall yield the right-of-way to pedestrians and to other traffic using the intersection. When the stoplight is emitting a steady yellow circular light on a traffic signal controlling traffic passing straight through an intersection or a steady yellow arrow light on a traffic signal controlling traffic turning at an intersection, vehicles facing the yellow light are warned that the related green light is being terminated or a red light will be immediately forthcoming. When the stoplight is

emitting a steady green light, vehicles may proceed with due care through the intersection subject to the rights of pedestrians and other vehicles as may otherwise be provided by law.

(3) When a flashing red light has been erected or installed at an intersection, approaching vehicles facing the red light shall stop and yield the right-of-way to vehicles in or approaching the intersection. The right to proceed shall be subject to the rules applicable to making a stop at a stop sign.

(4) When a flashing yellow light has been erected or installed at an intersection, approaching vehicles facing the yellow flashing light may proceed through the intersection with caution, yielding the right-of-way to vehicles in or approaching the intersection.

(5) When a stop sign, stoplight, flashing light, or other traffic-control device authorized by subsection (a) requires a vehicle to stop at an intersection, the driver shall stop at an appropriately marked stop line, or if none, before entering a marked crosswalk, or if none, before entering the intersection at the point nearest the intersecting street where the driver has a view of approaching traffic on the intersecting street.

(c) Control of Vehicles at Places other than Intersections.

(1) When a stop sign has been erected or installed at a place other than an intersection, it shall be unlawful for the driver of any vehicle to fail to stop in obedience thereto and yield the right-of-way to pedestrians and other vehicles.

(2) When a stoplight has been erected or installed at a place other than an intersection, and is emitting a steady red light, vehicles facing the red light shall come to a complete stop. When the stoplight is emitting a steady yellow light, vehicles facing the light shall be warned that a red light will be immediately forthcoming and that vehicles may not proceed through such a red light. When the stoplight is emitting a steady green light, vehicles may proceed subject to the rights of pedestrians and other vehicles as may otherwise be provided by law.

(3) When a flashing red light has been erected or installed at a place other than an intersection, approaching vehicles facing the light shall stop and yield the right-of-way to pedestrians or other vehicles.

(4) When a flashing yellow light has been erected or installed at a place other than an intersection, approaching vehicles facing the light may proceed with caution, yielding the right-of-way to pedestrians and other vehicles.

(5) When a stoplight, stop sign, or other signaling device authorized by subsection (a) requires a vehicle to stop at a place other than an intersection, the driver shall stop at an appropriately marked stop line, or if none, before entering a marked crosswalk, or if none, before proceeding past the signaling device.

(d) No failure to stop as required by the provisions of this section shall be considered negligence or contributory negligence per se in any action at law for injury to person or property, but the facts relating to such failure to stop may be considered with the other facts in the case in determining whether a party was guilty of negligence or contributory negligence.

History: 1937, c. 407, s. 120; 1941, c. 83; 1949, c. 583, s. 2; 1955, c. 384, s. 1; c. 913, s. 7; 1957, c. 65, s. 11; 1973, c. 507, s. 5; c. 1191; c. 1330, s. 22; 1975, c. 1; 1977, c. 464, s. 34; 1979, c. 298, s. 1; 1989, c. 285.

§ 20-158.1. Erection of "yield right-of-way" signs

The Department of Transportation, with reference to State highways, and cities and towns with reference to highways and streets under their jurisdiction, are authorized to designate main-traveled or through highways and streets by erecting at the entrance thereto from intersecting highways or streets, signs notifying drivers of vehicles to yield the right-of-way to drivers of vehicles approaching the intersection on the main-traveled or through highway. Notwithstanding any other provisions of this Chapter, except G.S. 20-156, whenever any such yield right-of-way signs have been so erected, it shall be unlawful for the driver of any vehicle to enter or cross such main-traveled or through highway or street unless he shall first slow down and yield right-of-way to any vehicle in movement on the main-traveled or through highway or street which is approaching so as to arrive at the intersection at approximately the same time as the vehicle entering the main-traveled or through highway or street. No failure to so yield the right-of-way shall be considered negligence or contributory negligence per se in any action at law for injury to person or property, but the facts relating to such failure to yield the right-of-way may be considered with the other facts in the case in determining whether either party in such action was guilty of negligence or contributory negligence.

History: 1955, c. 295; 1957, c. 65, s. 11; 1973, c. 507, s. 5; c. 1330, s. 23; 1977, c. 464, s. 34.

§ 20-160. Driving through safety zone or on sidewalks prohibited

(a) The driver of a vehicle shall not at any time drive through or over a safety zone.

(b) No person shall drive any motor vehicle upon a sidewalk or sidewalk area except upon a permanent or temporary driveway.

History: 1937, c. 407, s. 122; 1973, c. 1330, s. 24.

§ 20-161. Stopping on highway prohibited; warning signals; removal of vehicles from public highway

(a) No person shall park or leave standing any vehicle, whether attended or unattended, upon the paved or main-traveled portion of any highway or highway bridge outside municipal corporate limits unless the vehicle is disabled to such an extent that it is impossible to avoid stopping and temporarily leaving the vehicle upon the paved or main traveled portion of the highway or highway bridge.

(b) No person shall park or leave standing any vehicle upon the shoulder of a public highway outside municipal corporate limits unless the vehicle can be clearly seen by approaching drivers from a distance of 200 feet in both directions and does not obstruct the normal movement of traffic.

(c) The operator of any truck, truck tractor, trailer or semitrailer which is disabled upon any portion of the highway shall display warning devices of a type and in a manner as required under the rules and regulations of the United States Department of Transportation as adopted by the Division of Motor Vehicles. Such warning devices shall be displayed as long as the vehicle is disabled.

(d) The owner of any vehicle parked or left standing in violation of law shall be deemed to have appointed any investigating law-enforcement officer his agent:

(1) For the purpose of removing the vehicle to the shoulder of the highway or to some other suitable place; and

(2) For the purpose of arranging for the transportation and safe storage of any vehicle which is interfering with the regular flow of traffic or which otherwise constitutes a hazard, in which case the officer shall be deemed a legal possessor of the vehicle within the meaning of G.S. 44A-2(d).

(e) When any vehicle is parked or left standing upon the right-of-way of a public highway for a period of 48 hours or more, the owner shall be deemed to have appointed any investigating law-enforcement officer his agent for the purpose of arranging for the transportation and safe storage of such vehicle and such investigating law-enforcement officer shall be deemed a legal possessor of the motor vehicle within the meaning of that term as it appears in G.S. 44A-2(d).

History: 1937, c. 407, s. 123; 1951, c. 1165, s. 1; 1971, c. 294, s. 1; 1973, c. 1330, s. 25; 1985, c. 454, s. 6.

§ 20-161.1. Regulation of night parking on highways

No person parking or leaving standing a vehicle at night on a highway or on a side road entering into a highway shall permit the bright lights of said vehicle to continue burning when such lights face oncoming traffic.

History: 1953, c. 1052.

§ 20-162. Parking in front of private driveway, fire hydrant, fire station, intersection of curb lines or fire lane

(a) No person shall park a vehicle or permit it to stand, whether attended or unattended, upon a highway in front of a private driveway or within 15 feet in either direction of a fire hydrant or the entrance to a fire station, nor within 25 feet from the intersection of curb lines or if none, then within 15 feet of the intersection of property lines at an intersection of highways; provided, that local authorities may by ordinance decrease the distance within which a vehicle may park in either direction of a fire hydrant.

(b) No person shall park a vehicle or permit it to stand, whether attended or unattended, upon any public vehicular area, street, highway or roadway in any area designated as a fire lane. This prohibition includes designated fire lanes in shopping center or mall parking lots and all other public vehicular areas. Provided, however, persons loading or unloading supplies or merchandise may park temporarily in a fire lane located in a shopping center or mall parking lot as long as the vehicle is not left unattended. The prima facie rule of evidence created by G.S. 20-162.1 is applicable to prosecutions for violation of this section. The owner of a vehicle parked in violation of this subsection shall be deemed to have appointed any State, county or municipal law-enforcement officer as his agent for the purpose of arranging for the transportation and safe storage of such vehicle. No law-enforcement officer removing such a vehicle shall be held criminally or civilly liable in any way for any acts or omissions arising out of or caused by carrying out or enforcing any provisions of this subsection, unless the conduct of the officer amounts to wanton misconduct or intentional wrongdoing.

History: 1937, c. 407, s. 124; 1939, c. 111; 1979, c. 552; 1981, c. 574, s. 1.

§ 20-162.1. Prima facie rule of evidence for enforcement of parking regulations

(a) Whenever evidence shall be presented in any court of the fact that any automobile, truck, or other vehicle was found upon any street, alley or other public place contrary to and in violation of the provisions of any statute or of any municipal or Department of Transportation ordinance limiting the time during which any such vehicle may be parked or prohibiting or otherwise regulating the parking of any such vehicle, it shall be prima facie evidence in any court in the State of North Carolina that such vehicle was parked and left upon such street, alley or public way or place by the person, firm or corporation in whose name such vehicle is then registered and licensed according to the records of the department or agency of the State of North Carolina, by whatever name designated, which is empowered to register such vehicles and to issue licenses for their operation upon the streets and highways of this State; provided, that no evidence tendered or presented under the authorization contained in this section shall be admissible or competent in any respect in any court or tribunal, except in cases concerned solely with violation of statutes or ordinances limiting, prohibiting or otherwise regulating the parking of automobiles or other vehicles upon public streets, highways, or other public places.

Any person found responsible for an infraction pursuant to this section shall be subject to a penalty of not more than five dollars ($5.00).

(b) The prima facie rule of evidence established by subsection (a) shall not apply to the registered owner of a leased or rented vehicle parked in violation of law when said owner can furnish sworn evidence that the vehicle was, at the time of the parking violation, leased or rented, to another person. In such instances, the owner of the vehicle shall, within a reasonable time after notification of the parking violation, furnish to the courts the name and address of the person or company who leased or rented the vehicle.

History: 1953, c. 879, ss. 1, 1 1/2; c. 978; 1983, c. 753; 1985, c. 764, s. 32; 1985 (Reg. Sess., 1986), c. 852, s. 17; 1987, c. 736, s. 1; 1989, c. 243, s. 2.

§ 20-163. Unattended motor vehicles

No person driving or in charge of a motor vehicle shall permit it to stand unattended on a public highway or public vehicular area without first stopping the engine, effectively setting the brake thereon and, when standing upon any grade, turning the front wheels to the curb or side of the highway.

History: 1937, c. 407, s. 125; 1973, c. 1330, s. 26.

§ 20-165.1. One-way traffic

In all cases where the Department of Transportation has heretofore, or may hereafter lawfully designate any highway or other separate roadway, under its jurisdiction for one-way traffic and shall erect appropriate signs giving notice thereof, it shall be unlawful for any person to willfully drive or operate any vehicle on said highway or roadway except in the direction so indicated by said signs.

History: 1957, c. 1177; 1973, c. 507, s. 5; c. 1330, s. 28; 1977, c. 464, s. 34.

§ 20-166. Duty to stop in event of accident or collision; furnishing information or assistance to injured person, etc.; persons assisting exempt from civil liability

(a) The driver of any vehicle who knows or reasonably should know:

(1) That the vehicle which he is operating is involved in an accident or collision; and

(2) That the accident or collision has resulted in injury or death to any person;

shall immediately stop his vehicle at the scene of the accident or collision. He shall remain at the scene of the accident until a law-enforcement officer completes his investigation of the accident or collision or authorizes him to leave; Provided, however, that he may leave to call for a law-enforcement officer or for medical assistance or medical treatment as set forth in (b), but must return to the accident scene within a reasonable period of time. A willful violation of this subsection shall be punished as a Class H felony.

(b) In addition to complying with the requirement of (a), the driver as set forth in (a) shall give his name, address, driver's license number and the license plate number of his vehicle to the person struck or the driver or occupants of any vehicle collided with, provided that such person or persons are physically and mentally capable of receiving such information, and shall render to any person injured in such accident or collision reasonable assistance, including the calling for medical assistance if it is apparent that such assistance is necessary or is requested by the injured person. A violation of this subsection is a Class 1 misdemeanor.

(c) The driver of any vehicle, when he knows or reasonably should know that the vehicle which he is operating is involved in an accident or collision, which accident or collision, results:

(1) Only in damage to property; or

(2) In injury or death to any person, but only if the operator of the vehicle did not know and did not have reason to know of the death or injury;

shall immediately stop his vehicle at the scene of the accident or collision. A violation of this subsection is a Class 1 misdemeanor.

(c1) In addition to complying with the requirement of (c), the driver as set forth in (c) shall give his name, address, driver's license number and the license plate number of his vehicle to the driver or occupants of any other vehicle involved in the accident or collision or to any person whose property is damaged in the accident or collision. If the damaged property is a parked and unattended vehicle and the name and location of the owner is not known to or readily ascertainable by the driver of the responsible vehicle, the said driver shall furnish the information required by this subsection to the nearest available peace officer, or, in the alternative, and provided he thereafter within 48 hours fully complies with G.S. 20-166.1(c), shall immediately place a paper-writing containing said information in a conspicuous place upon or in the damaged vehicle. If the damaged property is a guardrail, utility pole, or other fixed object owned by the Department of Transportation, a public utility, or other public service corporation to which report cannot readily be made at the scene, it shall be sufficient if the responsible driver shall furnish the information required to the nearest peace officer or make written report thereof containing said information by U.S. certified mail, return receipt requested, to the North Carolina Division of Motor Vehicles within five days following said collision. A violation of this subsection is a Class 1 misdemeanor.

(d) Any person who renders first aid or emergency assistance at the scene of a motor vehicle accident on any street or highway to any person injured as a result of such accident, shall not be liable in civil damages for any acts or omissions relating to such services rendered, unless such acts or omissions amount to wanton conduct or intentional wrongdoing.

History: 1937, c. 407, s. 128; 1939, c. 10, ss. 1, 1 1/2; 1943, c. 439; 1951, cc. 309, 794, 823; 1953, cc. 394, 793; c. 1340, s. 1; 1955, c. 913, s. 8; 1965, c. 176; 1967, c. 445; 1971, c. 958, s. 1; 1973, c. 507, s. 5; 1975, c. 716, s. 5; 1977, c. 464, s. 34; 1979, c. 667, s. 32; 1983, c. 912, s. 1; 1985, c. 324, ss. 1–4; 1993, c. 539, ss. 373–375, 1260; 1994, Ex. Sess., c. 24, s. 14(c).

§ 20-166.1. Reports and investigations required in event of accident

(a) Notice of Accident.—The driver of a vehicle involved in a reportable accident must immediately, by the quickest means of communication, notify the appropriate law enforcement agency of the accident. If the accident occurred in a city or town, the appropriate agency is the police department of the city or town. If the accident occurred outside a city or town, the appropriate agency is the State Highway Patrol or the sheriff's office or other qualified rural police of the county where the accident occurred.

(b) Insurance Verification.—When requested to do so by the Division, the driver of a vehicle involved in a reportable accident must furnish proof of financial responsibility.

(c) Parked Vehicle.—The driver of a motor vehicle that collides with another motor vehicle left parked or unattended on a highway of this State must report the collision to the owner of the parked or unattended motor vehicle. This requirement applies to an accident that is not a reportable accident as well as to one that is a reportable accident. The report may be made orally or in writing, must be made within 48 hours of the accident, and must include the following:

(1) The time, date, and place of the accident.

(2) The driver's name, address, and driver's license number.

(3) The registration plate number of the vehicle being operated by the driver at the time of the accident.

If the driver makes a written report to the owner of the parked or unattended vehicle and the report is not given to the owner at the scene of the accident, the report must be sent to the owner by certified mail, return receipt requested, and a copy of the report must be sent to the Division.

(d) Repealed by Session Laws 1995, c. 191, s. 2.

(e) Investigation by Officer.—The appropriate law enforcement agency must investigate a reportable accident. A law-enforcement officer who investigates a reportable accident, whether at the scene of the accident or by subsequent investigations and interviews, must make a written report of the accident within 24 hours of the accident and must forward it as required by this subsection. The report must contain information on financial responsibility for the vehicle driven by the person whom the officer identified as at fault for the accident.

If the officer writing the report is a member of the State Highway Patrol, the officer must forward the report to the Division. If the officer is not a member of the State Highway Patrol, the officer must forward the report to the local law enforcement agency for the area where the accident occurred. A local law enforcement agency that receives an accident report must forward it to the Division within 10 days after receiving the report.

When a person injured in a reportable accident dies as a result of the accident within 12 months after the accident and the death was not reported in the original report, the law enforcement officer investigating the accident must file a supplemental report that includes the death.

(f) Medical Personnel.—A county medical examiner must report to the Division the death of any person in a reportable accident and the circumstances of the accident. The medical examiner must file the report within five days after the death. A hospital must notify the medical examiner of the county in which the accident occurred of the death within the hospital of any person who dies as a result of injuries apparently sustained in a reportable accident.

(g) Repealed by Session Laws 1987, c. 49.

(h) Forms.—The Division shall provide forms or procedures for submitting crash data to persons required to make reports under this section and the reports shall be made in a format approved by the Commissioner. The following information shall be included about a reportable crash:

(1) The cause of the crash.
(2) The conditions existing at the time of the crash.
(3) The persons and vehicles involved.
(4) Whether the vehicle has been seized and is subject to forfeiture under G.S. 20-28.2.

(i) Effect of Report.—A report of an accident made under this section by a person who is not a law enforcement officer is without prejudice, is for the use of the Division, and shall not be used in any manner as evidence, or for any other purpose in any trial, civil or criminal, arising out of the accident. Any other report of an accident made under this section may be used in any manner as evidence, or for any other purpose, in any trial, civil or criminal, as permitted under the rules of evidence. At the demand of a court, the Division must give the court a properly executed certificate stating that a particular accident report has or has not been filed with the Division solely to prove a compliance with this section.

The reports made by persons who are not law enforcement officers or medical examiners are not public records. The reports made by law enforcement officers and medical examiners are public records and are open to inspection by the general public at all reasonable times. The Division must give a certified copy of one of these reports to a member of the general public who requests a copy and pays the fee set in G.S. 20-42.

(j) Statistics.—The Division may periodically publish statistical information on motor vehicle accidents based on information in accident reports. The Division may conduct detailed research to determine more fully the cause and control of accidents and may conduct experimental field tests within areas of the State from time to time to prove the practicability of various ideas advanced in traffic control and accident prevention.

(k) Punishment.—A violation of any provision of this section is a misdemeanor of the Class set in G.S. 20-176.

History: 1953, c. 1340, s. 2; 1955, c. 913, s. 9; 1963, c. 1249; 1965, c. 577; 1971, c. 55; c. 763, s. 1; c. 958, ss. 2, 3; 1973, c. 1133, ss. 1, 2; c. 1330, s. 29; 1975, c. 307; c. 716, s. 5; 1979, c. 667, s. 33; 1981, c. 690, s. 14; 1983, c. 229, ss. 1, 2; 1985, c. 764, s. 33; 1985 (Reg. Sess., 1986), c. 852, s. 17; 1987, c. 49; 1993, c. 539, ss. 376, 377; 1994, Ex. Sess., c. 24, s. 14(c); 1995, c. 191, s. 2; 1998-182, s. 12.1; 1999-452, s. 19.

§ 20-169. Powers of local authorities

Local authorities, except as expressly authorized by G.S. 20-141 and 20-158, shall have no power or authority to alter any speed limitations declared in this Article or to enact or enforce any rules or regulations contrary to the provisions of this Article, except that local authorities shall have power to provide by ordinances for any of the following:

(1) Regulating traffic by means of traffic or semaphores or other signaling devices on any portion of the highway where traffic is heavy or continuous.
(2) Prohibiting other than one-way traffic upon certain highways.
(3) Regulating the use of the highways by processions or assemblages.
(4) Regulating the speed of vehicles on highways in public parks.
(5) Authorizing law enforcement or fire department vehicles, ambulances, and rescue squad emergency service vehicles, equipped with a siren to preempt any traffic signals upon city streets within local authority boundaries or, with the approval of the Department of Transportation, on State highways within the boundaries of local authorities. The Department of Transportation shall respond to requests for approval within 60 days of receipt of a request.

Signs shall be erected giving notices of the special limits and regulations under subdivisions (1) through (4) of this section.

History: 1937, c. 407, s. 131; 1949, c. 947, s. 2; 1955, c. 384, s. 2; 1963, c. 559; 1973, c. 507, s. 5; 1979, c. 298, s. 2; 1991, c. 530, s. 5; 1999-310, s. 1.

§ 20-171. Traffic laws apply to persons riding animals or driving animal-drawn vehicles

Every person riding an animal or driving any animal drawing a vehicle upon a highway shall be subject to the provisions of this Article applicable to the driver of a vehicle, except those provisions of the Article which by their nature can have no application.

History: 1939, c. 275.

Part 11. Pedestrians' Rights and Duties

§ 20-172. Pedestrians subject to traffic-control signals

(a) The Board of Transportation, with reference to State highways, and local authorities, with reference to highways under their jurisdiction, are hereby authorized to erect or install, at intersections or other appropriate places, special pedestrian control signals exhibiting the words or symbols "WALK" or "DON'T WALK" as a part of a system of traffic-control signals or devices.

(b) Whenever special pedestrian-control signals are in place, such signals shall indicate as follows:

(1) WALK.—Pedestrians facing such signal may proceed across the highway in the direction of the signal and shall be given the right-of-way by the drivers of all vehicles.
(2) DON'T WALK.—No pedestrian shall start to cross the highway in the direction of such signal, but any pedestrian who has partially completed his crossing on the "WALK" signal shall proceed to a sidewalk or safety island while the "DON'T WALK" signal is showing.

(c) Where a system of traffic-control signals or devices does not include special pedestrian-control signals, pedestrians shall be subject to the vehicular traffic-control signals or devices as they apply to pedestrian traffic.

(d) At places without traffic-control signals or devices, pedestrians shall be accorded the privileges and shall be subject to the restrictions stated in Part 11 of this Article.

History: 1937, c. 407, s. 133; 1973, c. 507, s. 5; c. 1330, s. 31; 1987, c. 125.

§ 20-173. Pedestrians' right-of-way at crosswalks

(a) Where traffic-control signals are not in place or in operation the driver of a vehicle shall yield the right-of-way, slowing down or stopping if need be to so yield, to a pedestrian crossing the roadway within any marked crosswalk or within any unmarked crosswalk at or near an intersection, except as otherwise provided in Part 11 of this Article.

(b) Whenever any vehicle is stopped at a marked crosswalk or at any unmarked crosswalk at an intersection to permit a pedestrian to cross the roadway, the driver of any other vehicle approaching from the rear shall not overtake and pass such stopped vehicle.

(c) The driver of a vehicle emerging from or entering an alley, building entrance, private road, or driveway shall yield the right-of-way to any pedestrian, or person riding a bicycle, approaching on any sidewalk or walkway extending across such alley, building entrance, road, or driveway.

History: 1937, c. 407, s. 134; 1973, c. 1330, s. 32.

§ 20-174. Crossing at other than crosswalks; walking along highway

(a) Every pedestrian crossing a roadway at any point other than within a marked crosswalk or within an unmarked crosswalk at an intersection shall yield the right-of-way to all vehicles upon the roadway.

(b) Any pedestrian crossing a roadway at a point where a pedestrian tunnel or overhead pedestrian crossing has been provided shall yield the right-of-way to all vehicles upon the roadway.

(c) Between adjacent intersections at which traffic-control signals are in operation pedestrians shall not cross at any place except in a marked crosswalk.

(d) Where sidewalks are provided, it shall be unlawful for any pedestrian to walk along and upon an adjacent roadway. Where sidewalks are not provided, any pedestrian walking along and upon a highway shall, when practicable, walk only on the extreme left of the roadway or its shoulder facing traffic which may approach from the opposite direction. Such pedestrian shall yield the right-of-way to approaching traffic.

(e) Notwithstanding the provisions of this section, every driver of a vehicle shall exercise due care to avoid colliding with any pedestrian upon any roadway, and shall give warning by sounding the horn when necessary, and shall exercise proper precaution upon observing any child or any confused or incapacitated person upon a roadway.

History: 1937, c. 407, s. 135; 1973, c. 1330, s. 33.

§ 20-174.1. Standing, sitting or lying upon highways or streets prohibited

(a) No person shall willfully stand, sit, or lie upon the highway or street in such a manner as to impede the regular flow of traffic.

(b) Violation of this section is a Class 2 misdemeanor.

History: 1965, c. 137; 1969, c. 1012; 1993 (Reg. Sess., 1994), c. 761, s. 17.

§ 20-175. Pedestrians soliciting rides, employment, business or funds upon highways or streets

(a) No person shall stand in any portion of the State highways, except upon the shoulders thereof, for the purpose of soliciting a ride from the driver of any motor vehicle.

(b) No person shall stand or loiter in the main traveled portion, including the shoulders and median, of any State highway or street, excluding sidewalks, or stop any motor vehicle for the purpose of soliciting employment, business or contributions from the driver or occupant of any motor vehicle that impedes the normal movement of traffic on the public highways or streets: Provided that the provisions of this subsection shall not apply to licensees, employees or contractors of the Department of Transportation or of any municipality engaged in construction or maintenance or in making traffic or engineering surveys.

(c) Repealed by Session Laws 1973, c. 1330, s. 39.

History: 1937, c. 407, s. 136; 1965, c. 673; 1973, c. 507, s. 5; c. 1330, s. 39; 1977, c. 464, s. 34.

Part 12. Sentencing; Penalties

§ 20-176. Penalty for misdemeanor or infraction

(a) Violation of a provision of Part 9, 10, 10A, or 11 of this Article is an infraction unless the violation is specifically declared by law to be a misdemeanor or felony. Violation of the remaining Parts of this Article is a misdemeanor unless the violation is specifically declared by law to be an infraction or a felony.

(b) Unless a specific penalty is otherwise provided by law, a person found responsible for an infraction contained in this Article may be ordered to pay a penalty of not more than one hundred dollars ($100.00).

(c) Unless a specific penalty is otherwise provided by law, a person convicted of a misdemeanor contained in this Article is guilty of a Class 2 misdemeanor. A punishment is specific for purposes of this subsection if it contains a quantitative limit on the term of imprisonment or the amount of fine a judge can impose.

(c1) Notwithstanding any other provision of law, no person convicted of a misdemeanor for the violation of any provision of this Chapter except G.S. 20-28(a) and (b), G.S. 20-141(j), G.S. 20-141.3(b) and (c), G.S. 20-141.4, or a second or subsequent conviction of G.S. 20-138.1 shall be imprisoned in the State prison system unless the person previously has been imprisoned in a local confinement facility, as defined by G.S. 153A-217(5), for a violation of this Chapter.

(d) For purposes of determining whether a violation of an offense contained in this Chapter constitutes negligence per se, crimes and infractions shall be treated identically.

History: 1937, c. 407, s. 137; 1951, c. 1013, s. 7; 1957, c. 1255; 1967, c. 674, s. 3; 1969, c. 378, s. 3; 1973, c. 1330, s. 34; 1975, c. 644; 1985, c. 764, s. 20; 1985 (Reg. Sess., 1986), c. 852, ss. 7, 17; c. 1014, s. 202; 1993, c. 539, s. 379; 1994, Ex. Sess., c. 24, s. 14(c).

§ 20-177. Penalty for felony

Any person who shall be convicted of a violation of any of the provisions of this Article herein or by the laws of this State declared to constitute a felony shall, unless a different penalty is prescribed herein or by the laws of this State, be punished as a Class I felon.

History: 1937, c. 407, s. 138; 1979, c. 760, s. 5; 1979, 2d Sess., c. 1316, s. 47; 1981, c. 63, s. 1; c. 179, s. 14.

§ 20-179. Sentencing hearing after conviction for impaired driving; determination of grossly aggravating and aggravating and mitigating factors; punishments

(a) Sentencing Hearing Required.—After a conviction for impaired driving under G.S. 20-138.1, G.S. 20-138.2, a second or subsequent conviction under G.S. 20-138.2A, or a second or subsequent conviction under G.S. 20-138.2B, the judge must hold a sentencing hearing to determine whether there are aggravating or mitigating factors that affect the sentence to be imposed. Before the hearing the prosecutor must make all feasible efforts to secure the defendant's full record of traffic convictions, and must present to the judge that record for consideration in the hearing. Upon request of the defendant, the prosecutor must furnish the defendant or his attorney a copy of the defendant's record of traffic convictions at a reasonable time prior to the introduction of the record into evidence. In addition, the prosecutor must present all other appropriate grossly aggravating and aggravating factors of which he is aware, and the defendant or his attorney may present all appropriate mitigating factors. In every instance in which a valid chemical analysis is made of the defendant, the prosecutor must present evidence of the resulting alcohol concentration.

(b) Repealed by Session Laws 1983, c. 435, s. 29.

(c) Determining Existence of Grossly Aggravating Factors.—At the sentencing hearing, based upon the evidence presented at trial and in the hearing, the judge must first determine whether there are any grossly aggravating factors in the case. The judge must impose the Level One punishment under subsection (g) of this section if the judge determines that two or more grossly aggravating factors apply. The judge must impose the Level Two punishment under subsection (h) of this section if the judge determines that only one of the grossly aggravating factors applies. The grossly aggravating factors are:

(1) A prior conviction for an offense involving impaired driving if:
   a. The conviction occurred within seven years before the date of the offense for which the defendant is being sentenced; or
   b. The conviction occurs after the date of the offense for which the defendant is presently being sentenced, but prior to or contemporaneously with the present sentencing.

Each prior conviction is a separate grossly aggravating factor.

(2) Driving by the defendant at the time of the offense while his driver's license was revoked under G.S. 20-28, and the revocation was an impaired driving revocation under G.S. 20-28.2(a).

(3) Serious injury to another person caused by the defendant's impaired driving at the time of the offense.

(4) Driving by the defendant while a child under the age of 16 years was in the vehicle at the time of the offense.

In imposing a Level One or Two punishment, the judge may consider the aggravating and mitigating factors in subsections (d) and (e) in determining the appropriate sentence. If there are no grossly aggravating factors in the case, the judge must weigh all aggravating and mitigating factors and impose punishment as required by subsection (f).

(d) Aggravating Factors to Be Weighed.—The judge must determine before sentencing under subsection (f) whether any of the aggravating factors listed below apply to the defendant. The judge must weigh the seriousness of each aggravating factor in the light of the particular circumstances of the case. The factors are:

(1) Gross impairment of the defendant's faculties while driving or an alcohol concentration of 0.16 or more within a relevant time after the driving.

(2) Especially reckless or dangerous driving.

(3) Negligent driving that led to a reportable accident.

(4) Driving by the defendant while his driver's license was revoked.

(5) Two or more prior convictions of a motor vehicle offense not involving impaired driving for which at least three points are assigned under G.S. 20-16 or for which the convicted person's license is subject to revocation, if the convictions occurred within five years of the date of the offense for which the defendant is being sentenced, or one or more prior convictions of an offense involving impaired driving that occurred more than seven years before the date of the offense for which the defendant is being sentenced.

(6) Conviction under G.S. 20-141.5 of speeding by the defendant while fleeing or attempting to elude apprehension.

(7) Conviction under G.S. 20-141 of speeding by the defendant by at least 30 miles per hour over the legal limit.

(8) Passing a stopped school bus in violation of G.S. 20-217.

(9) Any other factor that aggravates the seriousness of the offense.

Except for the factor in subdivision (5) the conduct constituting the aggravating factor must occur during the same transaction or occurrence as the impaired driving offense.

(e) Mitigating Factors to Be Weighed.—The judge must also determine before sentencing under subsection (f) whether any of the mitigating factors listed below apply to the defendant. The judge must weigh the degree of mitigation of each factor in light of the particular circumstances of the case. The factors are:

(1) Slight impairment of the defendant's faculties resulting solely from alcohol, and an alcohol concentration that did not exceed 0.09 at any relevant time after the driving.

(2) Slight impairment of the defendant's faculties, resulting solely from alcohol, with no chemical analysis having been available to the defendant.

(3) Driving at the time of the offense that was safe and lawful except for the impairment of the defendant's faculties.

(4) A safe driving record, with the defendant's having no conviction for any motor vehicle offense for which at least four points are assigned under G.S. 20-16 or for which the person's license is subject to revocation within five years of the date of the offense for which the defendant is being sentenced.

(5) Impairment of the defendant's faculties caused primarily by a lawfully prescribed drug for an existing medical condition, and the amount of the drug taken was within the prescribed dosage.

(6) The defendant's voluntary submission to a mental health facility for assessment after he was charged with the impaired driving offense for which he is being sentenced, and, if recommended by the facility, his voluntary participation in the recommended treatment.

(7) Any other factor that mitigates the seriousness of the offense.

Except for the factors in subdivisions (4), (6) and (7), the conduct constituting the mitigating factor must occur during the same transaction or occurrence as the impaired driving offense.

(f) Weighing the Aggravating and Mitigating Factors.—If the judge in the sentencing hearing determines that there are no grossly aggravating factors, he must weigh all aggravating and mitigating factors listed in subsections (d) and (e). If the judge determines that:

(1) The aggravating factors substantially outweigh any mitigating factors, he must note in the judgment the factors found and his finding that the defendant is subject to the Level Three punishment and impose a punishment within the limits defined in subsection (i).

(2) There are no aggravating and mitigating factors, or that aggravating factors are substantially counterbalanced by mitigating factors, he must note in the judgment any factors found and his finding that the defendant is subject to the Level Four punishment and impose a punishment within the limits defined in subsection (j).

(3) The mitigating factors substantially outweigh any aggravating factors, he must note in the judgment the factors found and his finding that the defendant is subject to the Level Five punishment and impose a punishment within the limits defined in subsection (k).

It is not a mitigating factor that the driver of the vehicle was suffering from alcoholism, drug addiction, diminished capacity, or mental disease or defect. Evidence of these matters may be received in the sentencing hearing, however, for use by the judge in formulating terms and conditions of sentence after determining which punishment level must be imposed.

(f1) Aider and Abettor Punishment.—Notwithstanding any other provisions of this section, a person convicted of impaired driving under G.S. 20-138.1 under the common law concept of aiding and abetting is subject to Level Five punishment. The judge need not make any findings of grossly aggravating, aggravating, or mitigating factors in such cases.

(f2) Limit on Consolidation of Judgments.—Except as provided in subsection (f1), in each charge of impaired driving for which there is a conviction the judge must determine if the sentencing factors described in subsections (c), (d) and (e) are applicable unless the impaired driving charge is consolidated with a charge carrying a greater punishment. Two or more impaired driving charges may not be consolidated for judgment.

(g) Level One Punishment.—A defendant subject to Level One punishment may be fined up to four thousand dollars ($4,000) and shall be sentenced to a term of imprisonment that includes a minimum term of not less than 30 days and a maximum term of not more than 24 months. The term of imprisonment may be suspended only if a condition of special probation is imposed to require the defendant to serve a term of imprisonment of at least 30 days. If the defendant is placed on probation, the judge shall impose a requirement that the defendant obtain a substance abuse assessment and the education or treatment required by G.S. 20-17.6 for the restoration of a driver's license and as a condition of probation. The judge may impose any other lawful condition of probation.

(h) Level Two Punishment.—A defendant subject to Level Two punishment may be fined up to two thousand dollars ($2,000) and shall be sentenced to a term of imprisonment that includes a minimum term of not less than seven days and a maximum term of not more than 12 months. The term of imprisonment may be suspended only if a condition of special probation is imposed to require the defendant to serve a term of imprisonment of at least seven days. If the defendant is placed on probation, the judge shall impose a requirement that the defendant obtain a substance abuse assessment and the education or treatment required by G.S. 20-17.6 for the restoration of a driver's license and as a condition of probation. The judge may impose any other lawful condition of probation.

(i) Level Three Punishment.—A defendant subject to Level Three punishment may be fined up to one thousand dollars ($1,000) and shall be sentenced to a term of imprisonment that includes a minimum term of not less than 72 hours and a maximum term of not more than six months. The term of imprisonment may be suspended. However, the suspended sentence shall include the condition that the defendant:

(1) Be imprisoned for a term of at least 72 hours as a condition of special probation; or
(2) Perform community service for a term of at least 72 hours; or
(3) Not operate a motor vehicle for a term of at least 90 days; or
(4) Any combination of these conditions.

If the defendant is placed on probation, the judge shall impose a requirement that the defendant obtain a substance abuse assessment and the education or treatment required by G.S. 20-17.6 for the restoration of a driver's license and as a condition of probation. The judge may impose any other lawful condition of probation.

(j) Level Four Punishment.—A defendant subject to Level Four punishment may be fined up to five hundred dollars ($500.00) and shall be sentenced to a term of imprisonment that includes a minimum term of not less than 48 hours and a maximum term of not more than 120 days. The term of imprisonment may be suspended. However, the suspended sentence shall include the condition that the defendant:

(1) Be imprisoned for a term of 48 hours as a condition of special probation; or
(2) Perform community service for a term of 48 hours; or
(3) Not operate a motor vehicle for a term of 60 days; or
(4) Any combination of these conditions.

If the defendant is placed on probation, the judge shall impose a requirement that the defendant obtain a substance abuse assessment and the education or treatment required by G.S. 20-17.6 for the restoration of a driver's license and as a condition of probation. The judge may impose any other lawful condition of probation.

(k) Level Five Punishment.—A defendant subject to Level Five punishment may be fined up to two hundred dollars ($200.00) and shall be sentenced to a term of imprisonment that includes a minimum term of not less than 24 hours and a maximum term of not more than 60 days. The term of imprisonment may be suspended. However, the suspended sentence shall include the condition that the defendant:

(1) Be imprisoned for a term of 24 hours as a condition of special probation; or
(2) Perform community service for a term of 24 hours; or
(3) Not operate a motor vehicle for a term of 30 days; or
(4) Any combination of these conditions.

If the defendant is placed on probation, the judge shall impose a requirement that the defendant obtain a substance abuse assessment and the education or treatment required by G.S. 20-17.6 for the restoration of a driver's license and as a condition of probation. The judge may impose any other lawful condition of probation.

(k1) Credit for Inpatient Treatment.—Pursuant to G.S. 15A-1351(a), the judge may order that a term of imprisonment imposed as a condition of special probation under any level of punishment be served as an inpatient in a facility operated or licensed by the State for the treatment of alcoholism or substance abuse where the defendant has been accepted for admission or commitment as an inpatient. The defendant shall bear the expense of any treatment unless the trial judge orders that the costs be absorbed by the State. The judge may impose restrictions on the defendant's ability to leave the premises of the treatment facility and require that the defendant follow the rules of the treatment facility. The judge may credit against the active sentence imposed on a defendant the time the defendant was an inpatient at the treatment facility, provided such treatment occurred after the commission of the offense for which the defendant is being sentenced. This section shall not be construed to limit the authority of the judge in sentencing under any other provisions of law.

(l) Repealed by Session Laws 1989, c. 691, s. 3.

(m) Repealed by Session Laws 1995, c. 496, s. 2.

(n) Time Limits for Performance of Community Service.—If the judgment requires the defendant to perform a specified number of hours of community service as provided in subsections (i), (j), or (k), the community service must be completed:

(1) Within 90 days, if the amount of community service required is 72 hours or more; or
(2) Within 60 days, if the amount of community service required is 48 hours; or
(3) Within 30 days, if the amount of community service required is 24 hours.

The court may extend these time limits upon motion of the defendant if it finds that the defendant has made a good faith effort to comply with the time limits specified in this subsection.

(o) Evidentiary Standards; Proof of Prior Convictions.—In the sentencing hearing, the State must prove any grossly aggravating or aggravating factor by the greater weight of the evidence, and the defendant must prove any mitigating factor by the greater weight of the evidence. Evidence adduced by either party at trial may be utilized in the sentencing hearing. Except as modified by this section, the procedure in G.S. 15A-1334(b) governs. The judge may accept any evidence as to the presence or absence of previous convictions that he finds reliable but he must give prima facie effect to convictions recorded by the Division or any other agency of the State of North Carolina. A copy of such conviction records transmitted by the police information network in general accordance with the procedure authorized by G.S. 20-26(b) is admissible in evidence without further authentication. If the judge decides to impose an active sentence of imprisonment that would not have been imposed but for a prior conviction of an offense, the judge must afford the defendant an opportunity to introduce evidence that the prior conviction had been obtained in a case in which he was indigent, had no counsel, and had not waived his right to counsel. If the defendant proves by the preponderance of the evidence all three above facts concerning the prior case, the conviction may not be used as a grossly aggravating or aggravating factor.

(p) Limit on Amelioration of Punishment.—For active terms of imprisonment imposed under this section:

(1) The judge may not give credit to the defendant for the first 24 hours of time spent in incarceration pending trial.
(2) The defendant shall serve the mandatory minimum period of imprisonment and good or gain time credit may not be used to reduce that mandatory minimum period.
(3) The defendant may not be released on parole unless he is otherwise eligible, has served the mandatory minimum period of imprisonment, and has obtained a substance abuse assessment and completed any recommended treatment or training program or is paroled into a residential treatment program.

With respect to the minimum or specific term of imprisonment imposed as a condition of special probation under this section, the judge may not give credit to the defendant for the first 24 hours of time spent in incarceration pending trial.

(q) Repealed by Session Laws 1991, c. 726, s. 20.

(r) Supervised Probation Terminated.—Unless a judge in his discretion determines that supervised probation is necessary, and includes in the record that he has received evidence and finds as a fact that supervised probation is necessary, and states in his judgment that supervised probation is necessary, a defendant convicted of an offense of impaired driving shall be placed on unsupervised probation if he meets three conditions. These conditions are that he has not been convicted of an offense of impaired driving within the seven years preceding the date of this offense for which he is sentenced, that the defendant is sentenced under subsections (i), (j), and (k) of this section, and has obtained any necessary substance abuse assessment and completed any recommended treatment or training program.

When a judge determines in accordance with the above procedures that a defendant should be placed on supervised probation, the judge shall authorize the probation officer to modify the defendant's probation by placing the defendant on unsupervised probation upon the completion by the defendant of the following conditions of his suspended sentence:

(1) Community service; or
(2) Repealed by Session Laws 1995 c. 496, s. 2.
(3) Payment of any fines, court costs, and fees; or
(4) Any combination of these conditions.

(s) Method of Serving Sentence.—The judge in his discretion may order a term of imprisonment or community service to be served on weekends, even if the sentence cannot be served in consecutive sequence.

(t) Repealed by Session Laws 1995, c. 496, s. 2.

History: 1937, c. 407, s. 140; 1947, c. 1067, s. 18; 1967, c. 510; 1969, c. 50; c. 1283, ss. 1–5; 1971, c. 619, s. 16; c. 1133, s. 1; 1975, c. 716, s. 5; 1977, c. 125; 1977, 2d Sess., c. 1222, s. 1; 1979, c. 453, ss. 1, 2; c. 903, ss. 1, 2; 1981, c. 466, ss. 4–6; 1983, c. 435, s. 29; 1983 (Reg. Sess., 1984), c. 1101, ss. 21–29, 36; 1985, c. 706, s. 1; 1985 (Reg. Sess., 1986), c. 1014, s. 201(d); 1987, c. 139; c. 352, s. 1; c. 797, ss. 1, 2; 1989, c. 548, ss. 1, 2; c. 691, ss. 1–3, 4.1; 1989 (Reg. Sess., 1990), c. 1031, ss. 1, 2; c. 1039, s. 6; 1991, c. 636, s. 19(b), (c); c. 726, ss. 20, 21; 1993, c. 285, s. 9; 1995, c. 191, s. 3; c. 496, ss. 2–7; c. 506, ss. 11–13; 1997-379, ss. 2.1–2.8; 1997-443, s. 19.26(c); 1998-182, ss. 25, 31–35.

§ 20-179.1. Presentence investigation of persons convicted of offense involving impaired driving

When a person has been convicted of an offense involving impaired driving, the trial judge may request a presentence investigation to determine whether the person convicted would benefit from treatment for habitual use of alcohol or drugs. If the person convicted objects, no presentence investigation may be ordered, but the judge retains his power to order suitable treatment as a condition of probation, and must do so when required by statute.

History: 1973, c. 612; 1981, c. 412, s. 4; c. 747, s. 66; 1983, c. 435, s. 29.

§ 20-179.3. Limited driving privilege

(a) Definition of Limited Driving Privilege.—A limited driving privilege is a judgment issued in the discretion of a court for good cause shown authorizing a person with a revoked driver's license to drive for essential purposes related to any of the following:

(1) His employment.
(2) The maintenance of his household.
(3) His education.
(4) His court-ordered treatment or assessment.
(5) Community service ordered as a condition of the person's probation.
(6) Emergency medical care.

(b) Eligibility.

(1) A person convicted of the offense of impaired driving under G.S. 20-138.1 is eligible for a limited driving privilege if:
   a. At the time of the offense he held either a valid driver's license or a license that had been expired for less than one year;
   b. At the time of the offense he had not within the preceding seven years been convicted of an offense involving impaired driving;
   c. Punishment Level Three, Four, or Five was imposed for the offense of impaired driving;
   d. Subsequent to the offense he has not been convicted of, or had an unresolved charge lodged against him for, an offense involving impaired driving; and
   e. The person has obtained and filed with the court a substance abuse assessment of the type required by G.S. 20-17.6 for the restoration of a driver's license.

A person whose North Carolina driver's license is revoked because of a conviction in another jurisdiction substantially equivalent to impaired driving under G.S. 20-138.1 is eligible for a limited driving privilege if he would be eligible for it had the conviction occurred in North Carolina. Eligibility for a limited driving privilege following a revocation under G.S. 20-16.2(d) is governed by G.S. 20-16.2(e1).

(2) Any person whose licensing privileges are forfeited pursuant to G.S. 15A-1331A is eligible for a limited driving privilege if the court finds that at the time of the forfeiture, the person held either a valid driver's license or a driver's license that had been expired for less than one year and
   a. The person is supporting existing dependents or must have a driver's license to be gainfully employed; or

b. The person has an existing dependent who requires serious medical treatment and the defendant is the only person able to provide transportation to the dependent to the health care facility where the dependent can receive the needed medical treatment.

The limited driving privilege granted under this subdivision must restrict the person to essential driving related to the purposes listed above, and any driving that is not related to those purposes is unlawful even though done at times and upon routes that may be authorized by the privilege.

(c) Privilege Not Effective until after Compliance with Court-Ordered Revocation.—A person convicted of an impaired driving offense may apply for a limited driving privilege at the time the judgment is entered. If the judgment does not require the person to complete a period of nonoperation pursuant to G.S. 20-179, the privilege may be issued at the time the judgment is issued. If the judgment requires the person to complete a period of nonoperation pursuant to G.S. 20-179, the limited driving privilege may not be effective until the person successfully completes that period of nonoperation. A person whose license is revoked because of a conviction in another jurisdiction substantially equivalent to impaired driving under G.S. 20-138.1 may apply for a limited driving privilege only after having completed at least 60 days of a court-imposed term of nonoperation of a motor vehicle, if the court in the other jurisdiction imposed such a term of nonoperation.

(d) Application for and Scheduling of Subsequent Hearing.—The application for a limited driving privilege made at any time after the day of sentencing must be filed with the clerk in duplicate, and no hearing scheduled may be held until a reasonable time after the clerk files a copy of the application with the district attorney's office. The hearing must be scheduled before:

(1) The presiding judge at the applicant's trial if that judge is assigned to a court in the district court district as defined in G.S. 7A-133 or superior court district or set of districts as defined in G.S. 7A-41.1, as the case may be, in which the conviction for impaired driving was imposed.

(2) The senior regular resident superior court judge of the superior court district or set of districts as defined in G.S. 7A-41.1 in which the conviction for impaired driving was imposed, if the presiding judge is not available within the district and the conviction was imposed in superior court.

(3) The chief district court judge of the district court district as defined in G.S. 7A-133 in which the conviction for impaired driving was imposed, if the presiding judge is not available within the district and the conviction was imposed in district court.

If the applicant was convicted of an offense in another jurisdiction, the hearing must be scheduled before the chief district court judge of the district court district as defined in G.S. 7A-133 in which he resides. G.S. 20-16.2(e1) governs the judge before whom a hearing is scheduled if the revocation was under G.S. 20-16.2(d). The hearing may be scheduled in any county within the district court district as defined in G.S. 7A-133 or superior court district or set of districts as defined in G.S. 7A-41.1, as the case may be.

(e) Limited Basis for and Effect of Privilege.—A limited driving privilege issued under this section authorizes a person to drive if his license is revoked solely under G.S. 20-17(2) or as a result of a conviction in another jurisdiction substantially equivalent to impaired driving under G.S. 20-138.1; if the person's license is revoked under any other statute, the limited driving privilege is invalid.

(f) Overall Provisions on Use of Privilege.—Every limited driving privilege must restrict the applicant to essential driving related to the purposes listed in subsection (a), and any driving that is not related to those purposes is unlawful even though done at times and upon routes that may be authorized by the privilege. If the privilege is granted, driving related to emergency medical care is authorized at any time and without restriction as to routes, but all other driving must be for a purpose and done within the restrictions specified in the privilege.

(f1) Definition of "Standard Working Hours".—Under this section, "standard working hours" are 6:00 A.M. to 8:00 P.M. on Monday through Friday.

(g) Driving for Work-Related Purposes in Standard Working Hours.—In a limited driving privilege, the court may authorize driving for work-related purposes during standard working hours without specifying the times and routes in which the driving must occur. If the applicant is not required to drive for essential work-related purposes except during standard working hours, the limited driving privilege must prohibit driving during nonstandard working hours unless the driving is for emergency medical care or is authorized by subsection (g2). The limited driving privilege must state the name and address of the applicant's place of work or employer, and may include other information and restrictions applicable to work-related driving in the discretion of the court.

(g1) Driving for Work-Related Purposes in Nonstandard Hours.—If the applicant is required to drive during nonstandard working hours for an essential work-related purpose, he must present documentation of that fact before the judge may authorize him to drive for this purpose during those hours. If the applicant is self-employed, the documentation must be attached to or made a part of the limited driving privilege. If the judge determines that it is necessary for the applicant to drive during nonstandard hours for a work-related purpose, he may authorize the applicant to drive subject to these limitations:

(1) If the applicant is required to drive to and from a specific place of work at regular times, the limited driving privilege must specify the general times and routes in which the applicant will be driving to and from work, and restrict driving to those times and routes.

(2) If the applicant is required to drive to and from work at a specific place, but is unable to specify the times at which that driving will occur, the limited driving privilege must specify the general routes in which the applicant will be driving to and from work, and restrict the driving to those general routes.

(3) If the applicant is required to drive to and from work at regular times but is unable to specify the places at which work is to be performed, the limited driving privilege must specify the general times and geographic boundaries in which the applicant will be driving, and restrict driving to those times and within those boundaries.

(4) If the applicant can specify neither the times nor places in which he will be driving to and from work, or if he is required to drive during these nonstandard working hours as a condition of employment, the limited driving privilege must specify the geographic boundaries in which he will drive and restrict driving to that within those boundaries.

The limited driving privilege must state the name and address of the applicant's place of work or employer, and may include other information and restrictions applicable to work-related driving, in the discretion of the court.

(g2) Driving for Other than Work-Related Purposes.—A limited driving privilege may not allow driving for maintenance of the household except during standard working hours, and the limited driving privilege may contain any additional restrictions on that driving, in the discretion of the court. The limited driving privilege must authorize driving essential to the completion of any community work assignments, course of instruction at an Alcohol and Drug Education Traffic School, or substance abuse assessment or treatment, to which the applicant is ordered by the court as a condition of probation for the impaired driving conviction. If this driving will occur during nonstandard working hours, the limited driving privilege must specify the same limitations required by subsection (g1) for work-related driving during those hours, and it must include or have attached to it the name and address of the Alcohol and Drug Education Traffic School, the community service coordinator, or mental health treatment facility to which the applicant is assigned. Driving for educational purposes other than the course of instruction at an Alcohol and Drug Education Traffic School is subject to the same limitations applicable to work related driving under subsections (g) and (g1).

(g3) Ignition Interlock Allowed.—A judge may include all of the following in a limited driving privilege order:

(1) A restriction that the applicant may operate only a designated motor vehicle.

(2) A requirement that the designated motor vehicle be equipped with a functioning ignition interlock system of a type approved by the Commissioner. The Commissioner shall not unreasonably withhold approval of an ignition interlock system and shall consult with the Division of Purchase and Contract in the Department of Administration to ensure that potential vendors are not discriminated against.

(3) A requirement that the applicant personally activate the ignition interlock system before driving the motor vehicle.

(g4) (Effective until July 1, 2000) The restrictions set forth in subsection (g3) of this section do not apply to a motor vehicle that meets all of the following requirements:

(1) Is owned by the applicant's employer.

(2) Is operated by the applicant solely for work-related purposes.

(3) Its owner has filed with the court a written document authorizing the applicant to drive the vehicle, for work-related purposes, under the authority of a limited driving privilege.

(g4) (Effective July 1, 2000) The restrictions set forth in subsection (g3) and (g5) of this section do not apply to a motor vehicle that meets all of the following requirements:

(1) Is owned by the applicant's employer.

(2) Is operated by the applicant solely for work-related purposes.

(3) Its owner has filed with the court a written document authorizing the applicant to drive the vehicle, for work-related purposes, under the authority of a limited driving privilege.

(g5) (Effective July 1, 2000) Ignition Interlock Required.—If a person's driver's license is revoked for a conviction of G.S. 20-138.1, and the person had an alcohol concentration of 0.16 or more, a judge shall include all of the following in a limited driving privilege order:

(1) A restriction that the applicant may operate only a designated motor vehicle.
(2) A requirement that the designated motor vehicle be equipped with a functioning ignition interlock system of a type approved by the Commissioner. The Commissioner shall not unreasonably withhold approval of an ignition interlock system and shall consult with the Division of Purchase and Contract in the Department of Administration to ensure that potential vendors are not discriminated against.
(3) A requirement that the applicant personally activate the ignition interlock system before driving the motor vehicle.

(h) Other Mandatory and Permissive Conditions or Restrictions.—In all limited driving privileges the judge shall also include a restriction that the applicant not consume alcohol while driving or drive at any time while he has remaining in his body any alcohol or controlled substance previously consumed, unless the controlled substance was lawfully obtained and taken in therapeutically appropriate amounts. The judge may impose any other reasonable restrictions or conditions necessary to achieve the purposes of this section.

(i) Modification or Revocation of Privilege.—A judge who issues a limited driving privilege is authorized to modify or revoke the limited driving privilege upon a showing that the circumstances have changed sufficiently to justify modification or revocation. If the judge who issued the privilege is not presiding in the court in which the privilege was issued, a presiding judge in that court may modify or revoke a privilege in accordance with this subsection. The judge must indicate in the order of modification or revocation the reasons for the order, or he must make specific findings indicating the reason for the order and those findings must be entered in the record of the case.

(j) Effect of Violation of Restriction.—A holder of a limited driving privilege who violates any of its restrictions commits the offense of driving while his license is revoked under G.S. 20-28(a) and is subject to punishment and license revocation as provided in that section. If a law-enforcement officer has reasonable grounds to believe that the holder of a limited driving privilege has consumed alcohol while driving or has driven while he has remaining in his body any alcohol previously consumed, the suspected offense of driving while license is revoked is an alcohol-related offense subject to the implied-consent provisions of G.S. 20-16.2. If a holder of a limited driving privilege is charged with driving while license revoked by violating a restriction contained in his limited driving privilege, and a judicial official determines that there is probable cause for the charge, the limited driving privilege is suspended pending the resolution of the case, and the judicial official must require the holder to surrender the limited driving privilege. The judicial official must also notify the holder that he is not entitled to drive until his case is resolved.

Notwithstanding any other provision of law, an alcohol screening test may be administered to a driver suspected of violating this section, and the results of an alcohol screening test or the driver's refusal to submit may be used by a law enforcement officer, a court, or an administrative agency in determining if alcohol was present in the driver's body. No alcohol screening tests are valid under this section unless the device used is one approved by the Commission for Health Services, and the screening test is conducted in accordance with the applicable regulations of the Commission as to the manner of its use.

(k) Copy of Limited Driving Privilege to Division; Action Taken if Privilege Invalid.—The clerk of court or the child support enforcement agency must send a copy of any limited driving privilege issued in the county to the Division. A limited driving privilege that is not authorized by this section, G.S. 20-16.2(e1), 20-16.1, 50-13.12, or 110-142.2, or that does not contain the limitations required by law, is invalid. If the limited driving privilege is invalid on its face, the Division must immediately notify the court and the holder of the privilege that it considers the privilege void and that the Division records will not indicate that the holder has a limited driving privilege.

(l) Any judge granting limited driving privileges under this section shall, prior to granting such privileges, be furnished proof and be satisfied that the person being granted such privileges is financially responsible. Proof of financial responsibility shall be in one of the following forms:

(1) A written certificate or electronically-transmitted facsimile thereof from any insurance carrier duly authorized to do business in this State certifying that there is in effect a nonfleet private passenger motor vehicle liability policy for the benefit of the person required to furnish proof of financial responsibility. The certificate or facsimile shall state the effective date and expiration date of the nonfleet private passenger motor vehicle liability policy and shall state the date that the certificate or facsimile is issued. The certificate or facsimile shall remain effective proof of financial responsibility for a period of 30 consecutive days following the date the certificate or facsimile is issued but shall not in and of itself constitute a binder or policy of insurance or

(2) A binder for or policy of nonfleet private passenger motor vehicle liability insurance under which the applicant is insured, provided that the binder or policy states the effective date and expiration date of the nonfleet private passenger motor vehicle liability policy.

The preceding provisions of this subsection do not apply to applicants who do not own currently registered motor vehicles and who do not operate nonfleet private passenger motor vehicles that are owned by other persons and that are not insured under commercial motor vehicle liability insurance policies. In such cases, the applicant shall sign a written certificate to that effect. Such certificate shall be furnished by the Division. Any material misrepresentation made by such person on such certificate shall be grounds for suspension of that person's license for a period of 90 days.

For the purpose of this subsection "nonfleet private passenger motor vehicle" has the definition ascribed to it in Article 40 of General Statute Chapter 58.

The Commissioner may require that certificates required by this subsection be on a form approved by the Commissioner. Such granting of limited driving privileges shall be conditioned upon the maintenance of such financial responsibility during the period of the limited driving privilege. Nothing in this subsection precludes any person from showing proof of financial responsibility in any other manner authorized by Articles 9A and 13 of this Chapter.

History: 1983, c. 435, s. 31; 1983 (Reg. Sess., 1984), c. 1101, ss. 30–33; 1985, c. 706, s. 2; 1987, c. 869, s. 13; 1987 (Reg. Sess., 1988), c. 1037, s. 78; 1989, c. 436, s. 6; 1994, Ex. Sess., c. 20, s. 3; 1995, c. 506, ss. 1, 2; c. 538, s. 2(h); 1995 (Reg. Sess., 1996), c. 756, s. 31; 1997-379, s. 5.6; 1999-406, ss. 4–6.

§ 20-179.4. Community service alternative punishment; responsibilities of the Department of Crime Control and Public Safety; fee

(a) The Department of Crime Control and Public Safety shall conduct a community service alternative punishment program for persons sentenced under G.S. 20-179(i), (j) or (k).

(b) The Secretary of Crime Control and Public Safety shall assign at least one coordinator to each district court district as defined in G.S. 7A-133 to assure and report to the court the person's compliance with the community service sentence. The appointment of each coordinator shall be made in consultation with the chief district court judge in the district to which the coordinator is assigned. Each county must provide office space in the courthouse or other convenient place, necessary equipment, and secretarial service for the use of each coordinator assigned to that county.

(c) A fee of one hundred dollars ($100.00) shall be paid by all persons serving a community service sentence. That fee shall be paid to the clerk of court in the county in which the person is convicted. The fee shall be paid in full within two weeks unless the court, upon a showing of hardship by the person, allows additional time to pay the fee. The person may not be required to pay the fee before beginning the community service unless the court specifically orders the person to do so.

(d) Fees collected under this section shall be deposited in the general fund.

(e) The coordinator shall report to the court in which the community service was ordered a significant violation of the terms of the probation judgment related to community service. The court shall then conduct a hearing to determine if there is a willful failure to comply. If the court determines there is a willful failure to pay the prescribed fee or to complete the work as ordered by the coordinator within the applicable time limits, the court shall revoke any limited driving privilege issued in the impaired driving case until the community service requirement has been met and in addition may take any further action authorized by Article 82 of General Statutes Chapter 15A for violation of a condition of probation.

History: 1983, c. 761, s. 154; 1983 (Reg. Sess., 1984), c. 1101, ss. 34, 35; 1987 (Reg. Sess., 1988), c. 1037, s. 82; 1989, c. 752, s. 109; 1995, c. 496, s. 9; 1997-234, s. 1.

§ 20-181. Penalty for failure to dim, etc., beams of headlamps

Any person operating a motor vehicle on the highways of this State, who shall fail to shift, depress, deflect, tilt or dim the beams of the headlamps thereon whenever another vehicle is met on such highways or when following another vehicle at a distance of less than 200 feet, except when engaged in the act of overtaking and passing may, upon a determination of responsibility for the offense, be required to pay a penalty of not more than ten dollars ($10.00).

History: 1939, c. 351, s. 3; 1955, c. 913, s. 1; 1987, c. 581, s. 5.

Article 3A. Safety and Emissions Inspection Program

Part 2. Safety and Emissions Inspections of Certain Vehicles

§ 20-183.3. Scope of safety inspection and emissions inspection

(a) Safety.—A safety inspection of a motor vehicle consists of an inspection of the following equipment to determine if the vehicle has the equipment required by Part 9 of Article 3 of this Chapter and if the equipment is in a safe operating condition:

(1) Brakes, as required by G.S. 20-124.
(2) Lights, as required by G.S. 20-129 or G.S. 20-129.1.
(3) Horn, as required by G.S. 20-125(a).
(4) Steering mechanism, as required by G.S. 20-123.1.
(5) Windows and windshield wipers, as required by G.S. 20-127. To determine if a vehicle window meets the window tinting restrictions, a safety inspection mechanic must first determine, based on use of an automotive film check card or knowledge of window tinting techniques, if after-factory tint has been applied to the window. If after-factory tint has been applied, the mechanic must use a light meter approved by the Commissioner to determine if the window meets the window tinting restrictions.
(6) Directional signals, as required by G.S. 20-125.1.
(7) Tires, as required by G.S. 20-122.1.
(8) Mirrors, as required by G.S. 20-126.
(9) Exhaust system, as required by G.S. 20-128. For a vehicle that is subject to an emissions inspection in addition to a safety inspection, a visual inspection of the vehicle's emission-control devices is included in the emissions inspection rather than the safety inspection.

(b) Emissions.—An emissions inspection of a motor vehicle consists of a visual inspection of the vehicle's emission control devices to determine if the devices are present, are properly connected, and are the correct type for the vehicle and an analysis of the exhaust emissions of the vehicle to determine if the exhaust emissions meet the standards for the model year of the vehicle set by the Environmental Management Commission. To pass an emissions inspection a vehicle must pass both the visual inspection and the exhaust emissions analysis. When an emissions inspection is performed on a vehicle, a safety inspection must be performed on the vehicle as well.

(c) Reinspection After Failure.—The scope of a reinspection of a vehicle that has been repaired after failing an inspection is the same as the original inspection unless the vehicle is presented for reinspection within 30 days of failing the original inspection. If the vehicle is presented for reinspection within this time limit and the inspection the vehicle failed was a safety inspection, the reinspection is limited to an inspection of the equipment that failed the original inspection. If the vehicle is presented for reinspection within this time limit and the inspection the vehicle failed was an emissions inspection, the reinspection is limited to the portion of the inspection the vehicle failed and any other portion of the inspection that would be affected by repairs made to correct the failure.

History: 1965, c. 734, s. 1; 1969, c. 378, s. 2; 1971, c. 455, s. 2; c. 478, ss. 1, 2; 1979, 2d Sess., c. 1180, s. 3; 1981 (Reg. Sess., 1982), c. 1261, s. 1; 1989, c. 391, s. 2; 1991, c. 654, s. 2; 1993 (Reg. Sess., 1994), c. 754, s. 1; 1995, c. 473, s. 2.

§ 20-183.8. Infractions and criminal offenses for violations of inspection requirements

(a) Infractions.—A person who does any of the following commits an infraction and, if found responsible, is liable for a penalty of up to fifty dollars ($50.00):

(1) Operates a motor vehicle that is subject to inspection under this Part on a highway or public vehicular area in the State when the vehicle has not been inspected in accordance with this Part, as evidenced by the vehicle's lack of a current inspection sticker or otherwise.
(2) Allows an inspection sticker to be put on a vehicle owned or operated by that person, knowing that the vehicle was not inspected before the sticker was attached or was not inspected properly.
(3) Puts an inspection sticker on a vehicle, knowing or having reasonable grounds to know an inspection of the vehicle was not performed or was performed improperly. A person who is cited for a civil penalty under G.S. 20-183.8B for an emissions violation involving the inspection of a vehicle may not be charged with an infraction under this subdivision based on that same vehicle.

(b) Defenses to Infractions.—Any of the following is a defense to a violation under subsection (a) of this section:

(1) The vehicle was continuously out of State for at least the 30 days preceding the date the inspection sticker expired and a current inspection sticker was obtained within 10 days after the vehicle came back to the State.

(2) The vehicle displays a dealer license plate or a transporter plate, the dealer repossessed the vehicle or otherwise acquired the vehicle within the last 10 days, and the vehicle is being driven from its place of acquisition to the dealer's place of business or to an inspection station.

(3) Repealed by Session Laws 1997-29, s. 5.

(4) The charged infraction is described in subdivision (a)(1) of this section, the vehicle is subject to a safety inspection or an emissions inspection and the vehicle owner establishes in court that the vehicle was inspected after the citation was issued and within 30 days of the expiration date of the inspection sticker that was on the vehicle when the citation was issued.

(c) Felony.—A person who does any of the following commits a Class I felony:

(1) Forges an inspection sticker.

(2) Buys, sells, or possesses a forged inspection sticker.

(3) Buys, sells, or possesses an inspection sticker other than as the result of either of the following:

a. Having a license as an inspection station, a self-inspector, or an inspection mechanic and obtaining the inspection sticker from the Division in the course of business.

b. A vehicle inspection in which the vehicle passed the inspection or for which the vehicle received a waiver.

History: 1965, c. 734, s. 1; 1967, c. 692, s. 3; 1969, c. 179, s. 1; c. 620; 1973, cc. 909, 1322; 1975, c. 716, s. 5; 1979, 2d Sess., c. 1180, s. 4; 1985, c. 764, s. 23; 1985 (Reg. Sess., 1986), c. 852, s. 17; 1993 (Reg. Sess., 1994), c. 754, s. 1; 1997-29, s. 5; 1999-452, s. 25.

Article 7. Miscellaneous Provisions Relating to Motor Vehicles

§ 20-217. Motor vehicles to stop for properly marked and designated school buses in certain instances; evidence of identity of driver

(a) The driver of any vehicle upon approaching from any direction on the same street, highway, or public vehicular area any school bus (including privately owned buses transporting children and school buses transporting senior citizens under G.S. 115C-243), while the bus is displaying its mechanical stop signal or flashing red stoplights, and is stopped for the purpose of receiving or discharging passengers, shall bring the vehicle to a full stop before passing or attempting to pass the bus, and shall remain stopped until the mechanical stop signal has been withdrawn, the flashing red stoplights have been turned off, and the bus has moved on.

(b) The provisions of this section are applicable only in the event the school bus bears upon the front and rear a plainly visible sign containing the words "school bus" in letters not less than eight inches in height.

(c) Notwithstanding the provisions of subsection (a) of this section, the driver of a vehicle traveling in the opposite direction from the school bus, upon any road, highway or city street which has been divided into two roadways, so constructed as to separate vehicular traffic between the two roadways by an intervening space (including a center lane for left turns if the roadway consists of at least four more lanes) or by a physical barrier, need not stop upon meeting and passing any school bus which has stopped in the roadway across such dividing space or physical barrier.

(d) It shall be unlawful for any school bus driver to stop and receive or discharge passengers or for any principal or superintendent of any school, routing a school bus, to authorize the driver of any school bus to stop and receive or discharge passengers upon any roadway described by subsection (c) of this section where passengers would be required to cross the roadway to reach their destination or to board the bus; provided, that passengers may be discharged or received at points where pedestrians and vehicular traffic are controlled by adequate stop-and-go traffic signals.

(e) Any person violating the provisions of this section shall be guilty of a Class 2 misdemeanor.

(f) Expired.

History: 1925, c. 265; 1943, c. 767; 1947, c. 527; 1955, c. 1365; 1959, c. 909; 1965, c. 370; 1969, c. 952; 1971, c. 245, s. 1; 1973, c. 1330, s. 35; 1977, 2d Sess., c. 1280, s. 4; 1979, 2d Sess., c. 1323; 1983, c. 779, s. 1; 1985, c. 700, s. 1; 1991, c. 290, s. 1; 1993, c. 539, s. 382; 1994, Ex. Sess., c. 24, s. 14(c); 1998-149, s. 10.

§ 20-218. Standard qualifications for school bus drivers; speed limit for school buses and school activity buses

(a) Qualifications.—No person shall drive a school bus over the highways or public vehicular areas of North Carolina while it is occupied by children unless the person furnishes to the superintendent of the schools of the county in which the bus shall be operated a certificate from any representative duly designated by the Commissioner and from the Director of Transportation or a designee of the Director in charge of school buses in the county showing that the person has been examined by them and is fit and competent to drive a school bus over the highways and public vehicular areas of the State. The driver of a school bus must be at least 18 years of age and hold a Class A, B, or C commercial driver's license and a school bus driver's certificate. The driver of a school activity bus must meet the same qualifications as a school bus driver or must have a license appropriate for the class of vehicle being driven.

(b) Speed Limits.—It is unlawful to drive a school bus loaded with children over the highways or public vehicular areas of the State at a greater rate of speed than 45 miles per hour. It is unlawful to drive a school activity bus loaded with children over the highways or public vehicular areas of North Carolina at a greater rate of speed than 55 miles per hour.

(c) Punishment.—A person who violates this section commits a Class 3 misdemeanor.

History: 1937, c. 397, ss. 1–3; 1941, c. 21; 1943, c. 440; 1945, c. 216; 1957, cc. 139, 595; 1971, c. 293; 1977, c. 791, ss. 1, 2; c. 1102; 1979, c. 31, ss. 1, 2; c. 667, s. 36; 1981, c. 30; 1987, c. 337, s. 1; 1989, c. 558, s. 1; c. 771, s. 6; 1991, c. 726, s. 22; 1993, c. 217, s. 1; 1993 (Reg. Sess., 1994), c. 761, s. 20.

§ 20-218.2. Speed limit for nonprofit activity buses

It is unlawful to drive an activity bus that is owned by a nonprofit organization and is transporting persons in connection with nonprofit activities over the highways or public vehicular areas of North Carolina at a greater rate of speed than 55 miles per hour. A person who violates this section commits a Class 3 misdemeanor.

History: 1969, c. 1000, s. 2; 1987, c. 337, s. 2; 1993 (Reg. Sess., 1994), c. 761, s. 23.

Article 7A. Post-Towing Procedures

§ 20-219.9. Definitions

As used in this Article, unless the context clearly requires otherwise:

(1) "Tow" in any of its forms includes to remove a vehicle by any means including towing and to store the vehicle;

(2) "Tower" means the person who towed the vehicle;

(3) "Towing fee" means the fee charged for towing and storing.

History: 1983, c. 420, s. 2.

§ 20-219.10. Coverage of Article

(a) This Article applies to each towing of a vehicle that is carried out pursuant to G.S. 115C-46(d) or G.S. 143-340(19), or pursuant to the direction of a law-enforcement officer except:

(1) This Article applies to towings pursuant to G.S. 115D-21, 116-44.4, 116-229, 153A-132, 153A-132.2, 160A-303, and 160A-303.2 only insofar as specifically provided;

(2) This Article does not apply to a seizure of a vehicle under G.S. 14-86.1, 18B-504, 90-112, 113-137, 20-28.2, 20-28.3, or to any other seizure of a vehicle for evidence in a criminal proceeding or pursuant to any other statute providing for the forfeiture of a vehicle;

(3) This Article does not apply to a seizure of a vehicle pursuant to a levy under execution.

(b) A person who authorizes the towing of a vehicle covered by this Article, G.S. 115D-21, 116-44.4, 116-229, 153A-132, 153A-132.2, 160A-303 or 160A-303.2 is a legal possessor of the vehicle within the meaning of G.S. 44A-1(1).

History: 1983, c. 420, s. 2; 1989, c. 743, s. 3; 1997-379, s. 1.7.

§ 20-219.11. Notice and probable cause hearing

(a) Whenever a vehicle with a valid registration plate or registration is towed as provided in G.S. 20-219.10, the authorizing person shall immediately notify the last known registered owner of the vehicle of the following:

(1) A description of the vehicle;
(2) The place where the vehicle is stored;
(3) The violation with which the owner is charged, if any;
(4) The procedure the owner must follow to have the vehicle returned to him; and
(5) The procedure the owner must follow to request a probable cause hearing on the towing.

If the vehicle has a North Carolina registration plate or registration, notice shall be given to the owner within 24 hours; if the vehicle is not registered in this State, notice shall be given to the owner within 72 hours. This notice shall, if feasible, be given by telephone. Whether or not the owner is reached by telephone, notice shall be mailed to his last known address unless he or his agent waives this notice in writing.

(b) Whenever a vehicle with neither a valid registration plate nor registration is towed as provided in G.S. 20-219.10, the authorizing person shall make reasonable efforts, including checking the vehicle identification number, to determine the last known registered owner of the vehicle and to notify him of the information listed in subsection (a). Unless the owner has otherwise been given notice, it is presumed that the authorizing person has not made reasonable efforts, as required under this subsection, unless notice that the vehicle would be towed was posted on the windshield or some other conspicuous place at least seven days before the towing actually occurred; except, no pretowing notice need be given if the vehicle impeded the flow of traffic or otherwise jeopardized the public welfare so that immediate towing was necessary.

(c) The owner or any other person entitled to claim possession of the vehicle may request in writing a hearing to determine if probable cause existed for the towing. The request shall be filed with the magistrate in the county where the vehicle was towed. If there is more than one magistrate's office in that county, the request may be filed with the magistrate in the warrant-issuing office in the county seat or in any other office designated to receive requests by the chief district court judge. The magistrate shall set the hearing within 72 hours of his receiving the request. The owner, the person who requested the hearing if someone other than the owner, the tower, and the person who authorized the towing shall be notified of the time and place of the hearing.

(d) The owner, the tower, the person who authorized the towing, and any other interested parties may present evidence at the hearing. The person authorizing the towing and the tower may submit an affidavit in lieu of appearing personally, but the affidavit does not preclude that person from also testifying.

(e) The only issue at this hearing is whether or not probable cause existed for the towing. If the magistrate finds that probable cause did exist, the tower's lien continues. If the magistrate finds that probable cause did not exist, the tower's lien is extinguished.

(f) Any aggrieved party may appeal the magistrate's decision to district court.

History: 1983, c. 420, s. 2.

§ 20-219.12. Option to pay or post bond

At any stage in the proceedings, including before the probable cause hearing, the owner may obtain possession of his vehicle by:

(1) Paying the towing fee, or
(2) Posting a bond for double the amount of the towing fee.

History: 1983, c. 420, s. 2.

§ 20-219.13. Hearing on lien

The tower may seek to enforce his lien or the owner may seek to contest the lien pursuant to Chapter 44A.

History: 1983, c. 420, s. 2.

§ 20-219.14. Payment to tower guaranteed

Every agency whose law-enforcement officers act pursuant to this Article, G.S. 115D-21, 116-44.4, 116-229, 153A-132, or 160A-303 shall by contract or rules provide compensation to the tower if a court finds no probable cause existed for the towing.

History: 1983, c. 420, s. 2.

Article 13. The Vehicle Financial Responsibility Act of 1957

§ 20-309. Financial responsibility prerequisite to registration; must be maintained throughout registration period

(a) No motor vehicle shall be registered in this State unless the owner at the time of registration has financial responsibility for the operation of such motor vehicle, as provided in this Article. The owner of each motor vehicle registered in this State shall maintain financial responsibility continuously throughout the period of registration.

An owner of a commercial motor vehicle, as defined in G.S. 20-4.01(3d), shall have financial responsibility for the operation of the motor vehicle as required by this section. The financial responsibility for a commercial motor vehicle shall be equal to that required in 49 C.F.R. §§ 387.3, 387.5, 387.7, and 387.11 for for-hire or private motor vehicles transporting property in interstate or intrastate commerce.

(b) Financial responsibility shall be a liability insurance policy or a financial security bond or a financial security deposit or by qualification as a self-insurer, as these terms are defined and described in Article 9A, Chapter 20 of the General Statutes of North Carolina, as amended.

(c) When it is certified that financial responsibility is a liability insurance policy, the Commissioner of Motor Vehicles may require that the owner produce records to prove the fact of such insurance, and failure to produce such records shall be prima facie evidence that no financial responsibility exists with regard to the vehicle concerned. It shall be the duty of insurance companies, upon request of the Division, to verify the accuracy of any owner's certification.

(d) When liability insurance with regard to any motor vehicle is terminated by cancellation or failure to renew, or the owner's financial responsibility for the operation of any motor vehicle is otherwise terminated, the owner shall forthwith surrender the registration certificate and plates of the vehicle to the Division of Motor Vehicles unless financial responsibility is maintained in some other manner in compliance with this Article.

(e) (Effective until October 1, 2000) Upon termination by cancellation or otherwise of an insurance policy provided in subsection (b) of this section, the insurer shall notify the Division of such termination; provided, no cancellation notice is required if the insurer issues a new insurance policy complying with this Article at the same time the insurer cancels or otherwise terminates the old policy, no lapse in coverage results, and the insurer sends the certificate of insurance form for the new policy to the Division. The Division, upon receiving notice of cancellation or termination of an owner's financial responsibility as required by this Article, shall notify such owner of such cancellation or termination, and such owner shall, to retain the registration plate for the vehicle registered or required to be registered, within 10 days from date of notice given by the Division either:

(1) Certify to the Division that he had financial responsibility effective on or prior to the date of such termination; or

(2) In the case of a lapse in financial responsibility, pay a fifty dollar ($50.00) civil penalty; and certify to the Division that he now has financial responsibility effective on the date of certification, that he did not operate the vehicle in question during the period of no financial responsibility with the knowledge that there was no financial responsibility, and that the vehicle in question was not involved in a motor vehicle accident during the period of no financial responsibility.

Failure of the owner to certify that he has financial responsibility as herein required shall be prima facie evidence that no financial responsibility exists with regard to the vehicle concerned and unless the owner's registration plate has on or prior to the date of termination of insurance been surrendered to the Division by surrender to an agent or representative of the Division designated by the Commissioner, or depositing the same in the United States mail, addressed to the Division of Motor Vehicles, Raleigh, North Carolina, the Division shall revoke the vehicle's registration for 30 days.

In no case shall any vehicle, the registration of which has been revoked for failure to have financial responsibility, be reregistered in the name of the registered owner, spouse, or any child of the spouse, or any child of such owner within less than 30 days after the date of receipt of the registration plate by the Division of Motor Vehicles, except that a spouse living separate and apart from the registered owner may register such vehicle immediately in such spouse's name. Additionally, as a condition precedent to the reregistration of the vehicle by the registered owner, spouse, or any child of the spouse, or any child of such owner, except a spouse living separate and apart from the registered owner, the payment of a restoration fee of fifty dollars ($50.00) and the appropriate fee for a new registration plate is required. Any person, firm or corporation failing to give notice of termination shall be subject to a civil penalty of two hundred dollars ($200.00) to be assessed by the Commissioner of Insurance upon a finding by the Commissioner of Insurance that good cause is not shown for such failure to give notice of termination to the Division.

(e) (Effective October 1, 2000) Upon termination by cancellation or otherwise of an insurance policy provided in subsection (b) of this section, the insurer shall notify the Division of the termination within 20 business days; provided, no cancellation notice is required if the same insurer issues a replacement insurance policy complying with this Article at the same time the insurer cancels or otherwise terminates the old policy, no lapse in coverage results, and the insurer sends the certificate of insurance form for the new policy to the Division. The insurer shall notify the Division of any new policy for insurance within 20 working days of its issuance unless the new coverage is a replacement insurance policy for a policy terminated by the same insurer. Any insurance company with twenty-five million dollars ($25,000,000) or more in annual vehicle insurance premium volume must submit the notices required under this section by electronic means. All other insurance companies may submit the notices required under this section by either paper or electronic means. The names of insureds and the beginning date and termination date of insurance coverage provided to the Division by the insurer pursuant to this paragraph shall constitute a designated trade secret under G.S. 132-1.2.

The Division, upon receiving notice of a lapse in insurance coverage, shall notify the owner of the lapse in coverage, and the owner shall, to retain the registration plate for the vehicle registered or required to be registered, within 10 days from date of notice given by the Division either:

(1) Certify to the Division that he had financial responsibility effective on or prior to the date of such termination; or

(2) In the case of a lapse in financial responsibility, pay a fifty dollar ($50.00) civil penalty; and certify to the Division that he now has financial responsibility effective on the date of certification, that he did not operate the vehicle in question during the period of no financial responsibility with the knowledge that there was no financial responsibility, and that the vehicle in question was not involved in a motor vehicle crash during the period of no financial responsibility.

Failure of the owner to certify that he has financial responsibility as herein required shall be prima facie evidence that no financial responsibility exists with regard to the vehicle concerned and unless the owner's registration plate has on or prior to the date of termination of insurance been surrendered to the Division by surrender to an agent or representative of the Division designated by the Commissioner, or depositing the same in the United States mail, addressed to the Division of Motor Vehicles, Raleigh, North Carolina, the Division shall revoke the vehicle's registration for 30 days.

In no case shall any vehicle, the registration of which has been revoked for failure to have financial responsibility, be reregistered in the name of the registered owner, spouse, or any child of the spouse, or any child of such owner within less than 30 days after the date of receipt of the registration plate by the Division of Motor Vehicles, except that a spouse living separate and apart from the registered owner may register such vehicle immediately in such spouse's name. Additionally, as a condition precedent to the reregistration of the vehicle by the registered owner, spouse, or any child of the spouse, or any child of such owner, except a spouse living separate and apart from the registered owner, the payment of a restoration fee of fifty dollars ($50.00) and the appropriate fee for a new registration plate is required. Any person, firm or corporation failing to give notice of termination shall be subject to a civil penalty of two hundred dollars ($200.00) to be assessed by the Commissioner of Insurance upon a finding by the Commissioner of Insurance that good cause is not shown for such failure to give notice of termination to the Division.

(f) The Commissioner shall administer and enforce the provisions of this Article and may make rules and regulations necessary for its administration and shall provide for hearings upon request of persons aggrieved by orders or acts of the Commissioner under the provisions of this Article.

History: 1957, c. 1393, s. 1; 1959, c. 1277, s. 1; 1963, c. 964, s. 1; 1965, c. 272; c. 1136, ss. 1, 2; 1967, c. 822, ss. 1, 2; c. 857, ss. 1, 2; 1971, c. 477, ss. 1, 2; c. 924; 1975, c. 302; c. 348, ss. 1–3; c. 716, s. 5; 1979, 2d Sess., c. 1279, s. 1; 1981, c. 690, s. 25; 1983, c. 761, s. 146; 1983 (Reg. Sess., 1984), c. 1069, ss. 1, 2; 1985, c. 666, s. 84; 1991, c. 402, s. 1; 1999-330, s. 4; 1999-452, s. 20.

§ 20-313. Operation of motor vehicle without financial responsibility a misdemeanor

(a) On or after July 1, 1963, any owner of a motor vehicle registered or required to be registered in this State who shall operate or permit such motor vehicle to be operated in this State without having in full force and effect the financial responsibility required by this Article shall be guilty of a Class 1 misdemeanor.

(b) Evidence that the owner of a motor vehicle registered or required to be registered in this State has operated or permitted such motor vehicle to be operated in this State, coupled with proof of records of the

Division of Motor Vehicles indicating that the owner did not have financial responsibility applicable to the operation of the motor vehicle in the manner certified by him for purposes of G.S. 20-309, shall be prima facie evidence that such owner did at the time and place alleged operate or permit such motor vehicle to be operated without having in full force and effect the financial responsibility required by the provisions of this Article.

History: 1957, c. 1393, s. 5; 1959, c. 1277, s. 3; 1963, c. 964, s. 5; 1975, c. 716, s. 5; 1993, c. 539, s. 388; 1994, Ex. Sess., c. 24, s. 14(c).